Praise fo

"This spler... e a
top choice ... ry.
Buchanan ... His
brief sum... are
downright ...

"A refreshi... ch,
Buchanan ... nto
just about ... hat
Europe's Tr... yet
the details ... *ry*

"The rema... of
a sharp bu... ay

"Buchanan ... ate
and gradua ... lly
written, it ... on
a diverse a...

"Buchanan ... ias
extremely ... lar
countries." ...

"Based on ... xt
contains a i ... or
element of ... ist
century. W ... al
panorama; ... ial
forces of ch ... its
new, still uncharted role in the world." *Carole Fink, The Ohio State University*

"*Europe's Troubled Peace* is a lucid, comprehensive assessment of the old continent's remarkable recovery from the depths of destruction and despair after the Second World War. In particular, the book provides a very useful treatment of the important political, economic, and cultural developments within the major countries as they struggled to redefine their roles in Europe and the world during and after the Cold War." *William R. Keylor, International History Institute, Boston University*

Blackwell History of Europe

General Editor: John Stevenson

The series provides a new interpretative history of Europe from the Roman Empire to the end of the twentieth century. Written by acknowledged experts in their fields, and reflecting the range of recent scholarship, the books combine insights from social and cultural history with coverage of political, diplomatic and economic developments. Eastern Europe assumes its rightful place in the history of the continent, and the boundary of Europe is considered flexibly, including the Islamic, Slav and Orthodox perspectives wherever appropriate. Together, the volumes offer a lively and authoritative history of Europe for a new generation of teachers, students and general readers.

Published

Europe's Uncertain Path: 1814–1914
R. S. Alexander

Europe between Dictatorship and Democracy: 1900–1945
Conan Fischer

Europe's Troubled Peace: 1945 to the Present, second edition
Tom Buchanan

Europe in the Sixteenth Century
Andrew Pettegree

Fractured Europe: 1600–1721
David J. Sturdy

In preparation

Europe: 300–800
Peter Heather

Europe in Ferment: 950–1100
Jonathan Shepard

The Advance of Medieval Europe: 1099–1270
Jonathan Phillips

Europe: 1409–1523
Bruce Gordon

Europe from Absolutism to Revolution: 1715–1815
Michael Broers

Europe's Troubled Peace

1945 to the Present

Second Edition

Tom Buchanan

A John Wiley & Sons, Ltd., Publication

Edition history: Blackwell Publishing Ltd. (1e, 2006)

Wiley-Blackwell is an imprint of John Wiley & Sons, formed by the merger of Wiley's global Scientific, Technical and Medical business with Blackwell Publishing.

Registered Office
John Wiley & Sons Ltd, The Atrium, Southern Gate, Chichester, West Sussex, PO19 8SQ, UK

Editorial Offices
350 Main Street, Malden, MA 02148-5020, USA
9600 Garsington Road, Oxford, OX4 2DQ, UK
The Atrium, Southern Gate, Chichester, West Sussex, PO19 8SQ, UK

For details of our global editorial offices, for customer services, and for information about how to apply for permission to reuse the copyright material in this book please see our website at www.wiley.com/wiley-blackwell.

Library of Congress Cataloging-in-Publication Data

Buchanan, Tom, 1960–
Europe's troubled peace : 1945 to the present / Tom Buchanan. – 2nd ed.
    p.   cm.
  Includes index.
  ISBN 978-0-470-65578-8 (pbk.)
1. Europe–History–1945–   I. Title.
  D1051.B83 2012
  940.55–dc23

A catalogue record for this book is available f[rom the British Library.]

Set in 11/13pt Dante by SPi Publisher Servic[es, ...]
Printed in Singapore by C.O.S. Printers Pte L[td]

3   2015

For Robert, Alex, and Francis

Contents

List of Maps   xi
List of Illustrations   xii
Acknowledgments for the Second edition   xiii
Acknowledgments for the First edition   xiv

Introduction: Europe's Troubles   **1**

1   The War and its Legacy   **8**
    Conquest and Occupation   8
    Collaboration   12
    Resistance   14
    Liberation, 1943–1945   17
    Neutral Europe   21
    The Human and Physical Cost   22
    Judgment   26
    Conclusion   29

2   Europe between the Powers, 1945–1953   **30**
    From Grand Alliance to Cold War, 1941–1947   30
    The German Question   35
    Marshall Aid and Economic Security   40
    NATO and the Defense of the West   44
    Culture and the Cold War   47
    Conclusion   50

3   Restoration, Reconstruction, and Revolution:
    Europe, 1945–1950   **51**
    A New Europe?   51
    Politics in Western Europe   53

Western Europe: Reconstruction and Welfare　　　　60
Scandinavia: Paths to Security　　　　62
Southern Europe: Dictatorship and Civil War　　　　64
The Soviet Union and Central and Eastern Europe　　　　67
Between East and West: Finland, Austria, and Yugoslavia　　　　72
Conclusion　　　　74

4　Consolidating Western Europe, 1950–1963　　　　75
Fears and Aspirations　　　　75
Towards Affluence: The Economy and Social Change　　　　78
From Korea to Berlin: The International Context　　　　82
"No Experiments": West Germany, Britain, and Italy　　　　87
France and Algeria　　　　91
Social Democratic Alternatives　　　　94
Conclusion　　　　96

5　Western Europe in the 1960s　　　　98
The Cultural Divide　　　　98
The New Society: Economic and Social Change　　　　103
The Limits to Reform: Italy, West Germany, and Britain　　　　106
The Enigmatic Republic: France, 1958–1968　　　　109
Revolt: Students and Workers, 1967–1969　　　　111
The Persistence of Dictatorship: Spain, Portugal, and Greece　　　　116
Conclusion　　　　118

**6　The Soviet Union and Eastern Europe,
from 1953 to the 1970s　　　　120**
New Societies, Recurrent Crises　　　　120
Khrushchev and de-Stalinization　　　　126
The Crisis of 1956: Poland and Hungary　　　　128
The Start of the Brezhnev Era　　　　131
East European Alternatives: Romania, Yugoslavia, Albania　　　　133
From Prague Spring to Brezhnev Doctrine　　　　136
Conclusion　　　　139

7　Western Europe in the 1970s: Downturn and Détente　　　　140
The Era of Détente　　　　140
Willy Brandt's *Ostpolitik*, 1969–1974　　　　142

The New Economic Insecurity   145
West European Politics   148
The Rise of Terrorism, c.1970–1981   152
Intellectual and Cultural Developments   154
Transitions: Spain, Portugal, and Greece   156
Conclusion   161

8   Western Europe in the 1980s: The Era of Thatcher,
    Mitterrand, and Kohl   162
    Towards the Post-Industrial Society   162
    Postmodern Cultures?   165
    The New Cold War   167
    Thatcher's Britain   168
    Mitterrand's France   171
    Helmut Kohl and West Germany   175
    Breaking the Mold? New Political Movements   179
    Southern Europe   181
    Conclusion   185

9   European Integration: From Rome to Maastricht,
    1957–1992   186
    Perspectives on Integration   186
    The Foundation of the EEC   192
    De Gaulle and the EEC, 1958–1969   194
    Stagnation, 1970–1984   197
    The Single European Act and "1992"   199
    Maastricht and After   202
    Conclusion   204

10 The Fall of the Communist Regimes: The Soviet
    Union and Eastern Europe, 1980–1991   205
    "All that is solid melts into air"   205
    Poland and Solidarity, 1980–1981   208
    Gorbachev and Soviet Reform, 1985–1990   211
    1989: The Fall of Communism in Eastern Europe   215
    German Reunification, 1989–1990   219
    The End of the Soviet Union, 1990–1991   223
    Conclusion   224

11   Europe after the Cold War   226
Building Europe?   226
West European Politics   230
Troubled Waters: Italy and Germany   233
Western Europe: The Economy and EMU   235
Post-Communism: Eastern Europe and the Former USSR   237
The Balkan Wars   242
Conclusion   246

12   Europe in the New Millennium   248
Diversity and Union   248
Memory and the "European Identity"   252
The "War on Terror" and the Security of Europe   256
West European Politics   259
The Politics of Intolerance   264
On Europe's Borders   266
From Financial Crisis to European Crisis   269
Conclusion   273

Notes   275
Guide to Further Reading   292
Index   301

Maps

1.1	The Nazi empire, autumn 1942	9
2.1	Postwar Germany and neighboring countries showing zones of occupation and administration	36
2.2	Europe in the Cold War	45
6.1	Communist eastern Europe, showing prewar boundaries	121
9.1	From the EEC to the EU: the growth of European integration, 1957–2004	188
11.1	National and ethnic distribution in Yugoslavia	243
11.2	The Dayton Peace Accord; shaded areas mark lands held in October 1995	244

Illustrations

1.1	The liberation of Paris, August 25, 1944: surrender of German troops	18
2.1	Advanced units of the 1st US army and the 5th Soviet Guard army meet at the destroyed bridge across the River Elbe at Torgau, April 25, 1945	31
4.1	The Berlin Wall in 1984	85
4.2	The Berlin Wall in 1984	86
5.1	Student leader Rudi Dutschke and Gaston Salvatore (on the right) on a Vietnam demonstration in Berlin, 1968	113
6.1	Soviet tanks enter Budapest during the Hungarian uprising (October 24–November 11, 1956)	130
7.1	The prime minister of the DDR, Willi Stoph, meets Chancellor Willy Brandt at Erfurt railway station, March 1970	144
7.2	General Franco and his designated successor, Juan Carlos, 1973	157
8.1	Erich Honecker and Chancellor Helmut Kohl listen to national anthems in Bonn, September 1987	178
9.1	From left to right: Jean Monnet, Robert Schuman, Konrad Adenauer, and Walter Hallstein meeting to sign a draft treaty of the Schuman Plan, March 1951	191
12.1	Holocaust Memorial, Berlin	253
12.2	Memorial to the forced laborers at Auschwitz concentration camp, Pere la Chaise cemetery, Paris	253
12.3	The Valley of the Fallen, Spain	255
12.4	German troops in Kosovo, 1999	259
12.5	Spain's defense minister Carme Chacon reviews a guard of honor during a ceremony at the defense ministry in Madrid, April 14, 2008	262
12.6	Nicolas Sarkozy and Carla Bruni, Egypt, 2007	263
12.7	Vladimir Putin and Silvio Berlusconi	263
12.8	2010: Greece, strikes and protest	271

Acknowledgments for the Second edition

I am most grateful to Tessa Harvey, History Editor at Wiley-Blackwell, for proposing a second edition of *Europe's Troubled Peace*. I would also like to thank the Project Editor Isobel Bainton for her help in preparing the revised manuscript and identifying illustrations. The major change in this edition is a new final chapter. This covers the period 2000–2011 and includes a few passages from the former Conclusion. Aside from some minor corrections the main body of the text is unaltered.

T.B.
Oxford
July 2011

Acknowledgments
for the First Edition

I would like to thank John Stevenson, the series editor, and Tessa Harvey, history commissioning editor at Wiley-Blackwell, for inviting me to write this book. Tessa and her staff have been unfailingly supportive and helpful as the project has come to fruition and I am particularly grateful to Angela Cohen for overseeing the final stages. The book was mainly written during sabbatical leave in Trinity term 2004: I would like to record my gratitude to the University of Oxford for granting me this period of leave, and to my colleagues at OUDCE, above all Christine Jackson and Diana Wood, for providing such magnificent cover both during my sabbatical and the year's secondment that preceded it. I am indebted to John Stevenson, Andrew Latcham, and Martin Conway for reading the manuscript at varying stages of completion and making invaluable comments and corrections. Martin, in particular, has provided tremendous support and guidance throughout the whole project. Any remaining errors in the text are, of course, my responsibility. A work of synthesis such as this inevitably rests above all on the research carried out by the many scholars who have written on the history of postwar Europe. I very much hope that, without unduly burdening the text with footnotes, I have adequately indicated my debt to them. I must thank Julia and the boys for all of their patience and understanding when I was working on the book during the long summer of 2004.

T.B.
Oxford
May 2005

Introduction
Europe's Troubles

In January 1995 the French President François Mitterrand, close to the end of his second term of office and, indeed, of his own remarkable life, made an emotional valedictory address to the European Parliament. He reminded the assembled MEPs of how World War II had brought "grief, the pain of separation, the presence of death – all as a result of the mutual enmity of the peoples of Europe." He went on to lay the blame for such suffering squarely on the nationalistic sentiments endemic in Europe at a time when "everyone saw the world from his or her own viewpoint, and … those viewpoints were generally distorting." Mitterrand praised those who, after the war, had been able to envisage a "more radiant future … based on peace and reconciliation." Yet he concluded by appealing to Europeans to continue the struggle to overcome their past, and warned that "nationalism means war!"[1] A few years earlier his peroration might have seemed fanciful; yet now western Europe was witnessing, as a rather forlorn observer, precisely such a devastating war of rival nationalisms in the former Yugoslavia (1991–5). In the mid-1990s imagery of "ethnic cleansing" in Bosnia, and even of starving prisoners in camps, uncomfortably connected Europe's present with the problems of its recent past.

Mitterrand spoke for a generation that had either participated in the war or whose lives had been directly affected by it (a group that included most leading European statesmen and women well into the 1980s). By their standards, the history of Europe since 1945 could well be viewed as a triumph, not so much in terms of the remarkable growth and diffusion of prosperity, but simply in terms of the avoidance of the war, dictatorship and mass killing which had plagued the continent between 1914 and 1945. But peace is, of course, more than simply the avoidance of war, and the long peace of the decades after 1945 rested on the deliberate creation of new institutional arrangements that made war between west European states unimaginable. In the course of the 1990s these arrangements began to be extended to include central Europe as well. This does not mean that

Europe's Troubled Peace: 1945 to the Present, Second Edition. Tom Buchanan.
© 2012 John Wiley & Sons, Ltd. Published 2012 by John Wiley & Sons, Ltd.

Europe was free from conflict after 1945. As we shall see, in addition to the unprecedented division of the continent imposed by the Cold War (c.1947–91) and the often brutal imposition of Soviet authority on its satellite states, the peace of Europe was regularly disturbed by political violence, by vibrant new political and social movements, and – in the case of both southern and eastern Europe – the pains of transition from dictatorship to democracy. Even so, by the end of the century Europe seemed smaller, tamer and more homogeneous than it had been prior to 1945, and a central theme of this book will be how this less dangerous (and in most ways better) Europe was created.

Because the war – and the lessons learnt from it – did so much to determine the evolution of Europe after 1945, Chapter 1 will examine the conflict and its legacy in some detail. This introduction, however, looks at the broader context, and asks what went so badly awry in Europe during the first half of the twentieth century, especially in the two decades after the end of World War I (1914–18). Six themes will be explored below: politics, international relations, the economy, social divisions, culture, and European imperialism. In each case the question to bear in mind is how the severe and chronic problems that were evident prior to 1945 could be overcome in the postwar era.

The hallmark of inter-war politics was the unprecedented richness of ideological variety and the absence of the kind of consensus that came to characterize politics in western Europe after 1945. In Spain during the 1930s, for instance, the whole political spectrum could be observed, from revolutionary anarchism and communism on the left, via an embattled liberalism to various brands of conservative and Catholic authoritarianism on the right. Understandably, the inter-war years have been viewed above all in terms of the failure of democracy. Quite apart from the establishment of Mussolini's fascist dictatorship in the early 1920s and Hitler's overthrow of the Weimar Republic in 1933, different forms of dictatorship became the norm during these years throughout eastern and southern Europe. In the Soviet Union, meanwhile, under Stalin's leadership the Communist Party embarked on an ambitious and ruthless program of industrialization and agricultural collectivization. By 1939 democratic government was limited to Britain, France, Switzerland, the smaller states of north-west Europe, and Scandinavia. Although a rather successful experiment in social democracy was under way in Sweden, on the whole the mood in the democracies was defensive and pessimistic. The future seemed to lie with the regimes of right and left that could mobilize their populations, either by terror or by appealing to class hatreds, nationalist or ethnic passions, and utopian visions.

Yet to concentrate on the anti-democratic forces of both ideological extremes ignores the degree to which democracy was itself part of the problem. In the late nineteenth and early twentieth centuries European states had undergone incomplete processes of democratization in response to the emergence of more educated, literate, and urban "mass" societies. Even in Britain universal suffrage (for all men and women aged 21 or over) was not achieved until 1928, while French women did not receive the vote until 1944. Democracy had come, in the words of British Prime Minister Stanley Baldwin, "at a gallop,"[2] and too rapidly for many European countries after 1918. Consequently, democracy came to mean many different things in the inter-war years, often negative. For some it represented an ungovernable cacophony of small interest groups; for others a means by which elites divided the corrupt spoils of office; while in Spain the coming of the reforming Second Republic in 1931 posed a deadly threat to the interests of the rich and powerful. It was, moreover, far from clear who the real democrats were. Many on the left, for instance, rallied to defend "bourgeois" democracy at the eleventh hour in the mid-1930s, but this was more a response to the threat of fascism than any genuine reconciliation. Such an instrumental approach to democracy was again evident in eastern Europe in 1945–8. In the West, a crucial task for politicians after 1945 would therefore be to identify democratic politics with prosperity and social harmony rather than with crisis and weakness.

In the sphere of international relations, the most spectacular failing was, of course, the inability to prevent the outbreak of a new European war in September 1939. The principal aggressors during the 1930s were undoubtedly Hitler and Mussolini, but their aggression emphasized the underlying failure to establish a new order for European security after 1918, whether based on the newly formed League of Nations or – more narrowly – on the strength of Britain and France. Much of the blame must attach to the Treaty of Versailles (1919), which humiliated Germany (through territorial losses and the imposition of reparations payments) without destroying the basis of its military and economic power. Moreover, the formation of a host of weak new states in central and eastern Europe out of the former Austro-Hungarian and Russian empires became a source of weakness as soon as Germany and the Soviet Union regained their strength. Even so, success had seemed tantalizingly close in the late 1920s, when the signing of the 1925 Locarno Treaty (which guaranteed the borders of western Europe) was followed by the temporary stabilization of Germany's Weimar Republic and the rescheduling of German reparations. Locarno fostered a belief that not only could Franco-German antagonism, the storm center of European instability since 1870, be overcome, but even that the time was ripe to take a significant step towards a "European Federal Union."[3]

Such optimism was destroyed in the early 1930s by the Depression, by the revival of nationalism, and above all by the advent of Hitler's Nazi regime bent on revising the Treaty of Versailles. By the mid-1930s the League had collapsed as an effective forum for resolving international disputes, and Britain and France were pursuing their national and imperial self-interest, rather than collective security, through the "appeasement" of Germany and Italy. At Munich in September 1938 war was averted, but only by presenting Hitler with the German-populated borderlands of Czechoslovakia. Meanwhile, the Soviet Union also pursued its own interests, opposing fascism in Spain during the Civil War (1936–9), but forging a nonaggression pact with Hitler in August 1939 when it became clear that the Western democracies would not form an alliance to contain him. Accordingly, when Britain and France did go to war on September 3, 1939 in response to Hitler's invasion of Poland, they lacked any worthwhile allies. The United States, which was still recovering from the Depression and was prone to powerful isolationist sentiments, leaned towards the democracies but remained officially neutral.

The problems of Europe owed much to a world economy which, dislocated by World War I, almost ground to a halt following the crash of 1929. The impact of the Great Depression was most visible in the more developed industrial nations: in the early 1930s unemployment peaked at 6 million in Germany, 3 million in Britain, and 13 million in the United States. International trade was hit hard, and by 1938 only the Scandinavian economies had restored their 1929 levels of exports. For most European countries 1929 was an economic benchmark not to be reached again until the late 1940s (and then rapidly surpassed). Although the crisis is often visualized in terms of idle factories, coal mines, and shipbuilding yards, across the continent farmers were confronted with a collapse in agricultural prices. Even in France and Germany, let alone eastern Europe, agriculture was still woefully unmechanized and many farmers were forced to abandon the market and await better times (which came during and after the war). Indeed, the one benefit of the Depression for the industrial world was the steady decline of international commodity prices which, paradoxically, made the 1930s a period of some affluence for those in work. Where manufacturing prospered it tended to be in the production of goods designed for an expanding domestic market, such as automobiles and household appliances. In 1938, for instance, there were already 1.2 million privately owned cars in Germany, and 2 million in Britain.

The political impact of the Great Depression was profound. High unemployment undermined confidence in the democracies – fatally in the case of Germany – and encouraged those most affected to turn to leaders offering extreme solutions. The German people rallied to Hitler's drive for full employment, even though the economy was increasingly geared not simply to recovery but to making war. In France the leftist Popular Front swept to power in the elections of May 1936 offering a new deal for the workers after a number of years of harsh deflation. However, its policies, which included a 40-hour week and the first paid holidays, soon encountered determined opposition from employers. Meanwhile, the apparent immunity of the Soviet Union from the Depression enhanced the attractiveness of communism throughout Europe. Economists were shocked by the scale of the crisis, but no new consensus emerged as to how to solve it. The ideas of the Cambridge economist John Maynard Keynes, whose work proved so internationally influential after 1945, were by no means generally accepted before the war. In the absence of any common international program for recovery, democratic governments turned to a range of short-term pragmatic measures, such as protectionism, imperial preference, currency devaluation, and cartelization. For their part, the fascist regimes resorted to autarky (self-sufficiency), barter agreements for raw materials, and, ultimately, the forcible seizure of resources by conquest.

The brief, carnivalesque experience of the French Popular Front, when workers occupied their factories and coal mines to reinforce the verdict of the ballot box, was a reminder of how Europe's social divisions could still erupt into class conflict. In Spain, an even more destructive blend of social, political, and religious violence marked the early months of the Civil War in 1936. European societies remained intensely class conscious: educational opportunities were still largely determined by wealth, social services were patchy and often rudimentary, and working-class budgets were still dominated by the costs of basic housing and nutrition. Inequalities were even greater in parts of rural Europe. Across southern Spain, Portugal, and Italy, for instance, landless laborers experienced extreme poverty and insecurity. In general, the Depression had served to reinforce the established social order, whether under a democracy such as Britain or an allegedly egalitarian dictatorship such as Nazi Germany. At the same time, however, powerful social solidarities survived the economic and political traumas of the inter-war years, such as the working-class culture of factory and community. Religion, too, played an increasingly important role in defining social and political identities. The Catholic Church, still deeply suspicious of democracy, proved remarkably adept at maintaining its autonomy under both democracies and dictatorships. Across Europe lay "Catholic Action" organizations such as the JOC (Young Christian Workers) flourished during the 1930s.

In many countries questions of race and ethnicity gained a remarkable and destructive new salience in the inter-war years. Violent anti-Semitism, of course, became central to the politics of the Nazis, if not to their political appeal. Once established in power, they proceeded to establish a "racial state,"[4] using both legal means and thuggery to separate out the German population from Jews and other minorities. However, it must be recalled that, while Nazi anti-Semitism was unparalleled in its extremism, awareness of ethnic difference had been heightened across the new states of central and eastern Europe after 1918. For instance, restrictions on numbers of Jews who could attend the universities and join professions were widespread by the 1930s. Moreover, many of these new states were undermined by ethnic differences, such as the resentment felt by Croats against a Serb-dominated Yugoslavia or by Slovaks against the Czech domination of Czechoslovakia. The question of Transylvania, where a large Hungarian population was placed under Romanian rule in 1919, remained highly contentious into the communist – and indeed into the post-communist – era.

Developments in both the high arts and in popular "mass" culture contributed to the instability in the inter-war years. The fractured, subversive impact of modernism in literature and the arts before 1914 was greatly amplified by World War I, which led many to question prewar assumptions about patriotism, religious belief, and technological progress. Indeed, the war, and the Russian Revolution of 1917 which it brought about, were not simply military and political convulsions, but immense cultural shocks in their own right. The culture of the 1920s reflected a world in which traditional values and hierarchies had been found wanting, but in which no new certainties had been established. The consequences were most striking in the artistic ferment of Germany's Weimar Republic, where culture rapidly became the focus of bitter conflict. Here, broadly modernist and democratic forms of expression, (such as the theater of Bertolt Brecht and Bauhaus design and architecture) clashed head-on with conservatives committed to preserving the cultural purity of the German *Volk* from "degenerate" influences.

It was inevitable that, due to the advent of new technologies and new forms of cultural activity, culture would be fiercely contested during the inter-war years. This applied most obviously to the advent of radio and the cinema, but also to advances in photography and propaganda. No authority – political or spiritual – could afford to ignore the opportunities offered by radio to communicate with the public in their homes, or the potential of cinema to shape dreams and desires. European dictatorships were fully alive to the importance of culture as a means of creating new concepts of community, whether racial or ideological. As the German critic Walter Benjamin observed in 1936, Nazism had achieved the "introduction of aesthetics into political life."[5] The Nazis' stage-managed rallies were used to show a nation on the march: ironically, their mastery of modern techniques of lighting and cinematography enabled them to create a mythologized past. Mussolini's regime was infatuated with the cinema, and built the Cinecittà film production complex in 1937. In the Soviet Union the initial modernism and abstraction of the immediate post-revolutionary era gave way in the 1930s to a "Socialist Realist" style that forced artists to celebrate the achievements of the Communist Party and its leaders. These contrasting "totalitarian" styles were, famously, juxtaposed in the rival pavilions at the Paris Exposition of 1937.[6]

Finally, it is important to note that, despite the immense destruction caused by World War I, Europe was still a preeminent force in the world. The British and French empires, in particular, were larger than ever after 1918, swollen with "mandates" (former territories of the defeated German and Ottoman Turkish empires) awarded by the League of Nations. Portugal, Belgium, the Netherlands, Italy, and Spain also retained significant colonial possessions. Empires remained highly attractive, as a mark of prestige and national pride, as an economic asset (providing raw materials and markets) during the Depression, and as a source of military recruits. Both Spain and Italy were engaged in bitter campaigns to expand their empires (Spain in Morocco in the 1920s; Italy in Abyssinia in 1935–6). However, empire also carried a cost. Britain and France, in particular, had to "think imperially" when considering grand strategy, and to be aware of the challenge from new imperial powers – such as Japan and the United States – in the Pacific. Colonial powers also had to combat the rise of nationalism (especially in India) and to prove that imperial rule brought genuine benefits to the colonized. In many respects, therefore, the European empires were living on borrowed time in the inter-war years. Although they survived World War II, it rapidly became apparent (to some countries more swiftly than others) that formal empire was no longer sustainable, and by the 1960s all of the leading European states had refocused their attention on Europe.

Europe on the verge of World War II provided, therefore, a diverse and bewildering spectacle. The fault lines of conflict ran not only between the nations of Europe, but also within them. If, to take Mitterrand's argument, the world was seen from a plurality of viewpoints, then these perspectives might just as well be ideological, national, or religious. What would the future hold? In the West there were the first glimmerings of how this dysfunctional Europe could be made to work. For instance, new economic thinking already envisaged a more constructive role for the state, and a balance between the needs of the free market and the provision of welfare. Moreover, the seeds of the idea had been sown that states would have to sacrifice some of their sovereignty in order to protect their vital interests. Yet the dictators, fascist and communist, were articulating their own very different prescriptions, and by the late 1930s they seemed to be in the ascendancy. All would hang on the unpredictable outcome of war.

1
The War and its Legacy

Conquest and Occupation

Between 1939 and 1942 most of Europe was united under German domination. At its greatest extent the territory occupied by Germany and its allies stretched from the Caucasus to the Atlantic coast of France, and from Greece to Norway (see Map 1.1). In addition to Britain and the USSR, only a small number of neutral states retained some degree of independence. Having rapidly overrun Poland and western Europe in 1939–40, Hitler took his greatest gamble by invading the Soviet Union in June 1941 ("Operation Barbarossa") while leaving an undefeated Britain in the rear. Although the Soviet resistance stiffened as German troops approached Moscow, vast tracts of territory and more than 3 million Red Army soldiers were lost in the first six months of combat on the Eastern Front. By September 1942, after a further successful campaigning summer, German forces stood on the Volga at Stalingrad, some 2,000 kilometers from Berlin.

What was the nature of this new German empire? According to Nazi rhetoric this was a "New Order," a hierarchy within which non-Germans would have their designated part to play. The "Germanic" peoples, such as the Dutch and Norwegians, might eventually be absorbed into the Reich, whereas the fate of the Slavs of eastern Europe would be resettlement and enslavement. Yet while there were those in the more privileged groups eager to collaborate on such terms (see below), Hitler had no intention of sharing power with them. The New Order enshrined Germany's domination of Europe, and its true nature was one of economic exploitation, political oppression, and increasingly severe racial persecution. The German war economy required immense amounts of labor, food, raw materials, and bullion which, apart from that which could be supplied by the neutral states, had to come from the conquered territories. The trade of

Europe's Troubled Peace: 1945 to the Present, Second Edition. Tom Buchanan.
© 2012 John Wiley & Sons, Ltd. Published 2012 by John Wiley & Sons, Ltd.

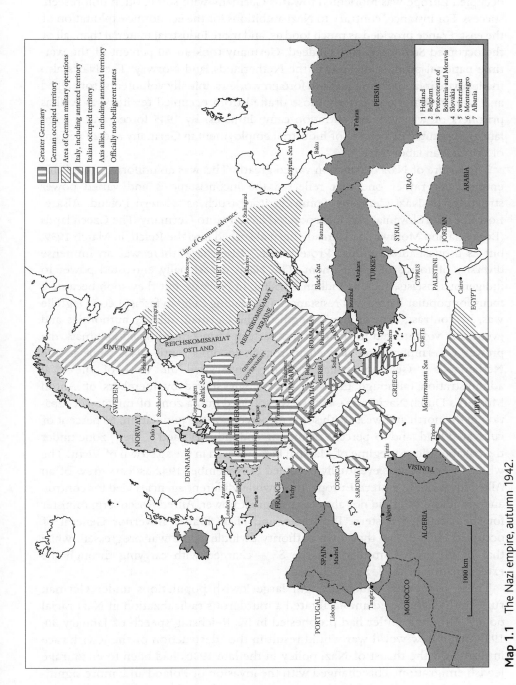

Map 1.1 The Nazi empire, autumn 1942.

Source: Jeremy Noakes and Geoffrey Pridham, *Nazism, 1919–1945*, vol. 3, *Foreign policy, war and racial extermination*, pp. 642–3 (Exeter University Press, Exeter, 2001 edn.). Used with permission.

occupied Europe was reoriented towards Germany with some, often unforeseen, success. For instance, contrary to Nazi ambitions for the economic exploitation of the east, France provided as much food as, and more industrial material than, all of the occupied Soviet territory.[1] Indeed, Germany took 30–40 percent of the wartime national product of France, the Netherlands, and Norway. The Nazis also made up their labor shortages with foreign workers, initially volunteers from allied and satellite states and latterly those drafted from occupied territory, as well as prisoners of war and concentration camp inmates. By 1945 forced and foreign labor constituted 25 percent of industrial employment in Germany and 20 percent of the civilian labor force.[2]

The nature of Nazi occupation varied greatly. This was no uniform, monolithic empire, but rather one that reflected the inconsistencies and varied power structures of Nazi Germany. Some territory (such as western Poland, Alsace-Lorraine, and Slovenia) was incorporated directly into Germany. The Czech lands (Bohemia and Moravia) had already been absorbed into the Reich, in March 1939, but as a quasi-autonomous "Protectorate." Elsewhere, there was an immense diversity of forms of government. The Nazis occasionally entrusted power to indigenous fascists, such as Vidkun Quisling in Norway, but they soon became a focus for popular hatred and resistance. The leading Belgian fascist Léon Degrelle was, by contrast, kept at arm's length by the German military authorities and eventually volunteered to fight on the Eastern Front. In occupied Denmark the prewar government was allowed to remain in office until 1943, while in the Netherlands a German civilian authority supervised the work of the local administration (although this was increasingly staffed by members of Anton Mussert's Dutch Nazi Party). France was divided into a zone of military occupation in the north and west (with some 67 percent of the population, 66 percent of cultivated land, and 75 percent of mining and industry) and a "free" zone under the collaborationist regime of Marshal Pétain, based in the spa town of Vichy. The whole of France was eventually occupied in November 1942 as fears grew of an Allied invasion. In eastern Europe, meanwhile, different agencies vied for control, and grandiose titles did not always carry great power. Alfred Rosenberg, minister for the Occupied Eastern Territories, and Hans Frank, Governor General of occupied Poland, saw their own authority dwindle as the war progressed, while that of Heinrich Himmler and the SS – charged with carrying through the extermination of the Jews – increased.

These conquests, which brought large Jewish populations under German rule, both encouraged and facilitated a murderous radicalization in Nazi racial policy. Although Hitler had prophesied in his Reichstag speech of January 30, 1939 that a new world war would result in the "destruction of the Jewish race in Europe,"[3] the thrust of Nazi policy in the late 1930s had been to encourage Jewish emigration. This changed with the invasion of Poland and, more significantly, with Operation Barbarossa, when SS special commandos (*Einsatzgruppen*) were detailed to murder Nazism's supposed ideological and racial enemies behind the front line. These units shot as many as 2 million men, women, and children in cold blood, often with the willing help of local populations. At the same time, senior Nazis began to speak of a "complete solution of the Jewish question within the German sphere of influence in Europe."[4] Further emigration was blocked and steps taken to organize the deportation of the Jews to occupied Poland. This policy was systematized at the Wannsee Conference of January 20, 1942, under the chairmanship of Reinhard Heydrich, where the organizational arrangements were made for Europe to be "combed through from west to east."[5] The purpose of this deportation was mass industrialized murder, initially pioneered at a number of smaller camps in Poland where Jews were killed by mobile gas vans. Most western Jews were sent to Auschwitz, a sprawling industrial and extermination complex where those deemed unfit to work (80–90 percent) were murdered in gas chambers on arrival. Those Jews selected to work for IG-Farben's synthetic rubber plant could only expect to live for three to four months – only one month if set to work in the associated coal mine.[6]

The "final solution" reflected the sense of power and boundless ambition felt by Nazi officials at the height of their supremacy within Europe. By late 1941 the Soviet Union seemed close to collapse and Britain was engaged in its own struggle for survival against the German U-boats in the Atlantic. Even the entry of the United States into the war following the Japanese attack on Pearl Harbor (December 7, 1941) made little initial difference as it would take almost a year for US servicemen to be deployed in action, and even then in North Africa rather than Europe. Moreover, war with Japan further stretched British resources and some 70,000 British and imperial troops capitulated at Singapore in February 1942. There were, however, also causes for concern on the German side, notably the very limited support that Germany received from its allies, and even from its Axis partner Italy. For all Mussolini's martial bluster, it soon became clear that Italy was ill prepared, both militarily and economically, for modern warfare. The Italian army suffered humiliating setbacks at the hands of the Greeks (October 1940) and the British in North Africa, while newly colonized Abyssinia was liberated in 1941. Half of Italy's modern and expensive battleship fleet was severely damaged at anchor in Taranto by British torpedo bombers. The war economy was inefficient, slow to expand, and crippled by a lack of energy resources which forced Italy into dependence on Germany. By 1942 Italy had sent 290,000 workers to Germany in exchange for supplies of coal and steel. Hitler's other allies, Hungary, Romania, and Bulgaria, were largely agrarian states. Their prewar authoritarian governments were already locked into economic dependence on Germany, and mainly concerned with rectifying their own territorial grievances. Alongside Finland, which joined the war on Germany's side to take revenge for the Soviet aggression directed against it in the winter of 1939/40, these allies were, at best, able to play an auxiliary military role on the Eastern Front.

Collaboration

Many in occupied Europe chose to collaborate with Nazi Germany, for a range of personal, ideological, and ethnic reasons. Collaboration was a far more complex phenomenon than its best-known image – of shaven-headed women humiliated after the liberation of France for sleeping with German soldiers – would suggest. In fact, collaboration represented a gradient down which all occupied populations might travel to some degree, and which might well go no further than the quite proper relations of local authorities with an occupying power. In cases of economic relations it was often difficult to tell where "business as usual" and an eye for profit elided into unacceptable levels of support for the German war effort. In France, for instance, contracts placed by the German authorities were not easily refused and, in any case, provided otherwise unobtainable employment for as many as 3 million workers. Yet their labor produced aircraft, shells, and uniforms, while French construction companies built the "Atlantic Wall" and a giant submarine base at Saint-Nazaire.[7] At the individual level, too, there were many gray areas. For instance, François Mitterrand, the future French president, slipped easily between working for the collaborationist Vichy regime and the resistance. In such cases, many would argue subsequently that they collaborated out of a sense of duty to protect their countrymen from the worst of the occupation. Some governments or heads of state opted to remain in post rather than seek exile, while Pétain famously described himself as the "shield" of France. Many lower-ranking officials and members of the police also continued in office, and some would undoubtedly have shared the Nazis' anti-communism and anti-Semitism. In all these cases, of course, the supreme test came when Nazi demands, notably for the deportation of the Jews, placed their own compatriots in danger.

   Collaboration requires a context, as the occupiers must be willing to work with the occupied. This was far less likely to be the case in eastern Europe where the prime Nazi objective was to create *Lebensraum* ("living space") for the expansion of the German race and to crush the indigenous Slavic population. In Poland, for instance, where Nazi (and, indeed, Soviet) policy was to destroy the prewar elites, collaboration was barely an option. Conversely, the Czechs, who were deemed to be semi-Germanic, enjoyed a relatively privileged status in their "Protectorate," retaining their own president and civil service. Here, collaboration was both possible and actively pursued, encouraged by the iron hand of Protector Heydrich in 1941–2. One major failing of Nazi rule was in the occupied Soviet territories, where resentment at Stalin's policies in the 1930s plus local anti-Semitism had created a reservoir of potential support. This was particularly strong in the Baltic states and eastern Poland, which had only been seized by the USSR in 1939–40. The Nazis encouraged the Balts, Belorussians, and Ukrainians to play an active role in the extermination of the Jews, and thousands of Ukrainian and Russian "Hiwi" auxiliaries served in the Wehrmacht. However, Nazi policy towards the region was blinkered by notions of racial superiority, and many opportunities were missed. Andrei Vlasov, a Red Army general captured in 1942 who turned against Stalin, was not allowed to form his "Committee for the Liberation of the Peoples of Russia" until September 1944, too late to influence events on the Eastern Front. Tellingly, German occupation policy was far more successful in the Caucasus, where the Wehrmacht was in charge and where local religious and cultural identities were respected.

Amongst those who wholeheartedly chose political collaboration, small minorities identified fully with Nazism and sought to integrate into the "New Order." For instance, some 50,000 Dutch, 40,000 Belgian, and 20,000 French volunteers served with the Waffen SS on the Eastern Front, alongside smaller numbers of Scandinavians. Such ideologically motivated collaborators tended to be prewar fascists who saw the Nazis as leading an international crusade against communism (and were greatly relieved when the Nazi–Soviet Pact was shattered by the German assault on the Soviet Union). There was, however, no automatic correlation between prewar and wartime political positions. Many conservative nationalists (such as Charles de Gaulle, who was often denounced as a "fascist" during his career) were above all patriots who detested the German occupation. Likewise, not all collaborators came from the right. A number were former socialists, such as Henri De Man in Belgium and Marcel Déat in France, who felt that the events of 1940 proved the failure of capitalism and parliamentary democracy. For them, to collaborate was to side – not necessarily in an opportunistic manner – with the new and enduring reality in Europe.

Other collaborators might not share Nazi goals or ideals but still saw the German victory as a chance to promote their own agenda for radical political change. For instance, Pétain had initially appeared as a reassuring figure amidst the chaos of July 1940. He enjoyed public support in negotiating an armistice and abolishing the Third French Republic (which was overwhelmingly approved in parliament by 569 votes to 80). However, Pétain's attempt to create a more traditionalist, Catholic, and xenophobic France under the trinity of "work, family, fatherland" alienated many who might have supported a more politically neutral regime. Instead, Vichy's assault on republican values and its ultra-conservative policies served to galvanize resistance. This was compounded from 1942 by the failure to protect the French people from the Nazi labor draft and the rounding up of the Jews (in which the French police played a crucial role). By this stage Pétain had lost control of his two principal assets which had given him some leverage with Berlin: control over the French fleet and the colonial empire. In 1942–4 Vichy's collaboration became increasingly overt under the premiership of Pierre Laval, and its paramilitary police force, the Milice, was effectively engaged in a civil war with the resistance.

Collaboration also offered opportunities to ethnic groups who welcomed German aggression as an opportunity to break up existing states and to assert their own cultural and political independence. Before the outbreak of war Germany had encouraged Slovak separatists to secede from the rump Czecho-Slovakia in

March 1939, and Slovakia became a German satellite state under the Catholic priest Joseph Tiso. Other examples included the fascist Ustasha in Croatia, some Flemish nationalists in Belgium, Breton autonomists in France, and Irish Republicans. Such groups might act as useful auxiliaries to Nazi rule, and as a means further to divide and rule the conquered, but if given too much authority their role could well prove counterproductive. For instance, once in power the Ustasha embarked on a murderous pogrom of Serbs, Jews, and Gypsies. Their intention was to create an ethnically homogenous greater Croatia, but their brutality generated considerable support for Tito's Partisans.

The legacy of collaboration was extremely influential in postwar Europe, and nothing, apart from the defeat of Nazi Germany itself, did more to discredit inter-war fascist ideology. The punishment of collaborators (see below) eliminated a whole tier of politicians and ideologues either through execution, imprisonment, removal of political rights, or simple popular disapproval. The attraction of fascism had hardly been destroyed, but it had been driven to disguise itself for decades to come. The specter of the "quisling" also hung over the Soviet domination of postwar eastern Europe and guaranteed a certain degree of autonomy for Soviet allies in the satellite states. Moreover, collaboration – alongside the resistance – sponsored a postwar political realignment as many who had formerly identified with the authoritarian right, such as Catholics, now came to see that their values could be enshrined in the democratic politics emerging from the war. In the process, a veil was drawn over the realities and complexities of collaboration that was not lifted until the subject was critically reexamined by historians and film-makers in the early 1970s.[8] It should also be remembered that, while the memory of collaboration remained generally negative, in parts of central and eastern Europe a more positive connotation survived. For instance, with the fall of communism in 1989/90 the Ustasha and Tiso regimes were often seen in Croatia and Slovakia as a brave first essay at independence.

Resistance

On August 25, 1944, General de Gaulle, leader of the Free French, arrived in Paris and proclaimed that it was a city "liberated by herself, by her own people, with the help of the armies of France."[9] Despite such rhetoric, no occupied country was in fact in a position to liberate itself during the war. Even though large resistance armies developed in some countries, notably Yugoslavia, Poland, Greece, and Albania, their success was ultimately dependent on the ability of the Allied armies to drive out the Germans. The case was made, tragically, in Poland where the advancing Soviet forces encouraged the Polish resistance to launch the Warsaw uprising (August 1944) and then held back while it was brutally crushed by the Germans. By October, some 15,000 Polish fighters and 200,000 civilians had died.

The extensive Slovak uprising of November 1944 was also defeated, and attempts by the French Maquis to confront German forces directly in the Vercors massif (July 1944) resulted in heavy losses. This is not to imply that the resistance movements were militarily irrelevant, as they played a significant role in disrupting communications, collecting intelligence, and assisting the escape of Allied airmen and prisoners. However, the resistance was as much to do with the future as with the present. Few countries conquered by the Nazis witnessed a simple restoration of the old order after the liberation, and the new politics was – to a degree at least – forged within the resistance.

Defeat was so complete and so disorienting in 1939–41 that there were very few resisters "of the first hour." In the case of France it was Pétain after all who embodied constitutional legitimacy, while de Gaulle – who claimed to speak in France's name from London – was merely a deserter supporting an apparently lost cause. In western Europe, unless one was the member of particular persecuted groups, it was generally possible to play a waiting game in a war that appeared to be almost over. In the absence of the communists, who did not explicitly support the resistance until June 1941, there was no coherent political leadership, and initially resistance was the somewhat eccentric choice of isolated individuals. As the war progressed, however, the context changed. Above all, the tightening of Nazi occupation policy propelled many into resistance – for instance, those fleeing compulsory labor service or Jewish deportation orders often formed the basis of the French Maquis in the hills. The changing tide of the war and the growing unpopularity of collaborators gave resistance a new legitimacy, despite the increasingly savage Nazi reprisals against civilian populations. In eastern Europe the situation was far starker. Here resistance – in the case of the Polish Home Army (AK), the Serb Chetniks, and later on the Russian Partisans – was from the outset a question of national survival in the face of the genocidal assaults of the Nazis and their allies. In Poland, the resistance was not only an armed movement, but also represented a remarkable attempt to sustain Polish culture and politics underground. For the Chetniks, resistance represented not only opposition to occupation but also a struggle to ensure that the Serbs maintained their dominant role if and when the kingdom of Yugoslavia was restored.

The development of the resistance was hugely influenced by the policies of Hitler's opponents. Churchill saw the potential benefits from an early stage, and in the summer of 1940 directed the new Special Operations Executive (SOE) to "set Europe aflame." More realistically, it would build up small intelligence networks which might eventually be capable of more sophisticated military operations. (SOE was later joined by the American Office of Strategic Services – OSS – the forerunner of the CIA.) The Western Allies came to play a decisive role as the main source of military and political support – witness Churchill's pragmatic decision in 1943 to favor the communist-led Partisans (now a quarter of a million strong) over the royalist Chetniks in Yugoslavia. Likewise, Churchill and Roosevelt eventually overcame their suspicions and decided to back de Gaulle even though, following the capture of Algeria, they initially saw more practical value in working with former Vichyites such as Admiral Darlan and General Giraud. However, while the resistance may have been a morale-raising myth in the dark days of 1940–1 and later a military asset, it was increasingly a political embarrassment given the prominence of communists in its ranks. The supreme allied commander Eisenhower claimed that it was worth five or six divisions at D-Day, but thereafter saw it as a politically divisive and "dissident" force in the rear of his advancing armies.[10]

For the communists, the decisive moment was the German invasion of the Soviet Union. This greatly simplified matters as most communists had been ardent anti-fascists during the 1930s and the Nazi–Soviet pact had made immense demands on their political discipline. Now, for the first time, a substantial political force that was used to operating in clandestinity joined the resistance. The Yugoslav Communist Party had, for example, been illegal for much of the inter-war period, and many leading Yugoslav communists had been involved with the International Brigades in the Spanish Civil War. In most countries the communists soon emerged as the largest resistance movement, sometimes, as in Greece and Yugoslavia, in bitter competition with other political forces. The success of the communist resistance in the Balkans was a source of mounting concern to the Allies as it heralded the formation of communist regimes at the end of the war in Yugoslavia, Albania and (very nearly) in Greece. At the same time, it should be noted that – at least until the advance of the Red Army into eastern Europe reduced the problems of communication – its independence was also a concern to Moscow. These political tensions were less overt in western Europe, where cooperation was more common. For instance, a broad-based French National Council of the Resistance (CNR) was established in May 1943 following the intercession of de Gaulle's emissary Jean Moulin, and a committee for the liberation of occupied northern Italy was forged in January 1944.

Like collaboration, resistance was a highly complex phenomenon that often belied its straightforwardly heroic image. The German bomb plotters, responsible for the unsuccessful July 1944 attempt to kill Hitler, contained many whose politics were profoundly authoritarian and nationalistic. The Polish resistance was equally heroic, but seemed unable to empathize with the plight of the Jews. The commander of the Polish Home Army reported to London in September 1941 that "the overwhelming majority of the country is anti-Semitic."[11] Many in the resistance movements were engaged just as much in civil wars – with collaborators and rival resistance groups – to determine the political future as they were in the struggle against the occupation. Moreover, the morality and political value of resistance violence was often questionable given the inevitability of reprisal. In March 1944, 335 Italian prisoners were killed in the Ardeatine caves in retaliation for the death of 33 German soldiers in a Partisan bomb attack in Rome. Although the German perpetrators were later brought to justice, some of the victims' families believed that the Partisans should also be punished for violating Rome's status as an "open city." Likewise, the assassination of Heydrich by Czech SOE agents in 1942 provoked harsh reprisals against the civilian population (including 173 slain in the village of Lidice).

In western Europe the influence of the resistance was immense, but its exact political character was surprisingly elusive. It proved too incoherent to determine the postwar political order, as many of its members had wished, and no single party was able to capture and channel its energies. The resistance had for the first time thrown together representatives of a wide range of political, religious, and social groups, enabling them to see beyond the rigid ideological positions of the 1930s. A character in Alberto Moravia's novel *Two Women* nicely captures this sense of stripped humanity prevalent in the latter stages of the war when he observes that "you and I are two human beings, and what we are, we are because of what we do and not because of any honours or degrees."[12] Thus, the resistance came to embody certain values – humanist, egalitarian, anti-fascist, and patriotic – that appealed across the somewhat constrained spectrum of postwar politics. None would turn the myth of the resistance to their advantage better than de Gaulle, draped in the cross of Lorraine and surrounded by a loyal coterie largely forged in exile. Yet in the 1970s the resistance would also be used to legitimize causes as varied as an anti-tax movement in Denmark and the violence of the Italian Red Brigade terrorists.

Liberation, 1943–1945

The course of the war hinged around the events of late 1942 and early 1943, with the German defeats in North Africa, and, above all, the great Soviet victory at Stalingrad in January 1943. Here, an entire army was destroyed and the myth of German military invincibility was shattered irretrievably. Although thereafter Germany was still capable of mounting powerful offensives, notably at Kursk (July 1943) and in the Ardennes (December 1944), the tide of war had clearly changed in the Allies' favor. On the Eastern Front a relentless series of Soviet offensives in the year after Kursk evicted the invaders from Soviet soil and brought the Red Army into Poland and the Balkans. Now Hitler's allies were steadily transformed into enemies, starting with the Allied invasion of Sicily which precipitated the overthrow of Mussolini on July 25, 1943. King Victor Emmanuel eventually led Italy into the Allied camp on September 8, 1943, although the "45 days" of confusion had allowed German troops to occupy the peninsula as well as the Italian zone of occupation in the Balkans and the Greek islands. Mussolini was rescued by German commandos and restored to lead the puppet "Republic of Salò" in the north. Hungary, too, was occupied in March 1944 when its ruler Admiral Horthy sought to withdraw from the war, and a government of the fascist Arrow Cross movement was imposed in October. However, Romania did successfully change sides in August 1944, and 110,000 Romanians died in

Figure 1.1   The liberation of Paris, August 25, 1944: surrender of German troops.
Photo © akg-images.

this new war alongside the 300,000 lost on the Eastern Front. Bulgaria and Finland
followed suit in September.

Meanwhile, the D-Day landings (June 6, 1944) by British, American, and
Canadian troops had opened the long-awaited "Second Front" in western Europe.
After desperate fighting in Normandy, in August the Allies broke out across
northern France and into Belgium (see Figure 1.1). By early 1945 German resistance was being squeezed between Allied armies advancing through the Rhineland,
Poland, the Balkans, and Italy. In the west an Allied army, now – unlike at D-Day –
predominantly composed of American troops, swept across the Rhine in March
1945. The Wehrmacht was rapidly collapsing, and more than 300,000 prisoners
were taken in the Ruhr pocket alone. Allied troops now fanned out to the east and
south, encountering the advancing Soviet forces south of Berlin. In central Europe
the Red Army had been delayed by stubborn resistance in Budapest (October
1944–February 1945), but it advanced more swiftly through Poland and Prussia. In
mid-April Marshal Zhukov opened his assault on Berlin, and some 78,000 Soviet
troops died amongst the ruins before the Red Flag was raised over the Reichstag
building. Hitler, having appointed Admiral Dönitz as his successor, killed himself
on April 30. Dönitz offered Germany's formal surrender on May 7 and delivered
up the German garrisons in Bohemia, Holland, Denmark, and Norway to the

Allies. He and his government were then unceremoniously arrested on May 23 by the Allied military authorities who were now Germany's true rulers.

Underpinning the military victory of the Allies was a fundamental shift in the balance of resources available to the two sides. In many respects, this outcome was implicit in Hitler's decision to go to war with both the USSR and the USA in 1941. If Hitler failed to win a swift victory in the east, and if a lasting alliance could be brokered between such ideologically disparate enemies, it was probable that a combination of Soviet manpower and US productive capacity would ultimately prevail. By the latter stages of the war, although the Allies could not always match the quality of the German equipment – notably in armored vehicles – they held a decisive advantage in sheer quantity. This imbalance was exacerbated for Germany by the distortions imposed by Nazi policy in the final stages of the war. Despite the success of Albert Speer, Hitler's Minister for War Production from 1942, in increasing production in the face of Allied strategic bombing, vital resources were diverted into the production of technologically advanced but unproven new weapons as well as, of course, into the extermination of the Jews (the "Holocaust"). The Nazis were fearful of alienating public support and slow to admit that Germany was involved in a "total war." Moreover, they were constrained by their own ideology. Female labor, for instance, was mobilized reluctantly and inefficiently, even though 13 million men were under arms. By contrast, the Allies approached the final phase of the war with single-minded lucidity. Difficult questions were postponed in the interest of maintaining the alliance (given that Soviet assistance was also thought to be needed in the defeat of Japan). The United States sustained the war efforts of both its principal Allies through the food, raw materials, and other resources made available under the lend-lease arrangements. The greater mobility of the Soviet forces, and their rapid advance in 1944, was greatly facilitated by American supplies, including 375,883 lorries, 380,135 field telephones, and a mountain of spam.[13] For Britain, US aid meant that extraordinary levels of resources could be directed into the war: 5 million men and women were in uniform and a further 5 million worked in the munitions industry.

In western Europe – and far more problematically in the east – Allied forces arrived as liberators. However, they were also the dominant presence in liberated Europe, with views on the new political structures that were emerging. At the most basic level there was still a war to be won and the Allies wanted to find local leaderships with which they could cooperate in preventing disorder. Prominent collaborators were removed from office, but there was considerable continuity amongst the police and bureaucracies (even though they may have been institutionally complicit in Nazi crimes). This generally meant the strengthening of local elites and the dashing of hopes that the liberation would immediately bring greater social justice: for instance, there was widespread social unrest by late 1943 in rural Sicily. Allied policy was also geared to prevent communist takeovers. In November 1944 Allied forces in Belgium protected the returned Pierlot government from pro-resistance demonstrators, while in Greece British troops found themselves engaged in conflict with the communist ELAS (National People's Liberation Army) forces in December 1944. Many members of the anti-communist Greek security battalions, set up under the pro-Nazi Rallis government, enrolled in the British sponsored National Guard (see Chapter 3). In Italy, however, where the influential Communist Party gave a pragmatic lead, an agreement that the resistance would rapidly surrender control of captured territory to Allied authorities and disarm was honored. On the Eastern Front, meanwhile, the Red Army imposed sympathetic governments in its wake and sought to reduce all opposition to Soviet control. In Poland, Soviet forces immediately came into conflict with the Polish Home Army.

In the short term, political power largely lay in the hands of those returning from exile. In some cases, such as Norway and the Netherlands, their legitimacy was such that the war could be treated as a mere parenthesis. Elsewhere, matters of sovereignty were more complicated. King Leopold III of Belgium, who had opted to remain in May 1940 while his government went into exile, had been spirited away by the retreating Nazis. His return in May 1945 opened the highly divisive "Royal Question" that was only resolved with his abdication in 1950. In France, de Gaulle was the man of the moment, but he had no authority beyond that granted him by the Allies and that derived from his own courage and vision during the war. His first task, therefore, was to assert his political supremacy over the resistance and throughout France. The situation was even more difficult for exiles in the Balkans and eastern Europe unless, as in the case of Greece, the Allies were willing to assist their return by force. Edvard Beneš, president of Czechoslovakia until he resigned after the 1938 Munich agreement, was able to return to power, but only by making a Faustian pact with Stalin. The exiled Polish government in London watched with mounting unease as the Soviets, on entering Polish territory in July 1944, created a puppet government in Lublin that was a rival to its own authority.

Although there was no immediate social revolution at the liberation, it was soon clear that the war years had greatly altered the balance of power within European societies. Europe was divided between winners and losers in a manner that transcended politics. War weakened the bonds of social class and reduced people's horizons to the level of the family and the locality. In a struggle for survival in the devastated landscape of Poland, even family and generational bonds were loosened as it was a tremendous advantage to be young and in good health. Some groups, above all farmers, had greatly benefited from wartime conditions and the opportunity for profit. As one British observer in northern Europe commented, any peasant farmer who had failed to clear his mortgage in 1940–1945 "was an exception."[14] Many businessmen had also prospered, even if they now required nimble footwork to avoid allegations of collaboration. Conversely, industrial workers had been greatly weakened as a collective force by the banning of trade unions and Nazi labor service, compounding the prewar impact of the Depression. Intimations of a leftward shift in European politics at the end of the war should therefore be qualified, as the underlying trend was in favor of the conservative blend of capitalism and welfare that came to be embodied in postwar Christian Democracy.[15]

Neutral Europe

A number of neutral countries – the Irish Free State, Spain, Portugal, Sweden, Switzerland, and Turkey – were able to stay out of the war. Neutrality itself offered no security, as the Nazi conquest of Belgium, the Netherlands, Denmark, and Norway demonstrated. Nor, despite the Swiss army's threat of a fight to the death in its mountain fastness (*réduit*), was this a victory of military deterrence. With the exception of Ireland, the neutrals remained independent because the limited inconvenience of overrunning them was outweighed by the benefits that they could bring to the Nazi war effort. In any case, the threat of invasion was largely irrelevant by mid-1940 when German troops either surrounded (in the case of Switzerland) or were well placed to intimidate the continental neutrals. They, in turn, were cut off from trade with or military assistance from the Allies and had little choice but to reorient their economies to the New Order.

There was little common political ground amongst the neutral states. General Franco's dictatorship had come to power with the military assistance of the Axis powers in the Spanish Civil War of 1936–9, and Franco had every expectation of joining the war on their side when he judged the conditions to be right. His fellow Iberian dictator, President Salazar of Portugal, conversely, led a country that was Britain's oldest ally and which had vital overseas imperial interests to protect. In Sweden, which had a Social Democrat-led coalition government, opinion was also largely pro-Allied and there was a lively anti-fascist exiled community. In Switzerland the country's somewhat apolitical traditions supported the pragmatism of Foreign Minister Marcel Pilet-Golaz who, on June 25, 1940, called on his countrymen to play their part in a Europe "very different from before."[16] Neutrality was unavoidable for Éamon de Valéra's Fianna Fáil government, given the history of Irish nationalism and the 1919–21 war of independence from Britain. This did not, however, prevent at least 40,000 southern Irish men and women from volunteering to serve in Britain's armed forces (while thousands more worked in its war industries).[17]

Neutral states assisted Germany both militarily and economically. Sweden agreed to allow unarmed German troops and supplies access to bases in northern Norway by rail, and after the June 1941 "midsummer crisis" permitted a German division to cross its territory to join the attack on the Soviet Union. Switzerland also allowed rail transit for the supply of German forces in Italy and engaged in a lucrative arms trade with Germany. Spain failed to enter the war, primarily because the price that Franco demanded (control of French North Africa and massive economic and military assistance) was too high. However, he did send some 45,000 volunteers to fight in the Blue Division on the Eastern Front, and provided the Germans with supply facilities for submarines as well as intelligence on British shipping in the Straits of Gibraltar. The neutrals were particularly valuable to the German war economy for the supply of metals such as high-quality iron ore (from Sweden) and steel-hardening tungsten and chromites from Spain, Portugal, and Turkey.[18] These three became the focus of desperate economic warfare as the Allies sought to buy up as much of the production as possible, while the rulers of these otherwise poor countries attempted to maintain the inflated prices. Most notoriously, Switzerland provided banking facilities that allowed the Nazis to utilize their plundered gold and other assets in international trade.[19] However, the Allies also received support from the neutrals. In August 1943 Portugal allowed Britain access to strategically valuable bases in the Azores, while Ireland shared intelligence and repatriated Allied personnel on its territory (while interning those from the Axis). For both sides, Lisbon was a center of intelligence-gathering and intrigue.

The neutrals gained few plaudits for their role in the war. Churchill criticized the Swedes' "calculated selfishness" and compared the policy of the Irish Free State highly unfavorably to that of Northern Ireland.[20] Franco, who avoided the fate of Hitler and Mussolini more by luck than judgment, faced a very difficult postwar struggle for the survival of his regime. Turkey overcame doubts about its vacillating role by declaring war on Germany – albeit late in the day – in February 1945. In all cases, the war conditioned the neutrals' postwar experience. For instance, Turkey and Portugal, although one-party states, emerged as pillars of postwar Western security while Franco's Spain was never wholly acceptable to west European opinion. For southern Ireland, too, the wartime "Emergency" heightened isolationist tendencies (it did not join the United Nations until 1955) and greatly reduced the prospects of Irish reunification. The Swedish and Swiss economies grew considerably during the war (GDP rose by 28 percent in the case of Sweden) and this contributed to their postwar prosperity. In both cases, however, their wartime collaboration cast a pall that was never wholly dispelled. Indeed, the question of restitution by Swiss banks, above all for the Jewish victims of Nazi plunder, was reignited in the 1990s.

The Human and Physical Cost

The extreme destructiveness of World War II was without precedent. The conflict was far less contained geographically than World War I, and this time the casualties were not borne primarily by the armed forces. Even Britain, the only European combatant not to face warfare on its own territory, suffered severe damage from aerial attack. At its worst, in central and eastern Europe, the war represented a murderous assault by the Nazis on those least able to protect themselves: Jews and other ethnic minorities, civilians, and Soviet prisoners of war. By such standards, the German atrocities on the Western Front, such as the massacre of 80 captured US soldiers at Malmédy, the execution of Allied commandos, and even bloody reprisals such as the murder of 642 French civilians at Oradour-sur-Glane in June 1944, were of a quite different order of magnitude.

By the end of the war some 6 million European Jews (some 67 percent of the prewar population) had been killed, either massacred by the *Einsatzgruppen* on the Eastern Front or deported to the camps where they were gassed or worked to death. Some 1 million Jews died at Auschwitz alone. The severest losses fell on the substantial Jewish communities of eastern Europe under Nazi control. Three million of the Jews in Poland perished (90 percent), as did 1 million (48 percent) of those in the Soviet Union. In western Europe, the fate of the Jews often depended on the collaborationist zeal of the local authorities. Seventy five percent of Dutch Jews were killed, and the French police often willingly assisted in the rounding up of Jews for deportation from France. The last regular rail shipment from Drancy (Paris) to the camps was on July 31, 1944, well after D-Day. However, the 8,000 Danish Jews were transported to safety in Sweden in October 1943, while some satellite regimes – such as that of Admiral Horthy in Hungary – also attempted to protect their Jewish populations. Quite apart from the loss of innocent life and the shattering of families, the social and cultural impact of the destruction of the Jewish populations on Europe was incalculable. Historic communities had been erased and the ethnic map of Europe redrawn. The Polish population, for instance, became far more homogenous as a result (as well as because of the expulsion of the Germans at the war's end). By 1945 Poland was 95 percent Catholic, as opposed to 68 percent in 1921.[21] Moreover, under the Nazi-imposed diaspora many Jews sought new and permanent homes in Palestine and the USA.

The Jews were the greatest – but by no means the only – victims of Nazi fanaticism. Up to half a million Gypsies were also killed, as well as 72,000 mentally handicapped Germans, systematically murdered in the "euthanasia" campaign of 1941. Many other groups were targeted, such as homosexuals, communists, and other political opponents. Nazi treatment of the 5.75 million Soviet prisoners of war was so brutal, including forced labor under inhuman conditions, that as few as 1 million survived their captivity.[22] Such inhumanity was by no means the preserve of the Nazis. In Bosnia, the epicenter of the struggle within Yugoslavia, the Croatian Ustasha embarked on a vicious campaign to "kill a third, convert a third and deport a third" of the Serb population. Meanwhile, both Serb and Croat nationalists directed violence against the Bosnian Muslims. In all, 1.5 million Yugoslavs – mainly civilians – died in the course of the war. The Soviet authorities also committed atrocities, notably following the annexation of eastern Poland and the Baltic states in 1939–40. Thousands of Polish officers were secretly murdered in the Katyn forest on Stalin's orders, a crime that was exposed by German forces in 1943.

Among the Allied states, the losses of the Soviet Union were by far the most severe, and almost beyond comprehension. In the winter of 1941/2 more citizens of Leningrad starved to death each month than the total number of Britons killed by bombs in the entire war.[23] It now appears that as many as 27 to 28 million perished in all (although Stalin, unwilling to reveal the USSR's weakness, only admitted to 7 million). These included 8.7 million Red Army soldiers and 19 million civilians (perhaps 1 million in Leningrad alone).[24] Some of these losses were, however, self-inflicted, such as the 13,500 soldiers executed for alleged cowardice during the battle of Stalingrad. More than a quarter of the 393,000 Chechens and 91,000 Ingush deported from their homes in the Caucasus to the deserts of Kazakhstan in early 1944, under suspicion of collaboration, eventually died.[25] Most of the survivors were unable to return home until the late 1950s. The USSR's physical loss was also immense: thousands of towns and villages were destroyed and vast amounts of industrial and agricultural assets removed to Germany. In the face of such appalling setbacks, the war represented a triumph for the organizational and motivational powers of the Communist Party, but also for Russian patriotism and initiative. The Red Army's victory over Nazism in the "Great Patriotic War" created a new legitimacy for the Soviet Union, and a symbolism more enduringly popular than that associated with the October Revolution of 1917.

Britain's wartime losses were dwarfed by comparison: some 264,000 soldiers and 90,000 civilians had died. Even so, Britain had made many sacrifices in its, for a time, solitary struggle against the Axis powers. The Luftwaffe's bombs in 1940–1, and later the V-1 and V-2 missile attacks in 1944, had caused considerable damage to economic infrastructure and housing stock. In all, some 110,000 buildings had been completely destroyed and 2 million more had suffered some damage.[26] Moreover, the British merchant marine had suffered grievous losses from German submarines. Above all, Britain had been forced to expend its national wealth to finance a global war effort. Overseas assets worth $21 billion had been turned into a $2 billion deficit. Britain, therefore, ended the war a bankrupt victor, in the shadow of the United States.

France had also suffered severely during the war: 250,000 were killed in the armed forces (while 1.5 million prisoners were forced to spend the war unproductively in Germany) and 300,000–400,000 civilians also died. However, the impact of the war was also physical and moral. If the swiftness of its collapse in 1940 spared France much material damage, the liberation proved slower and far more costly. For instance, the town of Caen was obliterated by Allied bombing during the battle of Normandy, although Hitler's vindictive order for the destruction of Paris was thankfully not implemented. In all, some 290,000 residential buildings were destroyed and the transport infrastructure lay shattered. By 1944 real GDP was only a half of the prewar level. Such losses could, however, be made good. Far harder to restore was a sense of French pride after the humiliation of occupation, and many aspects of postwar policy – such as the dogged defense of the empire and the pursuit of an independent world role – would reflect this.

Elsewhere in occupied Europe civilian casualties far exceeded those of the military. Six million citizens of prewar Poland died (including thousands under the Soviet occupation of 1939–41), of whom 150,000 fell in combat. The destruction was immense: Warsaw, for instance, was razed to the ground as a result of the 1944 uprising. Another peril of Nazi occupation was famine. The Red Cross estimated that 250,000 Greeks died between 1941 and 1943 as a result of food shortages caused by German requisitions and the dislocation of food production and supply.[27] Some 16,000 Dutch men and women also perished in the terrible winter of 1944/5 following the failure of the Allied thrust across the lower Rhine. Italy's losses were relatively light, given that it had been a major belligerent. Indeed, the Italian casualties, 291,000 in the armed forces and 180,000 civilians, were considerably lower than those suffered in World War I. Italy had exerted itself the least of all of the major powers and ended the war with a considerably enhanced engineering industry, allowing a relatively swift recovery after 1945.

By 1945 Germany appeared utterly devastated and transformed. The communist leader Walter Ulbricht wrote of his arrival in Berlin in May 1945 that "we could barely find our way through the rubble because of the smoke."[28] Up to 50 percent of the fabric of most larger cities had been destroyed, mainly in the Allied strategic bombing offensive, and 131 towns and cities had suffered more than 75 percent destruction.[29] The abiding image of the immediate postwar urban landscape was that of the *Trummerfrauen* ("women of the rubble") clearing the debris. Although estimates vary, as many as 7 million Germans had perished in the war, including 3.2 million civilians (many in the Allied bombing) and 85 percent of Germany's 125,000 Jews. In addition, in the closing stages of the war, German populations in the east were victims of the officially sanctioned vengeance of the advancing Red Army, driving them into flight. Between 6,000 and 9,000 civilians and wounded soldiers died with the sinking of the liner *Wilhelm Gustloff* in the Baltic on January 30, 1945. The final Soviet offensive was accompanied by the widespread rape of German women by Red Army soldiers, a danger that persisted well into the subsequent occupation.[30] In some respects, however, the image of abject defeat was deceptive. Allied bombing had flattened the cities and disrupted the railways, but had caused surprisingly little damage to the German war industry. Only 6.5 percent of machine tools had been destroyed in the war and, given the size of the Nazi investment program, the postwar capital stock in western Germany still exceeded the prewar level by one fifth.[31] Moreover, since 1942 Speer's armaments ministry had achieved enduring advances in productivity by imposing techniques of mass production (war production expanded threefold between 1942 and 1944). Accordingly, while Germany ended the war facing acute problems of economic, moral, and political reconstruction, its industrial potential remained huge (and was, indeed, realized in the 1950s). As we shall see, the fear that Germany would once more recover to endanger the peace of Europe remained a powerful force in the postwar era.

The end of the war was accompanied by the mass movement of populations.[32] Between 1945 and 1948 some 10 million Germans, including 3.5 million from the

Czech Sudetenland, were expelled from central and eastern Europe with the approval of the Allied powers. By 1951 more than a fifth of the West German population was composed of refugees. Polish and Czech peasants – some themselves victims of the Soviet seizure of the eastern borderlands – flocked to settle in former German farms and cities in one of the most sudden and profound ethnic transformations witnessed in Europe. Three million Germans remained as prisoners of war within the Soviet Union, the final 10,000 only returning after Adenauer's visit to Moscow in 1955. Elsewhere, some 11 million former forced laborers and prisoners of the Nazis were on the move. The successful return of many of them to their homes by the end of 1945 was a significant achievement for the Allied authorities, offset by the cynical forced repatriation, in line with Stalin's wishes, of Soviet refugees, exiles and anti-communist combatants. By September 1945, 2,272,000 had been handed over, many to a certain death, although some 500,000 remained in western Europe when the policy was relaxed in late 1945. Others, such as the 112,000 Spanish republican victims of an earlier conflict still in southern France in 1951, found themselves unable to return or, like many Jews, preferred emigration to a return to native countries made inhospitable or changed beyond recognition. The death of 42 Polish Jews in the Kielce pogrom of July 1946 was a savage reminder of the persistence of violent anti-Semitism in Europe after the Holocaust.

Judgment

In addition to imposing unconditional surrender on Germany and depriving it of its sovereignty, the Allied powers also criminalized their defeated enemies. This course of action was, needless to say, fraught with difficulty as no jurisdiction currently existed for trying war crimes and any trial was bound to smack of "victors' justice" – possibly turning the accused into martyrs. Moreover, many Germans were convinced that the Allied bombing was itself a war crime, and the Soviets had themselves been guilty of massacres and deportations in eastern Poland and the Baltic states between 1939 and 1941. Scrupulous care was therefore taken in prosecuting the surviving Nazi leaders and members of the German high command available for trial. (Some, such as Himmler and Goebbels, had joined Hitler in committing suicide, while others, such as Adolf Eichmann, had managed to flee.) The International Military Tribunal (with judges and prosecutors from the USA, USSR, Britain, and France) sat at Nuremberg for almost a year, and presented a huge volume of documentary evidence, as well as many eyewitnesses, of Nazi aggression and "crimes against humanity." Eventually, 11 of the 21 men in the dock were condemned to death, although Hermann Goering, the most defiant of the accused, succeeded in taking his own life first. Others were given lengthy prison sentences. Speer, who presented himself as a mere technocrat, received

20 years and was lucky to escape with his life. Alongside the prosecution of these individuals a number of organizations, notably the Nazi Party and the SS, were also tried and declared to be criminal, facilitating future trials. For all its flaws, Nuremberg served a very important function in cataloguing and providing irrefutable evidence (both documentary and visual) of the Nazis' crimes. It also created an important precedent by ruling against the defense that the accused were "obeying orders" and emphasizing, instead, personal responsibility. The precedent of Nuremberg also informed the establishment of the 1993 tribunal by the United Nations to investigate alleged war crimes in the former Yugoslavia.

By the time that the Nuremberg judgments were delivered on October 1, 1946, the Cold War had already begun to erode Allied unity, and future high-profile *international* trials – including a proposed one of businessmen – did not materialize. Nazi war crimes were thenceforth prosecuted at a national level in the countries where the atrocities had occurred, and eventually in Germany itself. For example, Karl Hermann Frank, the author of the Lidice massacre, was executed in Prague in May 1946, and 66 members of the Waffen SS were tried for the atrocity at Oradour in 1953 in Bordeaux. After the initial spate of prosecutions, trials punctuated the peace of postwar Europe less regularly but aroused ever more interest. Eichmann, the only major architect of the final solution still at large, was kidnapped from Argentina by Israeli agents, and tried and hung in May 1962. Between 1963 and 1965 there was a trial of former SS Auschwitz guards at Frankfurt, and, despite a majority of Germans opposing any further prosecutions, the statute of limitation for genocide was abolished in 1969. From the 1980s there was a new round of high-profile prosecutions of those complicit in Nazi war crimes, some of whom had previously been sheltered by their political or religious associates. These included the trials of Klaus Barbie (the murderer of Jean Moulin) in 1987, of the collaborator Paul Touvier in 1992, and of Maurice Papon, a Vichy police chief responsible for the arrest and deportation of 1,560 Jews, in 1997–8. As late as 1991 Britain introduced special war crimes legislation to allow the reopening of cases against those who had settled – in comfortable obscurity – after the war in the UK.

Alongside the quest for justice lay the larger question of the "de-Nazification" of German society, which had been agreed on as a goal by the Allied leaders at Yalta in February 1945. There was, however, a substantial difference of interpretation between the Western view – that this was a matter of individual screening to establish degrees of guilt – and the Soviet belief that de-Nazification would flow from the fundamental reform of the capitalist structures of German society. There were further differences within the Western powers as the United States favored a harsher process of de-Nazification prior to the intended withdrawal of US forces within two years of the war's end, while the British consistently favored a more pragmatic approach that would prioritize the rehabilitation of German society. Although policies and outcomes differed across the different occupation zones, the sheer scale of the task, combined with the need to revive the German economy and the pressures of the Cold War, tended to support the British view. From 1946 responsibility was devolved to German-run tribunals, and attempts were made to deal with the lesser cases by large-scale amnesties. By 1950 the tribunals had dealt with more than 6 million cases, of which a mere 1,700 were placed in the most serious category of offender, while two-thirds were immediately amnestied.[33] The new West German government brought the whole process to a close in October 1950. In many respects, the Allies had created the worst of all worlds: de-Nazification had been sufficiently intrusive to reinforce a sense of German grievance, yet it was easily circumvented and its real impact on German society had been very limited. Indeed, by the early 1950s at least 50 percent of West German civil servants were former Nazis. The British High Commissioner Sir Ivone Kirkpatrick recalled that in the early 1950s he constantly encountered "the ghosts of Hitler's Reich ... taking jobs in banks, commerce and industry."[34]

Very similar issues applied to the aftermath of collaboration, as governments were torn between the popular desire for national catharsis and the need to avoid social and economic upheaval. Such debates pitted the authority of the restored governments and the Allies, who sought to contain the purges and to protect business and administrative elites, against the desire of the resistance to broaden them as the basis for wholesale social change. These problems were first confronted in France where there were some 9,000 summary executions. Once the legal process had been initiated there were a further 767 executions, as well as some 26,289 prison sentences, 13,211 sentences of forced labor, and 40,249 punishments of "national degradation."[35] De Gaulle exercised clemency in two-thirds of the death sentences that he examined, refusing to pardon Pierre Laval but allowing Pétain to live his final years in prison (where he died in 1951).[36] There was less summary justice in Belgium, where the liberation occurred swiftly, although there were outbreaks of spontaneous violence against collaborators following the German surrender in May 1945. Of the 2,940 death sentences that were eventually passed only 242 were carried out.[37] As many as 12,000–15,000 people were killed in the confusion that enveloped the liberation of northern Italy, and Mussolini was captured and shot while fleeing dressed in a German uniform. His body was hung on display alongside that of his mistress in the Piazza Loreto, Milan. Thereafter, however, a remarkably restrained and short-lived legal purge was instituted, concerned far more with punishing active wartime collaboration than with any attempt to come to terms with two decades of Italian fascist rule.

In eastern Europe, where governments were under great pressure from both the USSR and local communist parties, postwar justice was far more overtly political. Often, the victors took the opportunity to crush their political opponents under the auspices of anti-fascism. For instance, Tito's resistance rival Mihailovic was tried and executed in 1946, and Archbishop Stepinac of Zagreb was imprisoned for collaboration. Perhaps 100,000 former Ustasha, Chetniks, and others were killed in Yugoslavia between 1945 and 1946.[38] The trial and execution of Monsignor Tiso, the former leader of Slovakia, was exploited by Czechs and communists as a weapon against both Slovak independence and the political power of the Catholic

Church in a reunited Czechoslovakia. Postwar trials and purges were also intended to facilitate rapid social change by stripping out the prewar elites. Across eastern Europe thousands of civil servants were dismissed either for collaboration with the Nazis or for their service under – legally constituted – authoritarian regimes. In the Soviet zone of Germany the fact that 75 percent of academic staff had fled or been purged from the six main universities eased a transition to a Marxist curriculum. There was also collective punishment of entire ethnic groups, such as the Germans of Poland and Czechoslovakia, who were forced to flee and whose lands were confiscated and redistributed.

Postwar "justice" was often ugly and sometimes unjust. Arbitrary distinctions were drawn between shades of collaboration or complicity with Nazism that varied from country to country and between zones of occupation. However, albeit more so in western Europe than the east, legal norms had been observed and the Nazis treated with greater fairness than they themselves had practiced or deserved. Above all, this was a process driven by the need to punish and to draw a line rather than to provide justice for the victims. The mood of the immediate postwar years was hard and uncompassionate. Too much had been seen and too much lost: the priority now was to construct a new social and political order rather than to dwell on the past. The amnesties introduced in France in 1950 and 1953, emptying the jails of all but the most serious collaborators, were symptomatic of the speed with which the war receded.

Conclusion

The defeat of Nazi Germany was only achieved at immense human and physical cost, and required the unprecedented alliance of the United States, the Soviet Union, and Great Britain. However, despite the remarkable initial victories of the German armed forces, the Nazi leadership contributed to their own defeat. The New Order was highly exploitative and did little to encourage active collaboration, while the German war effort was not fully mobilized until 1942. Moreover, the Nazis increasingly diverted resources into a racial and ideological war of extermination against their perceived enemies. The impact of the war on Europe was profound and long-lasting. Extreme right-wing ideologies were discredited, as were those prewar elites tainted with collaboration. In many countries the resistance (in which communist parties had often played a leading role) was poised to take power after the end of the war, or at least to form part of a new postwar political elite. Those countries which succeeded in remaining neutral profited from the economic assistance that they were able to provide, mainly to Germany. Following the liberation of 1944–5, the fate of Europe passed into the hands of the Great Powers. American and Soviet troops had been introduced into the heart of Europe: it could not have been predicted that they would not leave until the 1990s.

2
Europe between the Powers, 1945–1953

From Grand Alliance to Cold War, 1941–1947

On April 25, 1945 an advanced US patrol encountered Soviet troops on the River Elbe. Photographs record a moment of soldierly joy and relief: vodka was produced and there was wild dancing (see Figure 2.1). Yet there was also a touch of solemnity as an American lieutenant appealed to both sides to remember this day. One former GI recalled that "There were tears in the eyes of most of us. Perhaps a sense of foreboding that things might not be as perfect in the future as we anticipated."[1] In fact, barely 18 months later, amidst a welter of suspicion and bad faith, relations between the victorious powers had all but collapsed, while temporary zones of occupation were rapidly hardening into the postwar division of Europe. However, this incipient "Cold War" – so formative for the development of Europe over the next four decades – not only reflected the choices made by the powers after the defeat of Nazism but also the tensions within the wartime Grand Alliance itself. This chapter examines the nature of this unprecedented external intrusion into Europe's affairs, while Chapter 3 will look at how – within the context of the Cold War – the Europeans forged a new political and social order after 1945.

The Grand Alliance was above all a coalition devised to win the war. The prime objective on both sides was to hold it together until the defeat of Germany (and subsequently Japan) and to prevent any possibility of a separate peace. Detailed arrangements for the postwar world were, in general, shelved until the general peace settlement which never materialized.[2] The Casablanca agreement of January 1943, which committed Britain and the USA to the pursuit of unconditional victory, guided Allied policy more clearly in the last years of the war than did the Atlantic Charter of August 1941, which had proposed a postwar world founded on freedom and self-determination. Meanwhile, the exigencies of the wartime alliance

Europe's Troubled Peace: 1945 to the Present, Second Edition. Tom Buchanan.
© 2012 John Wiley & Sons, Ltd. Published 2012 by John Wiley & Sons, Ltd.

Figure 2.1 Advanced units of the 1st US army and the 5th Soviet Guard army meet at the destroyed bridge across the River Elbe at Torgau, April 25, 1945. Photo © akg-images.

had softened the bitter ideological differences of the inter-war years. It was, for instance, impolitic for Soviet officials to recall Churchill's attempt to crush the Bolshevik Revolution at birth, while prominent American diplomats such as Joseph Davies spoke glowingly of Stalin's achievements. None of this meant, however, that the members of the Grand Alliance had abandoned their – often incompatible – ambitions for the postwar world. Churchill dedicated himself to upholding the British empire in his November 1942 Mansion House speech, while Roosevelt, who was notoriously averse to any detailed planning, aspired to a new multilateral order based on free trade and close cooperation between the victorious powers. Stalin, for his part, fully intended to hang on to the border territories (the Baltic states, eastern Poland, and Bessarabia) gained in 1939–40 under the Nazi–Soviet Pact, while extending Soviet influence as far as possible into Europe.

Stalin's territorial claims were the first significant issue to trouble the Alliance. His position was hardly a strong one as Soviet forces did not reoccupy the border lands until 1944. However, the fact that the Red Army alone was fighting the Nazis in Europe, combined with the failure of the Allies to fulfill their promise of a "Second Front" in 1942, gave him an effective lever. Despite Allied misgivings, Roosevelt quietly agreed at the Tehran summit in November 1943 that the Soviet Union should keep its 1941 border (with compensation for Poland in German territory). The advance of Soviet troops into eastern Europe during 1944 raised further concerns, as pro-Soviet governments were installed in Bulgaria and Romania and a loyal Polish regime was established in Lublin. (Stalin had broken relations with the London-based Polish government in April 1943 when it had called for an inquiry into the Katyn mass graves, recently uncovered by the Nazis.) However, Stalin had no intention of antagonizing the Allies while the war continued and presumed that they would help to finance the Soviet Union's reconstruction. Indeed, in an apparent renunciation of Lenin's dream of world revolution, Stalin decided to dissolve the Communist International in May 1943. Moreover, his actions in eastern Europe seemed analogous to the Allies' behavior in liberated Italy, where the Soviet Union had been excluded from any significant role in the Allied Control Council. One way to assuage these tensions, much to Roosevelt's distaste, was to negotiate spheres of influence in the Balkans. In October 1944 Churchill traveled to Moscow and concluded the so-called "percentages" deal whereby the Soviets were guaranteed predominance in Romania (and less certainly in Bulgaria) while Greece fell within the British sphere. The Balkan agreement proved remarkably enduring: witness Stalin's limited support for the Greek communists during the civil war of 1946–9. Thereafter, attention focused ever more pressingly on the future of Poland and Germany.

The fate of both countries loomed large at the Yalta summit in February 1945, the second and last meeting of Stalin, Roosevelt, and Churchill. Yalta became a byword for the Cold War division of Europe. In reality, however, by this point there was nothing that the Western powers could do to dislodge the Red Army from its dominant position in eastern Europe, and Roosevelt felt that he had achieved the best outcome in the circumstances. It was agreed that the Lublin government would be expanded to include members of the exiled Polish administration, and that, under the terms of a high-sounding "Declaration on Liberated Europe," there would be free elections after the war. In any case, there were other important issues to be decided, such as the shape of the proposed United Nations Organization, the new eastern border of Poland, and the division of zones of occupation in Germany. At Churchill's insistence France was granted its own zone, carved out of the Anglo-US share. Furthermore, it was agreed that a commission should be established to assign the levels and distribution of German reparations, with 50 percent earmarked for the USSR. Roosevelt defended Yalta before Congress as a victory for the ideals of the Atlantic Charter, but there is some evidence that he rapidly became disenchanted with what had been accomplished. In late March he privately agreed with the more critical line on Soviet policy taken by Ambassador Averell Harriman in Moscow.[3] However, on April 12, 1945 the president died, to be replaced by the unknown and untested Harry S. Truman.

Although Roosevelt's death brought no initial change in US policy, Truman introduced a sharper note into relations with the USSR and a belief that both sides must honor their agreements. His domestic political position was also more cramped than that of his illustrious predecessor. For instance, Truman's decision to end lend-lease supplies as soon as the war in Europe was over hardly endeared him to the Soviets, but reflected the hostility of Congress to the US funding of its Allies' reconstruction. Truman was not the only newcomer at the third and final summit in Potsdam (July–August 1945). The Soviets were perplexed when, as soon as the results of the British general election were declared in late July, Churchill and Eden were replaced at the conference table by the new Labour Party Prime Minister Clement Attlee and his Foreign Minister, the bluff trade union leader Ernest Bevin. The Potsdam summit was inconclusive and demonstrated the rapid decline of the Grand Alliance. Interim arrangements for the occupation of Germany were agreed and a new border with Poland established on the Oder–Neisse river line, but the question of Germany's long-term future was not resolved (see below). Meanwhile, Stalin introduced a number of diversions such as a claim to part of the former Italian colony of Libya and the replacement of the Franco regime in Spain. The most significant moment came when Truman privately informed Stalin of the existence of the atom bomb, soon to be used against Japan. This was hardly a secret, due to the quality of Soviet intelligence, but it represented a blow to Stalin's strategy of defense in territorial depth. However, the Soviet response was publicly to refuse to attach any significance to the new weapon while, in secret, to pour vast resources into producing their own. For his part, Truman recognized the moral and logistical limitations of the atomic bomb as a means to enforce America's will.[4]

After Potsdam, American policy soon hardened in the face of what appeared to be the Soviet Union's relentless strengthening of its position and probing of that of its wartime allies. Noncommunist political forces were crushed in Bulgaria and Poland in defiance of the Yalta agreements and menacing moves were directed against Turkey in support of Stalin's claim on the Straits. On February 9, 1946 Stalin increased Western fears when, in a rare speech, he indicated that future "catastrophic wars" were unavoidable because the fair distribution of resources between nations was impossible under capitalism.[5] A few days later the Truman administration received muscular intellectual support for a tougher stance from the Soviet specialist George Kennan in his famous "Long Telegram" from the US embassy in Moscow. (His thesis was later honed in his equally famous anonymous article in the journal *Foreign Affairs*.) Kennan argued that the USSR was engaged in an unceasing, long-term ideological conflict with the West, and could only be resisted by "long-term, patient but firm and vigilant containment of Russian expansive tendencies."[6] The idea that Europe was already being partitioned by the Soviet Union was popularized for Americans by Churchill's March 1946

"Iron Curtain" speech at Fulton, Missouri. An early example of this policy of containment occurred in Iran, which had been occupied by the Allies during the war and from where Soviet troops were compelled to withdraw by US pressure in May 1946. In the course of 1946, therefore, many senior US officials came to see the USSR as a potential enemy. Indeed, by November 1946 Truman confided that he saw no difference between the Soviet Union, tsarism, and Hitlerism.[7]

The problem for the US administration, however, was that it was far ahead of the American people (as well as Congress) in its appreciation of a Soviet threat. Domestic opinion still expected a rapid postwar settlement in Europe, followed by the withdrawal of US forces, and the problems of the Balkans and of eastern Europe seemed too remote to stand in the way. Moreover, the USA had already substantially demobilized, so that the Soviet armed forces already enjoyed a clear advantage on the ground in Europe. The USA had reduced its armed forces from 10 million to 1.4 million between 1945 and 1947, and its defense budget from $81 billion to $13 billion per year. The Soviets, meanwhile, had reduced their armed forces from 12 million to some 2.8 million. What was required, therefore, was a means to dramatize the situation, in such a way that the American people would realize the need for unparalleled measures in a time of peace. An opportunity eventually presented itself in Greece, where British forces had been supporting the Greek royalist government against the communist guerrillas. On February 21, 1947 Britain informed the USA that, as of the end of March, it would be unable to continue to provide economic assistance. Truman seized his chance, and on March 12 appealed to Congress for funds for both Greece and Turkey. He argued persuasively that what was at stake was not the mere survival of two somewhat authoritarian regimes, but rather American leadership in a titanic struggle between the free world and "totalitarian" forces. "It must," he said, "be the policy of the United States to support free peoples who are resisting attempted subjugation by armed minorities or by outside pressures."[8] The Truman Doctrine (as it soon became known) was modest in its origins, as the president was, after all, initially only calling for economic aid. However, he had laid the foundation for an unprecedented ideological confrontation with Soviet communism both in Europe and, eventually, worldwide.

Truman's speech offered the American people a simple moral narrative which explained the need for new sacrifices in the containment of alleged Soviet expansionism. There are, however, alternative interpretations of the opening phase of the Cold War. One view, which is given greater salience by the events of 1947–9, emphasizes the success of west European politicians and social elites in drawing the United States into their defense by raising the specter of communism. Certainly, the role of Britain in precipitating the Greek crisis indicates how European governments could influence the pace at which the Cold War developed. At one extreme, this could be rendered as a triumph of European canniness over American naivety. A comment attributed to the French politician Pierre Mendès-France may easily apply to many European politicians in the early Cold

War: "Thank God for the communists: the bigger a fuss we make over the 'communist menace', the more dollars we shall get."[9] This is surely too glib, and fails to do justice to the hard-headedness of the Truman administration. But there is no doubt that the Cold War division of Europe would have been inconceivable without the firm foundation provided by European political forces on the center-left (such as the Labour Party in Britain and the Socialist Party in France) and of the center-right (Christian democrats in a number of countries) who adopted an anti-communist line in association with, and often in advance of, the United States.

From Stalin's perspective, meanwhile, the Soviet Union was quite legitimately attending to its own security needs in eastern Europe after the grievous losses that it had suffered in the war. Despite the wartime alliance, moreover, Britain and the USA had not ceased to be imperialist states, the interests of which were bound to conflict with those of the USSR just as surely as they would conflict with those of each other. There was, therefore, no great mystery about Soviet policy in the territory that it had occupied: as Stalin's colleague Molotov put it in 1974, "we had to consolidate our conquests."[10] Tellingly, he went on to say that "Of course, you had to know where to stop. I believe in this respect Stalin kept well within the limits." Certainly, Stalin was no warmonger. Indeed, his record both in World War II and later during the Korean War showed that he was highly cautious about involving Soviet forces directly in armed conflict. The problem was that Europe was rich with enticing possibilities for the Soviet leader in 1945–6. Communists had entered government in France, Italy, and Belgium, Germany was prostrate, western Europe appeared weak and leaderless, and Soviet military and political power was in the ascendant. The question was not, therefore, whether the Soviet Union should extend its authority into Europe, but how far, and what form that authority should take. The test case lay in Germany.

The German Question

The Allies had reached little prior agreement on the nature of a postwar German state (see Map 2.1). It had been decided at Yalta that the principles of the occupation should be "De-Nazification, Democratization, Demilitarization and Decentralization" in order to render Germany incapable of future aggression. However, each of the powers had a different view as to how this goal should be achieved. France, for instance, wished to see Germany split into a number of small states, with the Rhineland under its own domination. Although it was forced to abandon this strategy in the late 1940s, some elements of it survived in the attempt to absorb the mineral-rich Saarland (which was not returned to Germany until 1957). The USSR pursued, in effect, a dual-track policy by fastening communist political control over its zone of occupation while keeping alive the prospect of a united, neutral Germany under its influence. Britain and the USA had formally

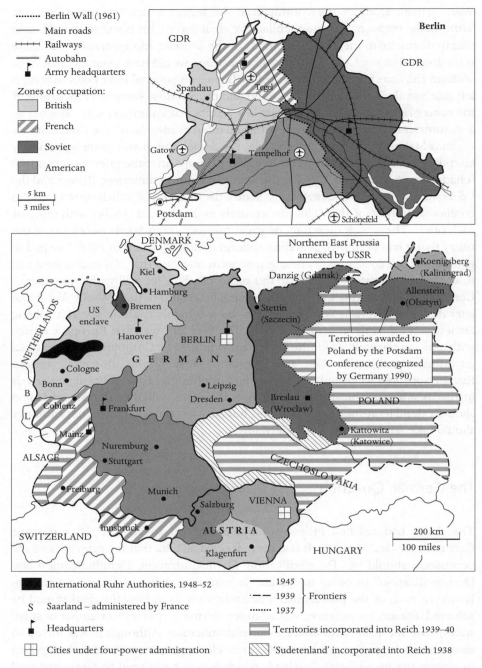

Map 2.1   Postwar Germany and neighboring countries showing zones of occupation and administration.

Source: Lothar Kettenacker, *Germany since 1945* (Oxford University Press, Oxford, 1997). Reprinted with permission.

adopted the 1944 Morgenthau plan, devised by the US Treasury Secretary, according to which Germany would be stripped of much of its industrial base and turned into a "pastoral" society. "Germany's road to peace" Morgenthau claimed "leads to the farm."[11] The plan had been extensively revised by May 1945, but it continued to influence the American occupation orders (JCS 1067) which were hostile to all but the most limited revival of the German economy. From the start, however, the British, who took control of the most industrialized zone (as well as of the largest and the least well fed population), adopted a more pragmatic approach to the occupation than the Americans (who controlled the more rural south).

Despite these highly divergent positions, a coherent policy was adopted at Potsdam (although it should be noted that France was not a party to the discussions). Germany was to be governed by an Allied Control Council (ACC) in Berlin, which had been placed under its own four-power occupation. During the occupation, Germany would be treated as a "single economic unit," with common policies for a broad range of activities. It was further agreed that reparations would be taken in kind by each power from its own zone, such that the German people would be left with sufficient resources to subsist without external support. The USSR would also be entitled to a quarter of the surplus capital equipment in the western zones, some of which had to be paid for in food and raw materials.[12] An agreement was reached in March 1946 on the exact levels of industry required to sustain the economic needs of the German people, which helped to calculate the Soviet entitlement. However, the reparations issue soon became a major cause of disharmony between the occupation authorities. In particular, the refusal by the Soviet Union (and France) to treat Germany as a single economic unit and allow the western zones access to food supplies forced Britain and the USA to subsidize their own occupied populations. Soviet reparations demands were seen as merely postponing the day when German industrial exports could begin to pay for essential imports into the Anglo-US zones. In May 1946 the head of the US occupation, General Lucius Clay, ordered that no more reparations should be sent eastwards. The dynamic of Allied policy had clearly shifted from the punishment of Germany to its economic rehabilitation: initially as a means of feeding its population, latterly as a potential ally in the Cold War.

Similar considerations underlay the Allies' changing attitudes to de-Nazification (see Chapter 1) and to demilitarization, which was primarily concerned with limiting Germany's war-making potential. Under the agreement of March 1946 the levels of German industrial production had been set at 75 percent of those of 1936. In addition, levels of certain key industries, such as steel and chemicals, were set much lower, while some war industries were to be completely eliminated. However, although there was some high-profile dismantling of war-related industries (for instance, the gantries of the Blohm and Voss shipyards were blown up), the original targets were never met. Following a fruitless meeting of the Council of Foreign Ministers in Moscow in March–April 1947, the British and

American authorities persuaded the French to join them in raising the level of industry to the 1936 figure and steel production was almost doubled. From the autumn of 1947 the list of plants for removal was reduced, and following the creation of the Federal Republic of Germany in 1949 a complete end to the program of dismantling was negotiated. The overall cost to West Germany has been estimated at 3.51 percent of gross fixed capital in the western zones.[13] In the Soviet zone, by comparison, it has been estimated that the occupation authorities seized some 30 percent of the region's 1944 industrial capacity,[14] either removing it altogether or establishing their own companies to run the factories. However, the motive was more the need for reparations to make up for Soviet wartime losses than demilitarization.

The very different political policies of the four occupying powers further widened divisions. In the western zones no political parties were initially permitted, and it was intended that German politics would be revived from the grassroots, with particular emphasis placed on institutional and educational reform. The United States was the first occupier to restore federal states, with appointed Minister Presidents, in its zone in September 1945. In the Soviet zone, conversely, some political parties were almost immediately legalized, allowing the authorities to use the Communist Party (KPD) as a further means of control. In this respect, however, Soviet policy was often counterproductive. The wholesale pillage of the economy of the eastern zone, as well as the widespread rape of German women by Red Army soldiers, created a deep resentment of the occupation and greatly reduced the political appeal of the KPD outside of the Soviet zone. As a result the KPD (from April 1946 known as the Socialist Unity Party – SED – following its forced merger with the Social Democrats) fared badly when free elections were held in the autumn of 1946. Thereafter, it had to resort to more overtly coercive methods in asserting its rule over the people of eastern Germany, many of whom had organized spontaneous anti-fascist committees and expressed strongly socialist views in May 1945.

In the course of 1946 the US government came to share the pragmatic view of Germany's future that had long been apparent to men on the ground such as Clay. It was evident that the unified authority established at Potsdam was ineffective, and that the choice now lay between prolonged dislocation and an economic and political restoration at the zonal level (or preferably a union of western zones). A zonal approach was now seen as the key to the economic recovery of Germany, which in turn was acknowledged as crucial to the well-being of western Europe. A shift in policy was signaled by Secretary of State James Byrnes in his speech at Stuttgart in September 1946. Crucially, Byrnes committed America to maintain its troop presence: "We are not withdrawing. We are staying here. As long as there is an occupation army in Germany."[15] He appealed for a return to the Potsdam principles, including the establishment of a German National Council, but also offered to unite the US zone as a single economic unit with any others willing to participate. Four months later, on January 1, 1947, the British and American zones merged to form the "Bizone," which took on many of the functions of a state, including an Economic Council under the liberal economist Ludwig Erhard. However, the French maintained the independence of their relatively small Rhineland zone (which had a population of only 5.9 million compared with some 40 million in the Bizone) until April 1949.

The formation of the Bizone started a process that would result in the formation of the Federal Republic of Germany (FRG) in May 1949 (as well as the German Democratic Republic (DDR) in the Soviet zone in October). At the Moscow conference in the spring of 1947, informal agreement was reached amongst the Western representatives on the desirability of moving towards West German statehood. However, a number of serious issues had to be addressed, notably France's security concerns. France was disturbed at the rapid rehabilitation of Germany, and particularly concerned that the loss of any control over the industrial Ruhr would make possible German revanchism while hampering its own reconstruction. However, the French were also aware of their diplomatic and economic weakness, and eager to benefit from the Marshall Plan which had been launched in the summer of 1947. Accordingly, the London Accords between France, Britain, and the USA in June 1948 allowed for the creation of a state in West Germany, on terms that would satisfy the French. In particular, it was agreed that the Allied occupation would continue, that a special board would monitor German demilitarization, and that the Ruhr would be placed under an (in the event toothless) international agency. Despite these concessions, however, France soon realized that Germany could not be held down indefinitely: hence the remarkable shift to a policy of reconciliation and integration of economic resources in the Schuman Plan of 1950 (see Chapter 3).

By 1948 the new Allied policy on Germany had clearly seized the initiative from the Soviet Union. In March 1948 the Soviet representatives left the ACC, effectively ending four-power control, when it was agreed that the western zones would participate in the Marshall Plan. The Allied currency reform of June 20, 1948, designed to ease the introduction of the Marshall Plan and eliminate the black market, was treated as a further provocation. Stalin, who was at the same time engaging in ideological conflict with his fellow communist Tito, responded by imposing a land blockade on the western sector of Berlin. This was a major test for the Allies as they could neither defend the city from military attack nor force the blockade. The only alternative to a war wanted by neither side was an unprecedented airlift which, by early 1949, was able to meet Berlin's basic supply requirements. Stalin admitted defeat and lifted the blockade in May 1949 after 321 days. The airlift had provided the West with valuable propaganda in the deepening Cold War, as well as doing much to convince the West Germans that the Allies were not only an army of occupation but were also committed to their defense. Berlin itself had become the first great symbol of an emerging "free world," epitomized in the dedication of a Freedom Bell before a crowd of 400,000 citizens (from east and west of the city) in October 1950.[16]

Marshall Aid and Economic Security

On June 5, 1947 the new US Secretary of State George Marshall made an address at Harvard in which he called on the United States to assist the economic recovery of Europe. This policy, he stated somewhat disingenuously, was not directed "against any country or doctrine but against hunger, poverty, desperation and chaos." Its purpose was to revive a "working economy" from which free institutions could grow, and the offer was open to all countries of Europe.[17] Although "Marshall Aid" did not begin to flow until 1948, the initiative marked a crucial stage in the Cold War division of Europe and, above all, in the US commitment to western Europe. Eventually, between 1948 and 1952, the European Recovery Program (ERP) would pump $13 billion-worth of aid (2.4 percent of US GNP at its peak in 1949) into the European economy.

Marshall had become convinced of the need for action while attending the Moscow conference in the spring of 1947. He came away with the impression that Stalin relished Europe's economic disarray, which American officials in Europe had been drawing attention to in colorful prose for some months. Will Clayton of the State Department had, for instance, written in May 1947 that "we have grossly underestimated the destruction to the European economy by the war ... Millions of people in the cities are slowly starving."[18] Although $9 billion had been spent in aid, both bilaterally and through the UN relief agency UNRRA, the level of agricultural production in western Europe still only stood at 83 percent of that of 1938. The comparable figure for industrial production was 88 percent, and for exports a mere 59 percent.[19] The lack of manufacturing strength meant that Europe suffered from a chronic dollar shortage and had run up a huge deficit in trade with the United States. The problem was not so much the loss of manufacturing capacity (although in many countries obsolescence was a serious issue) as the dislocation caused by the damage to transport infrastructure and the production of raw materials, especially coal. Furthermore, the collapse of the German economy and the loss of its coal supplies seriously affected its close neighbors and trading partners such as Denmark and Belgium. The severe winter of 1946/7, during which fuel supplies often failed, had thrown these shortcomings into sharp relief.

Two factors in particular underpinned the concerns of American officials. First, a direct connection was drawn between hunger and poverty and the rise of political extremism. As General Clay observed of the proposed ration allowance in Germany in March 1946: "there is no choice between becoming a communist on 1,500 calories [a day] and a believer in democracy on 1,000 calories."[20] One objective was therefore to prevent the political disintegration of western Europe and to restore a balance of power on the continent. Indeed, a key argument in the defense of the Marshall Plan before Congress was that economic aid now would preclude the need for expensive rearmament in the future. Secondly, Europe's problems signaled the failure of Roosevelt's idealistic vision of a rapid postwar economic recovery, based on free trade and overseen by new institutions such as the International Monetary Fund (IMF) and the UN's International Trade Organization. In particular, the goal of automatic currency convertibility – as agreed at Bretton Woods in July 1944 – was indefinitely postponed. A premature attempt to restore convertibility by Britain in August 1947, fulfilling the terms of Britain's postwar dollar loan, resulted in a financial crisis. One solution was a series of short-term loans to specific countries, such as those advanced to Britain and France in 1946. However, these were politically unpopular in the USA, where many critics complained that America was, in effect, subsidizing the British empire and the welfare state. The lesson was twofold. Not only was a new political rationale needed for American financial support (an economic analogue to the Truman Doctrine) but also loans were not enough. A sustained American intervention would be needed to force the European economy to become more integrated and productive, and thereby a stable long-term trading partner.

Marshall offered no blank check. Instead, it was left up to the Europeans, collectively, to make an appeal for US assistance and draw up a program of aid. Bevin and his French counterpart Bidault readily seized the initiative by convening a Conference on European Economic Cooperation (CEEC) in Paris for July 12, 1947. The conference was eventually attended by 16 west European states, while the interests of the western zones of Germany were also represented. The most pressing question was the response of the Soviet Union. It was not immediately apparent that the USSR would refuse to participate as Marshall had gambled that it would. Had the Soviets accepted, it is likely that they would have received very little aid,[21] but the moral high ground would have been lost. In the event the Soviet Foreign Minister Molotov arrived at the preparatory talks with Bevin and Bidault, only to walk out days later. The Soviets then browbeat the other east European governments – notably the Czechs – into following their policy. The Soviets interpreted the Marshall Plan (seen in the context of the recent departure of communists from government in France, Belgium, and Italy) as an aggressive act intended to consolidate American power in western Europe, which required a matching response in the east. In September Stalin convened the first meeting of the new Communist Information Bureau (Cominform) at Sklarska Poreba in Poland. Here, his lieutenant Zhdanov laid down the line that the world had divided into two antagonistic "camps" and that it was the task of communists to lead "the resistance to the American plan for the enthralment of Europe."[22] The hardening of attitudes after the Cominform meeting, above all the consolidation of communist power in Czechoslovakia in February 1948 (see Chapter 3), in turn did much to ease the passage of the Economic Cooperation Act through Congress in April.

What Molotov had balked at, but western Europe was willing to contemplate, was the many strings attached to Marshall Aid. In effect, the United States was willing to support those economies which were ready to model themselves on its own and to challenge entrenched attitudes on both sides of industry. In particular, the ERP promoted greater productivity on a "Fordist" mass production basis, an expansion of foreign trade, financial stability, and economic integration. There was much here that was controversial, especially at a time when the Europeans were increasing government expenditure on various forms of welfare state, and the ERP eventually emerged as a compromise between American ideals and west European realities. The draft bilateral treaties on which Marshall Aid was based contained a number of highly intrusive clauses, some of which (for instance, a requirement for the Europeans to register changes in exchange rates with the IMF) were dropped. However, clauses stipulating that 50 percent of aid should be carried in American ships and protecting the interests of American farmers were retained.

The CEEC had proved an unwieldy and fractious body, and eventually the administration of the ERP was entrusted to a new European Cooperation Agency (ECA) chaired by the former businessman Paul Hoffman. The ECA was independent of the State Department and, in Averell Harriman, possessed its own Special Representative in western Europe. It had numerous resources at its disposal, in particular the use of "counterpart funds" (the proceeds in local currencies of the sale of ERP goods). These were under the joint management of national governments and the ECA, with 5 percent reserved for the ECA alone, and were mainly spent on stabilization and infrastructure projects (such as the Monnet Plan in France). By mid-1951 the great bulk of Marshall Aid had been used to purchase food, feed and fertilizer ($3.192 billion), fuel ($1.567 billion), raw materials and semi-manufactured goods ($3.43 billion), and machinery and vehicles ($1.853 billion). The main recipients by mid-1951 were Britain ($2.7 billion), France ($2.4 billion), Italy ($1.29 billion), and western Germany ($1.29 billion).[23]

The most contentious aspect of the ERP was the American commitment to economic integration. For the Marshall Planners it was self-evident that western Europe (with a population of 270 million and a GNP of $160 billion) should seek to copy the single market of the United States (where 150 million people had a GNP of $260 billion).[24] They believed that this could be realized by placing the power to allocate resources in the hands of a supranational body – the CEEC's permanent successor, the Organization for European Economic Cooperation (OEEC). The principle of integration was not wholly unacceptable to the Europeans, even to Britain, so long as it could be implemented on their own terms and in line with their own interests (which were often divergent). However, none of them favored the supranational model, and American attempts to give greater powers to the OEEC were consistently stymied by the Europeans. For instance, the appointment of the Belgian Paul Henri Spaak, an enthusiast for greater European cooperation, as Director General was vetoed by Britain, and eventually the Dutchman Dirk Stikker was appointed with the inoffensive title of "Political Conciliator." Britain's eventual refusal to involve itself in any integrationist measures in 1949 was also a serious blow to the ECA, which had looked to Britain as the leader of Europe. The OEEC remained an important intergovernmental body, most notably as the vehicle for the September 1950 European Payments Union (which did much to restore intra-European trade). However, economic integration advanced during the 1950s on a far narrower front than had been envisaged under the Marshall Plan (see Chapter 9).

Marshall Aid was overtly political, and its function was to assert American leadership and undermine the communist left. The arrival of the first shipment of aid in Bordeaux was the occasion for a ceremony at which the socialist Transport Minister Pineau stated that "France owes her revival to the United States. This ship is symbolic of the common prosperity of the Free West."[25] Similarly, the $176 million of interim aid that the United States dispatched to Italy at the start of 1948 played a crucial role in the run-up to the watershed Italian election in April. Marshall underlined the point by threatening to withhold any further aid if the communists won. However, the ERP also represented a sustained effort to promote the "American way" of labor productivity and flexibility. This message was propagated through cinemas, pamphlets, and public meetings, as well as, in the early 1950s, through programs which sent workers and management to the USA to study American workplace methods. By 1952, 2,600 Frenchmen had visited the USA as part of some 200 teams. Another important area was labor relations, where the ECA's labor department worked closely with the American AFL/CIO union federation as well as the fledgling CIA to promote a more moderate and cooperative workforce. During this period the communist-led French CGT and the Italian CGIL, as well as the World Federation of Trade Unions, were all successfully split, and the anti-communist breakaway groups received US funding. However, the significance of American meddling should not be exaggerated, as in many respects the European unions split along well-established political fault lines that long predated the Cold War. US intervention can be seen, therefore, as the occasion, as much as the cause, of the restructuring of the trade union movement.

From June 1950, with the outbreak of the Korean War, the ERP was overshadowed by the US rearmament drive. By 1952 the United States was sending $1 billion in economic aid to Europe, compared with $4.8 billion of military aid under the Mutual Defense Assistance Program established in October 1949. However, American business investment in Europe rapidly expanded during the 1950s, and US military bases also brought an influx of dollars. By 1952 the GNP of western Europe had risen to 32 percent above the prewar level, although industry (up by 40 percent) had recovered significantly faster than agriculture (11 percent). In 1955 the ERP was wound up, with small amounts continuing to go to specific problem areas such as West Berlin and Yugoslavia. The exact contribution of the Marshall Plan remains highly contentious, and the idea that it single-handedly revived the European economies has been discredited by economic historians.[26] However, there is no doubt that the ERP was of immense political and psychological significance. It provided tangible evidence of America's commitment to a secure and prosperous western Europe, and offered a vision (or dream) of plenty and modernity that was not beyond the reach of ordinary Europeans. Politically, Marshall Aid polarized both Europe and the societies of western European between – as Hoffman put it – the party line and the assembly line.[27] In reality, however, ECA officials were forced to recognize that they faced an uphill struggle to convert European workers – who above all wanted social security – to the joys of the American way of life.

NATO and the Defense of the West

The Marshall Plan – and the Soviet response – marked a critical stage in the development of postwar Europe, clearly demarcating an emergent "western" Europe from an "eastern" Europe under Soviet domination (see Map 2.2). However, despite the United States' economic and political commitment, there was as yet no sign of the military guarantee which many European governments desired. In this they were not primarily motivated by fear of a direct Soviet attack. There is no evidence that such an offensive was intended, nor did the US and British high commands anticipate one. What governments did find worrying was the prospect of continuing Soviet pressures on the periphery, directed against countries such as Norway, which would weaken the resolve of western Europe as a whole. Accordingly, a long-term US military commitment to Europe came to be seen as essential to the political solidity of the West. There were, however, numerous obstacles in the way. Many west Europeans still perceived a revanchist Germany as a greater threat than the Soviet Union, and feared that the militarization of the West would merely hasten a German revival. Indeed, the Anglo-French treaty of Dunkirk, signed in March 1947, had specifically identified Germany as the potential enemy. For their part, many Americans were suspicious of military commitments and heeded George Washington's valedictory warning against "entangling alliances." Any military commitment to Europe would undoubtedly increase the prospects of US involvement in a war, while the stationing of troops in Germany (for political rather than military reasons) placed US servicemen in potential danger. However, it should be noted that, in spite of the Republican control of Congress after November 1946, there was remarkable political consensus behind Truman's foreign policy.

Pressures for a formal alliance mounted during 1948. In March the Dunkirk Treaty was extended to include the Benelux countries in the Brussels Pact which, in July, opened formal negotiations with the USA. The way was cleared by the Vandenberg resolution in the Senate (June 1948) which allowed the United States to take the unprecedented step of participating in a regional security pact. The talks were given greater impetus by the Berlin crisis, which exposed the West's military weakness. On April 5, 1949 the North Atlantic Treaty was signed by 12 states. The core of the alliance was provided by the USA and the five members of the Brussels Pact, while two countries, Norway and Denmark, joined under "minimum conditions." Norway informed the USSR that it would not allow

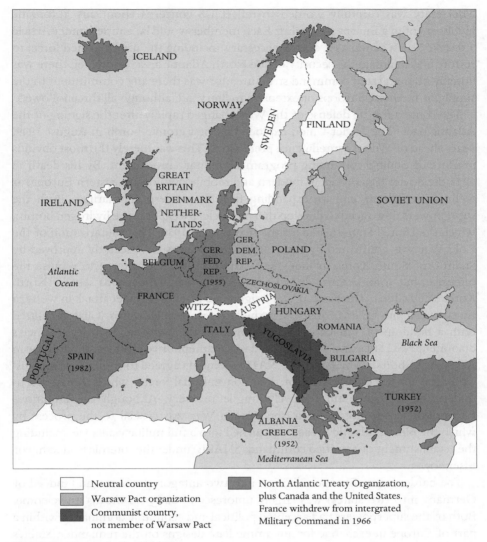

Map 2.2 Europe in the Cold War.
Source: William R. Keylar, *A world of nations* (Oxford University Press, Oxford, 2003), p. 42.

foreign troops to be based on its soil in peacetime, and in 1957 this was extended to include nuclear weapons. Portugal and Iceland were included primarily for their strategic significance, and from 1951 Iceland was defended by US troops. Italy chose to join despite the opposition not only of the communists but also of a section of the ruling Christian Democrats. These founding members were subsequently joined by Greece and Turkey (1952) and by West Germany (1955), but, contrary to American wishes, Franco's Spain remained beyond the pale.

The treaty was carefully worded to reflect US concerns about any automatic involvement in a European conflict. Each member would be entitled under Article 5 to take "such action as it deems necessary, including the use of armed force, to restore and maintain the security of the North Atlantic area." However, there was initially no integrated command structure, nor was there any commitment to the supply of further US troops or extensive military aid, although all three followed.

The context for the defense of the West changed rapidly after the signing of the Atlantic pact. The Soviet Union exploded its first atomic bomb in August 1949, years ahead of Western intelligence predictions. This was merely the most obvious product of Stalin's continuing program of military investment. By his death in 1953 the Soviet Union had 30 modern and mobile divisions in eastern Europe, as well as jet fighters and an expanding fleet of modern submarines. Both the superpowers now raced to develop thermonuclear weapons (the hydrogen bomb), which the United States tested for the first time in 1952. The militarization of the Cold War was confirmed by the North Korean invasion – secretly approved by Stalin – of South Korea in June 1950. The USA led a UN force to repulse the offensive, but soon became drawn into a costly war with troops sent by North Korea's ally China. The Korean War heightened fears of a Soviet attack in western Europe, and four US divisions were rushed to Germany. However, it also permitted both a build-up of US forces (as envisaged in the National Security Council's document NSC 68) and a US-sponsored rearmament drive amongst the European Allies. At Lisbon in February 1952, NATO members agreed to somewhat unrealistic targets for the enlargement of their conventional forces, which threatened to undermine Europe's still relatively fragile recovery. Although the ambitious Lisbon goals were not fulfilled, the Korean War was crucial to the process by which the North Atlantic Treaty was turned into a full military alliance, including the establishment of a unified command (SHAPE) under the totemic leadership of Eisenhower.

The hardening of Europe's division into two antagonistic blocs (and indeed of Germany into two states) was largely unforeseen but by no means unwelcome. Both of the superpowers had accepted political and economic dominance within a part of Europe in exchange for any immediate designs on the remainder. Stalin's note of March 1952, offering a united and neutral Germany, was a final reminder of how things might have turned out differently. The main victims of Europe's partition were the people of eastern Europe, who were cut off from the prosperity of the West and subjected to the full rigors of Stalinism. The main beneficiaries were undoubtedly the west Europeans, whose economic and military security were now assured. Britain was able to transfer the responsibility for defense of Europe to the USA and concentrate on salvaging what was left of its empire. For France, the stationing of American troops offered a solution to the threat posed both by the Red Army and a revived Germany, and allowed France to adopt a more constructive attitude towards Germany (although there were residual concerns about the "Anglo-Saxon" domination of NATO). The American military commitment had been encouraged and assiduously worked for by European governments – notably by politicians such as Bevin and the Belgian Prime Minister Paul Henri Spaak – and this has led some historians to argue, problematically, that western Europe now represented an "empire by invitation."[28] Clearly the American presence was by invitation, but it was hardly imperial in any conventional sense. Certainly, the United States did not impose its will by force as the Soviets did repeatedly in eastern Europe or, indeed, as the USA itself did in Central America and the Caribbean. The nature of this developing relationship remained unequal, but it was also subtle, mutually beneficial, and based on compromise.

Culture and the Cold War

The Cold War was not only a political, economic, and military confrontation: it was also a conflict of ideas conducted across all levels of culture, from radio propaganda and cartoons to high art. All sides in the Cold War came to appreciate the power of culture and would seek to harness it for their own ends. This is not to suggest that there was an equivalence in cultural life across the Cold War divide, as the controls on free expression in the Soviet bloc were far tighter than those in the West, even during the McCarthy era. Even so, in western Europe the growing patronage of the state, plus funding from US agencies and independent foundations, both transformed and none too subtly influenced cultural life in the postwar years. Here, the Cold War represented not only a riposte to Soviet communism but also, as we shall see, an attempt to define and build support for a "Western" liberal culture. Such a project was inevitably at odds with the influential cultural and intellectual movements which had emerged immediately after the war, such as the existentialist philosophy of Jean-Paul Sartre or Italian Neo-Realist cinema and literature. Both, in their own way, whether Sartre's advocacy of political nonalignment (of a leftist character) in his periodical *Les Temps modernes* or Neo-Realism's attempt to perpetuate the humanist optimism of the resistance, challenged the Manichaeanism of the Cold War.

In the Soviet Union cultural orthodoxy, somewhat relaxed during the war, was reimposed by the four decrees issued by Zhdanov from 1946 to 1948. These decrees, which affected Soviet culture well into the 1950s, addressed in turn the literary journals, drama, cinema, and music, and specifically criticized the work of such eminent figures as Akhmatova, Eisenstein, and Shostakovich. Zhdanov was restating the belief that there was "no place for neutral art in a classless society,"[29] and that there was no frame of cultural reference beyond the USSR – certainly not in the West. Under the paradigm of "Socialist Realism," Soviet writers and artists were expected to imbue their work with the principles of *narodnost* (people-mindedness) and *partiinost* (party-mindedness) and, above all, the cult of Stalin's personality. Works of art had to portray a positive, optimistic impression of the

Soviet Union: at its most absurd, a committee insisted that a bare-footed peasant girl be given shoes before a painting could be displayed.[30] Those who refused to obey the new strictures might suffer a worse fate than the loss of commissions. For instance, the Futurist artist Nikolai Punin was arrested in 1949 and died in a labor camp four years later. The anti-Western campaign went far further than the arts, as the late 1940s witnessed the victory within Soviet biology of Lysenko, a fanatical opponent of genetics whose bizarre theories blighted Soviet agriculture over the next decade. Tellingly, however, the still internationalist world of Soviet nuclear physics was able to resist these pressures so long as there was a prospect of creating a Soviet bomb.

Lysenkoism was deeply shocking to many intellectuals in western Europe who were otherwise sympathetic to Soviet communism, precisely because it flew in the face of its claim to scientific rationality. Even so, for a decade after the war communism was partially shielded from criticism in the West by the luster of anti-fascism and by an ignorance (or denial) of the realities of Stalinism. In addition, communism's appropriation of the mantle of European high art allowed it to benefit from the snobbery directed at the apparent shallowness and commercialism of American culture. Accordingly, Western communist parties, especially in France and Italy, continued to enjoy high levels of support from prominent figures in cultural life. Artists such as Picasso (who joined the French Communist Party in 1944) raised the profile of a series of communist-inspired campaigns of the period, notably the Europe-wide peace campaign launched in 1948. However, political engagement came with its own artistic cost. Picasso's anti-American *Massacre in Korea* (1951) seemed formulaic in contrast to the disturbing power of his *Guernica* (1937), while Sartre's literary production largely dried up after his espousal of communism in 1952.[31]

The most significant intellectual response in western Europe to the advent of the Cold War was a resurgent liberalism. European liberalism had seemed close to obliteration in 1945 after more than a decade of war, authoritarianism, and collectivism. Even prominent liberals such as William Beveridge and John Maynard Keynes were identified with policies that seemed closer to socialism. Liberalism was redeemed by intellectuals' growing disillusionment with the Soviet Union, and above all by the new credence given to the concept of "totalitarianism," which claimed that Stalinism, Nazism, and fascism were simply different facets of the drive for total political and social power. The persuasiveness of totalitarianism as an academic theory was underpinned by the revelations of defectors such as Victor Kravchenko, who confirmed the existence of the Soviet Gulag (labor camps), as well as the powerful impact on the Western imagination of novels such as George Orwell's *Nineteen Eighty-Four* (1949). Opposition to communism's "totalitarian" techniques and aspirations created the perfect banner behind which the noncommunist left of western Europe and the United States (including many former communists) could regroup around a moderate reformist politics. The fact that the costs of this activity were often met by secret subventions from the CIA was not recognized as an issue at the time: as Raymond Aron put it in 1951, "for an anti-Stalinist there is no escape from the acceptance of American leadership."[32] The crusade against totalitarianism, therefore, justified the liberals' collusion with the essential illiberalism of the Cold War state.

The liberal revival found its fullest expression in the Congress for Cultural Freedom (CCF), which was launched at a conference in Berlin in June 1950, attended by 121 intellectuals. Its immediate antecedent was the intellectual journal *Der Monat*, published by the US military authorities in Germany and edited by the former Trotskyist Melvin Lasky. Lasky had come to prominence when he intervened at the October 1947 German Writers' Congress to protest at the oppression of writers in the USSR. Significantly, on that occasion he was almost expelled by the US authorities as a troublemaker: one year later he was commissioned by them to edit *Der Monat* and win over the "atomized" German intelligentsia. The CCF, within which Lasky played a leading role, placed this mission on a west European-wide basis. It established numerous national centers and ran a series of influential journals (notably the English-language *Encounter* and the French *Preuves*) as well as many conferences and seminars. It purveyed a positive image of American culture to skeptical west Europeans, and demonstrated that the truncated Europe that emerged in the late 1940s still had a coherence and historic lineage as the heir to the Enlightenment. Politically, the CCF's center of gravity lay with the right wing of social democracy, and it played its part during the 1950s in winning the debate for Atlanticism and European integration within these parties of the center-left.

The pressures of the Cold War were felt keenly by many individual intellectuals, including those such as George Orwell who had avoided any simplistic desire to "take sides" during the ideological conflicts of the 1930s. Now, during his final illness in 1949, Orwell did just that: he had jotted down lists of intellectuals whom he saw as fellow travelers or otherwise suspect, for the benefit of the anti-communist propaganda wing of the Foreign Office.[33] Sartre was something of an exception as he had successfully charted a path of political neutrality during the early Cold War, although even he worked closely with the French Communist Party between 1952 and 1956. In general, however, no equidistance seemed possible and the idea of a pan-European intellectual life was dead. Thomas Mann spoke at the celebrations to mark the 200th anniversary of Goethe's birth in East Germany in 1949 on the condition that he gave the same speech as the one that he was intending to give in the West. Even so, he was bitterly criticized in the West – one German paper branded him as a "defendant of the Eastern world of torture"[34] – and he subsequently withdrew from public life. The apparent choice facing intellectuals was, indeed, nowhere starker than in Germany where many on the left, such as Arnold Zweig and Bertolt Brecht, felt honor-bound to settle in the anti-fascist East. Here they observed the growth of Stalinism with mounting apprehension and muted critical comment. Victor Klemperer, a Jewish survivor of the Third Reich and former anti-communist, chose an academic career in East Germany and membership of the Communist Party because, as he wrote in 1952, "with all our

weaknesses we are still the better people, the truth and the future are with us …"[35]
He fought a long and losing battle to convince himself that he believed this.

Conclusion

The division of both Europe and Germany between 1945 and 1949 was unforeseen
and without precedent. It has to be understood in the context of the rapid collapse
of trust between Stalin and the Western Allies, the advent of the Cold War as a
global struggle for political, strategic, and cultural supremacy, and the problems of
reconstruction in Europe and, more specifically, in Germany. The division of
Europe arose from a complex interplay of forces, involving not only the interests
of the United States and the Soviet Union, but also the desire of west European
elites for greater economic and military security. The crucial moment was the
decision to launch the Marshall Plan, as the United States' commitment to the
economic reconstruction of Europe inevitably had profound political and strategic
implications. It also defined which states would be included, and which excluded,
from the new "western Europe." After 1947 Stalin largely abandoned his hopes to
determine the future of the whole of Europe in return for establishing communist
control in eastern and central Europe. In 1949 the creation of NATO and the
establishment of the two German states established a new order in Europe that
would last until the end of the Cold War.

3
Restoration, Reconstruction, and Revolution
Europe, 1945–1950

A New Europe?

The postwar reconstruction of Europe was not only fashioned by the Great Powers, but also took place within the political and economic parameters set by the bitter experience of Depression, appeasement and war since 1929. With the minor exception of parties such as the neo-fascist MSI in Italy (established in 1946) the far right was not a viable political option. Even the British Conservatives under Winston Churchill, tainted by the Munich agreement and the mass unemployment of the 1930s, suffered a stunning election defeat in July 1945. The new watchwords were nationalization, welfare, and planning, although they were open to a wide range of interpretations in practice. It was not only the left that thought that *laissez-faire* capitalism had had its day: similar sentiments were expressed by the most conservative parties of the Czech National Front and even in the 1947 Ahlen program of the German Christian Democrat Union. Taken as a whole, however, the period from 1945 to 1950 in western Europe witnessed neither a sharp lurch towards collectivism nor a restoration of prewar economic and social conditions, but rather a new synthesis which meshed state-led modernization with a revival of business and the free market. In eastern Europe, conversely, reconstruction (which took place under the ever tighter control of the Soviet Union and national communist parties) represented a sustained attempt to create a new social and economic order.

With the obvious exception of Germany, the context for postwar political and economic life was the restoration of the nation-state, even if (as in the case of Poland) the borders, ethnic composition, and sovereignty of the prewar state had been profoundly altered. In this sense, at least, the nation-building legacy of 1918–19 was

Europe's Troubled Peace: 1945 to the Present, Second Edition. Tom Buchanan.
© 2012 John Wiley & Sons, Ltd. Published 2012 by John Wiley & Sons, Ltd.

preserved. Despite their internal collapse in the face of Nazi aggression, Yugoslavia and Czechoslovakia were successfully pieced back together, although in the former case on a new federal basis. Even the Baltic republics, the only states formally to lose their independence as a result of the war maintained the trappings of statehood and national cultures as Union Republics of the USSR. Wartime ideas of confederation in central and eastern Europe and dreams of a federal western Europe in some resistance circles came equally to naught. Apart from relatively powerless bodies such as the Council of Europe (1949), more substantial attempts at integration would have to wait until the 1950s. For the immediate future, policy continued to be forged by national governments rather than at the supranational level.

In the colonial sphere, however, the restoration of the authority of the European states did not go unchallenged. Indeed, in Algeria VE (Victory in Europe) day celebrations in May 1945 sparked anti-French riots in the town of Sétif and a violent backlash in which many thousands of Muslims perished. The British and Dutch empires in the Far East never recovered from defeat at the hands of Japan in 1942, and after 1945 each in turn was forced to grant independence to its most valuable colonial possession (India and Indonesia). Even so, the immediate postwar years did not witness the collapse of European imperialism, but rather a sustained attempt to reassert control and to adapt colonial relations to the needs of domestic reconstruction. Britain's Labour government, for instance, granted independence to India (1947) but worked assiduously to develop the economic potential of Malaysia and East Africa in the later 1940s. The Dutch did not give up their ambitions to recolonize Indonesia until prevailed upon to do so (or risk forfeiting Marshall Aid) by the United States in 1949. France became engaged in a protracted military conflict with the Vietminh in Indochina from 1946 onwards, and crushed a nationalist revolt in Madagascar in 1946–7. At the same time it restored its colonial trade so successfully that by 1949 a quarter of French imports and 40 percent of exports were in trade with the French Union (as the empire was now termed).

Domestically, too, states and elites struggled to restore their authority after the social and political upheavals of war. The mood was nicely captured by de Gaulle who, when introduced to a resistance leader who was a steel worker, advised him to return to the steelworks.[1] The resistance, for all its flaws, had fostered a unique kind of local direct democracy, such as the "free Greece" zones with their elected councils and people's courts organized by the communist EAM. As the war ended, many spontaneous bodies were created to protect workplaces from looting and to provide basic services, such as the German "antifas" committees or the Polish and Italian factory councils. Yet, although such committees might last for a number of years after the war, they were not destined to form the basis for a new participatory politics. This was partly because the forces of occupation or liberation preferred to deal with more familiar structures of authority, but also because national communist parties – the strongest force in the resistance – believed that their own authority would be best assured by a return to political normality. Therefore, apart from in areas where the occupation forces actively restricted it, such as in the western zones of Germany, there was a surprisingly rapid restoration of party political activity, even if the parties were often new.

The dislocations of the war's aftermath (see Chapter 1) were perhaps felt most profoundly by women. In Germany there were 2.5 million war widows, and women outnumbered men by 7 million, while 2 million Frenchmen were still absent at the war's end. Accordingly, many women faced unprecedented responsibilities as heads of household, but also privations that were often worse than those suffered during the war itself. In 1947 the French bread ration was cut to below occupation levels; in Vienna the availability of fresh vegetables returned to prewar levels by the late 1940s, but of meat not until the mid-1950s. In Britain, women who had accepted the need for wartime rationing were far less sympathetic than men to the continuation of austerity – and in certain respects, such as the bread rationing of 1946–8, its intensification – under the postwar Labour government. By the late 1940s house-wives, who by 1951 represented 66 percent of British women aged 20–64, were being assiduously courted by the main political parties.[2] Women's new political and social rights (such as the entitlement to vote for the first time in France, Italy and Belgium) seemed to count for little in the midst of a bleak struggle for survival. In the words of one female resident of Berlin, "after '45 no one thought about confronting the past. Everyone thought about how they were going to put some-thing in the pot ... and about how to start rebuilding and clearing away the rubble."[3]

In spite of the new legal equality accorded to women, a sustained attempt was made in many west European countries to restore an idealized family life after the war (although it should be noted that many women warmly embraced domesticity and the revival of fashion with the "New Look" of the late 1940s). In West Germany the family was seen as an institution that had survived Nazism and which would now form a bulwark against communism, and by 1950 the level of female employment was at its lowest since World War I.[4] In France pro-natalism was deemed a vital component of national security, and the French population grew from 40.1 million to 42.1 million between 1946 and 1951. Although there was an initial surge of women entering politics, the main political parties offered little encouragement and feminist move-ments were weak. In most European democracies the number of women elected to parliament dwindled after 1945–50. This social conservatism contrasted sharply with the situation in the communist East, where the promotion of women within the labor market (including in previously "male" spheres such as construction and heavy industry) was an important element in the social revolution of the late 1940s.

Politics in Western Europe

Immediate postwar European politics took place within a window of democratic opportunity which temporarily united the countries of northern and central Europe. Communist parties entered government in France, Italy, and Belgium, while even in the emergent Soviet sphere of influence a constrained form of democratic competition was initially allowed to take place, notably in Czechoslovakia. This window began to close in 1947 with the exclusion of the west European communists from power in May and the Soviet-imposed decision to refuse Marshall Aid in July, before being slammed shut with the Prague coup in February 1948. Even so, for much of industrialized Europe the immediate postwar years were to be sharply differentiated from the 1950s: political possibility, participation, and instability would give way to polarization, exclusion, and Cold War certainty. The politics of 1945–7 were characterized by a genuine if watchful Popular Frontism – almost an attempt to reenact the anti-fascist unity of the 1930s and make good its mistakes. There was an initial willingness to give communists the benefit of the doubt: thus, the president of the new World Federation of Trade Unions, which combined communists and noncommunists, was Sir Walter Citrine, a 1930s Cold Warrior *avant la lettre*.

The victory of the British Labour Party in July 1945 and the presence of communists in west European governments until 1947, as well as the success of socialists in a number of smaller countries such as Austria, the Netherlands, and Belgium, created the appearance of a dramatic shift to the left after the war. The left had without doubt helped to set the postwar agenda and to define the language of politics. However, the great achievement of 1945–50 in western Europe was the establishment of liberal democracies, economic recovery, and social welfare: all under the guarantee of American security. Socialist parties had played their part, but the most successful ones were those that had reoriented themselves towards Atlanticism and a mixed economy under the pressure of the Cold War. With hindsight, the most significant political development of these years was the emergence of new kinds of center-right parties – above all the Christian democrats – that were able to mobilize broad social and religious coalitions of support behind this postwar consensus. This was particularly important in the case of Germany and Italy as both had incomplete and unhappy experiences of democracy, and in neither case was democracy associated with prosperity or political stability.

The emergence of Christian Democracy was favored by a number of factors. First, the churches were the one institution that had, while remaining in occupied Europe, emerged from the war relatively untarnished by fascism and collaboration. (The criticism of the Papacy for its failure to do more for the Jews of Europe was not yet an issue at this time.) Christian democrat parties benefited from the moral authority of the churches, but also from the active support of their lay organizations such as Catholic Action. Secondly, Christian Democracy had the advantage of novelty and ideological flexibility. It contained elements of both left and right and appealed across class barriers. Moreover, lessons had been learnt from the past and where necessary – such as in Germany – Christian Democracy could genuinely present itself as a movement for all Christians, transcending its Catholic roots. Thirdly, with the onset of the Cold War, Christian Democracy could claim to be the natural leader of the Christian "West" against atheistic communism. In the immediate postwar years, the antithesis to communism was not capitalism, or even democracy, but the family and private property, both of which the churches stoutly defended. Christian Democracy's anti-communist credentials were burnished by the persecution of religion in eastern Europe in the late 1940s.

In this respect France was something of an exception as the Christian democratic Mouvement Républicain Populaire (MRP) failed to establish itself as a dominant center-right party after a very strong performance in the first postwar elections. The particular form of political stability that Christian democratic parties brought to Germany and Italy (see below) was notably absent in France. Instead, from 1947 the new Fourth Republic had to be governed in opposition to the two largest French political movements, the communists and the Gaullists, so that its very political legitimacy was constantly in question. The Fourth Republic came to be derided for its "revolving door" governments (26 in 14 years) and was unlamented on its demise in 1958. However, recent scholarship has emphasized that behind the instability lay real achievements in the Republic's early years; above all a powerful economic recovery, a successful German policy, and the defense of French security interests within an American-led West.[5] It was above all the Republic's problems in the colonial sphere in the 1950s that eventually laid bare its political frailty.

Charles de Gaulle had returned to France as prime minister at the head of a provisional government in August 1944, determined to restore the authority of the French state against the implicit challenge of the resistance (the CNR). De Gaulle brought the purges to an end and sought to heal France's wounds with the soothing myth that Vichy represented a mere "handful of malefactors." He also presided over some surprisingly radical social and economic reforms, including large-scale nationalization. However, his advocacy of a presidential system of government placed him at odds with the revived political parties following the elections of October 1945 and precipitated his resignation in January 1946. De Gaulle returned to politics in 1947 at the head of his RPF movement (Rassemblement du Peuple Français), which united a broad coalition behind Cold War anti-communism and support for a presidential republic. Although the RPF won 40 percent of the vote in the October 1947 local elections and more than 4 million votes in the 1951 national election, de Gaulle's stridency and the political violence that attended RPF meetings caused it to lose momentum. To de Gaulle's disgust, after 1951 the RPF became partially absorbed into the parliamentary system, and after 1953 he renounced politics in order to write his memoirs.

De Gaulle had been quick to deride the new Republic, the constitution of which was only backed by French voters at the second attempt, as "accepted by 9 million, refused by 8 million and ignored by 8 million."[6] The new Constitution was not radically different from that of the Third Republic, but placed even greater power in the hands of the parliament, making it essential that the main political parties should cooperate. This was accomplished during the era of "Tripartism" (1946–7), when power was shared between the MRP, the communists, and the socialists (the Section Française de l'Internationale Ouvrière / SFIO). However, a combination of domestic and international pressures made the communists' position untenable. In particular, France's reliance on force to restore its position in the colonies, the dependence on American loans to support the weak French economy, and the need for austerity measures meant that the communists could be outflanked to their left. Accordingly, when communist ministers supported striking Renault workers in May 1947 they were expelled from the government. Freed of office, the hostility of the communists, and especially of their CGT trade union federation, posed a threat to the stability of the Republic. In the autumn of 1947 the CGT launched a wave of strikes that were broken by the socialist Interior Minister Jules Moch. Subsequently, with CIA assistance, the CGT was seriously weakened by the breakaway of the more moderate Force Ouvrière. Thereafter, although regularly winning as much as 25 percent of the vote, the communists were stuck in a political cul-de-sac, and did not return to government until 1981.

From 1947 onwards governments were formed from the "Third Force" of the socialists, MRP and Radicals, whose internal disagreements were overshadowed by their joint opposition to the Gaullists and communists. However, the achievements of the "Third Force" governments were more positive than this might suggest. Above all, France abandoned its failed German policy and, following the creation of the German Federal Republic, forged a creative solution to its economic and security problems. On May 9, 1950 the MRP foreign minister Robert Schuman announced a remarkable volte-face: France and Germany (plus others that wished to join) would pool their coal and steel resources under an impartial authority, ensuring the participants access to the resources that they required. A year later six states combined to form the European Coal and Steel Community (ECSC). Schuman's comment that his proposal would make a future Franco-German war "not only unthinkable, but materially impossible"[7] concealed France's very real economic benefit but captured the magnitude of the prize that this swallowing of French pride had suddenly made attainable.

In the western zones of Germany the role of indigenous politicians was heavily circumscribed by the occupation authorities. However, once the British and Americans had decided that some form of political authority should be constituted within their zone, the question of West German party politics became a pressing one. It had been widely assumed that the Social Democrats (SPD) would play a leading political role. The SPD was, after all, a historic force that was already in power in a number of *Länder*, and led by Kurt Schumacher, whose resistance to Nazism gave him a clear moral stature. However, Schumacher's nationalism and desire for a unified Germany, plus his anti-clericalism and Marxist ideology, endeared him to neither the Allies nor many German voters. Moreover, the SPD had been weakened by the loss of its proletarian heartlands in the Soviet zone and was forced to compete for office in a truncated Germany that was more Catholic and less industrial than the Weimar Republic. Meanwhile, the liberal Free Democrat

Party (FDP), which only coalesced in December 1948, was too Protestant and too business-oriented to form a governing party. The survival of a number of small regional and extremist parties further raised the prospect of chronic political instability.

The problem was resolved by the emergence of the Christian Democrat Union (CDU), in close alliance with the Bavarian Christian Social Union (CSU), as a viable governing force. The CDU grew out of the pre-1933 Catholic Zentrum party, now revived as an interconfessional party open to Protestants (the CSU remained in effect a Catholic party until the mid-1950s). The CDU soon fell under the leadership of Konrad Adenauer, the mayor of Cologne between 1917 and 1933, who had suffered imprisonment under the Nazis and who was almost 70 when he entered national politics. Adenauer was motivated by a strong Catholic faith, ardent anti-communism, and a desire for reconciliation with Germany's Western enemies. He wanted to revive a strong and independent Germany and offered a far more nuanced rejection of the Nazi past than Schumacher. Crucially, however, he was willing to accept the partition of Germany in the short to medium term, only seeking reunification on his own terms, and he saw the road to German sovereignty as lying through economic and (in due course) military integration with the West. While these policies would lay him open to Schumacher's taunt that he was the "Chancellor of the Allies," they corresponded closely to the sentiments of many Germans.

The CDU was a cross-class movement with a strong trade union wing, and Adenauer initially had to compete with an influential social Christian current that advocated quasi-socialist policies and alliance with the SPD. However, Adenauer was able to outmaneuver his rivals, and the 1949 Düsseldorf program committed the CDU to a free market economy. Even so, Adenauer remained an atypical conservative, as his strong support for workers' participation in the Co-Determination Law of 1951 was to show. His belief in the free market reflected the growing influence of Ludwig Erhard who, as director of the Bizone's Economic Council, had pushed through the successful and highly popular price liberalization of June 1948. Although Erhard was naturally a liberal and close to the FDP, his decision to fight the 1949 election with the CDU greatly boosted its prestige. Moreover, his coining of the term "social market," which combined the maximum economic competition with social justice, provided Adenauer with a concept that softened the return to free-market capitalism. In 1949 he was able to present his election victory as a mandate "against the planned economy."[8]

Between September 1948 and May 1949 Adenauer chaired the Parliamentary Council of *Länder* representatives that devised the Basic Law. This was, in effect, the Constitution for the new German state, but left open the possibility of reunification. Every effort had been made to learn from the failures of the Weimar Republic (1918–33), which had been brought down not only by the rise of extremist parties but also by the abuse of presidential powers. Accordingly, it was agreed that this would be a federal republic, with substantial powers devolved to the *Länder*.

The Basic Law allowed for a weak presidency and a fixed four-year election cycle for the Reichstag. Governments could only be brought down by a "constructive vote of no confidence," so that a new majority must be ready to take power. The electoral system incorporated a 5 percent hurdle to keep out extremist minorities, and in the final resort the Constitutional Court could ban parties which were deemed (as was the case with the communists in 1956) to have undermined the "free and democratic" order. The new Republic was the very opposite of both Weimar instability and Nazi pretension: hence its capital was located in Bonn, a Rhineland backwater close to Adenauer's home. In addition to these constitutional arrangements, one powerful and highly respected institution, the central bank, was already in place prior to the formation of the Federal Republic. In March 1948 the Allies permitted the establishment of the Bank Deutscher Länder, which coordinated the monetary policy of the newly formed *Land* central banks across the Western zones. In 1957 this system was replaced by a single Bundesbank, entrusted with control over interest rates and charged to prevent inflation.

Despite the growing prestige of Adenauer and Erhard, the CDU/CSU achieved only a narrow victory over the SPD in the August 1949 election (31 percent to 29.2 percent). However, Adenauer was able to form a coalition with the FDP (11.9 percent) and won election as Chancellor by 202 votes out of 402. This weak start reflected the prevailing mood of political and economic insecurity as well as the survival of many smaller regional and extremist parties (including the communists) that collectively won some 28 percent of the vote. In the short term, matters worsened with the creation of a party for refugees from the East (the BHE) which won more than 1.5 million votes at the next election. However, during the next four years the combination of Adenauer's strong leadership with the remarkable economic recovery banished the ghosts of Weimar. In March 1953 the CDU/CSU won 45.2 percent, enough for an outright majority, and was able to absorb the small parties of the right. Adenauer offered an authoritarian brand of democracy, but he had demonstrated to Germans that a center-right party could deliver prosperity through the parliamentary system.

In Italy Christian Democracy faced a sterner challenge, both from a large and assertive Communist Party and from the expectation that the resistance (the "wind from the north") would open a new progressive era. The long, slow liberation of Italy had come to an end in April 1945 when the German Gothic line collapsed and there were resistance uprisings in the great northern cities. Under the terms of the December 1944 Rome Protocols there was an orderly transfer of power as Allied forces arrived. This accorded with the political "line" that the Communist Party (PCI) leader Palmiro Togliatti had implemented on his return from Moscow in March 1944. Given that there was no immediate prospect of revolution, the PCI proposed to work with the existing Italian authorities (the royal government of Marshal Badoglio) with a view to influencing the postwar political and social order. With the benefit of hindsight Togliatti's policy has been heavily criticized, as his studied moderation and participation in government prevented any fundamental overhaul of Italian institutions and brought the communists few political benefits. In his defense, Togliatti could not have anticipated the impact of the Cold War on Italy, nor the long years of political purdah that would be imposed on his party after 1948. Even so, the resistance failed to deliver substantial reforms beyond the referendum decision to abolish the monarchy (by 54 percent to 46 percent) in June 1946. Togliatti himself, as Justice Minister in the coalition government formed in December 1945, acted to moderate the anti-fascist purges through an ill-received amnesty in June 1946. Reform was also set back when the Action Party, the new radical force that had grown out of the resistance and provided the first postwar prime minister (Ferruccio Parri), dissolved after bitter internal disputes in 1946.

Togliatti's policy was based in part on a false assumption that the communists could turn their short-term coalition government with the Christian Democrat Party (Democrazia Cristiana, or DC) into a long-term partnership. The DC was established in September 1942 from remnants of the Partito Popolari (the first Catholic political party, dissolved by Mussolini in 1926) and young Catholic graduates. It was skillfully led by Alcide De Gasperi, who won the support of the Vatican while resisting its pressure to influence his policies and choice of political allies. When the war ended, the DC had rapidly emerged as the main conservative party, with a strong anti-communist and pro-Western stance, defending the family and the rights of property. Its main base was in the north, especially in the "White" Catholic areas of the Po valley. However, it was weaker in the south, where the neo-fascist MSI and the shorter-lived Uomo Qualunque (Common Man) movement enjoyed support from 1946 onwards.

The troubled Catholic–communist coalition was prolonged by the inconclusive election of June 1946 in which the DC, with 35 percent, trailed the 39 percent won by the combined vote of the PCI and its socialist (PSI) allies. During the next year the pressures for a decisive break were amplified by the Cold War. Thus, in early 1947 Giuseppe Saragat led an anti-communist faction out of the PSI and formed the Social Democratic Party, eventually joining the DC government. The DC came under acute political pressure from the severe inflation that hurt its middle-class supporters more than the working class (whose living standards were protected by the index-linking of basic goods). De Gasperi was also hurt by the peace treaty of February 1947 under which Italy lost all of its colonies, and had to pay compensation of $360 million to countries that had been victims of fascist aggression. Trieste, coveted by Yugoslavia, became a "free city" under international control, although it was soon returned to Italy. The treaty was a blow to De Gasperi's pro-Western strategy, but did not stimulate a nationalist backlash in Italy. Eventually, in May 1947 De Gasperi resigned and proceeded to form a center-right administration, excluding the communists from office. The new government was committed to tackling inflation with deflationary policies that resulted in high unemployment.

All eyes now turned to the April 1948 election. Not only was the future political direction of Italy widely deemed to be at stake, but the election was also (in the light of the Prague coup of February 1948) taken to be a critical juncture in the Cold War. There was open intervention from the Vatican and from the USA, as well as an early opportunity for covert action by the newly formed CIA. DC propaganda dwelt on the advantages of alliance with the USA: one poster pointed out that De Gasperi had "obtained free from America the flour for your spaghetti as well as the sauce to go on it."[9] The result was a crushing victory for the DC (48.5 percent) over the PCI–PSI alliance (31 percent). A few months later, on July 14, Togliatti was shot and wounded, sparking mass protests and even the specter of revolution. However, by then the moment had long passed and the left thought better of making a bid for power. There was now a new political order: the communists were permanently excluded from government, and Italy was locked into the "West" as a founding member of NATO. Meanwhile the DC consolidated its hold on power by building a clientelist base in the south to match its mass support in the north, abandoning most of its progressive ideals in return for immersion in the patronage of power.

Western Europe: Reconstruction and Welfare

Throughout western Europe, reconstruction was not simply an opportunity to restock and rebuild, but also to learn from and to remedy the mistakes of previous decades. Governments engaged in ambitious projects of national renewal, and did not allow the lack of funds to stand in their way. In France, for instance, the Monnet Plan (1947–52) envisaged a five-year program of industrial and infrastructural modernization that would finally allow France to stand up to the economic power of Germany. In Britain, the Labour government's goals were to promote greater economic productivity – hence maintaining the country's pretensions as a great power – while also removing the blight of social injustice. For Italy, there was the prospect (impossible under fascist autarky) of orienting its economy more firmly to international trade and competition, as well as tackling the backwardness of the rural south. Ultimately, however, such projects could only be fully realized through American aid, either funded by the ERP or on a bilateral basis, and this inevitably meant that an accommodation had to be struck between European and US visions for postwar Europe.

In the war's immediate aftermath, governments of all political persuasions had no qualms about resorting to nationalization and other forms of public ownership to achieve their economic objectives. De Gaulle and his successors nationalized gas, electricity, banks, and coal mines, as well as numerous private companies owned by pro-German collaborators. The British Labour government seized control of the so-called "commanding heights" of the economy, notably the Bank of England, the coal and rail industries, and the utilities. In Italy a somewhat different path was taken, as the postwar state inherited and reinvigorated Mussolini's giant public-sector corporations such as the IRI (Institute for Industrial Reconstruction). In each case these policies rested on a broad political consensus. In Britain, for instance, there was little opposition to the nationalization of coal and rail, as both had suffered from chronic under-investment in a myriad private hands. Moreover, at least between 1945 and 1947, west European governments enjoyed the valuable support of the communists and the trade unions in giving the highest priority to industrial production, even at the expense of low wages.

In most countries reconstruction was accompanied by a significant measure of social reform. Indeed, this was highly important for motivating workforces that had suffered wartime hardships followed by the long hours and reduced spending power of the postwar years. There was, however, no single model or blueprint. In Britain the 1942 Beveridge Report was broadly implemented by the Labour government as the basis for a comprehensive system of "cradle to the grave" social security, based on a unified system of national insurance. Labour's most enduring accomplishment was the creation in 1948 of a National Health Service, which provided free treatment for all at the point of delivery. In addition, the 1944 Education Act (passed by the wartime coalition) significantly expanded the scope of free, compulsory schooling. The British system, like that in postwar Sweden, typified a centralized social democratic model of universal welfare provision. In continental Europe, however, far more emphasis was placed on the devolution of responsibility to independent bodies such as the churches and trade unions. In France, for instance, the reforms of 1945–6 established a system of social security based on independently administered funds for all wage-earners. However, a fully comprehensive system covering all citizens was not introduced until 1967. Social reform was largely neglected in Italy, but there was a well-intentioned (if largely ineffective) attempt to promote land reform in southern Italy in 1949–50.

The reconstruction era brought profound, but hardly revolutionary, changes. From 1947 onwards, with the expulsion of the communists from a number of governments and the impact of Marshall Aid, free-market forces gathered strength while those of collectivism weakened. The turn towards liberalism and financial orthodoxy was encouraged by American policy both in Germany (where the United States dissuaded Britain from socializing the Ruhr industries and forced through the break-up of the major banks) and across the OEEC (through the use of ERP counterpart funds). However, it also reflected the fact that the left had suffered political defeat (in Italy and Germany), had fractured (as in France), or had simply a run out of ideas (as in Britain). In the latter case, for instance, the nationalization of the iron and steel industry in 1951, which was both profitable and efficient, proved far more divisive than earlier measures and was repealed when Labour left office. By late 1948 the president of the Board of Trade, Harold Wilson, saw political advantage in claiming to have lit a "bonfire" of economic controls. Nowhere was the ascendancy of economic liberalism more apparent than in the western zones of Germany, where the preparation for statehood was accompanied by measures such as the currency reform of June 1948 and the removal of price controls that accompanied it. Almost at a stroke, three years of black market trading, barter and suppressed consumption were ended. One commentator reported that "housewives strolled down the streets gazing in astonishment at shop windows – at shoes, leather handbags, tools, perambulators, bicycles, cherries in baskets ..."[10] However, it is important to note that Ludwig Erhard, architect of the price reforms, was seeking to create not only a free market but also a *freer* market than had previously existed, rid of cartels and other concentrations of economic power.

The outlook was hardly propitious for Europe's traditional economic elites in the immediate postwar years, and reconstruction brought to the fore a new managerial class. Such famous companies as Flick, Krupp, and IG Farben were brought to justice in the Nuremberg follow-up trials for their use of slave labor and plundering of deported Jews. In France, Louis Renault died in jail awaiting trial for collaboration, and his automobile company was nationalized. The French employers (the *patronat*), who had tended to side with Vichy rather than the Resistance, were at least temporarily cowed into silence. Although those tainted by the war proved remarkably adept at restoring their position in the 1950s, they now had to contend with a new technocratic elite, such as the products of the French ENA (the École Nationale d'Administration, established in 1945). In Italy the corporations and in Britain the boards of nationalized industries provided new avenues for introducing politicians and even trade unionists into the management of public enterprises.

The reconstruction of western Europe was remarkably successful, not only in terms of the surpassing of prewar levels of production, but also in the forging of an effective new balance between public and private interests. It was soon evident that reconstruction would not replace private enterprise, but rather steer it in a more equitable and efficient direction. The nature of the new synthesis varied greatly from country to country, but the broad outlines were clear: a greater involvement for the state, social welfare, and regard for the rights of workers. More than this, however, reconstruction had also created a greater sense of national unity and pride. The Monnet Plan, with its electrified railways and hydro-electric dams, not only created a more modern France but, as importantly, the popular image of a more modern France. While British reconstruction was not as visually seductive, a somewhat similar effect was created by the 1951 Festival of Britain with its futuristic "Skylon."

Scandinavia: Paths to Security

The experiences of the Scandinavian states of Sweden, Norway, and Denmark had proved highly divergent during the war (the case of Finland is examined separately below) and different conclusions were reached as to how to achieve security after the war. Swedes were eager to maintain the benefits of their neutrality into the postwar era, while Norwegians had emerged from the war strongly orientated towards the Western Allies and convinced that a defensive alliance was essential for guaranteeing their security. The northern region of Norway, it should be recalled, had been occupied by the Red Army until September 1945, and Norway now had a common frontier with the Soviet Union (at the expense of Finland). Denmark was equally vulnerable. Its border was now perilously close to East Germany, and it appeared to have merely traded one over-mighty neighbor for another. Between 1945 and 1949, therefore, Scandinavian diplomacy was dominated by the debate between the (primarily Swedish) advocates of a separate Nordic defense pact and those who envisaged some degree of integration with the defensive structures of the West. Following the failure of the Scandinavian summit at Karlstad in January 1949 Norway and (more reluctantly) Denmark moved to participate in the formation of NATO, while Sweden trusted to a neutrality that rested on its own economic and military strength. However, this regional failure did not preclude further common initiatives such as the Nordic Council (which first met in 1953), a common labor market (1954) and the development of the joint Scandinavian Airlines Systems (SAS) founded in 1946. Moreover, the Scandinavian input into the United Nations was disproportionately large: the founding Secretary General was the Norwegian Trygve Lie, and his most illustrious and activist successor was the Swede Dag Hammarskjöld (1953–61).

The divisive question of security aside, there was considerable political consensus in Scandinavia after 1945: above all, the ascendancy of social democracy was consolidated during this period. The Swedish Socialist Labor Party (SAP) was in office (usually in coalition) from 1936 to 1976; the Norwegian Labor Party won the election in October 1945 and remained in power until 1965, while the Danish Social Democrats, the largest party in the Folketing from 1924 to 2001, were in government from 1947 to 1950. This remarkable hegemony rested on a number of common factors. Perhaps most significantly, these were societies in which social and political consensus was highly prized, and in which agreements between the state, the parties, and their social partners had already been forged in response to the Depression in the 1930s. Therefore, social democratic parties, supported by cohesive trade union federations, came to embody a distinctively "Scandinavian" brand of politics, characterized by a commitment to social justice and high levels of welfare provision, paid for out of taxation and economic growth. Social democracy was almost proudly nonideological: dull, bureaucratic and in tune with cherished social and cultural values. Even when, as in Norway in the early 1950s, there was a lively debate between the parties over the extent of the "planned economy," the outcome tended to be merely a refashioning of the consensus.

The problem of postwar reconstruction varied greatly from country to country. In Sweden, of course, the issue did not arise, and the question was rather one of how the undamaged Swedish economy could best exploit its competitive advantage. By the late 1940s Sweden had a very powerful export-oriented economy, the success of which was based on high levels of technological investment, social harmony, and a protected domestic market. Social democratic governments worked closely with business, and during the 1950s companies such as the car manufacturers Volvo and SAAB became well-known brands throughout Europe. There were also differences between the experiences of the occupied countries, as Denmark had emerged largely unscathed from the war whereas Norway had suffered extensive damage to housing and infrastructure and had lost half of its valuable merchant fleet. Even so, Denmark experienced the slowest recovery of all Western states, with unemployment at around 10 percent until the mid-1950s. It was adversely affected by the disruption of trade with its major partners Britain and Germany after 1945 and the consequent lack of foreign currency for investment in its obsolescent industries. By 1949 a quarter of Danes had expressed the desire to emigrate to the United States.[11] Denmark was the principal Scandinavian recipient of US financial aid between 1945 and 1949, and the ERP played a significant role in the Danish recovery, above all in facilitating the large-scale mechanization of Danish farming. By contrast, Norway underwent frenetic economic growth after 1945, and levels of prewar output had been restored in both manufacture and agriculture by 1948. The key to success was a combination of intelligent economic planning, social solidarity and pay restraint, a commitment to conquering export markets, and efficient utilization of Norway's natural resources. Even so, these were hard years, and many goods were rationed until 1952 (and motor cars until 1960). In 1952 infamous "sugar queues" developed on the Norwegian–Swedish border when Sweden suddenly raised its sugar quota.[12] Across Scandinavia, however, postwar reconstruction had laid the foundations for the remarkable affluence of the later 1950s and 1960s, as well as the region's distinctive commitment to social equality.

Southern Europe: Dictatorship and Civil War

The democratic opportunities of 1945 meant little in the Iberian peninsula, where both the dictatorship of Salazar in Portugal and, more surprisingly, that of Franco in Spain managed to survive the end of the war. Although there were some similarities between the two regimes, not least a shared commitment to a bogus "organic" democracy, there were also substantial differences. Salazar had come to power in the aftermath of the military coup of 1926 but was careful to ensure that power in his "New State" lay in civilian hands (above all those of academics such as himself). While the army, the Catholic Church, and business and landowning elites were all highly supportive of the regime they were not allowed to dictate its policy. Franco acted far more as the arbiter between the powerful factions that had supported the "Nationalist" rebellion against the Republic during the civil war of 1936–9. The three main pillars of his regime were the army, the Church, and the

Falangist movement (FET). While Franco enjoyed immense prestige amongst those who had supported the Nationalist cause, his considerable political skills were generally devoted to balancing these discordant and often quarrelsome elements within the regime. In general, however, the radical and fascistic influence of the FET was in decline, especially after the defeat of the Axis powers, and by the later 1940s the reactionary character of the regime owed most to the Catholic Church, especially in the fields of education and social legislation.

Both regimes were highly repressive, although the repression in Spain was of an entirely different order from that administered by the PIDE secret police in Portugal. Franco had embarked on a punitive campaign against the Spanish Republicans at the end of the civil war and purged communists, Freemasons, and other perceived enemies from the professions. While the repression had passed its peak by 1942, there was no attempt at political reconciliation by a regime which gloried in – and claimed legitimacy from – its triumph over its "Red" enemies. The exiled opposition was weak and divided, and Franco succeeded in widening the divisions. The 1947 Law of Succession restored the Spanish monarchy (without a king) and kept alive monarchist hopes for a full restoration in the post-Franco era. Franco's agreement with the Bourbon pretender Don Juan in the following year, whereby his son Juan Carlos would be educated in Spain, drove a further wedge between the monarchists and the predominantly Republican opposition. The greatest threat to the Franco regime was not the opposition but its own mishandling of the economy, which combined autarky and international isolation with massive state intervention. The result was stagnation, corruption, and a thriving black market: 1929 levels of industrial production were not regained until 1950; agriculture did not recover to these levels until 1958.[13] The later 1940s were remembered as a time of hunger and poverty by many Spanish people, although the misery was too great to galvanize resistance. When Republicans launched a guerrilla campaign, emboldened by the Allied victory in 1945, they received little support from a traumatized and dejected rural population, and the insurgency had largely fizzled out by 1948.

Another important point of difference was that Franco, unlike Salazar, was an international pariah in 1945. Salazar's neutrality and his timely decision to allow Britain to establish bases in the Azores in 1943 guaranteed the survival of the dictatorship (and its African empire) in 1945. In addition, Portugal was allowed to join NATO in 1949. Franco, however, was widely seen as the creature of Hitler and Mussolini, and initially it seemed likely that he would share their fate. As Spain's wartime "neutrality" had leaned sharply towards the Axis powers, Spain was refused entry to the United Nations in 1945, as well as access to Marshall Aid and membership of NATO. In a further sign of disapproval, many UN member states withdrew their ambassadors between 1946 and 1950. Crucially for the regime's survival, however, this gesture was not backed up by more meaningful diplomatic or economic sanctions. Franco's guile and good fortune allowed the regime to survive until the advent of the Cold War, by which time his fascist antecedents counted less than his anti-communist credentials. In 1953 Franco struck a deal with the United States whereby it was allowed military bases in Spain (including air-fields for nuclear bombers) in return for economic assistance. The benefits were immense: this new international respectability, combined with the aid and the hard currency generated by the bases, guaranteed Franco's rule for the foreseeable future. However, there was also a cost. The bases were an affront to Spanish nationalism, undermining the ideological basis of the regime, and exposed Spain to Soviet nuclear assault without any guarantee of US protection.

The American presence also played a crucial role in the victory of the monarchist right in Greece during the civil war of 1946–9. The origins of the conflict lay in the Nazi invasion and occupation of Greece (April 1941) and the emergence of the communist EAM resistance movement and its military wing ELAS. By 1943/4 a complex struggle was under way. First, the resistance fought the Germans, who were backed by the collaborationist "security battalions"; secondly, within the resistance there was a contest for supremacy between EAM and other groups such as the British-backed EDES; and thirdly there was a debate over the postwar politi-cal order between the resistance and exiled politicians such as George Papandreou. When German forces began to withdraw from Greece in the autumn of 1944, EAM's attempt to fill the vacuum in Athens led to violent clashes with the arriving British and exiled forces in December. The communists' defeat and heavy losses, at a time when Stalin accepted that Greece lay within the British "sphere," resulted in the demobilization of ELAS and the formation of a provisional government.

Reconciliation proved impossible in postwar Greece. The communists regarded the new regime as undemocratic and the continuation of the repressive apparatus of the prewar Metaxas dictatorship. Accordingly, they boycotted the elections of March 1946 (which returned a right-wing monarchist majority) and the September 1946 referendum that restored the monarchy. From the right's perspective, the communists represented a continuing threat to stability, especially given the proximity of pro-Soviet regimes on three of Greece's borders. By late 1946 there was an escalating rebellion in rural northern and western Greece, culminating in the formation in October of the insurgent Democratic Army of Greece (DSE). The communists were backed by Yugoslavia, Albania, and Bulgaria, but crucially received only very limited support from Stalin. Even so, the DSE initially made good progress against an ill-prepared Greek army. By the spring of 1948 it was 26,000 strong. A half of the country and a third of the rural population were estimated to be under its control.[14]

The turning point in the civil war was the American decision, sanctioned by the Truman Doctrine, to take Britain's place as the regime's main external support. After March 1947 the United States poured military aid into Greece, as well as providing training in new counter-insurgency techniques. Unlike Stalin, Truman was willing to raise the stakes and turn Greece into the first battlefield in the Cold War. The DSE's lack of firepower was compounded by the loss of Yugoslav support following Tito's split with the Soviet Union, and poor tactics (in particular a tendency to be drawn into full-scale battles with a better-equipped enemy). The conflict was a success for the USA in its "containment" of communism in Europe, but also for the Greek right in convincing the United States that the defense of its reactionary policies represented a vital test of "freedom" against "totalitarianism." In this sense the Greek Civil War looked forward to counter-insurgencies in Latin America and Indochina in the 1960s and 1970s. For Greece, meanwhile, the cost was severe. More than 30,000 had perished in the civil war and 140,000 went into exile, while many remained in jail. Although relatively free elections were held in the 1950s, the civil war poisoned Greek politics for decades to come and a true democratization of Greek institutions had to await the fall of the 1967–74 military dictatorship.

The Soviet Union and Central and Eastern Europe

For Stalin, the victory over Nazism had not only proved that "the Soviet social system is a fully viable and stable form of organization of society," but also that it was superior to all others.[15] Even so, the magnitude of the task facing the ageing Soviet dictator in the years after 1945 was daunting. In addition to making good the country's massive material losses and reasserting the authority of the Communist Party in all spheres of Soviet life, the new territories on the western borders had to be integrated into the Soviet Union, and the extension of communist rule into eastern and central Europe overseen. Although some 9 million Red Army soldiers were demobilized, there was no sense of any postwar relaxation for Soviet citizens. The country remained on a war footing, with ever more resources diverted into heavy industry and the military, especially the program to develop a Soviet atom bomb. As in the 1930s, this was to be paid for by the peasantry, who were struck in the late 1940s with punitive levels of taxation, as well as enduring a terrible famine in 1946–7. Conditions were unspeakably harsh in a countryside depopulated by war. As one peasant widow recalled: "the village women took the place of men and horses."[16] Stalin's last years also saw a burgeoning of the Gulag, the vast empire of prison camps and colonies housing more than 2.5 million political opponents and criminals, administered by 240,000 guards, which became an important part of the Soviet economy in its own right.[17] The cost was appalling, but by a combination of the economic plunder of the Soviet zone of Germany, the imposition of ferocious labor discipline, and the exploitation of the peasants and Gulags the Soviet economy was restored, without the assistance of the West. Stalin bequeathed to his successors a state that would be able to confront the military power – if hardly the economic vitality – of the West.

Stalin, now often seen in his marshal's uniform rather than the unadorned tunics of the 1930s, unquestionably stood at the apex of the Soviet political system. Even so, he felt compelled to reassert his authority over the Red Army (the popular

Marshal Zhukov was demoted in 1946), the intellectuals (through Zhdanov's decrees) and his own close colleagues. While there was no return to the arbitrary, murderous violence of the 1930s within the upper echelons of the party (with the exception of a purge of the Leningrad party leadership in 1948–9), Stalin continued to make and break his colleagues with no regard to their true competence. As ever he demanded absolute loyalty: he even forced Molotov, one of his oldest allies, to divorce his wife when she came under political attack in 1948.[18] By the early 1950s Stalin and his inner circle had become enfolded in a fog of paranoia and conspiracy that culminated in the so-called "Doctors' Plot" of January 1953. Stalin's allegation that Kremlin doctors had murdered Zhdanov in 1948 was heavily laced with anti-Semitism. The dictator's own death on March 5, 1953 not only saved the lives of the doctors, but possibly also those of many Soviet leaders such as Lavrenty Beria. Certainly those closest to Stalin did not share the grief and disorientation of the Soviet public at the death of a man hailed as a military genius and savior.

By the time of Stalin's death, with the notable exception of Yugoslavia, the countries of central and eastern Europe had been absorbed into the Soviet empire, and now broadly shared a common political structure and common economic and social policies. However, if the end result was largely the same, the road traveled and the pace of change varied greatly. Despite Stalin's celebrated comment that "This war is not as in the past; whoever occupies a territory also imposes on it his own social system,"[19] Soviet power was not the only determinant of political change. After all, Czechoslovakia (where Soviet troops had withdrawn in November 1945) suffered a communist takeover, while Austria (from where the Red Army retained a zone of occupation) did not. Finland, which had been left prostrate but unoccupied in 1944, carved out a qualified independence. Thus, in explaining the communist takeover of central and eastern Europe, Soviet military power has to be weighed against a number of other factors. These included Moscow's wider political and strategic calculations, as well as the relative strengths of both indigenous communist parties and the resistance to communism.

A number of considerations smoothed the way for the communist seizure of power. Trust in the Western democracies as defenders of the independence of central and eastern Europe had been destroyed by the events of 1938–45. Edvard Beneš, the president of Czechoslovakia, was so appalled by the Franco-British betrayal of his country in September 1938 that he became fatally convinced that Stalin would be a guarantor of its postwar independence. Similarly, despite its traditional animosity towards Russia, Poland had no alternative other than to rely on the Soviet Union to protect its new western territories against potential German revanchism. Elsewhere in eastern Europe the USSR acted as the arbiter of competing national interests. Thus, Romania regained Transylvania from Hungary, but lost the Dobruja to Bulgaria; Lithuania lost its independence, but regained its lost capital of Vilnius from Poland; and Stalin sanctioned the liquidation of the central European minorities on the grounds that they were "a source of trouble and a Fifth column."[20] Throughout the region this web of territorial and ethnic adjustments served to enhance both Soviet power and the standing of local communists at a time when the West seemed to have little influence over or interest in its fate. Indeed, the West's willingness to sign peace treaties with Bulgaria and Romania in February 1947 was the signal for the final elimination of the opposition, including the execution of the Bulgarian leader Petkov. Similarly, the apparent questioning of the Oder–Neisse border between Poland and Germany by US Secretary of State Byrnes in September 1946 served to undermine the Polish anti-communist opposition.

Throughout eastern Europe the communists also benefited from the fact that prewar elites had been destroyed or discredited, either by their failure to resist Nazism or by their collaboration with it. Much of the Polish intelligentsia had been killed by the Soviets in the 1940 Katyn massacre or in subsequent Nazi atrocities. The communists skillfully exploited the widespread consensus that existed over the need to eliminate the social and ethnic weaknesses that had undermined these countries in 1937–9. They also recognized that sweeping land reform, nationalization, and the forced expulsion of minorities would be popular because so many stood to benefit. While the communists' policies were unexceptional – and indeed often less radical than those advocated by Social Democrats – their self-confidence, rooted in Marxist theory and the power and prestige of the Soviet Union, gave them the edge. As Milan Kundera described one such communist in his novel *The Joke* (1964), "He had the look all communists had at the time. He looked as if he'd made a secret pact with the future and thereby acquired the right to act in its name."[21] They also benefited from the emphasis that communism placed, especially in its Stalinist form, on ruthless *realpolitik*: the motto of the Czech leader Klement Gottwald was "The main thing is power and everything else is secondary."[22] With hindsight it is evident that a new political game was being played in central and eastern Europe, one in which only the communists understood the rules.

This play for power was, however, expressed in different ways across the region. The Yalta agreement had bought a share of government for noncommunists, and the result was a period of coalition rule. There were, however, limits to the pluralism of this period. Typically, even if they did not hold the most senior positions in government, communists made sure that they controlled key ministries such as those in charge of the police and land reform. Moreover, participation in coalitions acted as a trap for noncommunist parties while serving to delegitimize political activity beyond the coalition. Finally, the communists always had recourse to other political leverage, be it the ability to mobilize extra-parliamentary pressure or the presence of the Red Army and NKVD. In Hungary, for instance, the communists were able to break up the conservative Smallholders Party, which had won 57 percent of the vote to their own 17 percent in the elections of November 1945, by a campaign of intimidation and blackmail graphically referred to as "salami tactics."

There was a striking contrast between the case of Poland, where Soviet strategic interest dictated the rapid and brutal imposition of a subject government, and Czechoslovakia, where political pluralism lasted until 1948. Stanisław Mikolaijcyzk had returned from London to participate in the Polish government, and his Peasants Party soon restored its political dominance in the countryside. The communists, with a fragile political base, could not afford to engage Mikolaijcyzk in conventional politics. Accordingly, referendum results on political and economic reform in June 1946 were falsified, and the elections of January 1947 – in which the alliance of communists and socialists officially won a sweeping victory – were clearly rigged. Mikolaijcyzk, who had hoped that Poland could enjoy a status similar to that of Finland, was forced to flee in October 1947. In Czechoslovakia, where the Communist Party had been relatively strong before 1938, a five-party National Front was formed around the program of "national revolution." In the elections of May 1946 the communists emerged as the leading party with 38 percent of the vote, although performing far better in the Czech lands than in Slovakia. However, their new goal of "51 percent next time" suggested that even here, where the idea of a "parliamentary road to socialism" was most plausible, the communists had a somewhat instrumental approach to democratic politics. Certainly the elections resulted in a sharpening of tensions within the coalition. The communist-backed "millionaires' tax" in 1947, which divided the coalition and which was supported by extra-parliamentary pressure, gave a foretaste of the crisis of February 1948 (see below).

While these events exposed the ultimate pointlessness of competing within the coalition system, other forms of opposition were courageous but doomed. In the late 1940s armed resistance to Soviet annexation persisted in the Baltic states (especially in the forests of Lithuania) and in the western Ukraine, while in the Polish countryside as many as 60,000 Home Army fighters were still active in 1946. By the late 1940s there was a severe repression of the Catholic Church, including the imprisonment of the Hungarian Cardinal Mindszenty in 1949 and a failed attempt to implant an "underground" church in Czechoslovakia. However, the ability of Cardinal Wyszynski's Polish church to conclude an deal with the government in 1950 and protect some degree of autonomy (although serious harassment persisted until 1956) showed that there were limits to the "totalitarian" ambitions of these regimes, even at the height of Stalinism. Indeed, it is now evident that the communist parties experienced considerable difficulties in imposing their will on the societies that they governed. The skilled workers of Poland and Hungary, as well as the peasants of Yugoslavia, proved adept at resisting radical social change and often forced the communists to work with the grain of the existing societies.[23]

Such deeper patterns of social opposition cast doubt on the long-term viability of the new regimes, but in the short term communist parties had little difficulty in gaining a monopoly of power. Political rivals were destroyed (although some were allowed to survive as "front" parties) and socialist parties were forced into mergers. By early 1948 only the future of Czechoslovakia was uncertain, and the

Czech communists came under intense pressure from within the Cominform to bring matters to a head. In the event, in February 1948 it was three of their rival parties in the National Front that triggered the crisis by resigning from government in protest at a communist purge of the police. Crucially, however, they did not have the support of the socialists, who remained in office, and they failed to provoke the intervention of President Beneš and the army. A mobilization of workers' organizations and militia in Prague by the communists forced Beneš to accept the resignations and a reconstruction of the government. Soon afterwards the Foreign Minister Jan Masaryk, son of the state's founder, fell to his death from a high window, the victim of what is generally assumed to be political murder. Beneš, his hopes for an independent Czechoslovak democracy shattered for a second time, had again failed to give a strong lead in a moment of crisis. He was replaced as president by the communist leader Gottwald in June and died soon afterwards.

By the late 1940s, therefore, the countries of central and eastern Europe were converging on a Stalinist model. In each case the Communist Party had – by merger with the socialists – formed a new ruling political elite that enjoyed a monopoly of power. The new parties expanded rapidly: the Czechoslovak Communist Party grew from 475,000 members in July 1945 to 2.674 million in October 1948, following the seizure of power and the merger with the Social Democrats. In social and economic policy the goal was to copy the Soviet Union, with rapid collectivization of agriculture and the diversion of resources into heavy industry at the expense of consumer goods. This rapid change and political turbulence was the context for the spate of purges and show trials that convulsed eastern Europe after the Tito/Stalin split of 1948 (see below). The split presented Moscow with an opportunity to discipline the new Stalinist leaderships through division and terror, under the pretext of defeating the "Titoist" threat in other communist parties. There was no general logic to the purges. Although communist elites tended to be divided between those who had been based in Moscow during the war and those who had remained in their native land, in some countries (such as Hungary) the "Muscovites" triumphed, while in others (such as Romania) the "native" faction won. The Polish leader Gomulka, advocate of a communism more attuned to national conditions, was removed from office but allowed to live, whereas the Hungarian László Rajk was executed after a bizarre show trial. The only condition was that a scapegoat had to be found. In a scene reminiscent of Arthur Koestler's *Darkness at Noon*, Janos Kádár was sent to tell a reluctant Rajk that he must play his allotted role: "the Party has chosen you for the role of traitor, you must sacrifice yourself to the Party."[24] The shocking allegations against leading and trusted communists were widely believed at the time, and therefore their eventual exposure as lies was profoundly destabilizing. Rajk's reburial in October 1956 helped to trigger the Hungarian uprising, while the reassessment of the Czechoslovak show trials in the 1960s contributed to the Prague Spring of 1968.

Between East and West: Finland, Austria, and Yugoslavia

The Partisans' victory over the Chetniks, as well as the arrival of the Red Army on Yugoslav soil in October 1944, ensured that Tito's communists would control the destiny of postwar Yugoslavia. However, this was not simply a change in ruling elites; it also represented a genuine attempt to restore Yugoslavia on a new and more viable basis. The principal question was how to redress the ethnic tensions that had undermined the state before 1941, above all Croat resentment of Serb domination. Tito's response was to establish the new Yugoslavia as a socialist federal republic. The preponderance of Serbia was reduced by the devolution of power to six republics including one, Macedonia, carved out of Serbian territory. Tito, himself of Croat-Slovene extraction, hoped that the enmities of the past would dissolve into a new Yugoslav identity based on economic modernization and social equality. What he had not appreciated was that an even more effective cohesive force would soon be provided by the fear of Soviet invasion.

Between 1945 and 1947 the Yugoslav communists were Moscow's most enthusiastic supporters, and took a leading role at the first Cominform meeting in September 1947. However, from Stalin's perspective they were seen as dangerously independent and radical, a view reinforced by Tito's willingness to confront the West over his territorial claims on the Italian and Austrian border, as well as his proposal for a federation with neighboring Bulgaria. For their part, the Yugoslavs resented the patronizing Soviet attitude towards their legitimate aspirations – for instance, in 1945 they were asked "What do you need industry for? – in the Urals we have everything that you need."[25] Mounting tensions in 1948 culminated in Yugoslavia's expulsion from the Cominform on June 28 on the grounds that the Yugoslav leadership had succumbed to nationalism and "anti-Party and anti-Soviet views." Close observers noted that break with Moscow came as a "bitter psychological and intellectual blow" for Tito.[26] However, Stalin, who did not think that Tito could survive the split, had no plans for military action and was confounded when the vast majority of Yugoslav communists closed ranks against Moscow's pressure.

The most damaging consequence for Yugoslavia of the widening split was a Cominform economic blockade from late 1948 which, coinciding with mounting peasant resistance to agrarian reform, nudged Tito into a radical change of policy during 1949–50. Domestically, the attempts to reform agriculture were largely abandoned, allowing a rapid reversion to independent peasant land ownership by 1953. Politically, a deliberate attempt was made to offer an ideological alternative to Stalinism via greater devolution of power and, from 1952, the reinvention of the Communist Party as the "League of Communists." Most strikingly, in the international sphere Tito sought and received Western assistance. During 1949 the USA dropped its blockade of Yugoslavia and eventually sent both financial and military assistance, while in June 1950 Yugoslavia voted to condemn North Korean aggression at the UN. However, Tito had no intention of trading one bloc for another: instead he was able to demonstrate that some degree of equipoise (and from 1955 a formal "nonalignment") was now possible within Cold War Europe. Although after the death of Stalin there was an awkward rapprochement with the Soviet Union, Yugoslav independence was jealously guarded. Stalin's miscalculations had turned an attempt to discipline a minor ally into a damaging rift in the previously seamless world of international communism.

Two other states on the Cold War border, Finland and Austria, also struck an effective balance between East and West. In both cases, however, what emerged were political and economic systems oriented to the West alongside statements of neutrality that satisfied Soviet security concerns. While Finland had avoided occupation by concluding an armistice with the Soviet Union in September 1944, Austria, which had been "reunited" with the German Reich in 1938, ended the war under four-power occupation. There was a real danger that Austria might be partitioned like Germany, and there was even the possibility of an attempted communist takeover (although this seemed a distant prospect when the communists won a derisory 5 percent of the vote in the November 1945 elections). The avoidance of this fate owed a great deal to the maturity of Austria's politicians, symbolized by the veteran socialist Karl Renner, who became the first postwar president. The Socialist Party and the People's Party, which formed a successful coalition government, were essentially the same political forces that had fought a bitter class war in the 1930s. This was more than a mere political alliance as the parties laid the basis for far-reaching social consensus and bargaining (the so-called "consociational" model) involving their associated trade union, business, and farmers' organizations. The coalition saw off half-hearted communist bids for power (which had their roots in genuine working-class grievances) in 1947 and 1950, although full independence had to await the 1955 State Treaty under which Austria accepted permanent neutrality. Austria therefore emerged from these traumas with a far stronger sense of its own identity and nationhood, even if this was rooted in the polite fiction that it had been the "first victim" of Nazi aggression.

For Finland the cost of the wars with the Soviet Union of 1939–40 and 1941–4 was the loss of 12 percent of its territory, 13 percent of its national wealth, and the displacement of more than 400,000 internal refugees. Moreover, the Soviet Union demanded heavy reparations (in the form of commodities) that were not paid off until 1952, and the lease of a naval base. There were also political conditions: the trial of the politicians responsible for war in 1941, and the relegalization of the Communist Party, which had been banned in 1930. Despite these heavy blows, and without any obvious external counterbalance to Soviet power, Finland proved surprisingly resilient throughout the "danger years" of 1944–8. In the elections of March 1945 the communists (working through the SKDL umbrella organization) became the second largest party with 23.5 percent of the vote, and led a coalition government with the socialists and agrarians. Over the next three years Finland trod a delicate line between meeting Soviet demands and upholding its independence – for instance, the reluctant decision to refuse Marshall Aid made it far more vulnerable to Soviet pressure.

The crisis in Finnish–Soviet relations came in the spring of 1948 when Stalin demanded a military alliance, but eventually settled for an "Agreement of Friendship, Co-operation and Mutual Assistance" signed on April 6. The treaty (which was principally directed against Germany) committed Finland to resist any attack against the USSR through its territory, and precluded Finland from joining any alliance directed against the Soviet Union. In fact, Finland had got away lightly, as the agreement was essentially defensive and left it open to pursue other international relationships such as participation in the Nordic Council from the mid-1950s. Arguably Stalin had shown restraint following the furore over the Prague coup in February 1948 and in the knowledge of Finland's stern resistance in 1939–40. Subsequent events confirmed that the corner had been turned. In April 1948 the powerful communist Interior Minister was dismissed, and in the July 1948 elections the SKDL vote fell to 20 percent, allowing the socialist leader Fagerholm to exclude them from government. Even so, politicians were aware of the USSR's continuing readiness to meddle in internal Finnish politics, as incidents in 1958 and 1961 would clearly demonstrate. The long-term consequence was the quietly corrosive policy of self-censorship to avoid any provocation of the Soviet Union which, somewhat pejoratively, came to be known as "Finlandization."

Conclusion

The reconstruction of Europe was more than a question of making good the damage caused by World War II. Across Europe, governments were also concerned to tackle the broader socioeconomic and political weaknesses that had been so cruelly exposed during the inter-war years. In western Europe, for instance, democratic political regimes were established in Germany and Italy and a welfare state in Britain, while France underwent rapid modernization under the Monnet Plan. Although the balance varied from country to country, an effective synthesis was reached between the public sector and the free market that enabled industrial modernization and greater social justice. In eastern Europe, under communist control, a far more revolutionary transformation of the old social and economic order was undertaken. Meanwhile, a number of countries succeeded in straddling the Cold War divide, and Tito's Yugoslavia represented a genuine challenge to the hegemony of Moscow-line communism. In southern Europe dictatorship survived the war in Spain and Portugal, while in Greece a civil war eventually determined the country's "Western" political orientation.

4

Consolidating Western Europe, 1950–1963

Fears and Aspirations

During the 1950s and early 1960s, western Europe moved steadily towards a greater sense of security and stability. In Britain, West Germany, and Italy conservative and Christian democratic parties were in the ascendant, while in smaller countries such as the Netherlands and Austria there were stable coalition governments. The great anomaly seemed to be France, which witnessed not only the overthrow of the Fourth Republic in 1958 but also, with the Poujadist movement, the first great political insurgency of the postwar era. Even so, the crisis of 1958 was largely political in nature, concealing the rapid economic progress made since 1945. Under de Gaulle's Fifth Republic, France, too, would experience a decade of domestic stability. More generally, this was a period of transition and adjustment as the countries of western Europe passed from the armed peace of the early Cold War to the first glimmerings of détente, and from the austerity of reconstruction to thriving peacetime economies. There was, however, no overnight transformation: full currency convertibility was not restored until 1958, and many of the pleasures of "affluence" (the term popularized by J. K. Galbraith in 1958) did not become widely available until the 1960s. In West Germany even the per capita consumption of food was not restored to the prewar average until 1955/6, and as late as March 1957 a majority of German employees still worked a six-day week.[1]

Despite the steady improvements in living standards, the 1950s were a fearful decade. Fear of communism – as both an external and an internal threat – at the start of the 1950s elided subsequently into a more generalized fear of (in the graphic title of the German peace movement) "Atomic Death." Closer to home, Europeans were also apprehensive about their new-found prosperity. In July 1957 British

Europe's Troubled Peace: 1945 to the Present, Second Edition. Tom Buchanan.
© 2012 John Wiley & Sons, Ltd. Published 2012 by John Wiley & Sons, Ltd.

Prime Minister Harold Macmillan famously claimed that "most of our people have never had it so good," but went on to ask: "Is it too good to last?"[2] As late as 1966, following a mild economic downturn, 40 percent of West Germans still thought that another major crisis akin to that of 1929 was highly likely.[3] Although unemployment was generally low, such concerns helped to fashion a hard-working labor force and (until the early 1960s) low levels of industrial militancy.

The pervasive fear of communism, none too subtly manipulated by politicians, severely constrained public debate and political space. Visions of an "Asiatic" communism threatening Western civilization, stoked by shocking images of the Soviet repression of the Hungarian uprising in 1956, underpinned the appeal of Christian Democracy and helped to define a new "Atlanticist" social democracy. In an age of suspicion and willingness to think the worst, the threat of communism could be used to taint the left in general. In 1953, for instance, the West German Social Democrats' political opponents used slogans such as "Where Ollenhauer [the SPD leader] ploughs, Moscow sows" and "All roads of Marxism lead to Moscow."[4] Nor was communism simply subjected to rhetorical assault. In May 1952 a number of leading French communists were briefly arrested on trumped-up charges, and in 1956, after a long legal battle, the Communist Party in West Germany was banned and its offices closed. Conversely, the cleansing amnesia of the Cold War made former villains such as Franco semi-respectable and ended serious political opposition to German rearmament by the mid-1950s. The slate of the fascist era was quietly wiped clean as the jails were emptied of all but the most senior Nazis and collaborators.

Fear of the East did not necessarily imply infatuation with the United States, desperately desirable as its goods and lifestyles were to many. French communists decried the "coca-colonization" of Europe, and, indeed, the introduction of Coca-Cola into France, in 1950, was the occasion of considerable hand-wringing. However, ambivalence about the relationship with the USA went far beyond the left. Many German industrialists, for instance, desired the sheen of American mass production but feared the deleterious effect that its counterpart, mass culture, would have on their workforce. Louis Aragon's condemnation of the American "civilization of bathtubs and Frigidaires"[5] identified the sedating (and very welcome) effect that American culture might have on the lives of ordinary Europeans. At the same time, by the mid-1950s the destabilizing impact of American culture in Europe was also evident amongst the young: witness the sexual potency of Elvis Presley and the riots (as far afield as Oslo and Copenhagen) that accompanied the movie of Bill Haley's "Rock around the clock." The leather-jacketed *halbstarken* ("hooligan") youths in West Germany threw the sneer of the young Marlon Brando into the faces of their hard-working, conservative parents.

Such images were disturbing for many, but should not obscure the fact that during the 1950s west European societies remained deeply conservative. As the success of Christian Democracy demonstrates, the churches (and above all the Catholic Church) retained a considerable influence over social and political life.

Under the papacy of Pius XII (1939–58) the authority of the Vatican was consolidated and the more socialistic Catholicism of the French "worker priests" was firmly rejected. Church attendance appears to have held up well: in a 1956 survey 69 percent of Italians claimed to have attended mass that week, and 42 percent of Belgian adults in 1950 said that they attended church regularly. Many Catholics still lived within a network of religious associations such as Catholic Action, trade unions and farmers' associations. As late as 1959, 95 percent of Dutch Catholic farmers belonged to their confessional farmers' union, while in Belgium the Catholic trade union was stronger (with 731,000 members) than its socialist rival. The thicket of religious associations was at its most impressive in Italy, where there were 2.6 million members of Catholic Action and 1.6 million peasant families in the "Coldiretti" organization. The political implications were evident, not only in a country such as Italy, but also in the Netherlands where, until 1967, 80–90 percent of Catholics followed the lead of their bishops in voting for the Catholic Party at election time.[6]

Gender relations were also marked by an essential conservatism. The 1950s saw the triumph of an ideal of female domesticity advocated by conservative parties and the churches and reinforced by mass-circulation magazines such as *Elle*. There was precious little space for women in public life. The number of Italian female members of parliament fell from 41 in 1948 to 36 in 1953 and 17 in 1968; in France it fell from 42 in 1946 to 8 in 1958. In West Germany women constituted only 15 percent of members of political parties in the 1950s and 1960s. Although Article 3 of the Basic Law had established the principle of equality between the sexes, the old paternalistic Civil Code was not rewritten until 1957. Adenauer's Minister of Family Affairs, Franz-Josef Wurmeling, pointed to East Germany as an example of a form of gender equality "from which we want to protect ourselves and our women."[7] However, there was little sign that women were ready to contest their ordained place. Simone de Beauvoir's *The Second Sex* (1949), which saw marriage as a destiny to be avoided and motherhood as a trap, did not strike a significant chord until the 1960s. Women voters showed a partiality for conservative parties committed to defending the traditional family. As much as 60 percent of the Italian Christian Democrat vote was female, and a majority of women supported the arch-chauvinist de Gaulle.[8] Meanwhile, the experience of women in work was varied. In France the number of women in the workforce declined in the 1950s, but in West Germany the proportion was back to prewar levels by 1961. In all cases, however, women were largely restricted to unskilled and semiskilled jobs, and less well paid than men.

During a period dominated by conservatism and pressures to conform, critical voices were mainly heard in the cultural sphere, and were all the more effective for not being party-political. John Osborne's *Look Back in Anger* (first performed in May 1956) both transformed British theater and articulated the powerful tensions that were building up within an ostensibly more mobile and meritocratic society. The precocious Françoise Sagan's bestseller *Bonjour Tristesse* (1954) shocked and delighted readers with its depiction of the privileged young's hedonistic desires. It was not only Western mores and assumptions that were under scrutiny, but the very conventions by which culture had previously been transmitted. The absurdist French "New Theatre" of Eugène Ionesco and Samuel Beckett (whose *Waiting for Godot* was first performed in 1952) challenged conceptions of a proper play, just as the "New Novel" of Alain Robbe-Grillet and others denied the need for traditional narrative structures. In Italy, however, the most powerful social commentary of the Neo-Realist movement had come in the late 1940s (for instance, Vittorio De Sica's classic *Ladri di biciclette* (Bicycle Thieves) in 1948), and by the mid-1950s Italian film-makers were moving towards a more lyrical, expressive style prior to the full flowering of "art cinema" in the 1960s. It should also be noted that writers and film-makers in West Germany did not begin to engage profoundly with contemporary affairs and with the Nazi past until the late 1950s and 1960s, especially in the work of authors such as Günter Grass and Heinrich Böll. An early example was Grass's remarkable *The Tin Drum* (1959), which examined the Nazi era in a highly distinctive "magical realist" style, drawing on the author's early years in Danzig.

These independent voices had the power to prick consciences and stimulate debate. However, it should not be forgotten that Europe's cultural life – especially the cinema – was still dominated by mass-market products with no pretensions to influence public debate. Only about 10 percent of the films made in Italy between 1945 and 1953, for instance, were "Neo-Realist," and most of these were unsuccessful at the box office.[9] American movies remained highly popular with European audiences, as were European-made Westerns and even war movies. In France a determined effort was made to offer financial support to the domestic film industry, which contributed to the success of innovative film-makers such as François Truffaut and Claude Chabrol in the *Nouvelle Vague* (New Wave) of the late 1950s. Even so, across Europe, as the 1950s progressed the cinema's domination of popular mass culture was increasingly threatened by the rise of television, and film theaters closed in their thousands. Crucially, television was controlled by the state (the main exception being West Germany, where – to Adenauer's annoyance – the television channels were operated by the *Länder* rather than the federal government). Therefore, while television offered wonderful opportunities, at least during the 1950s it was hardly a vehicle for social and political criticism.

Towards Affluence: The Economy and Social Change

In the course of the 1950s western Europe put behind it not only the reconstruction of the later 1940s but also the poverty of the 1930s. If in the immediate postwar years the goal had been to restore prewar levels of production, by the 1950s sights were being recalibrated towards much higher goals. The targets of the Second

French Plan (1952–7) were comfortably exceeded, while the British Chancellor "Rab" Butler's aspiration in 1954 for standards of living to double in the next 25 years was soon exposed as absurdly unambitious.[10] Europe was launched on an unprecedented boom that overturned all previous expectations and consolidated the new belief in boundless economic growth, backed by full employment and low inflation. The boom grew out of a powerful and unique set of circumstances.[11] The USA, the most dynamic economy in the postwar world, had shared its machinery and productivist techniques through the Marshall Aid programs and had subsequently supplied military assistance and private investment. By 1950 the European Payments Union had created a framework to facilitate intra-European trade, which was greatly enhanced by the formation of the European Economic Community (EEC) in 1957 (see Chapter 9). Europe meanwhile benefited from low energy and raw material costs, and wage demands were kept in check by workers' share in the new prosperity and the formation of various forms of welfare state. Strikes were few and unions were often weak, politically divided, or drawn into new social partnerships (such as the West German co-determination arrangements and works councils). The French unions accounted for a mere 15 percent of wage-earners; in Italy, there were no strikes by the normally restive Fiat workers between 1954 and 1962. There was certainly nothing in democratic Europe to compare with the 1951 strike in Barcelona which spiraled from local grievances (over the increased cost of public transport) into an explosion of discontent at Franco's rule.

The European boom was driven forward by the remorseless, export-led growth of the West German economy, which recovered strongly after briefly faltering under the inflationary pressures of the Korean War. German machine tools, manufactured goods, and automobiles soon began to conquer new markets, especially within western Europe. The economy of the Federal Republic grew at the spectacular rate of 8.2 percent per annum during the 1950s, and for many this turnaround from the desolation of the mid-1940s seemed nothing short of an economic "miracle." The main components of success had, however, been present since 1945 in the form of a skilled, motivated, mobile, and cooperative labor force and high-quality industrial capacity. The task that Erhard and Adenauer successfully confronted, therefore, had been to create the conditions within which that potential could be realized. Their advocacy of free-market economics and tax breaks to support industrial investment was wisely tempered by a concern for the wider diffusion of prosperity. Thus, some 4 million new homes were constructed between 1950 and 1957 by a combination of public and private enterprise. Economic success was further underpinned by the anti-inflationary policies pursued by the central bank.

While the German recovery was exceptional, other European economies also experienced their own form of "miracle" during this period. French industrial output rose by 6 percent per year between 1952 and 1959, and (on the basis of an intense drive for mechanization) agricultural productivity grew somewhat faster than that of the economy as a whole (by 6.4 percent compared to overall growth of 5.2 percent per year between 1949 and 1962). There were, however, problems and constraints. France had grown heavily dependent on imported Middle Eastern oil by 1956, while the labor force (in spite of the baby boom and immigration) remained too small to meet demand, especially once half a million conscripts were sent to serve in Algeria. All of these factors contributed to the sharp economic crisis of 1957–8 and, hence, to the weakening of the Fourth Republic. The Italian economy, too, enjoyed remarkable success from the late 1950s. In particular, it responded well to the competition and new markets offered by the EEC, and Italy enjoyed an export boom driven by low wage costs and high-quality products (especially domestic appliances or "white goods"). The Italian "economic miracle" of 1958–63 launched the country on its rapid transformation into a modern industrial society, fuelled by mass migration from the agrarian south into the great northern cities. Likewise in Switzerland, the postwar surge of manufacturing, driven by worldwide demand for its specialist high-quality goods and pharmaceuticals, hastened the depopulation of the countryside and the transition to an essentially urban society.

There were, however, exceptions to the general success of the European economies. Britain, in particular, experienced sluggish growth (a mere 2–3 percent in the late 1950s and early 1960s) as a result of outdated machinery, inflexible labor relations, and government policy that lurched between expansion and deflation (the infamous "stop–go" cycle). The obvious shortfall in British performance when compared to its continental neighbors influenced the decision to make a belated bid for EEC membership in 1962 and also bred a sense of pessimism about Britain's perceived decline. Belgium, which had emerged from the war with its heavy industry relatively unscathed, also performed poorly in the 1950s. Its initial advantage was soon frittered away by the failure to tackle industrial obsolescence (especially that of the expensive domestic coal industry) and high labor costs. By contrast, the Netherlands adapted well to its changed postwar situation (above all, the loss of the greater part of its empire) through industrial reconstruction and a social consensus on the need for low, competitive wages. The Dutch were also greatly assisted by the revival of the German market for their agricultural products. The economy of Denmark also began to recover in the 1950s. Danish agriculture was successfully modernized and restructured, while manufacturers established niche products such as the phenomenally successful Lego children's toys.

The burgeoning prosperity of western Europe increasingly acted as a magnet for neighboring countries and populations. The 4 million East Germans who fled to the West before August 1961 provided the young skilled labor force demanded by the dynamic German economy. By 1963 West Germany was also host to 800,000 foreign workers, 297,000 of them from Italy. Italians also made up the largest contingent among the 155,000 immigrants per year who entered France between 1955 and 1961. In Britain some 180,000 immigrants had arrived from the countries of the "New Commonwealth" (primarily the Indian subcontinent and the Caribbean) by 1958. The economic attraction of western Europe was also evident in Franco's

Spain, where the heavily regulated economy was in crisis by the late 1950s. In 1957 Franco appointed a team of technocratic ministers from the Catholic Opus Dei organization who, against all of the dictator's instincts, oversaw the integration of Spain into the world economy. The 1959 "Plan for Stabilization and Liberalization" slashed public expenditure and opened Spain to foreign investment and tourism. Despite the pain of rising unemployment, during the 1960s Spain underwent remarkable growth. However, the great prize of EEC membership (for which Spain first applied in 1962) would have to await a matching political liberalization.

Western Europe's long boom inevitably brought profound social changes in its wake. Populations were relentlessly shifting from the countryside to the cities as the pull of industrial prosperity combined with the push of rural mechanization and poverty. In France, for instance, the urban population grew from 53.2 percent in 1946 to 61.7 percent in 1962, while in West Germany agriculture's share of the labor force fell from 22.1 percent to 13.3 percent between 1950 and 1960. Although the countryside experienced some benefits from growth, the new disposable income and expectation of continuing prosperity associated with "affluence" was experienced most immediately by city-dwellers in the later 1950s. Material possessions were not merely badges of affluence, but also profoundly influenced social and cultural behavior. Mass car ownership, for instance, bred a new individualism and pride, while also allowing thousands of Germans to drive to Italy and the south of France on camping holidays. In France there was one car per 17 inhabitants in 1951, but one for every seven in 1958. Car ownership rose between 1950 and 1960 from 0.5 million to 4.4 million in West Germany and 0.3 million to 1.9 million in Italy. The refrigerator, which reduced the need for daily shopping trips and made possible new tastes, was another icon of the period. Ownership of fridges in West Germany rose from 10 percent of households in 1955 to 51.8 percent in 1962–3.[12] Television (often initially watched in public) created a new sense of immediacy in shared national experiences (such as the coronation of Queen Elizabeth II in 1953 or West Germany's World Cup football victory over Hungary in 1954). However, perhaps the greatest impact of affluence was on the young, with the emergence in the late 1950s of the very concept of the "teenager" and a battery of new forms of consumption aimed at them (such as records and clothes).

Prosperity and increased holiday allowances also created greater demands for leisure and travel. The Germans led the way in pioneering mass tourism within Europe, overcoming initial fears of the lingering resentments of the war – sometimes brazenly. In 1957 Max Merten, head of the German wartime administration in Thessalonika, was arrested on his third visit to Greece as a tourist and given a 25-year sentence (although he was soon extradited back to Germany).[13] The nascent tourist industry was aided by the advent of jet travel, the ending of visa requirements within the EEC, and the creation of companies such as Club Med (1950) and Touropa (1951). Encouraged by the Franco regime, the Spanish Mediterranean coast, in particular, rapidly developed as a cheap but exotic holiday destination. There were 1.5 million foreign visitors to Spain in 1952, but 6 million in 1960, indicating that foreign holidays were no longer the preserve of the privileged elite. Even so, by no means everyone used their new leisure to travel abroad. Ninety percent of French workers received paid holiday in 1958, but only 30 percent chose to leave their homes.[14] Many British workers still preferred the regimented pleasures of the holiday camp or the traditional seaside resort.

Affluence widened the inequalities both between city and country and between social groups. The countryside could not remain untouched by social change. For instance, even in remote areas of southern Italy and Sicily surveys carried out in 1957–8 recorded greater access to television and the cinema for the young, as well as older generations disturbed by the relaxation of custom and the rise of "immorality."[15] Even so, across much of Europe the wholesale modernization of rural life – including the advent of electricity and running water – generally had to await the 1960s. Affluence also had profound political implications, as voters were increasingly looking to politicians not only to defend living standards but also to ensure that they continued to rise. As the Swedish socialist Olof Palme commented in 1958: "Providing a safety net, a minimum standard, was the problem of the 1930s. Maintaining our living standard is the goal of the 1950s."[16] For both conservatives and social democrats, moreover, the political impact of the new prosperity was difficult to read in the early 1960s. Socialists feared that social mobility would erode the established class loyalties on which much of their vote still rested: but conservatives and Christian democrats, for their part, had to confront the effects of the new materialism and the decline of deference.

From Korea to Berlin: The International Context

Although this period was bracketed by the Korean War at one end and the Cuban missile crisis at the other, by 1963 the threat of war in Europe had greatly receded. The prime symbol of this new stability was the construction of the Berlin Wall in August 1961 which, while hated by Germans, at least marked a new international acceptance of Europe's division. More positively, the July 1963 Nuclear Test Ban Treaty and the establishment of a "hotline" to avert future crises began to address European fears of nuclear conflagration. The new equilibrium was due in part to the failure of the Soviet Union under Nikita Khrushchev to gain a military advantage over the West. Despite talk of a "missile gap" during the 1960 presidential election campaign, the USA still enjoyed a lead of 4:1 in intercontinental ballistic missiles (ICBMs) and of 3:1 in long-range bombers. Khrushchev was reduced to idle boasting (in 1962 he would claim that the USSR had an anti-missile defense that could "hit a fly in outer space")[17] and dangerous gimmicks, such as the stationing of medium-range missiles in Cuba.

Greater security also reflected the successful transformation of NATO in the early 1950s from a paper treaty into a fully fledged military alliance, buoyed up by a costly rearmament program. While NATO could not match the Soviets and their allies man for man in central Europe, its forces, nestling under the US nuclear umbrella, were better equipped and better integrated than their opponents. Even so, the Atlantic alliance was contorted with numerous tensions, not least because the Soviet Union became a less belligerent adversary after the death of Stalin. Moreover, under the presidency of Dwight D. Eisenhower (1953–61), the USA hoped to scale down its manpower commitment to Europe. This was above all a matter of trust: could western Europe be confident that the USA would offer a credible deterrent to Soviet attack, especially once the USSR gained the capability to launch a nuclear strike at the American heartland? As de Gaulle reputedly put it, would an American president really risk New York or Chicago for Hamburg or Copenhagen?[18] For the Europeans, therefore, the presence of US troops was not only a deterrent to Soviet attack, but also, in effect, provided hostages to the US defense of Europe. This did not prevent Britain and France from seeking to acquire their own nuclear deterrents: the British bomb was tested in 1952 and the French in 1960. However, while the *force de frappe* became a symbol of French independence, the British bomb became a symbol of the loss of Great Power status. The next-generation British nuclear weapon (Polaris) was provided by the USA only after personal supplication by Harold Macmillan in 1962.

The alternative for the Europeans was to develop their own conventional military forces. However, not only was this economically unpalatable, but it also raised the specter of the rearmament of West Germany at a time when many still feared German militarism. Accordingly, the question of how this could be accomplished while at the same time guaranteeing the security of Germany's neighbors dominated the transatlantic politics of 1950–5. In October 1950 the "Pléven Plan" provided an integrationist solution which owed much to the success of the initial moves towards the creation of the coal and steel community. Under Pléven's proposed European Defence Community (EDC) Germany would be rearmed within the context of a European army. In effect, German troops would be placed under French command. There would also be a matching integration of defense procurement and a parallel structure for political integration. The EDC was supported by the USA and, reluctantly, by Adenauer because it offered a means for the restoration of full German sovereignty. The benefits for West Germany were immediate as under the General Treaty of 1952 the occupation was wound up, although the Allies retained unspecified rights to intervene in German affairs. In the event, the EDC failed to achieve ratification in the French parliament in August 1954, defeated by an unlikely alliance of communists and Gaullists. By now, however, much of the sting had been taken out of the issue, and a rational solution lay to hand. The 1948 Brussels Treaty was expanded to include West Germany and Italy, forming a new West European Union as a part of which a rearmed Germany could join NATO. In return, it had to renounce the production of atomic, biological, and chemical weapons, and to accept a continuing Allied military presence on its soil.

The US Secretary of State John Foster Dulles's abortive threat that the failure of the EDC would result in an "agonizing reappraisal" of the American position in Europe showed that there were limits to US power. Even so, America was unquestionably the decisive force in western Europe's international relations, especially when European ambitions conflicted with its own perceived interests. Most dramatically, in November 1956 Eisenhower forced the British and French to call off their attempt to retake control of the Suez canal from Egyptian President Nasser (see below). Suez amplified the resentment that France already felt towards the USA for its "betrayal" in Indo-China in 1954 and accelerated French involvement in European integration. Adenauer was visiting Paris when the British announced their ceasefire in Suez and told the French Prime Minister Guy Mollet that he should "make Europe your revenge."[19] France's humiliation also nourished de Gaulle's more independent foreign policy and anti-Anglo-Saxon posturing after his return to power in 1958. De Gaulle made his intentions clear on taking office by canceling nuclear cooperation with Italy and Germany and fruitlessly suggesting a Franco–British–US "directorate" of NATO. In March 1959 he withdrew the Mediterranean fleet from the integrated NATO command and refused permission for the United States to station atomic bombs on French soil.

The Suez crisis had been emblematic not only of the changed relationship between America and the European powers, but also of their changed relationship with the colonial world. In the face of nationalist rebellion, American pressures, and changed economic realities, the empires of Britain, France, and Belgium underwent rapid decolonization from the late 1950s. Only Portugal, said to be too poor to afford neo-colonialism, was apparently immune, although it was forced to give up its Indian enclave of Goa in 1961. With the sudden end of its colonial "mission," Europe had to come to terms with the emerging "Third World" (the term was coined in 1952).[20] The flows of population were now reversed. Thousands of white settlers returned home, above all the estimated 800,000 French *pieds noirs* fleeing Algeria after 1962, while from the mid-1950s Britain began to experience mass immigration from the Commonwealth. There was also a political dimension to this shift. By the end of the Algerian War, French students and intellectuals were accustomed to the idea that left-wing political inspiration was more likely to come from the peasant revolutionaries of Latin America and Indochina than from the Soviet Union.

Cold War tensions in Europe reached a peak with the Berlin crisis of 1958–61. The city was still under four-power rule and remained the one point of open access between East and West. As many as 60,000 East Germans traveled daily to work in the West and others crossed the border to shop for Western commodities (while West Berliners bought cheap bread and petrol in the East). Above all, by 1960 East Germans were fleeing into West Berlin at a rate of 4,000 per week and rising. For the ruling communists Berlin had become a "bleeding ulcer" that undermined the credibility of their state and threatened its viability. Their ambition was for East Germany to be recognized in the West, with Berlin as its capital. The crisis started in November 1958 when Khrushchev announced that the Soviet Union intended to sign a peace treaty with the DDR, and demanded that the West must now negotiate a Berlin settlement. The Soviet demands were initially met with a pragmatic response by Eisenhower, but the election of John F. Kennedy gave Khrushchev the chance to test a young and inexperienced president. At their meeting in June 1961 Khrushchev warned of the danger of war over Berlin; Kennedy's response, in a broadcast of July 25, was to pledge to defend the city. Importantly, however, no mention was made of the right of free movement across the divided city and this offered a taste of how the crisis could be resolved.

On the night of August 12/13, 1961 a well-planned East German operation to seal the border was carried out with sufficient secrecy to prevent any cohesive response from the Allies or the population of Berlin. Police, troops, and militia used barbed wire to create what was officially referred to as an "anti-fascist barrier" to prevent Western subversion. The Western response was muted, as there was only a garrison of 12,000 troops and the city was clearly indefensible. In private, Western leaders were relieved that – as in the words of the French Foreign Minister – "that settles the Berlin problem."[21] The Berlin Wall (7.5 miles of concrete and 116 watchtowers in its final form; see Figures 4.1 and 4.2) stabilized both

Figure 4.1   The Berlin Wall in 1984. Photo: Tom Buchanan.

Figure 4.2 The Berlin Wall in 1984. Photo: Tom Buchanan.

the East German state and Great Power relations in Europe. The wall's real victims were, of course, the divided families of Berlin and the estimated 200 people who died attempting to escape across it. While Kennedy was powerless to prevent the wall's construction, his forthright support for West Berlin as a "defended island of freedom" was much appreciated. His visit to Berlin in June 1963 marked the height of American popularity in Germany and some of the glamour was reflected onto the city's young mayor Willy Brandt, already hailed as the "German Kennedy." Kennedy raised the spirits of Berliners by recognizing that they had been "in the front lines for almost two decades."[22] In fact, however, Europe was soon to become a quiet front in a Cold War which would now be contested in Vietnam, Latin America, and Africa.

"No Experiments": West Germany, Britain, and Italy

During the 1950s, with the exception of France, there was a unique conservative domination of the major countries of western Europe. The term "conservative" is, of course, used guardedly of the Christian democratic parties given the progressive currents that continued to exist within them. However, it broadly describes their anti-communist, pro-capitalist, and pro-NATO policies in the 1950s. Adenauer's chancellorship lasted longer than the Weimar Republic; in Britain the Conservatives, under four different leaders, won three elections in a row, and came close to winning a fourth; in Italy the Christian Democrats entrenched themselves ever more deeply in power, although they were forced to share some of the spoils. Germany and Italy now had what Britain had possessed in the inter-war years and which they so dangerously lacked: parties of the center which possessed a "national" appeal and which could keep the middle classes satisfied within a parliamentary system. All three were highly effective electoral machines, adept at mobilizing their voters. All three also benefited from the uncompetitiveness of the left in opposition (although it is debatable whether the Italian communists were allowed to compete in any meaningful way). However, there were also significant differences. In particular, unlike the other two, which were built around the principle of strong leadership, the Italian Christian Democrats became increasingly factionalized after 1953.

The long domination by the center-right posed questions about the kind of democracy that was emerging in postwar Europe. This was less of an issue in Britain, with its long parliamentary tradition and independent civil service, but even so the third successive Conservative victory in 1959 posed the question "Must Labour lose?"[23] There was a fear that modern political and economic management could entrench one party in power indefinitely, as well as a belief that social change and the decline of the working class would turn Labour into a permanent minority. More pointedly, Adenauer's critics began to talk of an authoritarian *Kanzlerdemokratie* ("Chancellor democracy") which posed a threat to German democratic values. However, while Adenauer was undoubtedly high-handed and bullying, it is important to recall that his power was offset by the federal arrangements under the Basic Law, and also that he saw his role as a paternalistic one of educating a mistrustful population about the benefits of democracy.[24] The threat to democracy was most evident in Italy, where the Christian Democrat government's 1952 election law (dubbed the "swindle law") was intended to guarantee parliamentary domination for any alliance that could win more than 50 percent of the vote. This echo of Mussolini's 1923 "Acerbo" law backfired when the Christian Democrats won only 49.85 percent of the vote in the subsequent election. Far more sinister, however, was the party's ability to embed itself into the state and thereby create a complex web of patronage. As a whole, European postwar democracy was highly directed and nonparticipatory.[25] All too often pressure groups were de-legitimated by the smear of communism, whether the connection was real or not.

In Germany power revolved around Adenauer and his undiminished appetite for power. For the "Old Man" (*der Alte*) the CDU was a vehicle to win elections, and otherwise largely ignored, although he was responsive to the CDU's farming lobby and other interest groups. His political strategy, to make the CDU hegemonic on the center-right, bore fruit in the course of the 1950s with the absorption of most of the Christian Democrats' smaller rivals. In the 1957 election the CDU/CSU won a remarkable 50.2 percent of the vote on the dour slogan of "No experiments." Adenauer's electoral success rested on Germany's new prosperity and his ability to restore German sovereignty and pride, although he also benefited from the inflexibility of the Social Democrat opposition until its wide-ranging overhaul in 1959. He was a bruising politician, castigating Kurt Schumacher as a quasi-communist and, in 1961, giving free rein to vicious attacks on the patriotism and integrity of his young challenger Willy Brandt. Brandt later commented, with commendable restraint, that Adenauer's "relations with the truth were fickle and his chosen methods not invariably in the best taste."[26] Adenauer's authority was also stamped on the federal government. He took full advantage of his constitutional right to set policy guidelines for ministers, and could be brutal in his appointment and dismissal of colleagues. Adenauer rarely lost a political argument and tended to follow his instincts rather than expert opinion or the feelings of his own party. He clashed on numerous occasions with his finance minister Ludwig Erhard, whose free-market instincts urged caution over the EEC and the 1957 introduction of index-linked pensions. By the early 1960s, however, Adenauer's closeness to de Gaulle had allowed a dangerous gap to open within government between the so-called German "Gaullists" and the "Atlanticists" led by Erhard.

For all his success, Adenauer's record was besmirched by his attitude towards the Nazi past. Admittedly he forced through a reparations treaty with Israel in 1952, for the Jewish victims of Nazism, in the face of opposition from within his own party. However, alongside the Nuremberg trials, this was seen as a final settlement, allowing a veil to be drawn over the past. Nazi connections were now no impediment to high office: Theodor Oberländer, who had taken part in mass executions on the Eastern Front, sat in Adenauer's cabinet, and his State Secretary Hans Globke had written the commentary for the 1935 Nuremberg racial laws. In the 1950s there was little public discussion of Nazi crimes and the dominant image was one of the Germans as victims, above all of the Russians. Interestingly, a poll following Adenauer's death showed that 75 percent of Germans rated his release of prisoners of war (following his 1955 visit to Moscow) as his greatest achievement.[27] The cost of this selective memory became evident in the 1960s and 1970s when a younger generation began to ask questions of what their parents and grandparents had actually done during the Nazi era.

In the end, the uglier aspects of Adenauer's long rule precipitated his fall. His position had been weakened by the outcome of the 1961 election which forced him to form a new coalition with the FDP, having governed without them since 1956. Then, in October 1962 his government was shaken by the *Der Spiegel* affair, in which investigative journalism clashed head on with Adenauer's authoritarianism and the arrogance of his Defense Minister Franz Josef Strauss (the leader of the CSU). An article in *Der Spiegel* questioning Germany's readiness for war prompted a raid on its offices and the detention of a number of executives, while the journalist who had written the piece was, after a request by Strauss, arrested and returned to Germany by Spanish police. Adenauer's warning in the Bundestag of an "abyss of treason" failed to save Strauss, who was forced to resign by pressure from the FDP. The damage to Adenauer's authority was compounded soon afterwards by the Bundestag's reaffirmation of loyalty to NATO in its ratification of the Treaty of Paris. The old Chancellor, deemed a liability by many CDU colleagues, finally retired in October 1963. He had stayed too long, and the paramount question was whether his successor Erhard could meet the challenge of a revived SPD as well as managing the new and less deferential Germany revealed by the *Der Spiegel* affair.

Italian Christian Democracy was deprived of its most dominant and visionary postwar leader by the fall of De Gasperi following the electoral fiasco of 1953. Thereafter, the DC was reliant for its majority on the support of the smaller parties of the center-right, and the fact that there were fifteen governments between 1950 and 1963 gave rise to a sense of political instability. Such appearances were, however, deceptive. The prime minister was always a Christian Democrat and governing majorities were consistently drawn from the same shallow political pool. A combination of papal and American pressure ruled out any approach to the left, while the neo-fascist MSI was also excluded from office. The DC's only attempt to govern with the support of the MSI was swiftly terminated following riots in Genoa (where the neo-fascists were holding their congress) in June 1960. Italians were, it seemed, stuck with a Christian Democrat government that (under the restored system of proportional representation) lacked a clear majority.

The response of the DC, under the leadership of Amintore Fanfani from 1954, was to develop the party's institutional strength and reduce its dependence on the Catholic Church and business. Membership rose from 1 million in 1948 to 1.6 million by 1963, and DC influence was spread more widely, especially in the north-east, through the web of Catholic voluntary associations. Even more impressive, however, was the DC's ability to colonize the state and its agencies to gain control over the all-important levers of patronage. The formation of vast holding companies in the 1950s (such as the ENI, an empire of energy-related companies under Enrico Mattei) created immense economic fiefdoms under political control. Similarly, the public agencies for developing the south (notably the Cassa per il Mezzogiorno) offered the DC an alternative power base to the southern landowning notables, who had been disenchanted by the modest agrarian reforms of 1950. At a time when poverty was still endemic in the south, such patronage provided the basis for political power. In the words of one citizen of Naples: "The priest suggested to us that the only party was the DC ... I became a member because they said to me: 'If you don't become a party member you can't find work'."[28] While such practices smacked of corruption to northern Europeans, they were (with the partial exception of the communists) accepted across all parties until the early 1990s.

Amidst the rapid economic growth and social change after 1958, the DC began to look with increasing urgency for a new basis for its majority in government. Conditions were now ripe for an unprecedented opening to the moderate left.[29] There was a new Pope, John XXIII (1958–63), who did not share the Cold War mentality of his predecessor and a new American president, Kennedy, who actively favored social democratic reformism as a means to undercut communism. Moreover, the Italian Socialist Party, which took around 14 percent of the vote, had begun to distance itself from the communists after the Hungarian uprising. Aldo Moro, the DC secretary from 1959, embarked on the difficult courtship of the socialists which culminated in their decision to join his government in December 1963. The center of gravity of Italian politics had shifted towards the reformist left, but the DC's long rule had also been prolonged. It remained to be seen whether this center-left experiment would produce concrete reforms.

After the shock of defeat in 1945 the British Conservatives recovered well in the late 1940s, narrowly defeating the faltering Labour government in October 1951. Their revival was underpinned by organizational reforms intended to broaden the party's social base and a thorough reappraisal of policy (notably the 1947 Industrial Charter). The Tories returned to power accepting much of the Labour government's industrial and welfare reforms, but offering an attractive commitment to economic freedom. In the following years the remaining wartime controls and rationing were phased out, national service reduced, and taxes cut, all indicative of a belated return to normality. Churchill, his cabinet stuffed with aristocratic grandees, saved his energy for international affairs, and his government avoided any provocative steps in domestic politics. The Cabinet's rising star was Harold Macmillan, who implemented (and exceeded) the Conservatives' pledge to build 300,000 new homes. When Churchill finally retired in April 1955 he handed a strong position to his successor Anthony Eden, who was able to increase the Tory majority in the May 1955 election.

Eden soon squandered his advantage. He failed to impose his authority on his colleagues, and Conservative middle-class support was alienated by rising inflation (the concomitant of full employment). However, Eden's greatest failing was in the very field of foreign policy where he had established his reputation. In the course of 1956 he became dangerously obsessed with the Egyptian leader Nasser, who had nationalized the Suez Canal and whom Eden came to see as a reincarnation of the dictators of the 1930s. Egged on by the French, who had their own reasons for wishing to inflict a defeat on Arab nationalism, he embarked on a secret collusion with Israel. In early November 1956, ostensibly to restore order between Egyptian and invading Israeli forces, British and French troops stormed into the canal zone. Within days Eden, under pressure from the USA and close colleagues, had been forced to accept a ceasefire and eventual withdrawal. However, the Suez fiasco, which cruelly exposed Britain's international weakness and injected a new bitterness into party politics, made surprisingly little impact on Conservative fortunes. Eden, his health undermined, resigned in January 1957 to be replaced by Macmillan.

Macmillan, like his two predecessors, represented the minority anti-appeasement Conservatism of the later 1930s, and more than the others could also claim to be a true progressive in social policy. Much of his period in office was taken up with the handling of the economy. In particular, how could the twin problems of inflation and Britain's relatively slow economic growth be addressed without increasing social tensions? In this respect, there were clear limits to what Macmillan believed to be politically acceptable. In January 1958 he suffered the unprecedented resignation of his entire Treasury team when they demanded more substantial cuts in government expenditure than Macmillan was willing to concede. His preferred strategy for Britain's stumbling economic performance was the abortive first bid for EEC membership (1962–3), and the establishment in 1962 of the tripartite National Economic Development Council.

Macmillan was a masterful politician. However, like Adenauer he was undermined by a crisis that confronted a complacent political class with the reality of rapidly changing social values. In 1963 the Defence Minister John Profumo was forced to resign when caught lying to parliament over his relationship with the prostitute Christine Keeler. Macmillan's determination that "no British government should be brought down by the action of two tarts"[30] betrayed his lack of understanding of the new power of sex, scandal, and satire. The revelations of upper-class misbehavior, prostitution, and even hints of espionage shocked the "establishment" and entertained the public (not least via the relatively new medium of television). Macmillan resigned, officially on the grounds of ill health, in October 1963.

France and Algeria

The collapse of the Fourth Republic, and the opening phase of the Fifth, were inextricably bound up with the conflict in Algeria (officially a "police action" and never deemed a "war"). The rebellion by the National Liberation Front (FLN) on November 1, 1954 followed swiftly after France's crushing defeat at Dien Bien Phu (on May 7) and the subsequent decision to abandon Indochina under the Geneva accords. No similar withdrawal could be contemplated from Algeria, as it was no mere colony but a *département* of metropolitan France and the home to almost a million *pieds noirs* settlers. Algeria was at the same time an exotic dream of France "outre-mer," a valuable strategic and economic asset, and the focus for the French Republic's historic mission to "civilize" the native population. The problem was that for the Muslims (some 8.5 million by 1954, and with a birth rate 2.5 times higher than that of the settlers) the benefits of French civilization were arriving too little and too late. The more educated Muslims, who should have formed the core of an assimilated administrative elite, were increasingly responsive to the message of Arab nationalism emanating in particular from Nasser's Egypt. The French government's confidence that the revolt could be contained was shattered by the carnage in the Constantine region in August 1955, when 123 whites and alleged Muslim "collaborators" were massacred. Countless more Muslims were slaughtered in response. Constantine raised the specter not only of anti-colonial violence, but also of racial conflict and, indeed, in the eyes of many French politicians, of a struggle between civilization and barbarism.[31]

The escalating violence in Algeria impacted on a Fourth Republic that was already struggling for political stability and legitimacy in the face of communist and Gaullist hostility. After the 1951 election a succession of short-lived governments was created from the shifting and fractious center-right alliance. The Republic briefly seemed to have found its savior under the government of the neo-radical Pierre Mendès-France (June 1954–March 1955), a milk-drinking modernizer who wanted France to go beyond the "sterile" ideological divisions of the past and embrace a technological future. His lasting achievement was to secure an honorable French retreat from Indochina. Mendès-France represented the young urban France that was already reorienting itself away from empire towards a "modern" Europe. His antithesis was Pierre Poujade, a shopkeeper from the Lot who led a popular movement against taxation and the intrusive state. His Union de Défense des Commerçants et Artisans grew rapidly after 1953 and won 12 percent of the vote in the January 1956 elections. Although Poujade's political influence soon waned, his success gave voice to the pain of traditional small-town France and added to the Republic's political fragmentation.

The 1956 elections proved inconclusive and resulted in the government of the socialist leader Guy Mollet, whose "Republican Front" was committed to reforms in Algeria. In fact, confronted with *pied noir* pressure Mollet was soon forced into increasing France's military presence, and by the summer some 450,000 troops, many of them conscripts, were serving in Algeria. Mollet's abandonment of reform was an important element in the motivation of the small minority within France who began to fraternize with the FLN and even to work for its victory. Another factor was the French army's conduct during the "Battle of Algiers" in the spring of 1957. The FLN's decision to confront French power in the Algerian capital was militarily flawed, but the reliance of General Massu's paratroopers on torture allowed the rebels to win a propaganda victory. The battle, memorably recreated in Pontecorvo's 1966 film, pointed the way ahead: between 1957 and 1962 the French would win every battle but still lose the war. Even the Morice Line, that effectively sealed the porous Tunisian border after 1957 and which cost many FLN lives, could not redress the balance.

After the fall of Mollet in May 1957 a succession of weak and faceless governments squirmed under the mounting political and economic costs of Algeria. In

May 1958 the appointment of a government under Pierre Pflimlin, who was thought to favor a negotiated settlement, triggered a revolt by the *pieds noirs*. The colonists formed a Committee of Public Safety in Algiers and won the support of the French commander General Salan, who fatefully uttered the cry "Vive de Gaulle!" De Gaulle played a masterful political game in May 1958. He was conscious that events were running in his favor, but did not want to be seen to endorse military rebellion; nor did he wish to have his hands tied if he returned to power. However, public disenchantment with the Republic, combined with a genuine fear of military intervention on the mainland, delivered him the victory that he wanted. On May 29 de Gaulle was appointed prime minister by President Coty, with emergency powers for six months and a brief to undertake a "major reform of our institutions." Importantly, he had the support of many politicians from within the "system" such as Guy Mollet. Apart from the far left, opposition was limited to a few politicians such as Mendès-France and François Mitterrand. In September de Gaulle won overwhelming support for his proposals in a referendum, and in January 1959 he became the first president of the new Republic. He dismissed the Fourth Republic as a mere "parenthesis" and at his inauguration treated the outgoing Coty with contempt: his remarkable comeback was hardly celebrated with magnanimity. He now governed with broad, if somewhat ill-defined, powers (see Chapter 5). But the question that would dominate the first four years of his presidency would be whether – and on what terms – he could bring the Algerian conflict to a close.

De Gaulle had visited Algeria almost immediately on his return to power in June 1958. His comment to a group of settlers, "je vous ai compris" ("I have understood you"), was taken to mean that he supported their cause and, indeed, it is not clear exactly what his initial intentions were. However, from the start de Gaulle was determined, first, to act in the best interests of France and not of the *pieds noirs*, and secondly to achieve a military victory prior to any political solution. The offensive under General Challe in 1959 did, in fact, smash the FLN within Algeria. However, by now de Gaulle was aware that, given the diplomatic damage as well as the mounting internal dissent within France, this was no longer sufficient. In September 1959 he announced that, once security had been reestablished, a referendum would be held that could result in three options: secession and partition, full integration with France, or self-government. With this statement de Gaulle embarked on the endgame of the conflict: from now on his main enemies would be the settlers, their sympathizers, and the army. In January 1960 he faced down the "barricades week" revolt by the *pieds noirs* in Algiers, and in April 1961 he defeated an attempted military coup by Challe and Salan. On the latter occasion de Gaulle appealed directly to the conscripts in the so-called "Battle of the Transistors." De Gaulle's enemies now formed the OAS (Secret Army Organization) and engaged in a welter of terrorist violence against Muslims in Algeria and alleged traitors (including the president himself) on the mainland.

Algeria's future was decided at the Evian talks, and an agreement signed on March 18, 1962. By now de Gaulle was desperate to settle a conflict that, in his view, prevented France from fulfilling her destiny as a modern European power. Faced with the obduracy of the FLN he threw away most of his bargaining chips and betrayed many who had supported France in good faith. Under the settlement there would be a ceasefire and a progressive troop withdrawal; France would retain bases in the Sahara for five years and the great naval base at Mers el Kebir for 15; Algeria would remain within the franc zone and receive economic and cultural assistance. The white settlers must choose their nationality after three years, but few waited that long. The last days of *Algérie française* were marked by OAS violence and an exodus of *pieds noirs* to France. At least 10,000, and possibly as many as 100,000, members of the *harkis*, the Muslim militia that had supported the French authorities, were massacred, often with appalling cruelty. Although no official effort was made to save them, some 250,000 escaped to France to live in a bitter and often impoverished exile. If in de Gaulle's words France had finally "married her century,"[32] by now few in mainland France seemed to care about the cost.

Social Democratic Alternatives

Although Guy Mollet had assisted at its birth, the coming of the Fifth Republic was a disaster for the French left. The communists lost 1.6 million voters in the elections of October 1958, while the socialists, who held on to most of their support, were soon marginalized by de Gaulle. This was the latest in a series of, often self-inflicted, setbacks for the noncommunist left in the larger countries of western Europe. In Britain the Labour Party, having accomplished its historic program by 1951, subsided in opposition into bitter ideological strife. In West Germany, even after the death of Schumacher in 1952, the SPD struggled to move beyond the Marxist, anti-clerical, and anti-NATO policies that had blighted its electoral prospects. Nor were socialists immune from the social changes of the later 1950s. They seemed to have less and less to say to workers who were benefiting from the new prosperity, and socialist policies such as nationalization seemed increasingly irrelevant at a time when capitalist enterprise was beginning to deliver unprecedented prosperity. Significantly, the highly successful Swedish Social Democrats had never advocated extensive public ownership of the economy. The need to reach out to new sectors of the electorate in order to avoid political oblivion, as well as a necessary ideological adjustment to a rapidly changing social and economic context, resulted in profound debate in socialist circles during the 1950s.[33]

The most spectacular and influential "revisionism" came in Germany with the SPD's Bad Godesberg special congress of November 1959. The ground had been prepared over the preceding six years, notably by the economist Karl Schiller, and the SPD had already moved towards the CDU on issues such as co-determination and decartelization. At Bad Godesberg it went further and formally abandoned much of its ideological heritage. In the economic sphere there was a pragmatic new slogan: "As much competition as possible, as much planning as necessary." Moreover, the SPD proclaimed that it was no longer a party of the working class, but rather a "party of the whole people." Accordingly, the SPD reached out to churchgoers, noting that democratic socialism had its roots in Christian ethics and humanism, and to women (promising to protect young mothers from being forced to seek work).[34] A year later the transformation was completed when the SPD abandoned its "Plan for Germany" (which called for a denuclearized central Europe) and fully accepted German membership of NATO and the EEC. The results were hardly instantaneous as the SPD only entered office (and even then in coalition) in 1966. However, Bad Godesberg gave a vital and unmistakable signal that it was now willing to fight the CDU on its own terrain.

A less ordered and purposeful debate was also enacted in Britain. Here, the crucial text was Anthony Crosland's *The Future of Socialism* (1956), which challenged the sacred cow of nationalization and called for greater attention to consumption, leisure, and personal freedom. The impact of such revisionist thinking was blunted because it was identified with the right wing of a deeply divided party. The Labour leader Hugh Gaitskell's attempt to carry out his own Bad Godesberg by abolishing the clause of the Labour Party Constitution that committed it to public ownership (Clause IV) was defeated by traditionalists in 1959. The battle lines within Labour were, however, confusing. Gaitskell, in most respects a revisionist, was opposed to European integration, while the leading left-winger Aneurin Bevan spoke in favor of the British nuclear deterrent. On Gaitskell's premature death in 1963 the new leader, Harold Wilson, quietly led the Labour Party away from ideological division and towards power under a beguiling rhetoric of modernization.

While these debates were carried out in response to repeated defeats, elsewhere in Europe socialists had to rethink their new role within "affluent" societies while in government. The Austrian socialists held office in a coalition from 1945 to 1966, while, most significantly, the Swedish SAP was in government continuously from 1932 to 1976. In 1933 it had forged a "red–green" alliance with the Agrarian Party and laid the basis for a Swedish welfare state (the *folkhemmet* or "people's home") that was largely completed after 1945. The SAP's success rested on a homogenous working class and a strong, innovative trade union federation (the LO), combined with a willingness to work with other parties and social groups. Sweden enjoyed excellent industrial relations under the 1938 Saltsjöbaden agreement between unions and employees. Indeed by the 1950s the SAP, which had imposed an anti-inflationary wage freeze between 1949 and 1951, seemed if anything overly cosy with business. The regular private meetings with industrialists that were convened between 1955 and 1964 at the prime minister's country retreat were derided by opponents as "Harpsund democracy."

The wage freeze, of course, negated the unions' bargaining role. Their response, formulated by two researchers working for the LO and published in its 1951 report *Trade Unions and Full Employment*, became known as the "Rehn–Meidner model." Gösta Rehn and Rudolf Meidener's proposals were intended to achieve full employment, low inflation, and an efficient economy on a consensual basis and with limited state intervention. There were three core elements. First, higher rates of indirect taxation would reduce demand and keep wage rates steady; secondly, all employers should offer equal pay for equal work (on the basis of a rigorous job evaluation), forcing inefficient firms to modernize; and thirdly, an "active labor market" strategy would match workers to jobs. Although the model was not adopted wholesale by the SAP, key elements were put in place during the 1950s. Centralized national wage bargaining was imposed from 1956, a labor market board created in 1957–8, and higher indirect taxes were used during the boom of the early 1960s.

In the course of the 1950s Swedish socialists began to be concerned that they would be victims of their own success, and that their party's working-class base would be dissolved in affluence. Tage Erlander, prime minister from 1946 to 1968, opened the debate by warning in 1956 of the "discontent of rising expectations"[35] arising from full employment. In other words, the safety net created by the existing welfare arrangements could not meet all of society's new needs and there was a danger that the SAP would lose contact with white-collar workers. The answer proposed by Erlander and his young colleague Olof Palme was a "strong society," the centerpiece of which would be a compulsory supplementary pension scheme that would guarantee the participant's standard of living. Erlander was playing for high stakes as his proposal precipitated the collapse of the 1951–7 coalition with the Agrarians and triggered two years of political strife before the law was finally passed – by one vote – in May 1959. However, the outcome was worthwhile as the Social Democrats had demonstrated that they were no longer merely the party of the workers but of all wage-earners. The "Swedish model" clearly worked, but was it a model for the other social democrats? This was unlikely given the importance of consensual industrial relations and the Swedes' willingness to trade punitive rates of taxation for excellent welfare provision.

Conclusion

During the 1950s western Europe underwent a process of political and economic consolidation. The corner was turned on the austerity of the war years and the later 1940s, and by the end of the decade many Europeans were aware of a new affluence as a sustained economic boom got under way. Europe prospered under the guarantee of American military protection, and the resolution of the Berlin crisis (1961) created a new stability on the Cold War frontier. With the exception of France, the larger countries enjoyed stable government by political parties that were Atlanticist, conservative, and oriented towards the free market. However, social democratic alternatives were being developed in West Germany and, most notably, Sweden. All of the imperial powers apart from Portugal underwent processes of decolonization, and a number were involved in colonial wars. France fought two large-scale conflicts in Indo-China and Algeria: the latter destroyed the Fourth Republic and made possible the return to power of Charles de Gaulle in 1958. The decade was generally characterized by social conservatism, but there was evidence of a new questioning mood in the arts, while American popular culture made a powerful impact on the young.

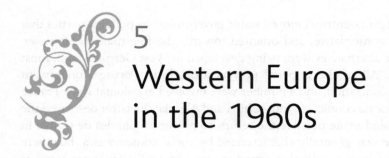

5
Western Europe in the 1960s

The Cultural Divide

Although the democratic and capitalist basis of modern western Europe was laid during the 15 years after 1945, fundamental change in social and cultural attitudes did not come until the ferment of the 1960s and early 1970s. The spirit of the 1960s was one of a profound skepticism and questioning, be it of the legitimacy of power and authority or the proper relationship between individuals and between classes. Umberto Eco has observed that the events of 1968 "profoundly changed the way all of us, at least in Europe, behave and relate to one another."[1] Indeed, in most areas of European life a clear continuity can be traced between the world that emerged from the 1960s and that of the century's end. However, it is important to distinguish between the changes that the 1960s set in train and those for which the radicals wished. There was much that now seems anachronistic about the politics of the 1960s, such as the revived language of revolution and class warfare. Other ideas popular in the 1960s, such as *autogestion* (workers' self-management), enjoyed a lingering influence but ultimately came to a dead end. Two further caveats need to be entered. First, conservatism (or in Richard Nixon's phrase the "silent majority") remained powerful and at times found its voice. For instance, the supporters of de Gaulle mounted their own mass mobilization on the streets of Paris in response to the events of May 1968, and went on to win an electoral landslide in June. Secondly, "the Sixties" is an elastic concept, difficult to delimit as a historical period. As we have seen, the pace of social and cultural change was already accelerating from the mid-1950s, and much permissive legislation was not passed until the early 1970s. Indeed, even within the decade of the 1960s the years 1968–9 represented an unanticipated crescendo of political and social unrest.

Europe's Troubled Peace: 1945 to the Present, Second Edition. Tom Buchanan.
© 2012 John Wiley & Sons, Ltd. Published 2012 by John Wiley & Sons, Ltd.

American culture – especially popular music – was ever more pervasive in Europe during the 1960s, yet in other respects the United States seemed more distant. US administrations, preoccupied with the escalating war in Vietnam, were prone to ignore Europe or even to see it as an economic rival. That view could be reciprocated, as J. J. Servan-Schreiber's best-selling *The American Challenge* (1967) pictured a Europe overrun with American investment and falling fatally behind a dynamic US economy. Vietnam eroded the Atlanticism of the 1950s and, especially for the young, transformed the USA from a protector into an imperialist aggressor. The first step taken by the West German terrorists Andreas Baader and Gudrun Ensslin was to firebomb a Frankfurt store in 1968, in retaliation for the American use of napalm in Vietnam. Growing suspicion of the USA was matched by the declining fear of the Soviet Union, although the August 1968 invasion of Czechoslovakia caused considerable shock (especially for the left). Even so, the new dialogue with the East in the late 1960s (notably the beginnings of West German *Ostpolitik*) made it far harder to demonize a Soviet Union which itself seemed diminished by its rift with communist China. The bi-polar world of the 1950s was shattering into many shards, the most attractive of which seemed to lie in the Third World.

This new relativism between East and West, and readiness to identify with the South, was vividly expressed in the intellectual life of the 1960s. The philosopher Herbert Marcuse heretically equated the "totalitarianism" of the new forms of social control in the technologically advanced societies of the West with that of the communist world in his *One-Dimensional Man* (1964). Jean-Paul Sartre, who had broken with the Communist Party in 1956, aligned himself fully with the FLN's struggle in Algeria in the late 1950s and discovered Cuba and China in the 1960s. In his preface to Frantz Fanon's *The Wretched of the Earth* (1961), Sartre defended the use of violence to smash white colonial power and restore humanity to the colonized masses. Régis Debray popularized the ideas of Che Guevara in his *Revolution in the Revolution* (1967) and was briefly incarcerated in Bolivia while trying to interview Guevara during his fateful last guerrilla campaign. There was, however, far more to the "Third Worldism" of the 1960s than a new and more exotic form of political tourism. One can also discern a genuine admiration for the achievements of Third World revolutionaries and a desire to learn from their example – however inappropriate the comparison may have been. For instance, the call by the German student leader Rudi Dutschke for a "long march through the institutions" was not a manifesto for gradualism, but rather envisaged the creation of "liberated zones in bourgeois society, which would be the equivalent of the areas freed by Mao's partisans in China."[2]

Strikingly, the avant-garde in cultural life came not so much from the arts, where there was considerable continuity with the trends established in the previous decade, but rather stemmed from the work of academics, especially in France. From the late 1950s onwards the underpinnings of "bourgeois" culture came under sustained critical assault from philosophers, anthropologists, psychoanalysts, and linguistic scholars. Although many were inspired by Marxism, their work was not party political, but rather an attempt to lay bare the underlying structures of authority and power. Structuralism, notably associated with the work of anthropologist Claude Lévi-Strauss and the psychoanalyst Jacques Lacan, drew heavily on the work of the linguistic theorist Ferdinand de Saussure (who had died in 1913). In place of human agency it emphasized the dominant role of structures and codes fashioned, above all, by language. In the later 1960s there was, in turn, a reaction against the certainties and apparent inhumanity of structuralism, notably in the highly influential thought of philosopher Jacques Derrida and the later works of historian Michel Foucault and cultural critic Roland Barthes. "Post-structuralism," which asserted the indeterminacy of meaning and the infinite possible interpretations of a text, challenged the concept of a canon of Western thought and literature. Moreover, as in the title of Barthes's famous 1968 essay, it proposed the concept of "the death of the author" and the elevation of the reader. The work of the post-structuralists was greeted with considerable suspicion (as well as attracting devout support) as it was seen as promoting a cultural relativism and anarchism within which there could be no meaningful standards of truth and quality. However, Derrida and others undoubtedly opened new vistas for research in the humanities, and made a crucial contribution to the cultural impact of postmodernism in the 1980s.

Foucault, in particular, seemed to represent a new image for the academic. No longer a distant, conservative figure locked in an ivory tower, the academic was now on the side of student radicals who were "not making a revolution: they are a revolution."[3] More generally, the European intellectual of the 1960s was questioning and independent, far removed from the complicity with the Cold War state that had been such a hallmark of the 1950s. In this respect, the revelation in April 1966 of CIA funding for the Congress for Cultural Freedom and *Encounter* magazine, which dealt a fatal blow to the former, represented a decisive moment. As in so much else, France had led the way towards this new activism with the 1960 manifesto signed by 121 intellectuals (some of whom were jailed) defending the right of French troops to disobey orders in Algeria. In Germany writers such as Günter Grass began to align themselves with the Social Democrats in the course of the 1960s and worked actively for an SPD victory. The German extra-parliamentary opposition of 1966–9 (see below) was backed by a wide range of intellectuals, notably Heinrich Böll and Hans Magnus Enzensberger. During the 1960s (and early 1970s) there was also a final surge of innovative Marxist thought, largely detached from its Soviet moorings, in the work of Louis Althusser and the German "Frankfurt School." European Marxists drew inspiration from Maoism and the Third World, or even from the reinterpretation of their own heritage. There was a new vogue for the humanist writings of the young Marx, while the critical theory of the Frankfurt School was seen to have particular relevance to understanding the consumer society. The work of Antonio Gramsci, who had died in prison in 1937, was used to map a new counter-hegemonic strategy for the

Italian Communist Party and, in particular, to cloak a departure from classic revolutionary politics.

These intellectual trends were reinforced by the rise of a less inhibited and more challenging popular culture, above all the advent of rock music. Here, assisted by the ubiquity of transistor radios, hi-fi, and television, the lead was taken by British and American musicians. The Rolling Stones were briefly deemed a gyrating, drug-taking threat by the British establishment; Bob Dylan shattered the convention of the three-minute popular song; and "swinging London" attracted the brightest talents of European art cinema such as Michelangelo Antonioni (with *Blow-Up*, 1966). The career of the Beatles encapsulated the evolution of popular culture, from the extraordinary success of their classic early pop songs, via Beatlemania and the conquest of the American charts, to their later embrace of the counter-culture, Indian mysticism, and pop art. Rock music, alongside the growth of concerts and festivals in the later 1960s, was a powerful vehicle for free expression and social mobility. It was closely linked to the growth of recreational drug-taking and relaxed sexuality that was gratifyingly offensive to older generations. By the end of the 1960s Europeans, especially the young, were party to a culture that was unprec-edented in its universality, explicitness, and freedom from government control. The result was not only liberating for west Europeans but also for those living under the neighboring dictatorships in Spain and Portugal (with the influence of mass tourism) or even East Germany (via television).

The Anglo-Saxon influence began to filter into continental Europe, first with home-grown rockers such as the Franco-Belgian star Johnny Halliday, and then with the hippies (such as the Italian *capelloni* or "long-hairs") of the mid-1960s. But Europe was quite capable of producing its own permissive societies (such as the relaxed attitude to pornography and drug-taking in both Amsterdam and Copenhagen in the later 1960s) as well as challenging cultural movements. The Dutch "Provo" movement, for instance, pitted anarchist wit against the "granite wall of bourgeois pettiness"[4] in the mid-1960s, and was dissolved once it became respectable. The Situationist movement, which was established in 1957 and drew on surrealism and anarchism, exerted considerable influence over the manner in which the French student radicalism of the late 1960s was experienced as both a political and a cultural event. In Italy there was a remarkable revival of popular political theatre in the later 1960s, most notably in the work of Dario Fo and his collaborators, who aimed to place themselves "at the service of the exploited, and to become their minstrels."[5] Fo's *Accidental Death of an Anarchist* (1970) offered a biting response to Italy's lurch into political terrorism and police brutality.

Television was the revolutionary medium of the 1960s and by the end of the decade few Europeans, even in the remoter villages, did not have access to a set. Television did not only entertain, even if many schedules were still dominated by game shows and state-controlled news programs. Some broadcasters – notably in Britain – were also beginning to explore its full potential by making realist drama, such as Ken Loach's *Cathy Come Home* (1966). At the same time television was becoming more commercial and shaping desires: the first TV advert in France (for Boursin cheese) was broadcast in October 1968, a decade after the first adverts in Italy and Spain. Not only goods were being marketed, as politicians learnt to use the new medium. Harold Macmillan became a consummate television performer in the late 1950s, but was then savaged by the BBC's satirical *That Was The Week That Was* in the final years of his premiership. Even de Gaulle deigned to give a televised interview, to great effect, in the second round of the 1965 presidential election. Television also enhanced the status of sport and created a new kind of celebrity: George Best and Johan Cryuff were not merely footballers but were also cultural figures in their own right, akin to film stars.

Just as in culture, the new politics of the 1960s represented a rejection of the paternalistic conservatism, and the constraints imposed by Cold War anti-communism, of the previous decade. In their very different ways, leaders such as Willy Brandt and Harold Wilson captured the youth, classlessness, and lack of deference so characteristic of the 1960s. But there was also a new desire for participation and self-expression outside the outmoded ambit of the existing parties, which had first surfaced in the "New Left" and anti-nuclear movements of the late 1950s. The impact was particularly visible on the left, which had, apart from a fleeting postwar moment, been historically divided between socialist and communist parties. By the late 1960s the revolutionary left was represented by a welter of small parties and "groupuscules," many inspired by Trotskyist and anarchist ideas largely invisible since the 1930s. The new focus for political activity, the street and the factory, also marked a return to the 1930s. Dutschke's "long march" did eventually occur, but in the short term could not compete with the excitement of direct action on campuses and piazzas. The decade also saw the rise of new political causes (such as environmentalism and human rights) and cleavages. In Belgium, for example, linguistic differences (between French- and Dutch-speakers) dominated the political agenda, divided politics, and threatened the country's viability. In Northern Ireland, the long-standing sectarian division between Catholics and Protestants was reconfigured in the late 1960s by the rise of a civil rights association. Civil rights marches, demanding an end to discrimination against Catholics in areas such as the allocation of housing, became the focus for violent rioting which eventually compelled the British government to send the army into the province in the summer of 1969.

There was striking proof that the old political alignments no longer applied in the changing role of the Catholic Church. In Italy student radicals often came from the Catholic campuses, while many priests were moving to the left under the influence of "Liberation Theology." Change was stimulated by the short but event-ful papacy of John XXIII. The new Pope, although already 77 years old on his accession, did much to unblock the church's responses to the changing postwar world. He opened the Second Vatican Council (or Vatican II, 1962–5) which initiated a less authoritarian church structure and a new tolerance towards other branches of Christianity. Moreover, the emphasis on universal human rights in the papal encyclical *Pacem in terris* (1963) applied to the Catholic-backed dictatorships of southern Europe just as much as it did to eastern Europe and the Third World. After the Council the church pulled back from direct intervention in politics, although maintaining a keen interest in issues such as divorce and abortion. Tellingly, the bitterest critic of Vatican II, Archbishop Marcel Lefebvre, objected not only to its liturgical reforms but also to the abandonment of the long anti-democratic tradition of the Catholic right. Falling church attendance in the 1960s and the decline of the lay associations weakened the social basis of Christian Democracy and pushed its political parties further towards interconfessionalism and even secularism. In the Netherlands the long-established division of society into separate "pillars" (for Catholics, Protestants, liberals, and socialists) underwent rapid decline in the late 1960s, introducing an unprecedented political volatility. The proportion of practicing Catholics voting for the Dutch Catholic KVP party fell steeply from 95 percent in 1956 to 72 percent in 1968,[6] and in the late 1970s the KVP fused with its Protestant rivals to form a united Christian Democrat Party. In 1972 the Austrian OVP party opened its membership "to Christians and to everybody accepting humanistic ideals."[7]

The New Society: Economic and Social Change

During the 1960s the postwar economic boom intensified and deepened, even if the growth rates of the 1950s could not be sustained. While the bases of success were largely unchanged (notably wage restraint and low energy prices), there was diversification away from the traditional industrial sectors towards high-tech industry. Growth was particularly striking in France, where one of de Gaulle's first measures on returning to power had been to commission a radical economic review. The Rueff stabilization plan of December 1958 called for harsh but effective measures: public spending was slashed, the franc devalued by 17.5 percent and trade extensively liberalized. Between 1959 and 1970 French growth of 5.8 percent of GDP per annum was the best in western Europe (compared with West Germany's 4.9 percent and a mere 2.9 percent for Britain).[8] There was a boom in French exports, especially within the EEC, from a rapidly modernizing industrial base. Italy also benefited greatly from the new European market, and the roaring growth of the late 1950s continued: in 1967 Fiat sold more cars within the EEC than any other firm.[9] However, there were also the first signs that the European economies might falter. West Germany experienced a sharp recession in 1966–7, following a rise in inflation and a first postwar budget deficit, but strong growth was restored in 1968. The French government was also forced to take sharp measures against inflation in 1963, while Britain's stumbling economic performance culminated in devaluation of the pound in November 1967.

Concomitant to continued growth was a further rise in urbanization and decline in the agricultural population. While agriculture became ever more extensive and productive, the small family farm lost its attractions compared to the lure of better-paid jobs in the cities. In France and Italy the 1960s marked the emergence of "modern" urban consumer societies within which the agricultural sector would still play a cherished – but hardly essential – role. The proportion working on the land in Italy fell from 42.2 percent in 1951 to 29.5 percent in 1961 and 17.2 percent in 1971. In France during the same period the proportion fell from greater than a quarter to less than a tenth of the working population, and in West Germany from 23.1 percent (1950) to 8.3 percent (1970). For those who remained in rural communities, however, the 1960s brought new comforts, such as belated connection to national power grids and mains water, and the ability to commute to work by car. A survey of the Italian village of Bonagente near Rome in 1969 showed that 20–25 percent of families owned cars and that most villagers owned both radio and television. There was a faith amongst the villagers that "prosperity and employment will continue."[10] Cushioned by the EEC's Common Agricultural Policy, a quiet revolution had taken place on the land, although there were already stirrings of concern as to the environmental consequences of the new large-scale, chemical-reliant farming.

The size of the industrial working class was largely unchanged during the 1960s, and the majority of new jobs were created in the expanding tertiary sector (such as banking, leisure, and the public sector). There was much talk of a "new working class"[11] of technicians and white-collar workers who were beginning to adopt a trade union identity. Although the traditional working class was neglected by the intellectuals, there were signs of mounting unrest following long years of pay restraint and managerial domination. In June 1962 the Fiat workers mounted their first major strike for many years, and the French miners' dispute of 1963 forced significant concessions from a government committed to restructuring the industry. The 1966 British seamen's strike against near-feudal conditions shocked a Labour government which was increasingly troubled by unofficial "wildcat" industrial action. Even so, there was nothing to prepare European governments for the upsurge of near-revolutionary syndicalism of the later 1960s and early 1970s.

The unacceptable face of urbanization was the growth of run-down *bidonvilles* in France where immigrant workers were forced to live, or the wretched conditions for many internal migrants from the south within Italy. The French government's plan to encircle Paris with new concrete satellite towns such as Sarcelles was ill conceived and gave rise to the *anomie* and depression dubbed "Sarcellitis." West Germany, cut off from the supply of labor from the East, now began to attract workers from Turkey, Yugoslavia, and Spain. The numbers of these *Gastarbeiter* ("guest workers") grew from some 280,000 in 1960 to a peak of 2.5 million in the mid-1970s. Both here and in Switzerland, where 30 percent of the workforce was composed of foreign workers by the early 1970s, "guest" laborers were denied many basic civil rights. Europeans might have been driving their own cars and taking foreign holidays in ever larger numbers, but access to opportunity remained heavily determined by class and, increasingly, race and nationality.

Social divisions were particularly evident in the field of education. Servan-Schreiber, for instance, had noted that not only did the USA produce many more graduates than the EEC countries, but that US children from working-class backgrounds were far more likely to have access to higher education.[12] Similar flaws were evident throughout the educational system. In France at the end of the 1950s, some 80 percent of children from managerial families would attend secondary school compared with 21 percent from the working class and a mere 13 percent from agricultural backgrounds.[13] This should not obscure the immense investments that were made in education during the 1960s at all levels. The Italian secondary school reform of 1962, for instance, triggered a rise in the numbers at school from 1,150,000 in 1959 to 1,982,000 a decade later. However, there was little attention to curriculum reform, and the failure to provide adequate resources resulted in high drop-out rates among the far larger numbers opting to stay on after the age of 14. The numbers of universities and (mainly middle-class) students also expanded massively. The student unrest of the 1960s did not so much reflect lack of access as the failure of universities to adapt their highly conservative methods of teaching and authoritarian administrations. Many students came to feel that universities existed to "churn out the trained personnel that is so essential for bureaucratic capitalism,"[14] just at a time when they were feeling less pressure to conform.

The dramatic social changes of the 1960s impinged directly and profoundly on the lives of women. Many more women were now entering the labor market, although some countries, notably the Netherlands, lagged far behind. There was a particularly marked increase in the number of married women and mothers in work. Women's work, even if still on disadvantageous terms compared to men, offered a route out of the boredom and disillusionment that many women now associated with the domesticity promoted in the 1950s. Women were also attending university in ever larger numbers. A survey of West German university faculty members in 1960 revealed that 64 percent opposed the presence of female students: even so, the proportion rose from 19 percent (25,000) in 1950–1 to 31 percent (130,000) in 1970–1.[15] The female graduates of the later 1960s were well placed to take advantage of the burgeoning opportunities in the public sector and the media.

The nature of family life was itself changing during the 1960s, and in particular there was a sharp fall in the birth-rate. This was due in part to the reduction in infant mortality and the declining economic imperative for large families, but it also reflected the advent of the contraceptive pill and the wider availability of other means of birth control. The pill became available in Britain in 1961 – where by 1964 it was being taken by 480,000 women – and slightly later in West Germany and the Netherlands. Other countries remained, however, more restrictive. In

France, access to birth control was conceded under the Loi Neuwirth of December 1967, but without any state financial support or publicity. In Italy, despite a public campaign from the mid-1950s onwards, the fascist-era law that banned publicity for contraception was not declared unconstitutional until 1971. In the Republic of Ireland, the only clinic that openly offered the pill was closed following the papal condemnation of birth control in the encyclical *Humanae vitae* (July 1968).[16] Here, the sale and distribution of all contraceptives remained illegal until 1979.

The pill, which gave women unprecedented control over their own fertility, came to symbolize what the British writer Margaret Drabble already perceived in 1967 as a "sexual revolution."[17] Although the true extent of changes in sexual practice in the 1960s remains open to debate, there was undoubtedly a new openness in the public discussion of sexuality. For instance, a pioneering series of magazine articles by Milana Mileni (published in October 1967 as *Italia sexy*) called for a "young Italy ... without taboos, without hypocrisy."[18] Meanwhile, established women's magazines such as *Elle* and *Marie Claire* swiftly adapted to reflect a readership that now felt comfortable discussing issues such as birth control, premarital and extramarital sex, and single parenthood. By the turn of the decade changes in lifestyle were becoming increasingly evident. In France, for instance, between 1969 and 1974 alone the proportion of children conceived out of wedlock rose from one-fifth to a quarter. Likewise, the marriage rate declined in France from the early 1970s onwards following a rise in premarital cohabitation.[19]

Politicians paid increasing attention to female voters during the 1960s. For instance, François Mitterrand made an issue of birth control in his unsuccessful 1965 presidential campaign, while in West Germany a law was passed in 1969 specifically to promote female employment. However, in political terms the 1960s largely proved a frustrating decade for women. One German social demo-crat complained that the party was hostile to young, educated middle-class women like herself, and that the SPD's women's section was more interested in the "size of the meat salad" at meetings than in influencing policy.[20] If the events of May 1968 represented a "psychodrama," as Raymond Aron would observe, then it was essentially a male one which consigned women to an auxiliary role. In May 1968 a Women's Action Council was established in Berlin, to challenge the male chauvinism so characteristic of the radical movement. The revived feminism which flourished in the 1970s was born of the belief that "men must learn to be silent."[21]

The Limits to Reform: Italy, West Germany, and Britain

During the 1960s the reformist left took office in three of the major European countries, although only in Britain (between 1964 and 1970) on the basis of a parliamentary majority. In West Germany the SPD acted as a junior partner in a

"Grand Coalition" with the CDU/CSU (1966–9) and in Italy the socialists joined four Christian Democrat-led coalitions between 1963 and 1969. Although these parties were refreshed with new leaderships and new ideas (at least in the first two cases), the experience of government proved in many respects frustrating. The limits to reform were demonstrated most starkly in Italy. The socialists lacked the political weight to carry through their ambitious program of administrative and social reforms, while for most Christian Democrats the "opening to the left" was far more to do with securing a majority than any genuine desire for change. Prime Minister Aldo Moro favored the alliance with the socialists more than most, but lacked the will to force change on his Christian Democrat colleagues and their associated interests. Indeed, greater change had occurred under Fanfani's reformist government of 1962–3 (such as educational reform) prior to the entry of the socialists into the coalition. Probably the main impact of the coalition was to change the socialists themselves. Not only did they complete their conversion into an Atlanticist social democratic party, but they also became ineluctably drawn to the spoils of office, with fatal consequences for their integrity.

The German SPD's opportunity for office followed the brief chancellorship of Adenauer's successor Ludwig Erhard (1963–6). Erhard had led the CDU to victory in 1965, but struggled to impose his authority on the government as economic difficulties mounted in 1966. Disagreement within the coalition over the correct economic counter-measures, compounded by the success of the neo-Nazi National Democratic Party (NDP) in *Länder* elections, created a sense of crisis and prompted Erhard's fall in November 1966. He was replaced by a Grand Coalition (with only the liberal FDP in opposition) under the CDU's Kurt-Georg Kiesinger. The fact that Kiesinger was an ex-member of the Nazi party occasioned much dismay in intellectual circles, but was balanced by the presence of Willy Brandt, a former anti-Nazi exile, as Vice-Chancellor and Foreign Minister. At one level the coalition was a success, as the economy soon recovered and the specter of the NDP was banished. Moreover, from the social democrats' perspective the experience of office smoothed the way towards their own political dominance after 1969. Yet in other respects the coalition brought dangers both for the SPD and for German democracy. The scope for reform was limited and the existence of a Grand Coalition galvanized the radical street politics of the "Extra-Parliamentary Opposition" (APO). Very much against his instincts (which were to open the SPD to the young radicals) Brandt found himself having to defend unpopular and heavy-handed legislation such as the 1968 Emergency Laws.

The constraints imposed by the Grand Coalition were particularly evident in foreign policy where Brandt (as Foreign Minister) found that real power resided in the Chancellor's office. Brandt, while mayor of Berlin, had shown that the division of Europe could be made porous by a "policy of small steps" (for instance, he had negotiated visits for families divided by the Berlin Wall over the Christmas of 1963). Kiesinger, however, remained wedded to the "Hallstein doctrine," first applied in 1957, according to which the Federal Republic claimed to represent the whole of Germany within its 1937 borders and refused to maintain diplomatic relations with any country that recognized the DDR.[22] Such steps as were possible, such as the 1967 establishment of relations with the Eastern bloc maverick Romania, were treated by the Warsaw Pact as an attempt to drive a wedge between its member states. At the Pact's meeting in April 1967 it was agreed that no other states should reach an agreement with the FRG until it had recognized East Germany and accepted the postwar Polish border. The lesson, confirmed by the 1968 invasion of Czechoslovakia, was that any future negotiations must start in Moscow and would require West Germany to make substantial concessions. Given that this was not politically feasible for the CDU, further progress in *Ostpolitik* clearly required an SPD-led government.

Brandt's SPD colleague Karl Schiller made a greater impact as Economics Minister. Schiller forged a successful partnership with the right-wing Finance Minister Strauss, and began to move economic policy away from Erhard's unfettered free-market principles. There was a greater emphasis on planning and Keynesian-style economic management, combined with a clear shifting of the balance towards the federal government and away from the *Länder* in economic matters. Schiller's economic success facilitated the SPD's rapprochement with the FDP, which was itself moving towards the center-left on economic and social issues. In addition, the FDP's young new leaders Walter Scheel and Hans Dietrich Genscher shared Brandt's desire for a diplomatic opening to the East. Indeed, the FDP was already calling for the recognition of the DDR. Therefore, in the election of September 1969 the choice was between a return to CDU/CSU government and a likely SPD–FDP coalition. The result was a close race which hung on the FDP's ability to exceed the 5 percent hurdle (in the event it won 5.8 percent). Kiesinger had already claimed victory when it became clear that Brandt had won a small majority. Brandt famously commented that "now Hitler has truly lost the war,"[23] although it was the legacy of Adenauer that would be buried by the new Chancellor's innovative and courageous policy towards the Federal Republic's eastern neighbors.

In contrast to Italy and West Germany, in Britain the left held the political initiative, especially once the Labour Party's slender majority of October 1964 was transformed into one of 97 seats in the election of March 1966. Harold Wilson had presented Labour in October 1963 as the party of modernity and technological progress, with no time for "restrictive practices or for outdated methods on either side of industry."[24] Once in government Wilson intended that planned economic growth would allow higher levels of social expenditure. The new Department of Economic Affairs (DEA) devised a National Plan envisaging (unrealized) growth of 3.8 percent per year for 1964–70. Labour's good intentions were, however, soon undermined by a succession of struggles to save the value of the pound in the face of an adverse balance of payments. Wilson's personal commitment to the exchange rate of $2.80 raised the political stakes, and the policy also heightened Britain's reliance on US financial assistance. The eventual decision to devalue to $2.40 in November 1967, accompanied by an austerity program, began to restore Britain's economic strength but demoralized Labour's working-class supporters. The National Plan, meanwhile, had been abandoned in 1966 and the DEA was itself wound up in 1969.

Wilson's government was also dogged by the revival of inflation and labor unrest, which were met by a wage freeze in 1966–7 and by a variety of nonbinding agreements with the trade unions. Wilson became increasingly exasperated by the unions' inability to control their own members and to act as responsible partners for government. In January 1969 he initially supported a White Paper for trade union reform, *In Place of Strife*, in which his Employment Secretary Barbara Castle called for strike ballots and a 28-day conciliation period before strikes could begin. However, the proposal was bitterly opposed by the unions, by Labour MPs, and even by key members of the Cabinet, and was eventually abandoned. A compromise "solemn and binding undertaking" by the unions on inter-union disputes was largely worthless. The unions' enjoyed a pyrrhic victory, however, as far more draconian measures to curb their privileges would be introduced under the future Conservative governments of Edward Heath and Margaret Thatcher.

For all Labour's apparent failure on core economic issues, the government could still claim to have a good reforming record. There was a torrent of significant social legislation after 1964 (some in the form of private members' bills), such as abolition of the death penalty, the legalization of abortion and male homosexuality, and easier access to divorce. Higher education was massively expanded, and Wilson claimed that his proudest achievement was the creation of the Open University, which used the new medium of television to offer distance learning to mature students. Comprehensive schooling was introduced (to be largely completed in the 1970s), as well as legislation concerning race relations and equal pay. Meanwhile the new Ministry of Technology, and prestige projects such as the Anglo-French supersonic airliner Concorde, helped to transform Britain's fusty image. Similarly, the decision to withdraw from imperial commitments east of Suez marked a sensible appreciation of Britain's true standing in the world, even if the logical corollary, membership of the EEC, was again vetoed by de Gaulle in 1967. In all, Britain was by 1970 a more permissive, open, and less hypocritical society. However, in the election of June 1970 these gains were not sufficient to offset the disappointment felt by Labour's working-class voters, and the Conservatives won an unexpected victory.

The Enigmatic Republic: France, 1958–1968

Immediately prior to his return to power, de Gaulle told a press conference: "Do you believe that, at sixty-seven, I shall start a dictator's career?"[25] The question was a tantalizing one, as for a number of years the exact nature of the Fifth Republic remained unclear. Was it simply a vehicle for de Gaulle's authoritarian rule – a modestly updated Bonapartism – and could the Republic outlast its founder? Certainly there were "Bonapartist" features of the new regime, such as the president's frequent recourse to direct communication with the people, over the head of parliament, via broadcasts and referenda. There were also uglier facets of de Gaulle's Republic, such as sweeping media control and over-reliance on the brutal application of force. For instance, as many as 200 Algerian protestors were murdered by police in Paris on October 17, 1961. Yet de Gaulle was hardly an unthinking conservative, and some of his attitudes (notably his anti-Americanism and suspicion of European integration) were similar to those of the communists. Moreover, the Republic created an environment in which new political parties could slowly emerge from the wreck of the old order. De Gaulle's greatest, if not wholly intentional, achievement was to create a new political system which could in turn be mastered by politicians other than him. Tellingly, his most dogged critic, François Mitterrand, who had denounced the Fifth Republic as a "permanent *coup d'état*,"[26] would find its institutions to his liking when he eventually became president in 1981.

The hallmark of the new Constitution, backed by 80 percent of voters in the referendum of September 28, 1958, was the diminution of the power and status of parliament and the elevation of the executive. Henceforward, the presidency would be indirectly elected by an electoral college of 80,000 notables and gain a range of new powers, such as the right to dissolve parliament and call referenda. The Constitution left unclear the question of how responsibility would be shared between the president and prime minister (who, unlike the president, was answerable to parliament). In the short term this seemed irrelevant given that, after the elections of October 1958, de Gaulle's followers and their right-wing allies controlled the assembly and the parties of the Fourth Republic were in disarray. De Gaulle's first prime minister, the loyal Michel Debré (1959–62), carried out the president's bidding even when, as over Algeria, he found the policy profoundly distasteful. Even so, in the early years of the new Republic, especially given the salience of Algeria, de Gaulle consistently expanded the presidential role and reduced the prime minister to little more than a chief executive. De Gaulle's parliamentary supporters grouped in the UNR (Union pour la Nouvelle République) were merely the "General's lobby fodder"[27] with no pretensions to set their own political agenda.

The end of the Algerian conflict precipitated a final settling of scores between de Gaulle and the opposition politicians, who viewed the growth of presidential power as a subversion of republican legality. De Gaulle's decision to replace Debré in April 1962 with Georges Pompidou, a former aide who had become a banker, was taken as an affront by parliament. The insult was compounded by his announcement (without consultation) of a referendum on a directly elected presidency. When censured by parliament in October, de Gaulle called fresh elections. The result was a double triumph: the referendum was carried by almost 62 percent, while in the parliamentary election the UNR came close to an outright majority and was able to govern with the support of Giscard d'Estaing's independents. De Gaulle had (with the exception of the communists) buried the parties of the Fourth Republic and earned himself a period of political tranquility.

De Gaulle's prime concern was with France's standing in the world, around which all other issues – such as a modernized economy or the fate of Algeria – revolved. At the heart of his foreign policy was a vision of an independent France at the head of a Europe free from superpower domination. De Gaulle undoubtedly managed to drag France out of the colonial quagmires of the 1950s and ensured that it could no longer be taken for granted. A nuclear-armed France was again a military power and the leading state within the EEC (see Chapter 9). However, there was little of substance behind his posturing, and his policies, while an irritation, never posed a serious challenge to US hegemony in western Europe. For instance, despite his 1966 decision to withdraw from the NATO joint command and to remove all foreign bases from French soil, de Gaulle did not wish to see US troops leave Europe. He strongly supported the US stance over Berlin and Cuba, and one of his last acts as president was to renew France's commitment to the North Atlantic Treaty in 1969. Although the French nuclear deterrent was said to point in all directions ("tous azimuts"),[28] there was no doubt that the main threat was still seen to lie to the east. Despite his excellent relations with Adenauer, moreover, de Gaulle's attempt to replace the USA as the main guarantor of West German security failed. Finally, de Gaulle's attempt to launch a private détente with the USSR, and his dream of a Europe united "from the Atlantic to the Urals,"[29] came to nothing. The crushing of the Prague Spring in August 1968 demonstrated that there was little that France alone could do to undermine the "politics of blocs."

Latterly, there was some evidence that the French public was tiring of de Gaulle. Even some ministers felt that he had gone too far with his infamous cry of "Vive le Québec libre" during his July 1967 trip to Canada, while his criticism of Israel after the Six Day War verged on the anti-Semitic. There was also evidence that his political position was weakening. In the presidential election of December 1965 a complacent de Gaulle was shaken by Mitterrand's strong performance in the first round, although he rallied to win easily in the run-off. In the March 1967 parliamentary elections Pompidou was pressed hard by a revived and more united left, and emerged with only a small majority. Thus, while the explosion of May 1968 could not have been predicted, there were already signs of a regime in trouble. The opposition was finally recovering and the French people seemed disenchanted with the ageing president and the pervasive authoritarianism that he symbolized.

Revolt: Students and Workers, 1967–1969

The events of May 1968 in France were by no means isolated, even if the clash between the old politics and the new was at its sharpest and most iconic in Paris. Student protest was widespread in the late 1960s not only within western Europe, but also, for example, in Spain and Yugoslavia. Italy was racked with endemic student and (increasingly) working-class unrest after 1967, and in West Germany a loosely organized radical movement flourished from the mid-1960s onwards. Although working-class participation was notably more marked in Italy and France than in West Germany, there were still many underlying common features. One was the rapid increase in the numbers of university students between 1960 and 1968: in France from 200,000 to 500,000, in Italy from 268,000 to 450,000, and in West Germany from 239,000 to 412,000. Students were crammed into massive lecture halls and outdated facilities, and had little contact with their professors. Universities such as Nanterre in Paris, the Free University in Berlin, and Trent in Italy became the incubators for a student politics that was swinging sharply to the left under the influence of the Vietnam War and a new sense of social and political injustice. In February 1968 the convening of an International Vietnam Congress in West Berlin, soon after the launching of the Vietcong's "Tet" offensive, demonstrated how the city was fast becoming a symbol not of the West but of the new anti-Americanism (see Figure 5.1). The stock of the communist parties fell rapidly amongst the young (as it would subsequently amongst workers) who now looked to Maoism and anarchism for inspiration. Correspondingly, the style of radical student politics shifted towards greater activism: debating societies gave way to the mass production of fly posters and even violent confrontation with the police and right-wingers. Soon, also, there were radical martyrs such as Benno Ohnesorg, shot dead by German police in June 1967 during a demonstration against the Shah of Iran's visit to Berlin.

Student unrest in France had initially trailed behind that in Italy and West Germany, but soon overtook it. The spark came from the grim new campus at Nanterre, next to a *bidonville* on the outskirts of Paris, where the movement was led by Daniel Cohn-Bendit, a student of German Jewish parentage. When the campus was closed on May 2 many students transferred their protest to the Sorbonne, which was also subsequently closed with many arrests. On May 10 some 20,000 demonstrating students began to erect barricades in the Latin Quarter, where they were attacked at 2 a.m. on May 11 by the hated CRS riot police. During the "Night of the Barricades" hundreds were injured or arrested, and 180 cars were destroyed. Crucially, the students maintained the support of the local population, many of whom sustained unprovoked violence to life and property from the CRS. They were also supported by the main trade union federations (CGT and CFDT), which called a general strike for May 13 in protest at police brutality. On the evening of May 11 Prime Minister Pompidou conceded many of the students' immediate demands, withdrawing the CRS and reopening the Sorbonne. This was, however, taken as a sign of weakness and, as one student leader put it, the goal now was nothing less than "to topple de Gaulle."[30]

The general strike of May 13 was well supported throughout France (as many as 1 million protested in Paris), but the unions soon lost control of the workers' movement. On May 14 workers at Sud-Aviation in Nantes decided to occupy their

Figure 5.1 Student leader Rudi Dutschke and Gaston Salvatore (on the right) on a Vietnam demonstration in Berlin, 1968. Photo © akg-images.

factory, and they were joined by workers at the larger factories (notably Renault) as well as by many school students. At the peak of the strike wave some 9 million workers were involved, paralyzing transport, the banks, and essential services. De Gaulle, who had been visiting Romania, returned to face an unprecedented challenge to his authority, and his acceptance of the need for reform only made matters worse. It was left to Pompidou to take active steps to end the strikes at the Grenelle talks with the unions on May 25–27. (His reward was to be dismissed as prime minister once the crisis had passed!) Pompidou conceded a 35 percent increase in the minimum wage and a 10 percent pay rise across the board, although in many workplaces this was deemed insufficient and there was no mass return to work. Indeed, in these remarkable circumstances it was very difficult for both unions and government to divine exactly what the workers did want.

Attention now reverted to the politicians. On May 28 Mitterrand, with foolish opportunism, called for a provisional government and announced his candidacy should de Gaulle step down. On the following day the president flew with his family to Baden-Baden to visit General Massu, commander of the French forces in Germany. Assured of the support of the military, de Gaulle returned with renewed confidence and called parliamentary elections. (The price of military support appears to have been an amnesty for the OAS terrorists.) On May 30 as many as 400,000 of the president's supporters demonstrated in Paris and reclaimed the streets from the left. The slogans of this reactionary crowd included "Cohn-Bendit à Dachau."[31] The counter-revolution had begun, and during June the police violently regained control of the factories and campuses. In the two rounds of voting on June 23–30 de Gaulle's followers won a landslide election victory, claiming 75 percent of the seats in parliament. Once de Gaulle had regained his self-belief, and galvanized his followers, the student movement soon fell victim to its own lack of clear objectives and any semblance of strategy. Even so, the impetus of May 1968 was merely transferred to a plethora of small left-wing parties and movements that would remain influential well into the 1970s.

The pace was very different in Italy's "creeping May." Many Italian campuses had been under student occupation since 1967, and by 1968 most universities were affected to some degree. The occupation of the Catholic University in Milan was particularly sobering as the students had typically been conservative and supportive of the Christian Democrats. When striking students were cleared out of the University of Rome in late February 1968 they decided to occupy the architecture faculty in its attractive location in the Valle Giulia. The open battle that ensued between students and police on March 1 marked an important milestone: the police had used violence against the privileged student elite for the first time, while, for their part, the students felt that they had unmasked the true repressive nature of the state. For the communist film-maker Pier Paolo Pasolini, however, they were "spoilt brats" who in attacking the police were beating up "the sons of the poor."[32] The Italian working class also displayed a new militancy in 1968, rebelling against the low wages and paternalism of the Italian factories (from many of which unions were excluded). When workers went on strike in the textile mills of Valdagno in April 1968, they symbolically attacked the statue of Gaetano Marzotto, whose family dominated the town. In many factories new autonomous leaderships developed, such as the Unitary Base Committee established in Milan's Pirelli factory in February 1968.

The Italian unrest intensified during 1968 and culminated in the "hot autumn" of 1969, when contract renewal in the engineering sector gave rise to seemingly endless strikes and demonstrations. If the campuses were quieter now it was because many student radicals had switched their attention to the factories – some took industrial jobs while others sold radical papers at the gates. However, the "hot autumn" represented no mere transference of middle-class militancy, but rather a new political self-expression and autonomy for the working class. The result was sweeping concessions by management (including a 40-hour week and new rights for trade unions) that were enshrined in law by the Labour Charter of May 1970. While the consequences were damaging for the Italian economy, the industrial militancy had created a new sense of equality and self-worth amongst working people. The decade ended darkly, however, with a bomb in the Piazza Fontana, Milan, which killed 12 people. The police immediately suspected the anarchists, one of whom died falling from a window in police headquarters. In fact, the bombing was later to be revealed as a right-wing provocation and the first taste of the neo-fascist "strategy of tension" intended to undermine the democratic republic. Tragically, one legacy of 1967–9 would be a turn to violence by the extremes of both left and right.

In West Germany there was no crescendo to match May 1968 or the "hot autumn," but rather a steady growth in student militancy throughout the 1960s. It had its organizational basis in the Socialist Student League (SDS), which had been expelled from the SPD in 1961, and in the Extra-Parliamentary Opposition of 1966–7. Its most charismatic leader was Rudi Dutschke, an East German refugee studying in Berlin who was shot and gravely wounded by a right-wing assailant in April 1968. By the late 1960s a distinctive radical counter-culture had emerged in Berlin and a number of other German cities. The radicals were angry at the absorption of the SPD into the Grand Coalition but also reveled in the political opportunities that this created. The principal difference between the events in West Germany and those in France and Italy was the absence of any substantial working-class involvement. Even when the trade unions did make common cause with the students, for instance in opposition to the 1968 Emergency Laws, they broke ranks once their own concerns had been addressed. The unrest was framed by the memory of the ill-starred Weimar Republic, as both left and right accused the other of endangering German democracy. The students were quick to denounce the media magnate Axel Springer as a "fascist," and held his tabloid newspapers responsible for creating a climate of hatred directed against leaders such as Dutschke. Conversely, even some leftist intellectuals saw the student unrest as a form of "left fascism." Jürgen Habermas argued that, by "using the university for pseudo-revolutionary adventures," the students had missed the chance to push for lasting institutional reforms,[33] By the late 1960s the SDS had become heavily factionalized and in March 1970 it disbanded. As in Italy, a small minority was now ready to turn to terrorist violence.

The radicalism of the late 1960s seemed to have little immediate political impact, although, indirectly, it brought an end to de Gaulle's career. The president had sought to renew his popular support by calling an otherwise inconsequential referendum on reform of the Senate in April 1969. Instead, he united his critics and resigned after losing by 47 to 53 percent. The election of Pompidou as his successor brought little real change, however. Although the former prime minister had proclaimed that "I am not General de Gaulle,"[34] he was broadly loyal to his policies. In the longer term, however, a new political generation had been forged that influenced both the revived French Socialist Party and the German SPD in the 1970s. By 1973 more than half the SPD members were new, 66 percent of them under the age of 35, while in France Michel Rocard's PSU, which joined the Socialist Party in 1973, acted as a bridge for many of the "'68-ers" to enter mainstream politics. The radicals also surfaced in a wide range of "new social movements" (such as feminism and environmentalism) and eventually in the Green parties of the 1980s. Aftershocks were also visible in the rise of more democratic, participatory political structures, such as the establishment of regional councils in Italy. Beyond that, perhaps the most enduring impact of 1968 lay in wider changes in social and political attitudes. By the 1970s there had been considerable liberalization of the media and education throughout western Europe, and there was less deference towards authority in all its forms. The more permissive and individualistic society of late twentieth-century Europe may not have been in many respects what the radicals of the 1960s wanted, but it certainly offered an alternative to what one French pupil in June 1968 had called the "predetermined path which leads nowhere."[35]

The Persistence of Dictatorship: Spain, Portugal, and Greece

The Greek military coup of April 21, 1967 was a sharp reminder that the democratic consolidation of postwar Europe was restricted to the north and west of the continent. In southern Europe various forms of dictatorship survived well into the 1970s and, indeed, there were justified fears that Italian democracy, too, might succumb to a military or neo-fascist plot. With hindsight, however, it is clear that most of the factors that precipitated the end of dictatorship in southern Europe between 1974 and 1975 were already visible in the 1960s.

   In Spain and (more hesitantly) Portugal, the dictatorships sought to ride the tiger of economic growth. The Spanish economic liberalization of the late 1950s brought spectacular rates of growth of GDP (7.5 percent per year between 1960 and 1973), booming exports, and (just as in France and Italy) a swift decline in the rural population. Meanwhile foreign tourists, even if largely corralled on the Mediterranean coast, brought with them both prosperity and new cultural and sexual mores. By 1970 there were some 30 million foreign visitors to Spain a year. The Portuguese economy also grew, especially as there was a boom in inward investment (taking advantage of the country's spectacularly low wages) once Portugal joined the European Free Trade Area (EFTA). Development was, however, far more modest than in Spain as Salazar, rightly fearing the political impact of economic modernization, kept the brakes on. As a consequence agriculture remained highly backward, and between 1960 and 1974 some 1.5 million Portuguese went to work abroad (mainly in France and Germany). Remittances became a vital prop for the economy, along with the beginnings of a tourist industry on the beaches of the Algarve in southern Portugal. In both countries the industrial elites hankered after membership of the EEC, and were aware that this could only follow political liberalization.

In other respects, however, the experience of the Iberian dictatorships differed. In Spain an array of new, if as yet disunited, opposition movements emerged in the 1960s. These included a resurgence of working-class protest led by the clandestine communist unions (CCOO), and the rise of the militant Basque nationalist group ETA which, from 1968, took up armed struggle against the regime. University students (who were primarily the children of the elite) were also increasingly active in their opposition to the regime and, in 1965, forced the abolition of the official Falangist student union. Particularly damaging was the loss of the support of that former pillar of the regime, the Catholic Church. The Catholic hierarchy was by the late 1960s advocating political neutrality and the defense of human rights. Loss of support amongst Spain's 18,000 priests was striking: by 1969 some 25 percent considered themselves socialists, while only 2.4 percent were Falangists.[36] In both the Basque country and Catalonia, priests were particularly prominent in monitoring the regime's human rights abuses. Despite these setbacks, however, the regime remained confident that it could retain control over the process of modernization, and moderate government ministers such as Manuel Fraga pushed for limited change. In 1966 press censorship was abolished and, in December of that year, Spaniards voted overwhelmingly in a referendum in favor of cosmetic political reforms. Above all, Franco moved to resolve the delicate question of his succession when in 1969 he finally appointed Juan Carlos as his heir. In this way Franco retained the political initiative, as Juan Carlos had effectively usurped the right of his father (Don Juan) to the throne. (His legitimacy was only fully accepted when Don Juan renounced his claim to the throne in May 1977.) Franco had, it seemed, groomed the young prince and now dictated the terms under which he would govern.

Salazar also had to deal with opposition, such as the popular candidature of General Delgado for the presidency in 1958, but the real threat to his regime lay in Africa. Although chronically underdeveloped, the African empire remained economically valuable to Portugal, as well as the home for some 350,000 settlers (mainly small-scale farmers). In the course of the 1960s, nationalist guerrilla movements developed in Angola, Mozambique, and Guinea-Bissau. Although these insurgencies could be contained by a combination of military force and the assassination of their leaders, the financial strain and the cost to Portugal's international reputation escalated steeply. Between 1960 and 1971 military requirements rose to 45.9 percent of government expenditure,[37] and an army in Africa of 150,000 men could only be sustained by lengthy compulsory military service (itself sapping for the domestic economy). The colonial war radicalized the professional officers, many of whom felt that the intransigence of the regime had doomed them to a struggle that they must eventually lose. However, although this resentment led directly to the overthrow of the regime in 1974, in the short term the dictatorship seemed secure. In 1968 Salazar was incapacitated (he died in 1970) and he was replaced by Marcello Caetano, an academic lawyer. The new prime minister was loyal to the founding principles of the "New State," but presided over a limited period of prosperity and liberalization. From 1971, however, even this pallid "Lisbon spring" gave way to renewed repression.

The Colonels' coup in Greece was a response to the same modernizing social and political trends that were undermining dictatorship elsewhere in southern Europe. In the decade after the civil war Greece had been dominated by a right-wing anti-communist establishment which held power through the manipulation of the electoral system. In the 1960s it found itself challenged by a rejuvenated democratic opposition led by George Papandreou, advocate of "relentless struggle" for reform. In November 1963 Papandreou's Centre Union formed a minority government and in February 1964 won a landslide election victory with nearly 53 percent of the vote. He embarked on a program of educational reforms and freed those still in jail for their role in the civil war. Following a struggle for control of the Ministry of Defence, however, Papandreou was forced to resign by the young King Constantine in July 1965, opening a period of extreme political unrest. When fresh elections were scheduled for May 1967, a military junta led by Colonel George Papadopoulos seized power. The king and the United States both went along with the coup, although Constantine was soon forced into exile after plotting with monarchist officers. The junta retained the support of the bureaucracy, judiciary, and church, but the new regime's pig-headed traditionalism and unthinking savagery appalled public opinion and galvanized opposition. Thousands of opponents were detained and tortured, provoking criticism by the Council of Europe, and in November 1973 as many as 80 students were killed when an occupation of Athens Polytechnic was ended by force. There was certainly never any prospect of establishing a stable basis for the Greek dictatorship equivalent to that achieved over so many years in Spain and Portugal.

Conclusion

The 1960s represented the watershed in the history of Europe since 1945. The decade is inevitably associated with generational revolt by the young, symbolized by the events of May 1968 in Paris. However, the student radicalism must be seen in the context of far more extensive social and cultural change, in particular the growth of prosperity and affluence, liberal reforms in the realm of social and sexual behavior, the rise of a new, more critical intellectual culture, and the declining authority of the churches. The new mood reflected a general optimism born of prosperity and the decline of superpower rivalry in Europe. Indeed, the United States was now often seen less as a protector than as an aggressor in Vietnam.

It should also be noted that the radicalism of the 1960s was by no means restricted to the young: in both France and Italy there were also remarkable mobilizations amongst industrial workers. Although the radicals did not achieve all of their objectives, the Sixties set western Europe on a path towards both greater personal freedoms and new solidarities with respect to feminism, the Third World, and the environment.

6
The Soviet Union and Eastern Europe, from 1953 to the 1970s

New Societies, Recurrent Crises

On June 17, 1953, barely three months after the death of Stalin, striking workers took to the streets across East Germany in protest against a sudden 10 percent increase in work norms. Although the uprising was swiftly crushed by the Red Army, it prefigured greater challenges to Soviet dominance over eastern Europe[1] in Hungary (1956), Czechoslovakia (1968), and Poland (1980–1). However, while the dysfunctional aspects of communist rule loom large in this period, and the history of eastern Europe can appear as an unfolding series of crises, that is far from the whole picture. This was also a time of profound economic and social transformation, as well as one in which the communist regimes sought – with some success – to establish new bases for political legitimacy and stability. Despite recurrent crises, a new and very distinctive way of life was developing in eastern Europe, and there was no immediate prospect of it coming to an end (see Map 6.1).

The Soviet Union's ability to contain these threats to its dominance – by force if necessary – ensured that it remained the dominant factor within eastern Europe. However, the Soviet Union's own position was less certain following the death of Stalin. Its ideological lead in the communist world, once taken for granted, was challenged in the 1950s by Yugoslavia and in the 1960s by China. Stalin's successors, eager to bring Yugoslavia back into the fold, played a dangerous game with Tito in the mid-1950s. The joint agreement signed by Tito and Khrushchev in June 1956, which stated that "the paths of socialist development vary according to the country and the conditions that prevail there,"[2] tore up a central tenet of Stalinism and encouraged those agitating for radical change in Poland and Hungary. Similarly, the Chinese attack on Soviet "revisionism" in the 1960s provided an opportunity for Romania to carve out a substantial degree of independence

Europe's Troubled Peace: 1945 to the Present, Second Edition. Tom Buchanan.
© 2012 John Wiley & Sons, Ltd. Published 2012 by John Wiley & Sons, Ltd.

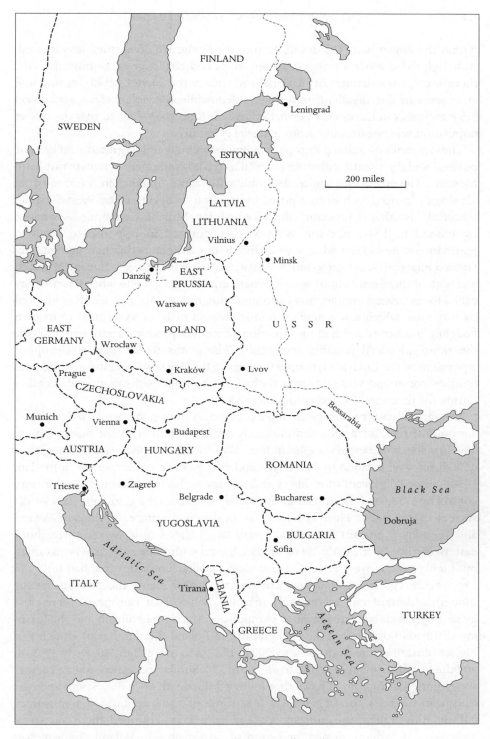

Map 6.1 Communist eastern Europe, showing prewar boundaries.
Source: Robin Okey, *Eastern Europe, 1840–1980* (Hutchinson, London, 1982), p. 217.

within the Soviet bloc. Domestically, too, the Soviet Union seemed less assured. Although there was no prospect of any sustained challenge to communist rule, there were the stirrings of nationalism within the Soviet republics and the emergence of the "dissident" movement. Meanwhile, the violent clashes over food price increases in the city of Novocherkassk in June 1962 showed that the Soviet population was not immune from material grievances.

The countries of eastern Europe remained strikingly unintegrated, and lines of political and diplomatic influence (as well as trade) continued to radiate out from Moscow. The east European leaders only truly came together in the face of an ideological threat, such as that posed by the Prague Spring or by West German *Ostpolitik*. Neither Comecon (the Council for Mutual Economic Assistance established in 1949) nor the Warsaw Pact (formed in response to German rearmament in 1955) had a supranational dimension. Stalin had consistently favored bilateral – and exploitative – relationships with the east European states, and both of these institutions were dormant until the early 1960s when Khrushchev called for increased military and economic integration. His initiative was blocked by Romania, which saw a new economic division of labor as a threat to its own fledgling industries and had no intention of merely producing raw materials for the more advanced socialist economies. There was to be no east European equivalent of the EEC. Soviet hopes for turning the Warsaw Pact into an integrated military command were similarly dashed by the poor performance of its allies during the invasion of Czechoslovakia in 1968.

The face of eastern Europe changed profoundly during the first two decades of communist rule, a transformation closely modeled on that of the Soviet Union. The first step was a rapid state-led industrialization; the second was the emergence of a distinctive, if pallid by Western standards, form of consumerism in the late 1950s. Some 90 percent of industry and commerce had been brought under state control by 1953,[3] and the industrial landscape was marked by giant new steel works such as that at Nowa Huta in Poland. With the significant exceptions of Poland and Yugoslavia, peasant farming had very largely been collectivized throughout eastern Europe by the early 1960s, although even within the collective farms small but highly productive private plots remained. Balkan countries that had until the 1940s been regarded as "peasant Europe" were now laying the foundations for modern industrial and increasingly urban societies. East Europeans were now increasingly well educated (even if compulsory Marxism-Leninism and the learning of Russian dominated the curriculum). In Poland the number of students in higher education rose from some 95,000 in 1947/8 to more than 250,000 in 1965/6, and the number of faculties rose from 162 to 350. Similar increases occurred across the region.[4] During the "Thaw" that followed the death of Stalin, Soviet and east European societies also began to display some of the trappings of a consumer culture. Although private domestic space remained very cramped, there was a new awareness of fashion, design, and even of advertising. In Poland, for instance, where private business had almost ceased to exist in the early 1950s, some 10,000 private shops and kiosks were set up in 1957 alone[5] and self-service supermarkets began to appear in the early 1960s. The launch of the East German Trabant car in 1958 was further evidence of the refocusing of the economy towards the consumer, even if private car ownership remained limited.

The communist parties governed in the name of the working class and the industrial workforce grew steadily, even in countries where, before the war, industrialization had been very limited. In Romania, for instance, the working class grew from 23.7 percent to some 40 percent of the population between 1956 and 1966 and in Bulgaria from 29.2 percent to 42 percent during the same period.[6] All too frequently, however, communist regimes found themselves at odds with the workers: the period covered by this chapter opens with the East German protests of 1953 and closes with the Polish strikes of 1970 (where there was worse to come in 1976 and 1980). One solution was to privilege the status and wages of skilled industrial workers, although this became increasingly difficult to sustain as the economic situation worsened in the 1970s. Another was to promote egalitarianism: hence the remarkable flatness of wage differentials between manual and white-collar workers in 1960s Czechoslovakia helped to maintain working-class support. The communist regimes also encouraged social mobility so that in Bulgaria, for instance, by 1966 more than half of all directors of enterprises were former workers who had had no secondary education.[7] However, the rise of a technocratic elite (or "intelligentsia") in the 1960s created its own political problems. The technocrats possessed the skills needed to run increasingly complex economies, but were impatient with the ideological straitjacket imposed by communist rule. Apart from the working class and the intelligentsia, and given the marginalization of the pre-communist middle class, the only other important social grouping was the party bureaucracy itself. Milovan Djilas, the Yugoslav dissident and former high-ranking communist, caused controversy when he described the bureaucracy as *The New Class* (1957). While this attribution raises sociological questions, Djilas's attack on a self-appointed clique with access to material privilege and increasingly separate from those it claimed to represent clearly struck home: he received a seven-year jail sentence.

The experience of women under communist regimes was profoundly mixed, as radical emancipatory intentions often gave way to compromise with entrenched social attitudes. Women rarely achieved high political office (the principal exception being the Bulgarian leader Todor Zhivkov's daughter Ludmilla). Communist regimes did promote women within the labor force, with far more generous state nursery provision than was available in western Europe, although women were unlikely to obtain the skilled (and better-paid) industrial jobs. On average women's pay trailed far behind that of men, and this was particularly noticeable in the professions, such as medicine, which educated women had entered in large numbers. The family unit remained central, and within it women carried the greatest burden of housework and childcare. There was nothing in eastern Europe to match the challenge to male attitudes posed by feminism in the West from the late 1960s. One observer noted that the mantra of Western feminism, that "the personal is political," carried little attraction for women living in societies in which "the reality and the danger is that the private becomes political too often."[8] Even so, women's social rights were promoted. For instance, most communist regimes legalized abortion between 1955 and 1957, and contraception was generally available. An exception was Romania which, in 1967, effectively banned abortion as part of an attempt to increase the birth-rate. East Germany did not legalize abortion until 1972, but free contraception and childcare resulted in an abortion rate that was, by 1988, a half that of Poland and a quarter that of the Soviet Union.[9] For all of their flaws, the communist regimes undoubtedly offered greater opportunities to women, especially those with families, within the labor market, and after 1989 many would look back to the *Muttipolitik* (as the provision for mothers was referred to in East Germany) with some regret.

Although these were one-party states, they were far from monolithic. One of the most striking features of the 15 years after the death of Stalin was the willingness of east European communist intellectuals to challenge the system from within. "Reform communists" tested Soviet-style communism against Marx's own commitment to truth and human emancipation and found it wanting. They had few illusions about the Soviet Union. Zdeněk Mlynář, a leading figure in the Prague Spring, had studied in Moscow in the early 1950s and was shocked not so much by the poverty that he encountered as by the "absence of values." He was struck by the manner in which many Soviet citizens "tried to keep politics utterly separate from their personal lives."[10] Reform communists did not question the "leading role" of the Communist Party, but believed that it should govern with greater consent and democracy (in the sense of public participation rather than political pluralism). In the cultural sphere Imre Nagy, the prime minister of Hungary in November 1956, attacked the idea of party control: "this method precludes the search for reality and truth, the exchange of ideas and, above all, criticism."[11] Reform communism's simplest and most famous formulation was that of Alexander Dubček in July 1968: "Socialism with a human face."[12]

There were very clear limits to change, as the Soviet response to the Czechoslovak reform movement showed in 1968, but communist regimes could not ignore the question of economic reform. The overall Comecon growth rate of industrial production fell from 13.3 percent in 1951–5 to 9 percent in 1961–2 and 7.5 percent in 1962 as the reconstruction boom came to an end. Moreover, by all indices the gap between the Comecon countries and the West was widening: for instance, agricultural productivity in western Europe had risen by 50 percent over prewar levels by 1963, while in the east it barely exceeded the level of 1934–8.[13] Stalinist central planning – which had proved brutally effective in the postwar era – was of little value by the 1960s when economies were becoming more oriented towards consumer goods and technological innovation. The command economy had resulted in an uneven supply of poor-quality goods, giving rise to queuing and corruption, but the obvious alternative – a price mechanism within a market economy and the threat of unemployment – was politically unacceptable. Accordingly, the most radical economic reform took place beyond Moscow's control in Yugoslavia, and even here liberalization was balanced by socialist measures such as workers' self-management. Within the Soviet bloc the most effective reformer was the Hungarian leader János Kádár, whose New Economic Mechanism (1968) scrapped central planning, introduced profit incentives, and led to a glut of home-produced food. Reform elsewhere, including the "Kosygin" reforms in the USSR, was hamstrung by lack of ambition and political dogmatism in its implementation. The late 1960s represented the moment at which the communist economies forsook any real prospect of competing with the West.

Even so, some states, notably Bulgaria and East Germany, enjoyed reasonable success during this period. Under the wily leadership of Todor Zhivkov, who became leader of the Communist Party in 1954, Bulgaria did not find itself at loggerheads with the USSR as did its socialist neighbors Romania and Yugoslavia. A healthy trading balance with the USSR (exporting agricultural produce in return for Soviet energy and machinery) ensured solid economic growth, assisted by the development of light industry and Black Sea tourism. Zhivkov also promoted a moderate Bulgarian nationalism, while accepting the security offered by the Soviet Union within a volatile region. East Germany, meanwhile, gained a new stability once its survival had been assured by the construction of the Berlin Wall in 1961. Of course, stability was due in part to the existence of a highly intrusive police state under the control of the Stasi which, by 1975, had some 60,000 paid employees and controlled a legion of informers.[14] Yet this was also a society with – by east European standards – a high standard of living, especially during the early years of Erich Honecker's leadership (1971–89) when greater resources were diverted into consumer goods. Although there were dissenting voices, East Germany was marked by a high level of participation in the Communist Party (one in five citizens were members) or its many political, social, and cultural satellite organizations.

Despite the heavy levels of repression and censorship throughout the USSR and eastern Europe, opposition continued to be voiced. Its main weakness was that it took many different forms which, at least until the 1970s, did not make common cause. Working-class unrest tended to be spontaneous and could be highly politically damaging, but until the advent of Solidarity in 1980 the workers did not mount a sustained challenge. Their demands were largely material, and timely concessions often proved effective in defusing protest in the short term. Conversely the students, who were increasingly prominent critics in the late 1960s, were primarily concerned with expanding intellectual and political freedoms. Their closest allies were those in the cultural sphere (such as the Czech film directors of the mid-1960s "New Wave" or playwright Václav Havel) who exploited chinks in state control to poke absurdist fun at authority and question the heroic official myths of the war. The third main source of opposition was the churches, although their position varied profoundly from country to country. In states where religion was heavily repressed, such as the USSR and Czechoslovakia, an autonomous – let alone critical – voice was impossible. Here, the churches were often heavily penetrated by the state and could be forced into collaboration. Yet where the churches were stronger – notably in Poland – they also had interests to defend (such as seminaries and access to schools) and the temptation was to reach an understanding with government. In the 1960s a number of east European regimes (such as Hungary in 1964 and Yugoslavia in 1966) concluded concordats with the Vatican. When the churches chose to criticize the regime, the issues at stake – such as Cardinal Wyczynski's condemnation of abortion and birth control – often did not have the support of students and intellectuals. The great achievement of the Polish opposition in the later 1970s was to break down the barriers between opponents of the regime and to create the first truly comprehensive resistance to communism in eastern Europe.

Khrushchev and de-Stalinization

On Stalin's death power passed to a "collective leadership," within which Georgi Malenkov (who took control of the government) was the first among equals. The Communist Party, which had been weakened in the later Stalin years, was entrusted to Nikita Khrushchev, while Lavrenty Beria controlled the secret police. Despite the uneasy relations between the Soviet leaders, who in June 1953 united to defeat and kill the dangerous Beria, none wanted to return to Stalin's terror or personal domination, and they realized that the only alternative was to base communist rule on a higher standard of living and increased personal freedoms. As many as 1 million prisoners were immediately released from the Gulag and agricultural taxes were cut. In the international sphere, the Korean War was swiftly brought to a close and the first moves made towards a "peaceful coexistence" with the West, while diplomatic relations were restored with Stalin's *bête noir* Yugoslavia. Khrushchev, who soon emerged as the main rival to Malenkov, did not differ greatly from him on policies (and, indeed, eventually implemented many of his ideas). Perhaps more significant was Khrushchev's restoration of the authority of the Communist Party and his development of a power base amongst both party cadres and the military and industrial elites, many of whom felt threatened by the pace of Malenkov's proposed reforms. When Malenkov was forced to resign in February 1955 (on the grounds of "rightist deviation") he was not executed like Beria, but simply assigned a lowly government ministry. The clear signal was that in the post-Stalin era political disagreements would no longer be resolved by arbitrary violence.

Between February 1955 and June 1957 (when he finally defeated his remaining rivals), Khrushchev struggled to assert his authority. In the process he decided to break with Stalin's legacy: a difficult task for someone who had been one of Stalin's lieutenants since the 1930s and was closely implicated with his policies. In February

1956 Khrushchev addressed a closed session of the CPSU's XX congress, mounting a four-hour assault on Stalin's crimes, his "cult of the individual leader,"and his incompetence during the war. He drew a careful distinction between Stalin and Lenin, for instance in the latter's use of terror, to avoid completely discrediting the Communist Party. Even so, the "secret speech" was political dynamite and unofficial copies were soon in circulation both in the USSR and abroad. Khrushchev was deeply concerned by the powerful forces of change that he had unleashed, especially in eastern Europe, where the attack on Stalin contributed to a near-disastrous collapse of Soviet authority. Indeed, by the start of 1957 Khrushchev was already rowing back, telling his hosts at a Chinese reception in Moscow that "the term 'Stalinist', like Stalin himself, is inseparable from the high title of communist."[15]

The complexity of "the Thaw" (the term made famous in Ilya Ehrenberg's novella of 1959) was most visible in cultural policy, where Khrushchev still believed that it was the task of the Communist Party to determine the "main aim of creative work."[16] Accordingly, de-Stalinization represented, at best, a crab-walk towards greater artistic freedom. In 1958 Boris Pasternak was forced to decline the Nobel Prize for literature, having had *Dr Zhivago* privately published in the West in 1957, yet in 1961 Khrushchev personally approved the publication of Solzhenitsyn's devastating account of the Gulag, *One Day in the Life of Ivan Denisovich*. He later commented of this decision that he had been impressed by the realism of Solzhenitsyn's writing, and believed that "in order to prevent a repetition [of the crimes of the Stalin era] we had to brand the truth firmly into literature."[17] Although the cultural "thaw" ended with Khrushchev's outspoken attack on modern art while visiting a Moscow exhibition in December 1962, there was no return to the constraints of high Socialist Realism.

Khrushchev's attack on Stalinism was in part a political maneuver against his rivals, but was also a tribute to his belief in the victory of Soviet communism once it had been restored to true Leninist principles. Khrushchev came from a peasant family and had benefited from Stalin's social revolution of the 1930s, rising through the party hierarchy. His instincts were radical and egalitarian – for instance, unlike Stalin he mounted a militant campaign against Christianity, and in 1958 he insisted that all students should prepare for higher education with two years of manual labor. He was certainly no advocate of market reforms or pluralism: instead, he believed that the Soviet Union's future success should rest on political mobilization and technological prowess. In 1956 he famously declared that the USSR would "bury" the West by peaceful means, and he took the launch of the satellite *Sputnik* (1957) and Yuri Gagarin's pioneering space flight (1961) as proof of the superiority of the Soviet system. According to the Communist Party's new program unveiled in October 1961, the USA would be overtaken in per capita production by 1970, and communism constructed "in the main" by 1980.[18] How was this to be achieved? Given that terror was no longer an option, Khrushchev's main tool was inspiration and emulation, and a great deal rested on his ability to use the Communist Party (which grew from 6.9 million to 11 million members during his tenure) to galvanize economic growth. However, Khrushchev's incessant tinkering with the party apparatus alienated vested interests. More importantly, his policies were not rewarded with success, notably in the critical area of agricultural production. The failed harvest of 1963, in part the result of Khrushchev's own overly ambitious policies in the mid-1950s, gravely weakened his leadership.

Khrushchev presented a novel image of the Soviet leader to the outside world. He was willing to travel abroad and made historic visits to China, India, and the USA. The West found his earthy charm attractive but unpredictable, while many Soviet citizens felt that his behavior was gauche and unstatesmanlike. This would have counted for little had his saber-rattling brought appreciable gains. Instead, he suffered defeat over Cuba, while the collapse of relations with China raised the specter of a new and powerful enemy in Asia. Khrushchev had invested heavily in nuclear weaponry, and scaled down the Red Army from 5.7 million to 3 million men over a period of ten years, but had not delivered greater security. Having lost the confidence of senior political and military leaders, he was summoned to an emergency meeting of the Communist Party Praesidium in October 1964 and sacked. Tellingly, Khrushchev hailed the meeting at which he was overthrown as a "victory for the party."[19] He became the first Soviet leader to live out his final years in anonymous retirement (1964–71) and even to see his illicitly recorded memoirs published in the West.

The Crisis of 1956: Poland and Hungary

The perils of de-Stalinization running out of control were nowhere more evident than in Poland and Hungary, where the internal disputes within the Communist Party leaderships coincided with wider social and political convulsions. The outcomes were, however, very different: in Poland the crisis was successfully managed, while in Hungary it resulted in a popular uprising and Red Army inter-vention. In both cases the purges of the late 1940s had placed loyal Stalinists in charge, implementing harsh, Soviet-style political and economic policies. The Hungarian leader Mátyás Rákosi gloried in being "Stalin's most adept pupil."[20] By 1953 both societies were prone to mounting discontents, not only due to the collapsing standard of living and lack of political freedom, but also to the national humiliation of Soviet domination. In Poland the presence of a Red Army mar-shal, Rokossowski, as Defense Minister was particularly resented; in Hungary one of the first gestures of the 1956 uprising was to cut the hammer and sickle from the national flag. After Stalin's death Moscow swiftly imposed a change of policy in Hungary, and Rákosi had to accept his reformist rival Imre Nagy as prime minister. Nagy was the advocate of a "New Course" in economic policy, shifting the balance from heavy industry to consumer goods and slowing, or even reversing, collectivization. Although Nagy was sacked in 1955, his supporters led a mounting anti-Stalinist clamor during 1956, egged on by news of Khrushchev's "secret" speech. The Petőfi circle of young intellectuals held a series of well-attended public seminars which subjected recent events in Hungarian history to critical review.

At this point events in Poland intervened. Large-scale rioting broke out in Poznan on June 28 and 29, 1956 over demands for higher pay. The demonstrations took on an anti-communist dimension, and during their suppression Polish security forces killed 53 civilians. After the violence at Poznan the leadership of the Polish Communist Party (PZPR) could not conceal the scale of popular discontent, articulated by the numerous workers' councils which had recently sprung up. The only alternative to a complete collapse of communist control was to rehabilitate the former leader Gomulka, who had languished under house arrest between 1949 and April 1956. Khrushchev initially attempted to block Gomulka's return and descended on Warsaw to express his concerns. He also ordered Soviet troops to advance on the Polish capital, but backed down when it seemed that Polish forces would put up resistance. Accordingly, on October 20, 1956 Gomulka was appointed to lead the PZPR, and 500,000 Poles publicly celebrated his return to power. In reality, however, a compromise deal had been struck. Gomulka restored Communist Party rule, brought anti-Soviet sentiments under control, and kept Poland inside the Warsaw Pact, in return for the restoration of a degree of Polish pride and independence. Marshal Rokossowski departed, along with numerous other Soviet officers, and Poland gained some control over the Soviet troops on its territory. In addition, Gomulka won a free hand domestically, enabling him to reverse collectivization, raise wages and reintroduce religious education in schools.

In Hungary, meanwhile, the Kremlin (under pressure from Tito) had forced Rákosi to resign in July 1956. However, by replacing him with his close colleague Ernő Gerő it did nothing to still the mounting discontent. The reburial of László Rajk, victim of the show trials, on October 6 was attended by thousands, and the writer Béla Szász hoped that an epoch of "lawlessness, arbitrariness and moral decay"[21] would be buried with him. On October 23 a large demonstration, led by students, rallied in solidarity with Poland and was addressed by Imre Nagy. Although Nagy, the only communist who enjoyed any popular support, urged the crowd to return home, a monument to Stalin was smashed and the "Radio Hungary" station besieged: demonstration was turning into nationalist and anti-communist revolt. The Communist Party's response was to appoint Nagy as prime minister (in the hope that he would act as a Hungarian Gomulka) and to seek Soviet military assistance. Soviet tanks entered Budapest on October 24, although, without infantry support, many were destroyed by the "Molotov cocktails" of the bands of students and young workers now defending the capital.

After four days of fighting, and following an appeal from Nagy, Soviet forces withdrew. However, Khrushchev's position soon hardened when the lynching of members of the secret police in Budapest increased the political pressure on the Soviet leader to take a robust line against a "fascist" counter-revolution.

Figure 6.1 Soviet tanks enter Budapest during the Hungarian uprising (October 24–November 11, 1956). Photo © akg-images/Erich Lessing.

Coincidentally, the Suez crisis presented the opportunity for military action while the West was divided and distracted. The Soviet leadership decided on this course of action on October 31, and Khrushchev spent the next few days consulting other east European leaders, notably Tito and Gomulka. In addition to military intervention a political strategy also took shape. On November 1 János Kádár, the leader of the recently reformed Hungarian Communist Party, who had suffered imprisonment under Rákosi, presented himself to the Soviet embassy and was spirited away to Moscow. He would return in the wake of the Red Army as the leader of the new government. In Budapest, meanwhile, Imre Nagy now sided openly with the rebels: on November 1 he declared Hungary's neutrality and threatened to withdraw from the Warsaw Pact. He had already legalized the political parties of the 1945–8 era on October 30, and a new government was formed in which the "new" Communist Party shared power with Smallholders, Social Democrats, and members of the revolutionary armed forces.

On November 4, 1956 the Red Army launched its attack on Budapest (see Figure 6.1). Little formal resistance was possible, and Nagy and other leaders – having ordered Hungarian forces to remain in barracks – took refuge in the Yugoslav embassy. By November 11 all armed opposition in Budapest was crushed. More than 700 Soviet troops and some 2,500 Hungarians had died in the fighting, and 200,000 had fled into exile by the end of 1956. Nonviolent resistance continued in the provinces into 1957, often led by spontaneously organized committees and workers' councils. Kádár's new government cooperated with the Soviet authorities in a fierce repression. Between 1957 and 1960 some 13,000 were interned, and by

1961 350 had been executed for their role in the rebellion. International opinion was outraged – but powerless to help – when Nagy and other leaders, under a promise of safe passage from their refuge, were seized and eventually executed in June 1958. Hungary had punctured US rhetoric about the "liberation" of subject peoples and graphically reinforced the Cold War division of Europe.

The worst of the repression was over by 1962, when Kádár commented that henceforth "those who are not against us are with us."[22] Kádár presided over a surprisingly effective restoration of political control (far more so than that in Czechoslovakia after 1968) legitimated by improved standards of living as well as by the unspoken trauma of November 1956. His "alliance" policy of the 1960s presented the Communist Party as the patriotic defender of Hungarian interests, steering a path between the excesses of Rákosi and the revolutionaries of 1956 and deserving broad national support. The "goulash communism" of the 1960s and 1970s promised all Hungarians a full stomach, facilitated by market reforms. Hungary came to enjoy the highest level of freedom of expression in eastern Europe (within implicit boundaries) and, in consequence, did not possess a large "dissident" movement. Kádár was unusual amongst east European leaders in his willingness tolerate Western rock music and other cultural influences – for instance, he permitted the import of Wurlitzer jukeboxes playing Western records in 1957 and allowed the emergence of a Hungarian rock music scene.

It is instructive to compare Hungary's development after 1956 with that of Poland. For all the hopes aroused by Gomulka's return, by the late 1960s his rule had slipped into sclerotic dictatorship and he was a principal enemy of the reformist Prague Spring. Under pressure from the hard-line "Partisan" faction within the PZPR, his responses to internal dissent became increasingly coarse and brutal. Concerned at Polish sympathy for Israel during the Six Day War of June 1967, Gomulka presided over an "anti-Zionist campaign" which pandered to the anti-Semitism of the Partisans. In March 1968 he crushed a movement of students demanding an end to censorship, and by early April some 2,700 had been arrested and a number of faculties closed. (The students had objected to the banning of a production of Adam Mickiewicz's 1831 anti-Russian play *The Forefathers*.) Eventually, in December 1970, Gomulka was forced to resign when working-class protests against a 17 percent increase in the price of meat were bloodily suppressed. His successor, Edward Gierek, inherited an incipient economic and social crisis. By that stage there seemed little question as to which of the two countries had had the better deal in the longer run.

The Start of the Brezhnev Era

Although Khrushchev was replaced by another collective leadership, Leonid Brezhnev (the General Secretary of the CPSU) had consolidated his hold on power by the early 1970s. Brezhnev, who died in office in 1982, was an extremely effective operator of the Soviet political system, described by his adversary Henry Kissinger as a "mixture of crudeness and warmth ... cunning and disarming."[23] Although his rule was famously denounced by his eventual successor Mikhail Gorbachev as an "era of stagnation," this applies more accurately to the latter years when Brezhnev was incapacitated by ill health, and ignores the attempt at economic reform in the 1960s.[24] Perhaps a fairer judgment would be that Brezhnev brought unprecedented stability at home and a new respect for Soviet power abroad, but that his policies also carried within them the seeds of decline. There is no question that Brezhnev led a conservative reaction (that was welcomed by the Soviet elites) against Khrushchev's radicalism and unpredictability. His policy was encapsulated in his 1971 slogan: "the stability of cadres." In other words, once his power was secure, no member of the ruling elite (the *nomenklatura*) need fear for their status or material interests. The result was gerontocracy. The average age of the Politbureau rose from 55 to 68 (1966–82) and of the Central Committee from 56 to 63. By the end of Brezhnev's rule, moreover, 75 percent of the latter body had joined the CPSU before 1950, 82 percent were of working-class or peasant origin, and 97 percent were male.[25] Political power was concentrated in the hands of Brezhnev's long-serving appointees such as Foreign Minister Andrei Gromyko and KGB chief Yuri Andropov. The reformist aspirations aroused by Khrushchev amongst the *shestidesyatniki* (the "generation of the Sixties") were deep frozen. In the Soviet republics Brezhnev gave more power to non-Russians in the local communist parties, trading short-term stability for the longer-term cohesion of the union.

The new regime had initially promised change, and after 1965 Prime Minister Kosygin presided over tentative economic reforms intended to give more autonomy to managers and to provide greater incentives for productivity. There was also a new openness to international technological collaboration, such as the agreement with Fiat to set up the Togliatti car plant at Stavropol. However, after the crushing of the Prague Spring in 1968, Kosygin's reforms became politically embarrassing and they were abandoned by the early 1970s. Economic life returned to the characteristic Soviet system, whereby individual plants and managers muddled through. Even so, the 1960s were still a time of rapid economic growth, and the chronic decline of the Soviet economy set in only after 1973.[26] The Soviet economy grew by 5–6 percent per annum in the 1950s and 1960s, compared to 3.7 percent per annum in 1971–5 and 2.7 percent per annum in 1976–80.[27] Although resources were still heavily diverted into defense and related industries, there was increasing access to consumer goods. By 1970, 61 percent of urban households and 32 percent of rural ones owned a television (which would be ubiquitous a decade later),[28] although car ownership was still very limited. In the interests of social harmony the regime was willing to turn a blind eye to the burgeoning "shadow economy" that made access to consumer goods possible. The greater opportunity and prosperity in the cities acted as a magnet for the rural population, despite substantial investment in the countryside. The rural share of the population fell from 46.7 percent to 34.4 percent in the 20 years after 1965 and agriculture, increasingly a preserve of women and the old, began to underperform seriously in the 1970s. However, the small private plots remained highly productive and by the 1960s provided 70 percent of the nutritional needs of rural families.

During the 1960s the Soviet authorities were confronted with the problem of a small but courageous "dissident" movement. The struggle was clearly an unequal one, and those convicted could be sent to jail, labor camps, and even mental hospitals. Even so, some leading critics such as Andrei Sakharov, a member of the Soviet Academy of Sciences, or the novelist Alexander Solzhenitsyn, could not be easily ignored or silenced. In 1970 Sakharov and the historian Roy Medvedev sent an open letter to Brezhnev appealing for a "gradual democratization" of Soviet life.[29] The 1960s also saw the rise of "self-publishing" or samizdat (a play on the name of the state publisher, Gosizdat). Sakharov and others eventually came to reject the Soviet system in its entirety, but the roots of dissidence in the 1960s lay in an idealization of pure Bolshevism and a sense of the lost opportunities of the 1920s, prior to the consolidation of Stalin's power. Roy Medvedev's *Let history judge* (which was published abroad in 1968) argued that had it not been for the early death of Lenin, the "genuinely socialist and democratic tendencies" within communism might well have triumphed over Stalinism.[30] The dissident movement lacked purchase within Soviet society, and samizdat documents gained a far wider circulation in the West than was ever possible within the USSR. There were, however, also loyal critics of the regime who found a niche within official journals and research institutes. While they did not take risks with their liberty, and remained fundamentally loyal to the communist ideal, it was this stratum that would provide the intellectual vibrancy behind Gorbachev's *perestroika* in the 1980s.

East European Alternatives: Romania, Yugoslavia, Albania

During the 1950s Tito's Yugoslavia offered the main socialist alternative to Soviet-style communism. Yugoslav communism was a deliberate inversion of Stalinism: workers' "self-management," the decentralization of power, and a nonaligned foreign policy took the place of central planning, Communist Party hegemony and Soviet-centered "internationalism." However, while it had its admirers, there were many contradictions within the Yugoslav model. Tito was still a Leninist in his commitment to communist rule and did not confuse devolution of power with political pluralism. He encouraged the Hungarian reformers but needed little persuasion to endorse the suppression of the 1956 uprising when it seemed likely that communism itself would be overthrown. He balanced out the ethnic forces within Yugoslavia with increasing agility (to the advantage of groups such as the Bosnian Muslims), but during the 1950s sanctioned a bloody repression of the Albanians of Kosovo. The architect of that violence, and Tito's *éminence grise*, was the Serb Alexander Ranković, head of the UDBA secret police.

By the 1960s Yugoslavia was increasingly preoccupied with the tensions produced by rapid economic growth. The new prosperity was due not only to liberalization, but also to the precious hard currency generated by the advent of mass tourism and by the large numbers of Yugoslavs working abroad. Twelve million tourists visited Yugoslavia in 1966, bringing an income of $230 million, and by 1973 over 500,000 Yugoslavs were working in West Germany.[31] Prosperity brought wider differentials of wealth and provoked internal political disputes between centralizers and liberals. The former were primarily Serbs who believed that national resources should be utilized to help the more backward southern regions, and that this required a strong central state and party. The liberals, mainly drawn from the more developed northern republics of Croatia and Slovenia, argued that more resources should be allocated to the republics (especially as the lucrative tourist industry was primarily sited on Croatia's Illyrian coast). Tito temporarily sided with the liberals, although he was aware of the dangers of setting in train disintegrative forces. In 1966 he brought down the over-mighty Ranković and reined in the UDBA which, it transpired, had even placed Tito himself under surveillance.

The reformists in turn were assailed both by hardliners and by critics to their left, and their position was not helped by the initial economic hardship produced by reform. The journal *Praxis*, an influential forum for Marxist critics of the regime, argued that Yugoslavia was "getting the worst of both worlds": the commercialization of capitalism and the political monopoly of east European communism.[32] Some of the 1967 elections (which were contested for the first time on the basis of a choice of candidates) were won by grizzled old Partisans fighting on a pro-Serbian, anti-reform platform. In June 1968 Belgrade students launched a nationwide protest. The movement was inspired by the recent events in Paris and by police violence closer to home, but the students' slogans (such as "Down with the Red Bourgeoisie!" and "More Schools, Fewer Automobiles!") also rejected the new materialism.[33] The unrest was eventually defused by the Warsaw Pact invasion of Czechoslovakia in August and the fear that Yugoslavia, which had strongly supported Dubček, might also be threatened. During 1968, and especially in the latter months, 100,000 new members under the age of 25 rushed to join the League of Communists.

Tito's other problem was his native Croatia, where by the early 1970s the tide of reform was beginning to move beyond acceptable bounds. The local Communist Party leaders were pushing for greater independence for Croatia and tried to play the dangerous card of Croat nationalism (at a time when it was thriving amongst guest workers in West Germany). The "Zagreb spring" of 1970–1 was characterized by student agitation and the rise of the Croat cultural organization Matica Hrvatska, which soon became, in effect, a political party. In the summer of 1971 Tito bluntly warned the Croat leaders that "others [i.e., the Soviets] are watching" and "Do we want to have 1941 again?"[34] Eventually, when Zagreb students went on strike in November 1971, Tito sacked the Croat leaders, banned Matica, and purged the Communist Party of nationalists (including Franjo

Tudjman, the future president of independent Croatia). The restoration of authority was a tribute to the respect owed to the 78-year-old Tito, as well as the real fear of civil war and foreign intervention. Tito's longer-term solution to the governance of Yugoslavia was the more confederal Constitution of 1974, which indicated that he was willing to allow decentralization so long as it was clear that separatism would not be tolerated. However, while buying time Tito was also stoking up the centrifugal pressures that would bring disaster to Yugoslavia after his death in 1980.

During the 1960s a number of states took advantage of Moscow's loosening grip on eastern Europe to win a greater degree of independence. The most extreme case was that of Albania, where the communist dictator Enver Hoxha, having fallen out with Tito and then Khrushchev, accepted Chinese patronage in 1961. Hoxha not only received Chinese aid, but also imitated Mao's cultural revolution in 1966–7 so that Albania became the most overtly atheistic of the socialist states. After the death of Mao in 1976, Hoxha in turn broke relations with China and pursued a policy of complete isolation. Albania had been too remote from China to become a complete satellite of Beijing, and too insignificant to be missed by the Warsaw Pact (which it had quit in 1968). Instead, under the leadership of Hoxha, who died in 1985, it evolved into a Stalinist backwater, both terrifying and pitiable in its poverty and autarkic backwardness.

A far more subtly independent policy was pursued by the Romanian Communist Party (RWP) under the leadership of Gheorge Gheorgu-Dej and, after his death in 1965, Nicolae Ceauşescu. Gheorgu-Dej had, during the 1950s, turned the RWP from a party dominated by Jews and other minorities into a party of young ethnic Romanians. The rights of the 1.5 million Hungarians in Transylvania were progressively curtailed (their Hungarian Autonomous Region was finally abolished in 1968), and Jewish emigration was encouraged. In 1958 Romania secured the withdrawal of Soviet troops from its territory. However, the real turning point was Gheorgu-Dej's successful defiance of Khrushchev in 1964 over Comecon integration. Thereafter Romania increasingly ploughed its own furrow: in 1967 it led the way in establishing diplomatic relations with West Germany and Israel (which had become a pariah in the Soviet bloc after the Six Day War). Ceauşescu banned Warsaw Pact exercises on Romanian territory and denounced the invasion of Czechoslovakia in 1968. He also cultivated an awareness of Romania's ancient "Dacian" heritage to emphasize its difference from other Slavic Warsaw Pact states. His independence from Moscow made him the darling of the West in the 1970s, earning him – as president after 1974 – numerous invitations for state visits and Most Favored Nation trading status for his country. But Ceauşescu was no liberal, and his "national communism" was intended primarily to legitimate communist rule by identifying it with Romanian national pride. He was careful not to push his criticism of the Soviet Union too far and, internally, was set to become a dictator whose ambition to remodel his country was on a par with Stalin's.

From Prague Spring to Brezhnev Doctrine

The Soviet-led crushing of the "Prague Spring" reform movement in August 1968 marked a turning-point in postwar eastern Europe. The crisis had its origins in the history of Czechoslovak Stalinism, which was curiously out of sync with that elsewhere in central and eastern Europe. A monstrous statue of Stalin was dedicated in Prague as late as 1955 (and dynamited in 1962), while the show trials started later and continued longer than under other regimes (lasting from 1949 to 1954). The principal victims were the Communist Party General Secretary Rudolf Slánský, who was executed, and the Slovak communist Gustav Husák, who was given a life sentence for "bourgeois nationalism." The new leader Antonín Novotný (who from 1957 held a dual role as General Secretary and president) presided over a slow and cagey retreat from Stalinism, abandoning his colleagues in order to divert attention from his own role in the terror. Husák was released from jail, and in 1963 the Supreme Court declared most of the show trial verdicts invalid. But this was not enough to prevent the emergence of a powerful coalition of forces for change in the mid-1960s, including reform communists, Slovaks (advocating a federal state), and economic reformers such as Ota Šik (the architect of the December 1966 market reforms). The pressure for change was underpinned by Czechoslovakia's very poor economic performance: indeed, the country was so badly affected by the recession of the early 1960s that the 1961–5 plan had to be abandoned in 1963. Beyond the ambit of the Communist Party, the mid-1960s also witnessed the emergence of a hippy (*manicky*) counterculture amongst students and others in Prague: precisely the groups who would be quick to press for greater freedom once the door to reform had been opened.

Lacking support from Moscow, Novotný was forced to stand down as party leader in January 1968 (and subsequently as president in March) and was replaced by the 46-year-old Slovak Alexander Dubček. Although Dubček's appointment was a trigger for change, he himself was, initially at least, a cautious and centrist figure. Over the next eight months he was increasingly torn between the popular demands for radical reform, on the one hand, and the fears of the USSR and other socialist neighbors on the other. It must be emphasized, however, that Dubček's goal was not to introduce a multi-party democracy, let alone restore capitalism, but rather to bury Stalinism and build mass support for Czechoslovak communism through a rectification of past mistakes. He was strangely naive in his belief that he would be allowed the freedom to pursue a reformist path so long as Czechoslovakia remained within the Warsaw Pact. He did not believe that a Soviet invasion would happen, and many years later concluded that "I do not see what I could or should have done otherwise ... we were bound by a valid alliance treaty, and Czechoslovakia was avoiding anything that might throw doubt on her loyalty."[35] Thus, the Communist Party's "Action Program" of April 5, 1968 sought to satisfy the USSR by pledging to maintain the party's "leading role" and loyalty to the Warsaw Pact while, at the same time, offering an end to censorship, federalism and a "socialist market." Dubček hailed the program as a "first step towards a new democratic model of Socialist society."[36]

Alarmingly for Moscow, the relaxation of censorship in Czechoslovakia on March 4, 1968 had produced a welter of public debate, pushed forward by the press and by nonparty organizations such as K231 (for those imprisoned in 1948). Many of the satellite parties of the National Front began to take a more independent stance, and there were even plans to reestablish an independent Social Democratic Party. On May Day the usually well-ordered march was peppered with irreverent slogans such as "Long live the USSR – but at its own expense." The widely endorsed "2,000 words" manifesto by the writer Ludvík Vaculík in June, which called on citizens to be ready to take up arms to defend reform against "foreign forces," was bitterly resented by the Soviet leaders. Dubček's decision to bring forward the date of the Czechoslovakian Communist Party's 14th congress to September 9 – which raised the prospect of his gaining a mandate for radical reform – in effect set the timetable for the Soviet invasion.

By the early summer, therefore, the USSR was seriously concerned about events in Czechoslovakia, which seemed dangerously reminiscent of those of 1956. The Kremlin was also under pressure from the Polish and East German leaders, Gomulka and Ulbricht, both of whom feared the spread of the Czech contagion to their own regimes. (In March, Polish students had been heard to chant that "Poland is awaiting its own Dubček."[37]) The Soviets too feared that the unrest would spill into the Ukraine and the Baltic states. In a series of Warsaw Pact meetings Dubček was, in effect, given an ultimatum to change course and restore political order. The Soviet leaders became convinced that he was weak and deceitful, and on August 6 the Politbureau agreed that there must be an invasion before the meeting of the 14th congress. Although there was no real evidence that Dubček had lost control, the Politbureau saw no reason to take a chance. On August 17 it voted unanimously to "provide assistance" to the Czechoslovak people to prevent the overthrow of socialism in their country. On August 20–21 Warsaw Pact forces (primarily composed of Red Army troops but with substantial military contingents from other states) swiftly overran Czechoslovakia. The Czech leaders condemned the invasion but instructed their forces not to resist. The Central Committee building was seized at gunpoint and Dubček and his colleagues arrested. Zdeněk Mlynář, watching from Dubček's office, was stunned by the thought that they were now threatened by "the same soldiers you welcomed and embraced joyfully on May 9, 1945, with whom you drank vodka …"[38]

Almost immediately, however, the Soviet plan began to break down. President Svoboda refused to swear in a new government of Czech hardliners who had been in secret communication with Moscow. Instead, he flew to Moscow on August 23 for direct negotiations with the Soviet leaders. His hand was strengthened by the extent of nonviolent resistance to the invasion, and by the convening, in secret, of the Communist Party congress on August 22. The congress called for Soviet withdrawal and elected an even more reform-minded Central Committee. On August 28 the Soviet leaders gave way and restored Dubček and his colleagues to office. However, under a secret protocol the Czech leaders agreed to dismantle the reforms, invalidate the congress, sack reformers such as Ota Šik, and allow Soviet troops to remain on a temporary basis. Dubček and Svoboda had won a pyrrhic victory as – while aiming to preserve something of the reforms – they had agreed to do Moscow's dirty work. The result was a slow unraveling of the achievements of the Prague Spring. Censorship was remorselessly reimposed, reformist leaders were – one by one – removed from office, and the universities purged of political opponents. Under the Moscow treaty of October 16 the Czechs conceded the right for Soviet troops to be stationed on their soil. An agreement on federation between Slovakia and the Czech lands, implemented in January 1969, provided the only lasting institutional legacy of 1968 but was a source of resentment to some Czechs, who felt that the Slovaks had sold them out.

The betrayal of reform by Dubček and the other senior leaders did not end resistance, but it broke its spirit. The self-immolation of the student Jan Palach in January 1969, calling for an end to censorship, was symptomatic of the despair that many now felt. Dubček himself was finally forced to resign following the March 21, 1969 anti-Soviet riots sparked by a Czech ice hockey victory over the USSR. His place was taken by Husák, the former political prisoner, who was accorded a degree of credibility by his bitter hostility to Novotný. In fact, Husák's regime was to be one of total subservience to Moscow and a return to Novotný-era authoritarianism. Leaders of the Prague Spring such as Dubček were expelled from the party (he was eventually consigned to work as a mechanic in the Slovak forestry administration), as were 250,000 ordinary members in 1970 alone. Husák's "normalization" was based on what the novelist Milan Kundera referred to as a "massacre of culture."[39] While there were no show trials or executions, many leading intellectuals were forced to recant, to take menial jobs, or to go into exile. Significantly, however, unlike Hungary in the 1960s, no political relaxation was possible, and the communist regime remained one of the harshest in eastern Europe. Instead, with the state's tacit approval, many Czechs quietly developed their own private sphere. By the early 1980s, for instance, some 31 percent of Prague householders owned a *chata* (weekend cottage).[40]

The Warsaw Pact invasion profoundly affected not only Czechoslovakia and the Soviet "bloc" but also world communism. Milovan Djilas's comment regarding the Hungarian revolution, that it inflicted a wound on communism which "can never be completely healed,"[41] is perhaps even more appropriate to the suppression of the Prague Spring. First, it was clear that no further ideological dissent or experimentation would be permitted within the Soviet bloc. Three months later the Soviet leader articulated the so-called "Brezhnev doctrine," according to which force could now be used when "forces hostile to socialism are threatening to turn a socialist country back to capitalism."[42] Secondly, the Prague Spring was a final attempt to reform communism from within, and to rescue the kernel of humanity and idealism from the husk of Stalinism. Thereafter, the new opposition movements of the 1970s and 1980s would seek to remove communism completely, using a new language of human rights, and had no illusions that it could be reformed. As the Polish opposition leader Jacek Kuroń commented in 1980, there was no point in dreaming of a future socialist utopia when "what we have here *is* Socialism."[43] Kuroń's insight was mirrored by the somewhat defensive self-description of the Soviet bloc in the 1970s as "actually existing socialism." Finally, the invasion was deeply shocking to many west European communists. It brought Soviet relations with the Italian Communist Party (PCI) to breaking point and set the PCI on the road to "Eurocommunism" (accepting the Western model of democracy). However, as the exiled Hungarian writer François Fejtő observed with remarkable prescience in 1969, there was one glimmer of hope: "that the next Dubček will emerge in the nerve centre of the system: Moscow."[44] Indeed, Mikhail Gorbachev, who had become a friend of Zdeněk Mlynář as a student at Moscow University and was in many respects the true heir of reform communism and the Prague Spring, represented the nemesis for Brezhnevite communism.

Conclusion

The Soviet Union underwent considerable political change in the decades following the death of Stalin, and faced repeated challenges to its authority in eastern Europe. Khrushchev's principal achievement was to break with Stalinist terror; Brezhnev brought a new stability to Soviet life, which eventually turned into stagnation. In international relations, Khrushchev relied unduly on bluff and bluster, but his successor was able to establish military parity with the United States. Both men were willing to sanction the use of force to maintain control in eastern Europe, in Hungary (1956) and Czechoslovakia (1968). However, the restoration of authority in these countries proved progressively more difficult. A number of regimes in the region were able to increase their freedom of action during this period, although none went so far as Yugoslavia. Both in the USSR and the "People's Democracies" communist rule represented an alternative path towards modernity to that pursued in the West, and distinctive new societies and cultures were emerging that were more than a pale and warped reflection of the West.

7

Western Europe
in the 1970s
Downturn and Détente

The Era of Détente

Although the Berlin crisis of 1958–61 had drawn the sting from the Cold War in
Europe, East–West relations remained deep frozen until the late 1960s. Change
was facilitated both by shifts in the global balance of power and by the determination
of European politicians (notably Willy Brandt) to ease tensions at the regional
level. The resulting process of engagement became known as "détente" (or
"relaxation"), but was characterized by distrust not only between the USA and the
USSR but also between the superpowers and their European allies. For all of the
benefits that it brought, détente was at best a strategic pause within a Cold War
that both sides still believed that they could win.

Superpower détente had three principal roots. First, under Brezhnev the USSR
had gained a rough nuclear parity with the USA, so that the Soviets could now
claim, in the words of Foreign Minister Gromyko, that no international problem
could be resolved without the participation of the Soviet Union.[1] While many in
the USA were dismayed by the loss of military preponderance, Henry Kissinger
(National Security Adviser and subsequently Secretary of State, 1969–77) believed
that there was an opportunity for creating a new international equilibrium.
Secondly, the United States had been seriously weakened by its costly involvement
(and looming defeat) in Vietnam. Its influence in the Third World had been greatly
reduced, while that of the USSR had correspondingly grown, and Vietnam had
taken some of the warmth out of relations between the USA and its European
allies. Thirdly, the Soviet Union had been engaged in border skirmishes with China
during 1969 and feared the prospect of conflict on both its European and Asian
fronts. These fears were amplified by Nixon's bold decision to visit Beijing in
February 1972. Détente therefore offered rewards for both sides. From a Soviet

Europe's Troubled Peace: 1945 to the Present, Second Edition. Tom Buchanan.
© 2012 John Wiley & Sons, Ltd. Published 2012 by John Wiley & Sons, Ltd.

perspective, it would help to contain China and might drive a wedge between the USA and western Europe. The Soviets also saw no incompatibility between détente and the expansion of their ideological influence in the Third World. For the USA, détente offered a way to manage superpower relations during a time of relative international weakness and internal disharmony which was soon to be compounded by the Watergate scandal.

The major achievement of superpower détente was SALT (the Strategic Arms Limitation Treaty), signed by Nixon and Brezhnev at the Moscow summit of May 1972. The treaty acknowledged the "strategic equivalence" between the powers and set out clear limits to their nuclear arsenals as well as (in an associated treaty) their anti-ballistic missile systems. SALT (in tandem with Brandt's diplomatic successes) undoubtedly created a new sense of international understanding, although it also posed again de Gaulle's awkward question about how far the United States would go to defend western Europe. Thereafter, however, the returns started to diminish and suspicions mounted on both sides. The Soviet Union was aggrieved when the United States excluded it from any role in the October 1973 Arab–Israeli war, dashing its aspirations for parity. For the United States' part, after Nixon's resignation in 1974 US administrations became increasingly convinced that détente was merely a cloak for Soviet ambitions in the Third World (notably in the former Portuguese colonies of Angola and Mozambique). The SALT 2 treaty, signed by President Jimmy Carter in June 1979, was bitterly attacked in Congress and was never ratified.

Détente continued to make progress at the European level, although the Soviet gains were more problematic than appeared at first sight. In the absence of a formal peace treaty after World War II, the USSR had long demanded that the West should accept the postwar territorial status quo. This was conceded in the final act of the Conference on Security and Cooperation in Europe (CSCE) signed in Helsinki by thirty-five states (including the USA) on August 1, 1975. Although the Helsinki Accords appeared to have confirmed the existing borders, "Basket III" (which dealt with human rights issues) opened the Soviet bloc to unprecedented criticism and scrutiny. Even prior to Helsinki, the West had increasingly exploited the USSR's vulnerability over human rights. For instance, the commercial agreements signed during the 1972 Moscow summit had been abandoned when the US Congress linked them to progress on Jewish emigration from the Soviet Union. There was also at this time a discernible shift amongst west European intellectuals towards greater criticism of Soviet human rights abuses. In France, in particular, the exile of the Nobel prize-winning novelist Alexander Solzhenitsyn in 1974 and the publication of his *The Gulag Archipelago* in French translation proved influential. The particular significance of Helsinki, however, was that the communist regimes had very publicly agreed to observe norms of conduct that clearly differed from those that they practiced, and this provided an opening for small groups of oppositionists in the USSR and eastern Europe. The most significant of these was the Czechoslovakian "Charter 77," launched in

January 1977, which welcomed the Helsinki Accords but noted that these "basic rights in our country exist, regrettably, on paper only."[2] Although it remained a small organization primarily of Czech intellectuals, Charter 77 provided a vital link between the surviving reform communists and a wider opposition that rejected Soviet-style communism outright. Even so, the costs were high: of the leaders, Václav Havel spent some four years in jail (1979–83), while Jan Patočka died as a result of his mistreatment in prison.

From a US perspective détente ended in December 1979 when Soviet troops invaded Afghanistan and Carter imposed sanctions on the USSR. Whatever understanding may have existed between the superpowers collapsed in a welter of misperception: where the United States saw an act of Soviet imperialism, the USSR saw itself as containing dangerous instability in its own backyard. If the Soviets had hoped to weaken US leadership in Europe through détente, however, the European response to Carter's call for sanctions showed that they may have succeeded. Brandt's successor Helmut Schmidt had no intention of renouncing the new economic and cultural links with the East at Carter's behest. The French Foreign Minister said that it would be "enormous stupidity" to relinquish the gains of détente, and President Giscard d'Estaing accepted an invitation to visit the Kremlin in May 1980.[3] Clearly European and American interests had diverged during the 1970s, but this uncooperative attitude also reflected European exasperation with Carter's indecision and moralizing. However, the point should not be pushed too far as on December 12, 1979, immediately prior to the Soviet invasion, NATO had taken the momentous decision to install American Cruise and Pershing missiles in Europe as a riposte to the Soviet deployment of medium-range SS-20 missiles. Significantly, this "twin-track" decision (so called as the threat of deployment was intended to encourage Soviet arms reductions) had been taken in response to pressure from west European governments (many of them center-left) desperate for reassurance that the USA remained committed to their defense.

Willy Brandt's *Ostpolitik*, 1969–1974

The *Ostpolitik* ("eastern policy") by which West Germany's new Chancellor sought to improve the Federal Republic's relations with its eastern neighbors was closely connected with détente but also quite distinct from it. While it suited both super-powers to see progress towards improved relations between the two Germanies, both were concerned that the process might run out of control, with potentially destabilizing consequences. The main impetus came from Willy Brandt, perhaps the most intriguing statesman produced by postwar Europe and a man uniquely suited to this complex mission. Brandt was by origin a left-wing socialist who had fled to Norway when the Nazis came to power (and thence to neutral Sweden in 1940). His anti-Nazi credentials gave him great moral stature outside Germany, while his years as mayor of West Berlin, and above all his determination to engage with the East after the construction of the Berlin Wall, provided him with an unequalled experience in this sphere. However, the fact that he had taken Swedish citizenship, and that "Willy Brandt" was in fact a pseudonym for a man born as Herbert Frahm, was often held against him by his domestic critics.

Brandt did not face an easy task as, in addition to conducting a very difficult negotiation, he also had to deal with entrenched opposition on his own side. He eschewed the conservative-minded Foreign Office and preferred to work through Egon Bahr, his close colleague from Berlin days. West Germany was bitterly divided over *Ostpolitik*, and many feared that Brandt would give away too much in the pursuit of reconciliation. To take one graphic example, when Brandt visited Warsaw to sign the treaty with Poland, he famously knelt in homage at the site of the ghetto that had been liquidated by German troops in 1943. He later recalled that his action was spontaneous: "From the bottom of the abyss of German history, under the burden of millions of victims of murder, I did what human beings do when speech fails them." However, in Germany a poll showed that only 41 percent deemed his action "appropriate," and 54 percent of 30–60-year-olds rejected it.[4] (Meanwhile, some Poles muttered that he had not knelt at the tomb of their Unknown Soldier.) His diplomacy was also severely tested when, much to the embarrassment of the Stasi, Brandt was greeted by rapturous crowds during his historic visit to East Germany in March 1970. He did his best to calm the mood, realizing that *Ostpolitik* could offer no instant liberation and that there was nothing to be gained in needlessly embarrassing his hosts.

Brandt was fortunate that by 1969 Moscow was ready to negotiate, its confidence bolstered by the suppression of the Prague Spring, and hopeful that rapprochement with the West would bring economic benefits. The result was the Moscow Treaty of August 1970 under which West Germany recognized the existing borders in eastern Europe – implicitly accepting the existence of East Germany and the loss of German territory to Poland. However, the Soviets allowed the Federal Republic to issue an accompanying letter in which it reserved the right to work for the peaceful unification of Germany. In a television broadcast from Moscow, Brandt denied that anything had been lost "that had not long since been gambled away [by Hitler]," and confirmed that the "results of history" must stand. He urged West Germans to cease dwelling on the events of the past and to "found our relationship with the East anew" on the basis of present realities.[5] The Moscow Treaty opened the way to a hectic round of diplomacy, and treaties were concluded with Poland (in December 1970), and with Bulgaria, Hungary, and Czechoslovakia (all in 1973). The new warmth in relations with the Soviet Union soon brought economic benefits as well. Between 1969 and 1979 West German trade with the USSR increased sixfold, and the USSR became a major supplier of natural gas.

Attention now shifted to the question of relations between the two Germanies and the future of Berlin (which was still in the hands of the wartime Allied powers) (see Figure 7.1). Therefore the tortuous negotiations between the East and West

Figure 7.1   The prime minister of the DDR, Willi Stoph, meets Chancellor Willy Brandt at Erfurt railway station, March 1970. Photo © akg-images.

Germany (again handled by Bahr) were intimately connected with the four-power talks on the status of Berlin. The resulting September 1971 Quadripartite Agreement accepted the status quo in Berlin and proposed that there should be guaranteed land access to West Berlin. The details were finalized by the two German governments in the December 1971 transit accords and the May 1972 treaty governing traffic between the two states. While the status quo was hardly satisfactory, the agreements increased the security of West Berlin and meant that the life of its citizens became progressively more "normal." The agreements also enhanced contacts across the divided city not only at the level of telephone calls but also, increasingly, of day visits.

In negotiating the formal treaty between the two Germanies, the wording was everything. The East Germans were desperate for international recognition and legitimacy, but adamant that they represented not only a separate state but also a separate nation. The negotiations were played out against mounting political polarization in West Germany, and in April 1972 the CDU/CSU opposition came very close to defeating Brandt on a "constructive vote of no confidence." However, the Chancellor's nerve held and in November 1972, having precipitated an election, he won a clear mandate for *Ostpolitik*. For the first time, by 45.9 percent to 44.8 percent, the SPD took a greater share of the vote than the Christian Democrats. In December 1972 the "Basic Treaty" was signed whereby the two German states mutually recognized each other's existence. The treaty was largely of symbolic value, but made progress possible on a range of issues: the two Germanies both became members of the United Nations in September 1973, and they exchanged "permanent representatives" (in other words, ambassadors) in May 1974. Soon afterwards, Brandt fell victim to a spy scandal when it was revealed that his close aide of the previous two years, Günter Guillaume, was an East German agent. However, neither his social democratic successor Helmut Schmidt (1974–82) nor the more conservative Helmut Kohl (1982–98) departed from the principles of his *Ostpolitik* (although Kohl was more willing to toy with German nationalism). Indeed, in 1983 the Bavarian right-winger Franz-Josef Strauss, a bitter opponent of Brandt in 1972, negotiated a massive loan that propped up the ailing East German economy.

With hindsight, there is little doubt that *Ostpolitik* was a necessary and logical – but also courageous – break with the legacy of Adenauer. It greatly enhanced the security of central Europe and did much to improve the life of ordinary East Germans, while also giving new international confidence and stature to West Germany. However, the relationship with the rulers of East Germany was morally ambiguous and has remained highly controversial. *Ostpolitik* had set out to challenge the status quo but increasingly seemed to defend it. So much had been invested in the relationship with the East German government (and other east European regimes) that West German politicians came to fear instability. Perhaps the most disturbing moment came in December 1981 when Helmut Schmidt, who was visiting East Germany at the time, initially refused to condemn the Polish authorities' declaration of martial law and merely regretted that it had "now proved necessary."[6] The one eventuality which the proponents of *Ostpolitik* had not bargained for (and which they even feared) was that the people of eastern Europe might have an active role to play in the destruction of communist rule.

The New Economic Insecurity

Europe's enhanced sense of security during the 1970s was accompanied, paradoxically, by a new economic insecurity. As a result of the October 1973 Arab–Israeli war, the Organization of Petroleum Exporting Countries (OPEC) imposed an eventual 400 percent increase in the price of crude oil and placed a temporary embargo on states that supported Israel (such as the USA, Portugal, and the Netherlands). The ensuing panic in the import-dependent states of western Europe highlighted the lack of any coordinated response and triggered a recession in 1973–5. Even in Europe's strongest economy, West Germany, unemployment rose to more than 1 million (4.1 percent) in 1975 and there was no return to the very high rates of growth achieved before 1973. The situation was far worse in weaker economies such as those of Italy and Britain. In Britain inflation peaked at

26.9 percent in August 1975, and by 1977 unemployment stood at 1.5 million. Italy, which relied on oil for 75 percent of its energy in 1973, recorded an average of 15 percent per annum inflation during the 1970s. The steady rise in official Italian unemployment figures was only offset by a burgeoning black economy. France, which maintained one of the higher rates of economic growth in western Europe during the 1970s (2.3 percent per annum), suffered latterly from persistent unemployment (1.5 million) and inflation (of around 10 percent). Talk of a "golden age" of postwar economic success gave way after 1973 to a pessimistic and morbid language of "malaise" and "disease."

The 1973 oil shock sent a stark message that the economic buoyancy of the previous two decades was at an end, and had important public policy implications (such as stimulating investment in nuclear power and warmer relations with the Arab world, as well as accelerating the exploitation of North Sea oil and gas). However, it was by no means the sole cause of the new uncertainty. Just as significant was the weakening US economy, which by 1971 was running a substantial trade deficit under the heavy cost of the Vietnam War. The Nixon administration was far more disposed than its predecessors to see western Europe as an economic rival and to act unilaterally in defense of its own interests. Nixon is reputed to have said "We'll fix those bastards," and under the Nixon–Connally measures of August 1971 did just that: the convertibility of the dollar was suspended and a temporary 10 percent surtax imposed on imports.[7] The fixed exchange rates of the Bretton Woods era gave way to flexible bands on both sides of the Atlantic (such as the European "snake") and a preference for floating currencies to boost exports, even at the cost of inflation.

The problems of the 1970s also had their roots within Europe. The labor unrest of the late 1960s had required generous pay settlements and had strengthened the trade unions, while in Italy wage indexation tied the government's hands. The labor militancy of 1968–9 continued into the new decade, which was marked in some countries by highly conflictual industrial relations. Britain was embarking on more than a decade of labor unrest bracketed by coal miners' strikes in 1972 and 1984–5. Governments also had to bear the cost of social reform and the expansion of the welfare state: public expenditure rose from 38 percent of gross domestic product in 1967–9 to 46 percent in 1974–6.[8] In addition, both Europe and the USA were confronted with rising competition from Japan and other Asian economies. The Japanese economy overtook those of both Britain and West Germany in the 1960s, and Japan was now presenting a formidable challenge in the automobile and electronics markets. By contrast, many west European industries seemed uncompetitive and willing to shelter behind protection and state subsidies. Governments' industrial policy, intended to "pick winners" and promote "national champions," lapsed all too easily into the propping up of ailing industries to preserve jobs.

The mainly center-left governments of western Europe responded to the recession of the mid-1970s with classic Keynesian measures – increasing government expenditure to boost demand – but they no longer seemed to work. Governments were confronted with the new phenomenon of "stagflation" whereby, instead of being able to trade off inflation for unemployment, levels of both rose. Expans ionary measures had boosted wages without increasing productivity. Government policy was heavily influenced by the belief that high levels of unemployment were politically unacceptable. For instance, the prospect of 1 million unemployed forced a policy "U-turn" on Edward Heath's Conservative government in 1972, and he later insisted that "no government could exist on any other terms" than the pursuit of full employment.[9] This wisdom was already being questioned by monetarist economists such as Milton Friedman, who argued that the taming of inflation through control of the money supply should be governments' top priority. However, the monetarists' prescriptions proved to be far more influential (and even then in Britain more than in continental Europe) in the 1980s.

Not all European economies performed poorly in the 1970s, and those that rode out the storm most effectively were those with a strong corporatist framework. In West Germany, for instance, the social democrat government (supported strongly by the Bundesbank) emphasized the need to control inflation, and received support from trade unions that were willing to moderate their demands in return for longer-term benefits. Accordingly, the Federal Republic maintained its export-led competitiveness and, after the blip of 1974–5, staved off unemployment until the early 1980s when it was very hard hit by the second OPEC price rise of 1979. This "Modell Deutschland"[10] was attractive to politicians such as Raymond Barre (prime minister of France, 1976–81) but proved very difficult to replicate: nowhere else did the memory of the 1920s ensure such strong public aversion to inflation. In Sweden and Austria, too, unemployment was kept at bay. Although the Swedish socialists lost power in 1976, their policies of binding wage bargaining combined with heavy taxation to fund a generous welfare state and emergency job creation schemes remained in place. Likewise in Austria, where the socialists were in power from 1971, the highly sophisticated social partnerships between government, employers and unions ensured economic stability.

In spite of these successes, and although even in the worst-hit economies there was no return to the misery of the 1930s, it was evident that the assumptions underpinning the postwar boom – such as the availability of cheap fossil fuels and labor, international economic stability, and social harmony – had been under-mined. Politicians now surveyed a changed economic landscape. Many of the tensions of the 1960s had, after all, been those of growth and optimism: students who felt that they did not have to prepare immediately for the world of work; workers who struggled for greater dignity in the workplace as well as a greater material rewards; and welfare states paid for out of endlessly expanding economies. The new mood was neatly captured by the Labour Party politician Tony Crosland's famous comment, "The party's over."[11] Indeed, political economy after 1973 was to be dominated by stubborn levels of unemployment and inflation, the attempt to reconcile conflicting claims to limited resources, and a new questioning of the role of the state. The response to the downturn of the 1970s was particularly depressing for the advocates of European integration (see Chapter 9) as EEC member states had clearly preferred economic nationalism to the prospect of a coordinated recovery. Nontariff barriers and other forms of state subsidy proliferated, while intra-European trade languished, and plans for further integration (such as monetary union) now seemed ludicrously ambitious.

West European Politics

Social democratic and reformist governments finally received their chance in a number of countries in the 1970s, although, as we have seen, in the least propitious of circumstances. The widespread public expectation of reform was sustained by the continuation of the social and political activism of the late 1960s. At the same time, politicians were buffeted by the world economy and the failure of the established tools of economic management. Even so, the center-left's electoral record was a good one. The German social democrats led coalition governments with the FDP from 1969 to 1982, while the British Labour Party held office, if increasingly perilously, between 1974 and 1979. In Austria and Sweden socialist governments were dominated by the larger-than-life personalities of Bruno Kreisky and Olof Palme, both of whom claimed an international role far beyond the weight of their respective countries. The Italian communists made sweeping advances in the city and regional elections of June 1975, and between 1976 and 1978 stood on the threshold of national power, forcing the Christian Democrats into a new burst of reformist energy. Even when the left was not actually in power, as in France, it strengthened its position. A new Socialist Party (PS) was launched in 1971 under the leadership of François Mitterrand, successfully combining the remnants of the old SFIO with newer leftist currents of the 1960s. Although the PS suffered electoral reverses in 1974 and 1978, progress could at last be made towards achieving Mitterrand's vision of a "large hegemonic Socialist Party which, in order to govern, will soon be supported by centrists and communists."[12]

Far more so than in the past, politicians had to respond to a range of pressures that went beyond party politics or well-established interest groups. The explosion of direct action in the late 1960s had carried over into a richer and more sustained popular politics in the early 1970s. The British government was eventually forced to bail out the Upper Clyde Shipbuilders yard following a work-in which started in the summer of 1971, and the French government was put under similar pressure by a widely supported occupation of the Lip watchmaking factory in 1973. A 1971 confrontation between French farmers and the army over the future of the Largac massif turned into a decade-long *cause célèbre* for ecologists, Maoists, and others on the left. In Italy large-scale collective protest continued well into the 1970s, and new tactics emerged such as *autoriduzione* (mass refusal to pay higher service charges). The Italian student unrest of 1977 was strongly reminiscent of that of the 1960s, egged on by leftist professors such as Antonio Negri. In West Germany the campaign by local "citizens' initiatives" against nuclear power marked the rejection by many young people of Helmut Schmidt's SPD and fostered the emergence of the Green Party.

One hallmark of the politics of the 1970s was the decentralization of power. This was clearly a response to the conflicts of the previous decade, and a recognition by politicians of left and right of the need to reduce the gap between governments and governed. On his election in 1969 Willy Brandt had promised Germans that "we do not stand at the end of our democracy, we are only just beginning,"[13] while the Gaullist Jacques Chaban-Delmas (prime minister of France, 1969–72) proposed a "New Society" of greater democratic openness. Valéry Giscard d'Estaing, French president from 1974 to 1981, believed that France should be "governed from the centre"[14] but initially at least posed as a liberalizer. One very obvious concession to youth was the reduction of the voting age to 18 in both France and West Germany. In Italy decentralization took the form of the creation of a new tier of elected regional authorities and the institution of the right to call a referendum (following the collection of 500,000 signatures). In France, Giscard d'Estaing went some way to liberalizing the broadcast media, which under de Gaulle had been little more than the mouthpiece of the state, by dismantling the ORTF (Office de la Radio et de la Télévision Française) and abolishing the Ministry of Information. However, his main political reform backfired when the 1977 election for the restored office of mayor of Paris was won by his bitter rival (and former prime minister) Jacques Chirac. Many governments discussed ideas for "industrial democracy," and in West Germany co-determination was extended in 1976 to all firms with more than 2,000 employees. Scottish and Welsh nationalist parties made a political breakthrough in the British elections of 1974 and forced a fading Labour government to grant (unsuccessful) referenda on the devolution of power in March 1979.[15]

The new feminism of the 1970s, a particularly influential factor in social reform, owed much to the militancy of the late 1960s while, at the same time, representing a critique of it. Women's liberation movements such as those in Britain and France adopted the diverse, nonhierarchical mode of organization of "1968," but rejected the macho heroics of many of its leaders. Feminists, who felt that the "liberation" of the 1960s had merely made women more available for the fulfillment of male desires, now wanted to rewrite the political agenda. Alongside the completion of more traditional demands such as legal and workplace equality, they placed a new emphasis on the personal and the need to prefigure change in daily life. Clearly, the pressure for action on women's rights came not only from feminist organizations but also from far broader social trends, such as women's growing role in the trade unions and the continuing increase in female graduates. Even so, feminist campaigning undoubtedly played a central role in promoting politically sensitive issues such as abortion (often in league with concerned doctors and other professionals). In France the publication of a manifesto in April 1971 signed by 343 prominent women who admitted to having had an illegal abortion galvanized debate. A limited legalization of abortion was eventually passed in 1975, and needed the support of the opposition when only 99 out of 314 deputies of Giscard d'Estaing's majority supported it. In Italy 800,000 signatures were collected for a referendum on abortion, but the politicians preferred to pass a compromise measure in 1978 (under which some two-thirds of doctors exercised their right not to practice abortion). This limited reform was confirmed by referendum in 1981, when 67.9 percent voted against a Catholic proposal to restrict abortion to cases when the woman's life was in danger. The abortion issue also played a central role in the emergent German feminist movement, although the 1974 reforms were initially blocked by the Constitutional Court.

If this can be seen as a decade of reform, however, reformism was clearly running out of steam by the late 1970s as political pressures abated and belt-tightening reduced the scope for largesse. Helmut Schmidt was a very able political and economic manager, but he lacked Brandt's commitment to democratization or his appeal to the young. Giscard d'Estaing's liberalizing zeal soon faded, and he was mocked for his failure to abolish a death penalty which he personally abhorred. Under his second prime minister, the acerbic Raymond Barre, his government became associated with politically damaging austerity. The Labour governments under Harold Wilson (1974–6) and James Callaghan (1976–9) were preoccupied with Britain's economic crisis, and at one point even had to seek a loan from the IMF. Under Callaghan, Keynesianism was abandoned in favor of proto-monetarist deflation, with some initial success. However, the attempt to hold down public-sector pay increases brought on a fatal bout of industrial unrest in early 1979 (the so-called "Winter of Discontent") which contributed to Labour's heavy election defeat in May 1979.

Although the west European communist parties did not taste power in the 1970s this was a decade of some optimism for them, albeit one that ended in disappointment. After their vocal – if often hedged – criticism of the suppression of the Prague Spring, communists felt increasingly free to chart their own ("Eurocommunist") course. The communist parties of Italy, France, and Spain finally recognized what had long been self-evident: that they were no longer revolutionary organizations and were committed to the defense of parliamentary democracy. This was taken furthest in Italy, where the PCI's new leader Enrico Berlinguer launched the idea of a "historic compromise" between communism and Christian Democracy in 1973, and even accepted Italy's place in NATO. Communist electoral success in June 1976 resulted in a government of "national solidarity" between 1976 and 1979, whereby the communists offered parliamentary support to a reformist Christian Democratic government. However, the anticipated political benefits failed to materialize, and Berlinguer's strategy turned the socialists, under the thrusting leadership of Bettino Craxi, into determined adversaries. Eurocommunism enjoyed far less purchase in France, where the Communist Party held on to 20 percent of the vote and a membership of 500,000.

The party's dogmatic leader Georges Marchais, still very much in thrall to the Soviet Union, missed numerous opportunities for political renewal and became alarmed at the rise of François Mitterrand's socialists. In an astonishing fit of pique, the communists preferred to break up their alliance with the socialists (1972–7) rather than see Mitterrand lead a united left to victory in the 1978 parliamentary elections. Such crude thinking could not stave off the PCF's political irrelevancy for long. The Spanish and Portuguese communists, who might well have expected to be rewarded by voters for their long-standing opposition to dictatorship, were likewise marginalized during the transition to democracy by socialist parties that carried less visible baggage from the past.

This was a very difficult decade for the Christian democratic parties of the center-right. The Italian DC vote was lodged at just over 38 percent during the 1970s, and in 1976 stood only 4 percent ahead of the communists. The DC only remained in power because a communist government was still unimaginable (and specifically ruled out by the United States). In France the center-right was rendered increasingly vulnerable by the division between the heirs of de Gaulle and Giscard d'Estaing's more liberal centrism. By 1978 this had been consolidated into two ill-matched political parties, the neo-Gaullist Rassemblement pour la République and Giscard's Union de Démocratie Français. The loss of four elections in a row by the West German CDU/CSU (1969, 1972, 1976, and 1980) was a bitter experience for Adenauer's successors, although after Brandt's triumph in 1972 the Christian Democrats at least regained their position as West Germany's most popular party. In the late 1970s they also had to contend with Franz Josef Strauss's threat to take his CSU out of the coalition, although this receded when Strauss was defeated as CDU/CSU candidate for Chancellor in the bitterly fought 1980 election. The Austrian People's Party was excluded from power by the socialists between 1970 and 1987 and cast around with increasing desperation for a vote-winning political identity. In Belgium the Christian Democrats split in 1968 into separate Flemish and Francophone parties, and during the 1970s lost voters to regional rivals and even to the socialists. The travails of Christian Democracy also reflected wider political changes. Most notably, there was abundant evidence of the declining power of religion as a mobilizing force in politics and of the widening gulf between public attitudes and traditional Christian morality. For instance, the Italian referendum on divorce of May 1974, which had been called by Catholics, resulted in the unequivocal endorsement of the December 1970 reform (by 60 percent to 40 percent) and a heavy defeat for the Christian Democrats. An intervention by the Catholic bishops in the West German election of 1980, on the issues of divorce and abortion, failed to save Strauss. Long years in office had also left Christian Democracy organizationally weak. For instance, Helmut Kohl's victories of the 1980s owed much to his ability to restore the CDU after becoming its National Secretary in 1973 (between 1969 and 1980, CDU membership rose from 304,000 to 694,000).[16]

The problems of the center-right during the 1970s were even more palpable in Britain, where Edward Heath's Conservatives had surprisingly won office in June 1970.

The Conservative leadership's pre-election conference at Selsdon Park had given rise to the misapprehension (popular among many Tory activists) that this would be a right-wing government intent on ending postwar state interventionism. Such hopes were soon dashed as Heath prioritized growth and jobs (even nationalizing the ailing Rolls Royce company). In 1972 he introduced a statutory prices and incomes policy that he had specifically ruled out in the election campaign: one of many "U-turns" later held against him by his critics. Heath achieved one major success in negotiating Britain's entry to the EEC in January 1973, but his government collapsed in 1973/4 amidst a mounting sense of national crisis brought on by industrial conflict and the oil shocks. In February 1974 Heath called and narrowly lost an election, having appealed for public support in his battle with the unions. His ill-fated administration became a paradigm on the Tory right of how not to govern, and fuelled a backlash against the postwar settlement in all its forms. The principal beneficiary was Heath's former Education Minister Margaret Thatcher, who challenged him successfully for the party leadership in early 1975. The Conservative Party was reborn under Thatcher as a uniquely British blend of middle-class fears and working-class aspirations, and there was no equivalent in European Christian Democracy to the anti-socialist populism that swept her to power in 1979. If anything, a closer analogue was the Danish Progress Party, which won over 15 percent of the vote on an anti-tax and anti-bureaucracy platform in 1973.

The Rise of Terrorism, c. 1970–1981

Political violence reached levels during the 1970s, which, with the exception of France, had not been seen in western Europe since before the war. More than 400 people died during Italy's "Years of Lead," while the "Troubles" in the British province of Northern Ireland claimed some 2,000 lives between 1969 and 1980. The violence was particularly associated with Marxist groups such as the West German "Red Army Faction" (RAF, also known as the "Baader–Meinhof gang") and the Italian "Red Brigades," although it by no means came exclusively from the left. In Italy, for instance, the far right's "strategy of tension" was intended to destabilize society through indiscriminate violence, and possibly to provoke an authoritarian takeover. As the decade progressed, increasingly sophisticated terrorist groups demonstrated their ability to strike at the heart of the establishment, such as in the kidnap and murder of the leading Italian politician Aldo Moro (1978) and of the German industrialist Hanns Martin Schleyer (1977), and the killing of Lord Louis Mountbatten by the IRA in 1979. Such attacks could be highly politically effective. The assassination of Franco's right-hand man Luis Carrero Blanco by ETA in December 1973 helped to smooth the transition to democracy after the dictator's death (although ETA would, in turn, torment Spain's democratic governments).

Terrorism also brought a new vulnerability to the daily life of ordinary citizens. Twenty-three died when the IRA bombed a Birmingham pub in 1974, the Italian fascist bomb at Bologna station in August 1980 left 85 dead, and a bomb (also planted by the far right) at the September 1980 Munich Oktoberfest killed 12.

The terrorist groups were often by no means isolated from society. A poll of July 1971 showed that 25 percent of West Germans under 30 admitted to a "certain sympathy" for the RAF. As many as one in 20 said that they would be willing to offer them shelter overnight, and the figure was far higher in northern Germany.[17] A number of prominent German intellectuals, while by no means endorsing violence, felt concern that the state's anti-terrorist campaign might sap the fragile underpinnings of the liberal society. Thus, in Heinrich Böll's novel *The Lost Honour of Katherina Blum* (1974), the life of a woman innocently involved with a terrorist is destroyed by the ruthlessness of the police and mass-circulation press. During the Moro kidnapping the novelist Leonardo Sciascia stated publicly that he could take no side between the terrorists and a corrupt Christian Democrat state.[18] Both Irish and Basque radical nationalism succeeded in building significant electoral support, as witnessed by the success achieved by their political wings in the early 1980s. Herri Batasuna won 16.5 percent in the vote for the first autonomous Basque parliament in March 1980, and Sinn Fein became a significant presence in Ulster politics during the 1980s. In 1981 the IRA hunger striker Bobby Sands was elected from jail as a Member of Parliament and in the UK elections of 1983 Sinn Fein won 13.4 percent of the vote in Northern Ireland.

There was no single root cause for this upsurge in violence. Clearly the IRA and ETA were forged in the very specific grievances of the Basques and of the Catholic population of Northern Ireland. The IRA's gunmen, for instance, were only able to reestablish themselves within the Catholic/Nationalist community because the peaceful civil rights movement of the 1960s was violently blocked by the Unionist/Protestant majority. However, in most cases one can discern a trajectory from the political activism of the late 1960s to the hardened, violent attitudes of a minority in the 1970s. This is not to argue that political violence was the inevitable consequence of 1960s radicalism, but rather that it was one of the many paths that led on from it. The Italian Red Brigades were created by former student radicals who went from nonviolent solidarity with the working class to increasingly violent activity in its name. The medium was a highly politicized culture within which violence seemed justified against a "fascist" Italian state allegedly sheltering behind a mask of democracy. In the words of one repentant leader, they had been "addicts of ideology. A fatal drug."[19] Violence was also encouraged by a number of contingent factors, such as the rise of terrorism in the Middle East and the new availability of powerful and compact guns and explosives. In 1970 the core of the RAF received rather farcical training from the PLO/Fatah in Jordan, and they also obtained assistance from the East German authorities. Another factor was the unpreparedness and the political ineptness of governments. The IRA was greatly boosted by the British government's introduction of internment in 1971 (which alienated even moderate Catholics), while the West German decree of January 1972 that excluded all those deemed to be "extremists" from jobs in public service was a gross overreaction.

Eventually, of course, the authorities gained the upper hand. The British government was able to contain the Northern Ireland conflict within, in the words of one government minister, an "acceptable level of violence," by mounting an extensive counter-insurgency operation. Indeed, by 1972 there were more than 20,000 troops in the province. However, a political solution proved elusive so long as the extremists on both sides chose to oppose it, and a power-sharing agreement that restored devolved government to the province in 1973 was wrecked a year later by a Unionist strike. In both Italy and West Germany governments adopted a policy of firmness, although the Moro kidnapping (March–May 1978) was a terrible ordeal for members of the Christian Democratic establishment, many of whom had enjoyed Moro's patronage. Under a new Italian anti-terror law in 1979, bail was all but abolished for terror suspects, and from 1981 mass trials were mounted of members of the Red Brigades. Opinion was already shifting against the Brigades as a result of Moro's murder, and when a communist factory worker was assassinated in Genoa in January 1979 more than 200,000 workers demonstrated their opposition. In West Germany the government won approval from the *Länder* for the unprecedented centralization of policing, and most of the leaders of the Baader–Meinhof gang had been captured by 1974. Even from jail, however, they were able to harass the state during a trial that lasted almost two years. In October 1977, following a failed hijacking by Palestinian sympathizers, Baader and two others died in a suicide pact at Stammheim prison. Although the IRA and ETA campaigns were far from over, indigenous terrorism, and the nihilistic radicalism that had nurtured it, was less of a central issue during the 1980s.

Intellectual and Cultural Developments

In culture as in politics, the radicalism of the late 1960s and early 1970s began to lose its dominant position in the course of the decade. This trend was most pronounced in France, where there was a backlash (often championed by former Marxists) against both Marxism and the unthinking idealization of revolution in the Third World. As we have seen, the impact of Solzhenitsyn was considerable, but so too, in the later 1970s, was the mounting evidence of the inhumanity of revolutionary regimes in China, Vietnam, and Cambodia. The plight of the refugee Vietnamese "boat people" in 1979 united a constellation of French intellectuals in humanitarian sympathy: in Sartre's words, "We don't care about their politics any more, we're concerned with their lives."[20] By now, however, Sartre (who died in 1980) was a declining force in French intellectual life. The new stars of the mid-1970s were the media-friendly "New Philosophers" such as Bernard-Henri Levy.

Intellectual fashion now favored a liberal, anti-socialist outlook, allied to a new suspicion of foreign political models and distaste for political violence. More profoundly, by the late 1970s the value of any all-encompassing models of social modernization, be they Marxist, nationalist, or technological, was increasingly being questioned and found wanting. Indeed, in his highly influential "report" of 1979 the French philosopher Jean-François Lyotard diagnosed the essence of the "postmodern" (which will be examined in more depth in Chapter 8) as an "incredulity towards metanarratives," and called for a "war on totality."[21]

The most striking cultural development of the 1970s was the central role played by the arts – above all cinema – in reopening national debates about fascism and World War II. In France, for instance, Marcel Ophuls's *The Sorrow and the Pity* (1971) and Louis Malle's *Lacombe Lucien* (1974) both critically examined the reaction of ordinary French citizens to the German occupation. Ophuls's documentary, in particular, cast an unnerving light on the everyday accommodations made by the occupied and did much to undermine the Gaullist myth of the French as a "nation of resisters." In Italy, Fellini's *Amarcord* (1973) and Bertolucci's *1900* (1973) offered contrasting views of Italian fascism as a phenomenon rooted in Italian society, while a spate of films addressed the Holocaust. West German cultural life also gained a new maturity from the mid-1960s, not only in the literature of Grass and Böll, but also in the so-called "new German cinema." The share of the domestic market taken by West German movies had actually shrunk from 47.3 percent (1955) to 8 percent in 1978.[22] However, the quality of German films was now world-class, and directors such as Werner Herzog and Wim Wenders achieved unprecedented success in the Anglo-Saxon world. Moreover, from 1974 onwards legal changes ensured a very high level of subsidy for the film industry from German television. This facilitated a brief, feverish burst of creative activity (Rainer Werner Fassbinder alone produced 40 films in 15 years before his death in 1982). German films played a central role in the critical reevaluation of the recent past, not only the Nazi era but also (for instance, in Fassbinder's *The Marriage of Maria Braun* (1979)) the "economic miracle," and even (in the films of Margarethe von Trotte) the radicalism of the early 1970s. Interestingly, however, it was an American television series on the Holocaust, watched by a West German audience of some 20 million in 1979, which had the greatest popular impact. Film-maker Edgar Reitz responded with the mammoth television series *Heimat* (1984), which examined the Nazi era through the prism of a remote German village in the Hunsrück mountains. The film was criticized for its failure to deal with issues such as the Holocaust, and prefigured the intense debate over "revisionism" within the German historical profession in the mid-1980s (see Chapter 8).

Britain remained largely immune to these critical reflections on the war, and continued to bask in the glow of a Churchillian "finest hour" (although the popular television comedy *Dad's Army* mocked the petty snobbery of wartime British society). The street parties that celebrated Queen Elizabeth II's silver jubilee in the summer of 1977 consciously evoked the deferential wartime mood.

However, the emergence of punk rock, which was at its most creative and subversive in 1976–7, showed how far British culture had in fact changed. Punks set out to shock with tuneless loud music, provocative lyrics, swearing on prime-time television, and a clothing style derived from the sex industry. Although it was, in part, a response to the high levels of youth unemployment, punk was not truly a sociological phenomenon. Rather, it represented a revolt in favor of style, spontaneity (or "anarchy") and nonconformity, bringing to the fore designers such as Vivienne Westwood and injecting images of sexual transgression into the cultural mainstream. Punk also forged contacts with West Indian reggae music, and played a vital role in the growth of a genuine multicultural awareness amongst the young. Although the leading bands, such as the Sex Pistols, were short-lived, punk had a profound impact on the music and fashion industries in Britain, as well as – in the longer term – on the arts in general. It was also influential in Europe, notably in Germany (where punk was associated with a revival of rock music sung with German lyrics) and even Slovenia (see Chapter 10). In such countries, punk's use of the swastika and other totalitarian imagery – which in Britain had merely caused a mild *frisson* – had far more disturbing implications.

Transitions: Spain, Portugal, and Greece

The fall of the south European dictatorships in the mid-1970s had significant ramifications for Europe as a whole, making possible the southward expansion of European integration in the 1980s, and offering a foretaste of how even more sweeping change in eastern Europe could be facilitated in the 1990s. The size of the task was daunting, as in Spain and Portugal (and arguably in Greece) entire generations had been raised under authoritarian rule. Moreover, rapid and potentially destabilizing change would be required if these relatively backward economies were to aspire to integration with the European Community. The experience of southern Europe gave rise to intense interest in the process of what became known as the "transition to democracy." However, the appearance of a wave of democratization in the mid-1970s,[23] or of some standardized process of "transition," needs to be qualified. Not only did the reasons for the fall of these dictatorships vary profoundly, but also there was no agreement as to what new political and social order should take their place. While external forces such as the European Community, the Socialist International or, indeed, the CIA might seek to influence events, the outcomes were decided above all by the choices made by domestic politicians.

In Spain the trigger for change was the long-awaited death of Franco on November 20, 1975 (see Figure 7.2). However, while democratic reform was widely supported and anticipated, the adherents of the old order remained strongly placed in the army and political institutions. Juan Carlos was immediately crowned king,

Figure 7.2 General Franco and his designated successor, Juan Carlos, 1973.
Photo © akg-images.

but it was far from clear what role he would play. Hard-line Francoists presumed that, having been groomed as Franco's successor, he would perpetuate the dictatorship, while many in the opposition thought that his reign would end in a swift restoration of the republic. In fact, the king soon signaled his commitment to change and, in mid-1976, replaced his conservative prime minister, Arias Navarro, with the 43-year-old Adolfo Suárez. This was a crucial appointment as, although Suárez had been a servant of the Franco regime and a former head of state television, he shared the king's reformist vision. The two men made an effective team: the king retained the loyalty of the army, while Suárez possessed the political skills to persuade a majority of the regime's supporters that the future lay with an opening to democracy. In November 1976 the Law for Political Reform passed the Cortes by 425 to 59 (as well as gaining 95 percent support in a referendum), clearing the way for free elections, a free press, and the legalization of political parties. Most strikingly, the Communist Party, demonized for so many years, agreed to abandon its hopes for a *ruptura* (a radical break with Francoism) in return for a place in Suárez's more gentle transition. This support was valuable, as under the Pact of Moncloa (October 1977) Suárez won communist and cross-party support for industrial restraint in return for social reform.

The elections of June 15, 1977 were a victory for Suárez's hastily assembled Unión de Centro Democrático (UCD) which took 34.3 percent of the vote. The UCD acted as a haven for former Francoists who were making the awkward transition to democratic politics, and was clearly seen by voters (especially women) as a safe choice that would not provoke the military. The Socialist Party, under the youthful leadership of Felipe González, came second with 28.5 percent, marginalizing the communists (9.3 percent). The principal task of the new parliament was to agree a new constitution, which was overwhelmingly endorsed in a referendum of December 1978. The only significant dissent came from the Basque country, where ETA campaigned against a document that made no provision for self-determination. In the event 55 percent of Basques abstained and 24 percent voted against the Constitution, but Suárez was able to offer just enough autonomy under the "Statute of Gernika" to win the support of moderate Basques without alienating the army.

The dismantling of the regime was accompanied by equally rapid cultural change after Franco's death. During the latter Franco years, writers and film-makers had successfully developed an elliptical, allegorical style that allowed them to investigate Spain's recent past within the flexible limits set by state censorship. For instance, movies such as Víctor Erice's *The Spirit of the Beehive* (1975) examined the repression and rural backwardness of the early Franco years through the eyes of children. By contrast, the transition – above all the abolition of film censorship in December 1977 and the guarantee of free expression under the 1978 Constitution – produced a flood of outspoken social and political comment in the arts and the media. In addition, the relaxation of the regime's moral puritanism (as well as the weakening of the church's social leadership) promoted a new wildness and hedonism, expressed in an appetite for violent and sexually explicit movies and magazines. The new freedoms were particularly welcome in the Basque country and Catalonia which had been subject to cultural repression under Franco. The Catalan language, for instance, had been banned in education, and the publication of books in Catalan – although legal since 1946 – had stagnated under the dictatorship. Moreover, the wholesale arrival in Catalonia of immigrants from other parts of Spain during previous decades meant that perhaps a half of the population could not speak Catalan by the end of the 1970s. However, under the autonomy permitted by the new Constitution there was a strong revival of Catalan (including the establishment of successful Catalan television and radio channels) during the 1980s.[24]

Despite his further victory in the March 1979 elections, Suárez's position was eroded by ETA violence and mounting threats of a military coup. He eventually resigned in January 1981, forced out by the disintegration of the ever fractious UCD. On February 23 the investiture of his successor was halted when Lieutenant Colonel Tejero of the Civil Guard stormed the Cortes and held the deputies prisoner. Tejero was in league with leading military officers, and the army even came onto the streets in Valencia, but the coup was halted in its tracks by the king's dramatic live TV broadcast at 1.15 a.m. on February 24. Juan Carlos made clear that he would not tolerate any attempt to "disrupt by force the democratic process," and the mass of uncommitted officers followed his lead. "23F" was the turning point: the most prominent hard-line opponents of democracy had been smoked out and defeated. Within two years González's Socialist Party had swept to power and Spain was set on the path to full integration with western Europe. The leadership of the king, the restraint of the political parties, and the bankruptcy of the far right had made possible a peaceful, if troubled, transition. Much had been gained, but something had also been lost, as the price of the transition had been the so-called "Pact of Forgetting." In other words, to facilitate the headlong rush away from the authoritarian past there would be no reckoning with the crimes of the civil war and Franco era. For some, therefore, the transition was tinged with a sense of dishonesty, incompleteness and private suffering.

While the Spanish transition was essentially managed by the political class, a far more revolutionary break occurred in Portugal. By 1973–4 the Caetano government had lost the support of many army officers, who formed the clandestine Armed Forces Movement (MFA). A natural leader emerged in General Spínola (the former commander in Guinea-Bissau), whose book *Portugal and the Future* (February 1974) caused a sensation by calling for Portugal's integration with Europe and a political settlement in the colonies. On April 25 the MFA overthrew Caetano in a bloodless coup, promising political liberty. Spínola was appointed president and the political parties – banned for many years – jostled to establish themselves. The coup unleashed forces that were difficult to control, and marked the beginning of a period of turbulence that lasted for the best part of two years. The army radicals soon fell out with the politically naive Spínola, who had not wished to dismantle the empire, but rather place it on a federal basis, and forced him from office in September 1974. Portugal lurched to the left as the Communist Party grew rapidly in strength. In October 1974 the socialist Foreign Minister Mário Soares visited the USA and was told by Kissinger that he would be the Portuguese Kerensky (the liberal Russian politician whose government had been overthrown by the Bolsheviks in 1917).[25]

The revolution reached its peak between March and November 1975. The radical officers constituted an unelected Council of the Revolution as the supreme authority in the state, and there was extensive land reform and nationalization of industry. However, the revolutionary forces were far less powerful than appearances suggested. The officers had no political party behind them, while communist support was primarily limited to the poor laborers of the south and the Lisbon working class. Elections in April 1975 showed a clear majority in favor of democratic change: Soares's socialists won with 38 percent while the communists won a mere 12.5 percent. In the summer there was an explosion of anti-communist violence across the more Catholic and smallholding north of the country, and 49 Communist Party offices were burnt. It seemed as if Portugal might descend into civil strife, but after an abortive left-wing coup on November 25, 1975 the military radicals collapsed. The emerging leader, the moderate officer Ramalho Eanes, successfully steered the country between the shoals of revolution and counter-revolution.

Under the April 1976 constitution it was agreed that Portugal would make a "transition to socialism" under the watchful eye of the Council of the Revolution and an autonomous military. The revolution's economic reforms were deemed irreversible, and the Constitution could not be altered until 1981. In June 1976 Eanes was elected president with a landslide 61 percent support, and won a second term in 1980. In reality, however, a return to normal politics was well under way. With the independence of Mozambique and Angola (in June and November 1975) politicians could now focus on Portugal's collapsing economy. The severe unemployment and rampant inflation were only worsened by the arrival of some 700,000 former African colonists. The political parties progressively reasserted their authority, even despite the death in 1980 of Portugal's most charismatic civilian politician and leading critic of the army, Francisco Sa Carneiro, in a plane crash. Portugal's transition had been protracted due to the revolutionary ferment of 1974–5, but by the mid-1980s the army had finally been excluded from politics and brought under civilian control.

The Greek military junta, headed by Dimitrios Ioannidis following the overthrow of George Papadopolous in 1973, was brought down by a failed foreign adventure. In 1959 Greece and Turkey had come to an agreement on independence for Cyprus from British rule (with provisions for the Turkish minority) under the presidency of Archbishop Makarios. However, successive Greek governments had continued to harbour dreams of *Enosis* (union with Greece). The junta, which was facing mounting opposition as well as severe economic problems, now used the former EOKA terrorist Nikos Sampson to destabilize Makarios's government. On July 15 Sampson overthrew (but failed to capture) Makarios in a coup that was clearly supported by the junta. Five days later Turkey invaded Cyprus, and in the course of the summer the island was, in effect, partitioned. The ham-fisted pursuit of *Enosis* had resulted in a division of Cyprus on ethnic lines (accompanied by a forcible exchange of populations) that would endure into the next century. The junta's attempt to mobilize for war was shambolic, and Ioannidis was sacked by his colleagues who, in desperation, invited the former conservative prime minister, Constantine Karamanlis, to return from his Parisian self-exile to take charge.

Karamanlis presided over a remarkably rapid dismantling of the dictatorship and restoration of democracy. He legalized all of the political parties, notably the communists, and held elections in November in which his New Democracy Party won 54 percent of the vote. The following month Greeks voted in a referendum, by 69 percent, to abolish the monarchy. Karamanlis also withdrew Greece from NATO's military command (recognizing popular anger at US support for the junta), and made it clear that there would be no war over Cyprus. (However, relations with Greece's NATO ally Turkey remained very poor – and often on the brink of war – well into the 1980s). Finally, Karamanlis purged the judiciary, the civil service and – more slowly than many would have wished – the military. The Colonels and their associates were tried for their crimes in 1975 and a number of death sentences were commuted to life imprisonment. The Greek transition went far beyond a mere restoration of the pre-1967 status quo (albeit minus the king): it represented a fundamental break with the authoritarianism of the past half-century. Greek politics remained unusually impassioned, clientalist, and polarized, but henceforth would be conducted within the terms of the Constitution and supported by more democratic institutions. The seal was set on Greece's transformation by the events of 1981: accession to the European Community and the peaceful transfer of power to Andreas Papandreou's socialist PASOK party following an electoral landslide (see Chapter 8).

Conclusion

The 1970s represent something of a transitional decade that defies simple characterization. The radicalism of the late 1960s and early 1970s gave way to a greater suspicion of socialism, in both political and intellectual circles, towards the end of the decade. The great postwar boom came to an end, large-scale unemployment and inflation made unwelcome returns, and the oil shocks of 1973 and 1979 marked the end of an era of cheap energy. Governments, mainly of the center-left, struggled to come to terms with the new challenges and constraints that these changes represented, as well as with the new scourge of urban terrorism. Conversely, détente, at both the superpower and the European levels, created a greater sense of security, and *Ostpolitik* marked the emergence of West Germany as a mature international actor. Perhaps the most optimistic development came in southern Europe, where the dictatorships in Spain, Portugal and Greece all fell in the mid-1970s, and were eventually replaced with democratic governments after complex processes of political transition.

8
Western Europe in the 1980s
The Era of Thatcher, Mitterrand, and Kohl

Towards the Post-Industrial[1] Society

The 1980s were a pivotal decade in western Europe's postwar economic development. Trends were established and policies formulated which not only dominated the European economy until the end of the century (and beyond), but also proved highly influential during the transformation of eastern Europe during the 1990s. Although national experiences varied greatly, there was a general convergence during the decade on "neo-liberal" economic policies, the decline of manufacture and heavy industry, the rise of the tertiary sector, and the reduction of national sovereignty in economic decision-making. There was also a tacit acceptance of higher levels of unemployment and – despite the continuing growth of welfare provision – of urban poverty (often linked to the problems faced by racial minorities). The emergence of a new consensus hardly seemed plausible at the start of the decade when ideological polarization had never seemed so acute: in 1981 the free-marketeering policies of Margaret Thatcher confronted the social-ist experiment of François Mitterrand. The consensus, therefore, owed much to the failure of the latter and the unacceptability (in its cruder forms) of the former.

Thatcher's policies (see below) offered Europe a vision of a "de-industrialized" future. British manufacturing output fell by 17 percent in the opening years of Conservative government (1979–81), the workforce of the steel industry plunged from 220,000 (1974) to 54,000 (1986), and the coalmining industry underwent severe contraction. Meanwhile, the tertiary sector (notably financial services) rose to some two-thirds of total output by the early 1990s, and levels of industrial

Europe's Troubled Peace: 1945 to the Present, Second Edition. Tom Buchanan.
© 2012 John Wiley & Sons, Ltd. Published 2012 by John Wiley & Sons, Ltd.

productivity at last began to rise to compete with those of Britain's main competitors.[2] The British case was exceptional, but many of its components were far from unique. It was, after all, the socialist Mitterrand who embarked on the restructuring of the state-owned French steel and automobile industries with the loss of thousands of jobs in 1984. Indeed, in the guise of neo-liberalism, Thatcher's policies proved highly influential. By the late 1980s governments of both left and right were seeking to deregulate and liberalize their economies, while prioritizing the battle against inflation through reduction of budget deficits. There was a new recognition that the duty of government was to assist wealth creation rather than to run the economy. The era of ambitious industrial policies and state subsidy was drawing to a close, and the *coup de gräce* was delivered by the Single European Act (1986) and the "1992" program for completion of the free market within the European Community.

There were, however, two very significant ways in which Britain could not offer a lead to Europe. First, most member states saw increased economic integration as a vital weapon in the struggle for economic stability (see Chapter 9). For them, participation in the Exchange Rate Mechanism from 1979 (which Britain only joined grudgingly in 1990) was not only a means of reducing currency volatility, but also provided a helpful financial discipline for curbing inflation. In Italy, for instance, the result was institutional reform and single-figure inflation by the mid-1980s. Moreover, most continental countries did not share Thatcher's fears about the loss of national sovereignty, and were willing to link their currencies to the Deutschmark. Secondly, Thatcher's attempt to free the labor market by breaking the unions was unpalatable in much of northern Europe, where strong unions were seen as partners in the management of wage demands.

These trends did not merely connote an ideological revolution; they were also a recognition of Europe's changing place in the world economy and of profound changes in the nature of work. Although manufacturing industry held its own in certain countries (such as Italy, with its plethora of small family firms) it was clear that the traditional core of west European industry had had its day. Quite simply, coal, steel, and many manufactured goods could be imported more cheaply from emerging economies which enjoyed lower labor costs. But for the Common Agricultural Policy (CAP), the same would also have applied to agricultural produce. Moreover, it was logical that a Europe that was turning away from traditional industries should seek to take advantage of the growing economic potential of computerization and high technology, as well as the opportunities presented by a more leisured society.

The social impact of these trends was profound, above all for the shrinking industrial working class. Proletarian identity was being challenged by the loss of factory jobs, by greater social mobility and educational opportunity, and by greater female equality. Across Europe, trade unions declined in membership and influence during the 1980s. By 1980 some 2 million of the 5 million members of the Italian CGIL were pensioners, while in France membership of the trade unions fell to less than 10 percent of active wage-earners during the Mitterrand years. In Spain the socialist UGT federation declined from some 1,460,000 members in 1979 to a mere 666,000 in 1988 (under a socialist government). The defeat of the Fiat strike in 1980 symbolized a new era of industrial stability in Italy, while Rupert Murdoch's decision to sack his Fleet Street printworkers and move to new high-tech facilities in 1986 was evidence of the new brutalism in British industrial relations. Elsewhere, however, the unions remained a significant force. In West Germany the metal workers led a campaign in 1984 for a 35-hour week, and eventually settled for a 38.5-hour week and a pay rise. Across Europe in the late 1980s the unions (encouraged by Jacques Delors, president of the European Commission) were quick to recognize the new opportunities for workers' rights offered by the latest phase of European integration.

The main beneficiaries of these changes were the new "yuppy" middle class and working women. Tax reform and deregulation provided an environment favorable to an enterprising, young and socially mobile stratum that embraced rather than feared the advent of information technology and often wanted to run their own businesses. The hallmarks of the new phenomenon were individualism, a vogue for style and design and, especially in Britain, ostentatious wealth created by the deregulation of financial services. The 1980s also saw the rise of women within the workforce, often married women returning to work in part-time jobs. In West Germany 43 percent of married women worked in the late 1980s (compared with 25 percent in the early 1950s) and the average length of break from work after having a child fell from 15 to eight years.[3] In some countries (notably Sweden) there was very generous state child-care provision to encourage women to work, while in Germany a law passed in 1986 by the conservative government tilted the balance the other way: child-rearing was recognized as akin to paid work and pension rights were granted to housewives. The increasing prominence of women in the workplace added to the pressure on the unions to shed their traditional male image and demanded a response from politicians. Mitterrand created a Minister for Women in 1981, and in Norway eight out of 17 members of Gro Harlan Brundtland's 1986 cabinet were women.

The 1980s were a disorienting time for many. Europe's modest economic recovery was accompanied by drastic restructuring, suggesting a far more insecure (or flexible) future for the workforce. Nowhere was this disorientation felt more keenly than on the left. The failure of Mitterrand's socialist policies in 1981–3 (as well as the abandonment of a radical scheme for economic democracy in Sweden) seemed to spell the end of any real social democratic alternative to capitalism. With the failure of socialism on a national scale, many on the left increasingly transferred their ambitions to the European level. However, the neo-liberals by no means had it all their own way. There was still scope for well-managed public enterprise: witness the success of Elf-Aquitaine in France, and of Romano Prodi as director of the Italian state-holding company IRI. Even in Britain social expenditure continued to grow as a percentage of GDP, and in southern Europe considerable steps were taken to enhance welfare provision. Moreover, despite the new individualism, the decade was marked by new solidarities. The 1986 Chernobyl disaster graphically demonstrated the interconnection of environmental concerns, even across the Cold War divide, while the British "Live Aid" concert of 1985 showed how satellite technology could be used to unite a vast international audience behind the cause of famine relief in Africa.

Postmodern Cultures?

During the 1980s some of the cultural consequences of long-term social and economic change became evident. This was most noticeable in architecture where, since the 1970s, there had been a reaction against the functionalism and brutality of the modernist style that had been so dominant in the postwar world. In 1977 the critic Charles Jencks identified a "postmodern" movement in architecture, distinguished by an eclectic and playful approach to style and design, as well as an awareness of architectural history and the context in which a building was located. To its detractors, however, postmodern architecture merely offered an amorphous pastiche of previous styles. The movement came of age with a highly influential session at the 1980 Venice Biennale on "The Presence of the Past in Architecture." The British architect James Stirling's Neue Staatsgalerie in Stuttgart, completed in 1984, is often cited as the best European example of the new style, which was more fully developed in the USA. The reaction against modernism was also evident in music, and audiences generally welcomed the abandonment of elitist, abstract compositions for a more referential, melodious style. As the German-based composer Krzysztof Penderecki put it: "I had no intention of composing atonal clusters forever or dense, opaque harmonies …"[4]

The question was whether "postmodernism" was simply a reaction against the excesses of "modernism," or if – as a number of leading intellectuals began to argue in the late 1970s – it represented a new phase in the social and economic development of the industrialized world. For Jean-François Lyotard and others, postmodernism was no mere passing style, but a "condition" which related to profound changes such as the advent of post-industrialism, the growth of more pluralist, multicultural societies, and the decline of all traditional hierarchies and explanatory frameworks (be they ideologies, social classes, the nation-state, or the patriarchal family). Jean Baudrillard went even further in arguing that the rise of new media and information technology represented – in effect – a new reality. Postmodernism, which rapidly gained ground in the academic world during the 1980s, aroused fierce controversy. Even its advocates often found it hard to agree on how it should be applied, and they also undermined their case by writing in an opaque and jargon-laden fashion.

Even so, the concept is undoubtedly helpful in looking at the Europe of the 1980s, as it offers a means of bringing together a range of otherwise disparate phenomena, six of which are identified below. However, whether they amounted to a new "postmodern" era, or were merely the intensification and fulfillment of trends evident since at least the 1960s, remained hotly disputed. In politics, this was a decade in which the dominant ideologies of postwar Europe faced an unprecedented challenge from new environmentalist, regionalist, and feminist movements (see below). Secondly, gender roles were profoundly tested, not only by feminism and changes in the labor market, but also by more open gay and lesbian lifestyles. Thirdly, the widespread deregulation and commercialization of broadcast media, as well as the coming of satellite and cable television, vastly expanded consumer choice and helped to break down barriers between high art and popular culture. The most representative cultural artifact of the 1980s was the pop video, which frequently paid homage to (or plundered) well-known images and genres. Fourthly, there were ever greater opportunities for consumption, with easy access to credit and new hypermarkets offering a dazzling range of goods both from within Europe and from the global economy. Fifthly, there was an explosion in leisure and tourism. By 1986, for instance, West Germany spent 10 percent of its GDP on leisure, and 66 percent of the population went on holiday[5] to increasingly distant destinations. Finally, there was a significant change in western Europe's relationship with the past: a new knowingness of how the past could be shaped to suit the needs of the present. In the words of Umberto Eco in the postscript to his bestseller *The Name of the Rose*, the past "must be revisited: but with irony, not innocently."[6] Hence, the industrial past, like rural life before it, was repackaged as the "heritage industry," and former coal miners found a new productive life serving the tourist trade.

There was no guiding hand behind these changes and, indeed, there was much that seemed contradictory. Margaret Thatcher, for instance, was the leading advocate of deregulation, but a die-hard supporter of the centralized British state and of traditional morality. In France the state intervened more than ever in cultural life under Mitterrand and his Culture Minister Jack Lang. Yet, although many of Mitterrand's architectural projects (such as the Louvre pyramid) were in a modernist vein, this was also a government that permitted the establishment of European Disneyland (denounced by some on the left as a "cultural Chernobyl")[7] outside Paris in 1985. Cultural change was at its most pronounced in Spain, where established authority was in abeyance after the death of Franco. Here, the political transition had collapsed decades of cultural change into a few short years: witness the frenetic "la movida" (the youth "scene") that swirled around the bars of Madrid and Barcelona. These dramatic changes were encapsulated in the remarkable international success in the 1980s of the gay film-maker Pedro Almodóvar, whose movies dealt with sexual desires and practices with an openness that would have been quite inconceivable under Franco.

Postmodernists sought to describe, rather than offer a judgment on, the "postmodern condition." Jencks, for instance, readily accepted that there were both advantages and disadvantages to, say, the increase in communication, the rise of leisure time and the decline of traditional "Fordist" manufacture. On balance, however, they celebrated the greater plurality, egalitarianism, and empowerment of postmodern life. Yet other critics roundly deplored the effects of media deregulation throughout western Europe, arguing that it had produced a trivial-ized culture of game shows and soap operas, lacking in meaning and values, and reduced to the lowest common denominator. In fact, however, the cultural changes of the 1980s looked rather tame compared to those (notably the advent of the Internet, digital technology, e-mail, and the mobile phone) that accompanied the communications revolution of the 1990s.

The New Cold War

The somewhat reluctant retreat from détente under Carter accelerated into a "new" Cold War[8] following the election of Ronald Reagan in 1980. Reagan's two-term presidency (1981–9) caused grave disquiet in western Europe, where his attempt to restore American pride and world leadership (seasoned with simplistic anti-Soviet rhetoric) was widely seen as warmongering. Reagan launched an arms build-up far greater than that initiated by Carter (there was an increase of $32.6 billion on Carter's already enhanced military budget of $200.3 billion). Many suspended programs, such as the B1 bomber, were revived, and World War II battleships were readied for service in a crude display of power projection. As before, the Cold War was largely fought in the Third World, notably in Afghanistan, and without Carter's regard for human rights. No aspect of US policy caused more concern in Europe than the Reagan administration's support for repressive right-wing regimes in Central America and its funding of the rebels (or "contras") fighting against the Sandinista revolution in Nicaragua.

Reagan's presidency therefore sharpened the divisions between Europe and the USA, and the old actor's folksy charm, so effective in domestic politics, did not travel well. With the exception of Margaret Thatcher, his closest military and ideo-logical ally, European leaders were decidedly ambiguous in their response to Reagan and saw him as dangerously unpredictable. They feared that his cherished Strategic Defense Initiative (SDI, or "star wars") would merely increase instability when it was announced in March 1983, and they were appalled when, at the October 1986 Reykjavik summit, he offered Mikhail Gorbachev the prospect of eliminating all nuclear weapons. They were also deeply concerned at Reagan's fiscal irresponsibility, as the USA's massive budget deficit resulted in higher interest rates in Europe. Even the much-vaunted special relationship with Britain was shaken by the unannounced American invasion of Grenada (of which the queen was head of state) in October 1983 and by America's initial even-handedness between Britain and Argentina over the Falklands conflict (March–June 1982).

West European governments preferred détente to Reagan's belligerency, and they refused to follow US leadership if it conflicted with their own economic or security interests. They forced the USA to back down over proposed economic sanctions against the USSR following the imposition of martial law in Poland, and in April 1986 would not allow American planes (flying from Britain) to use their air space for the bombing of Libya. Only West Germany supported the US boycott of the 1980 Moscow Olympic Games. There was, moreover, no sign of a new Cold War in relations between the two Germanies: if anything, economic assistance and political contacts intensified in 1983–4. However, European governments continued to desire – and expect – US protection. Britain and West Germany pressed ahead with the deployment of Cruise and Pershing missiles in November 1983 in the face of a "hot autumn" of mass demonstrations. Indeed, opposition was such that the projected deployment was never carried out in the Netherlands. To America's pleasant surprise, France's new socialist president, François Mitterrand (a consistent critic of Soviet power), supported the NATO deployment.

Ironically, European leaders cared little more for Reagan's quest to be remembered as a "peacemaker" during his second term, although in reality the impetus for change came primarily with the advent of Mikhail Gorbachev as leader of the USSR in March 1985 (see Chapter 10). Gorbachev was initially viewed with some suspicion in the West, and Helmut Kohl even claimed in October 1986 that he was a master of propaganda akin to Joseph Goebbels. Once Gorbachev's sincerity had been accepted, Reagan, to his credit, swallowed his innate anti-communism and seized the chance for genuine progress on arms reduction. From a European perspective, however, the Reagan–Gorbachev relationship raised the prospect that agreement might be reached between the superpowers with little regard for their own interests. Britain and France were particularly concerned that their nuclear deterrents might be compromised. Even so, the results were momentous. In December 1987 the Intermediate Nuclear Forces (INF) Treaty scrapped the entire arsenal (Soviet and US) of medium-range missiles that had menaced Europe's security. The way was now opened for far-reaching talks to reduce both strategic nuclear weapons and conventional forces in Europe.

Thatcher's Britain

In May 1979 Margaret Thatcher led the Conservatives back to power, having defeated the incumbent Labour Party by 43.9 percent to 36.9 percent. As we have seen, Thatcher's policies and governing style owed much to the bitter experience of Edward Heath's government (1970–4). More than that, her government represented a repudiation of principal elements of Britain's "postwar consensus," above all the quest for full employment. A sustained attempt would be made to reverse what Sir Keith Joseph, her ideological mentor, termed the ever-tightening "ratchet" of socialism since 1945.[9] Thatcher appealed above all to a middle class who resented inflation, trade union power, and rising crime. However, she also won over significant sections of the skilled working class who now aspired to greater social mobility, and one of her most popular early policies was to facilitate home ownership through the sale of publicly owned housing. In place of Heath's vacillations, Thatcher offered leadership by "conviction." The main objectives of what became known as "Thatcherism" were to reduce the power of the state and increase the freedom of the individual, while restoring Britain's international prestige and self-confidence. Her policies were sustained by the plethora of think tanks that had led the neo-liberal counter-attack in the late 1970s, and also bore the intellectual imprint of monetarist economics.

Thatcher's radical policies were particularly audacious given the initial weakness of her political position. Her immense popularity amongst the Conservative Party's rank and file was less evident amongst her parliamentary colleagues. Many senior Tories (the so-called "Wets") questioned the social divisiveness of her policies, but they were never a coherent internal opposition and had been decisively defeated by 1981. Thatcher was also helped by the civil war that broke out within the Labour Party in opposition. A powerful left wing emerged under the leadership of Tony Benn, while many on the party's right broke away to establish the Social Democratic Party (SDP) in 1981. Labour's very public divisions, and the intellectual bankruptcy exposed by its defeat in 1979, rendered it unelectable until the 1990s and helped Thatcher to endure two deep troughs of mid-term unpopularity. The seal was set on her recovery by military victory over the Argentinian junta in the Falklands conflict, which elevated Thatcher from a mere politician into a successful war leader. In the June 1983 election landslide the Conservatives (with 42.4 percent) gained a parliamentary majority of almost 200 MPs. The Labour Party recorded its worst share of the vote since 1918 (27.6 percent) and was almost overtaken by the SDP–Liberal Alliance (25.4 percent).

Thatcher's deflationary policies during her first term hardly courted popularity. Cuts in taxation and expenditure, combined with high rates of interest and exchange, devastated the country's manufacturing industry. Unemployment soared to 3 million in January 1982, mocking the Conservative's pre-election slogan of "Labour isn't working," but Thatcher shrugged off calls for a policy "U-turn." The key moment came in the autumn budget of 1981 when, in the depths of the recession, Chancellor Geoffrey Howe stood Keynesian orthodoxy on its head and opted for further deflationary measures. The economy started to pick up in time for the 1983 election, but unemployment and intense urban deprivation remained. The government was shaken by a series of inner-city riots between 1980 and 1985, often sparked by friction between the police and racial minorities. One casualty of the recession was the government's espousal of strict monetarism, as the high levels of unemployment, which cut tax income while increasing benefit payments, made it impossible to meet the government's targets for reduction in public expenditure. Thatcher, whose ideological verve was generally balanced with pragmatism, was also well aware that certain parts of the public sector (such as the National Health Service) were too politically sensitive to be cut.

Thatcher's greatest achievement, which had eluded her predecessors of both parties, was reform of the trade unions. Unlike Heath, who had sought to impose a complete new legal framework for industrial relations, her government legislated against specific manifestations of union power such as mass picketing, the lack of pre-strike ballots, and the closed shop. She also avoided confrontation with her most powerful union adversary, the coal miners, until conditions were in her government's favor. In this way Thatcher outmaneuvered the unions, already weakened by unemployment and by the advent of new technologies, and kept public opinion on her side. Between March 1984 and February 1985 she took on and defeated the coal miners in a bitter year-long struggle that encapsulated her divisive decade in office. The miners were hamstrung by the new legal constraints, crushed by heavy policing, and let down by a leftist leadership that refused to seek democratic legitimacy for the strike. Their defeat exposed the industry to rapid decline and doomed many mining villages to poverty and social dislocation. Thereafter, far from playing a decisive role in national politics, the unions were on the defensive, and union membership fell from 13.5 million in 1979 to 9.5 million in 1991.

Privatization of state-owned assets, which became Thatcher's most imitated policy, was not attempted on a large scale until after the 1983 election. Even then the government was slow to realize that the real benefit lay not in the income generated for the Exchequer but rather in promoting popular capitalism. A swath of industries and utilities (such as gas and telecommunications) was sold from the mid-1980s, creating unprecedented opportunities for small share-owners. Privatization became the cutting edge of Thatcher's attempt to make the British people more enterprising and individualistic. The state sector, 11.5 percent of GDP in 1979, was halved during the following ten years, while the proportion of adults owning shares rose from 7 percent to 20 percent. However, much of the sheen was lost in the stock market crash of 1987, and later privatizations of complex and controversial industries (such as nuclear power and the run-down railway network) proved far less successful. Thatcher's ardent economic liberalism was not replicated in her government's social policies, which espoused a highly repressive morality. Ministers were quick to blame contemporary social problems on the permissiveness of the 1960s and, although there was no sustained attempt to overturn the reforms of that period, action was taken to ban the promotion of homosexuality by publicly funded bodies. Likewise, little progress was made on women's rights under Britain's first female prime minister. Thatcher's liberalism was also strangely centralizing. Local democracy was curbed, and the Greater London Council (GLC), which had fallen under Labour control, was abolished after a damaging political struggle.

Even in opposition, in 1975–9, Thatcher had been an outspoken critic of détente, and gloried in the title "the Iron Lady" bestowed on her by an official Soviet newspaper (she later commented that "they never did me a greater favour").[10] In office she was a staunch Atlanticist and defender of Britain's nuclear deterrent at a time when the Labour Party was advocating unilateral nuclear disarmament. However, she supported political and economic reform in eastern Europe, and was one of the first Western leaders to identify Gorbachev's potential before he took office. Her belligerence in relations with the European Community was initially effective (Britain received a "rebate" on its budget contributions in June 1984), but it was far less influential once European integration entered a more intense phase in the later 1980s. Thatcher was an increasingly isolated figure, not only at European summits but even within her own government, and the successful challenge to her leadership was triggered by Sir Geoffrey Howe's resignation from the cabinet over European policy. She had been rendered increasingly vulnerable by the economic downturn of the late 1980s and by a deeply unpopular reform of local taxation (the "poll tax") which had sparked violent disturbances. Thatcher had clearly lost her political touch, and many of her own MPs had come to see her as an electoral liability. In November 1990 she was forced to resign when she was challenged for the leadership and taken to a second ballot by Michael Heseltine.

Margaret Thatcher dominated British politics in the last fifth of the twentieth century, but did she have any significance for continental Europe? A number of European leaders sought to emulate her confrontational style, with mixed results, notably Jacques Chirac during his unsuccessful period as French prime minister (1986–8), as well as the Conservative Poul Schluter in Denmark and Wilfred Martens in Belgium. In Greece, Theodore Mitsotakis posed as the "Greek Thatcher" while prime minister (1990–3). Thatcherism, in its pure union-busting, deregulating form, has, however, proved difficult to export to western Europe, given the value placed on consensus, the prevalence of coalition governments, and the cross-class basis of Christian Democracy. Thatcher's legacy is far more evident in the emerging post-communist states of the 1990s, where free-market politicians such as Václav Klaus were less inhibited in their admiration for a woman whom they regarded as a heroine of the Cold War. Moreover, historians are now beginning to argue for the importance of Thatcher's impact on European integration, not only for opening the Community to market forces through the Single European Act, but also as the advocate of the most viable alternative to the dominant model of integration since the mid-1980s.[11]

Mitterrand's France

François Mitterrand was an unlikely socialist leader for the late twentieth century. He was a man of bourgeois Catholic upbringing who was initially a centrist politician and had served in almost half of the short-lived governments of the

Fourth Republic. His politics were anti-communist and anti-Gaullist, and he became the best-known critic of the Fifth Republic during the 1960s. He was a consummate political tactician, possessed of immense resilience and patience, who survived setbacks that would have finished the career of a lesser politician (such as his ill-timed bid for power in May 1968). His socialism was principled rather than programmatic: he was an intellectual with a profound sense of the republican tradition in French politics and a strong belief in social justice and human rights. It was only in 1971 that he found a reliable vehicle for his ambitions when he was elected First Secretary of the recently formed Parti Socialiste (PS), bringing weight and experienced leadership to a party riven with ideological factions and personal animosities. His goal was simple: to break the monopoly of the right within the Fifth Republic and to revive the left as a governing force. To do so, he would need to work closely with the communists even if (as they were well aware) in the long term he aimed to overtake and marginalize them.

In spite of the communist sabotage of the "Union of the Left" in 1977, Mitterrand was by 1981 in a position to bid for power without the support of a formal alliance. Giscard d'Estaing's popularity had been eroded by unemployment (which had risen fairly modestly under his presidency) and by his perceived aloofness. Giscard was further weakened by divisions in the conservative camp and the failure of his Gaullist rival, Chirac, to support him once eliminated from the contest. In a remarkably effective campaign, Mitterrand tapped into the widespread desire for change (winning votes particularly among women and the young) but also depicted himself reassuringly as "La force tranquille." The man dubbed the "eternal loser"[12] in 1978 took 26 percent of the vote in the first round and then defeated Giscard with 51.75 percent in the second. Mitterrand immediately dissolved parliament and in June the socialists won an absolute majority, giving the left a degree of power unrivalled even by the success of the Popular Front in 1936. Just as importantly, Mitterrand had won on his own terms, as the communists had backed him but he was not beholden to them. His decision to include four communist ministers in Prime Minister Pierre Mauroy's cabinet may have worried the United States, but in fact it represented an astute tactical move (especially once austerity measures were required in 1983).

Mitterrand's victory was greeted by ecstatic crowds on the streets of Paris. Fully aware of the symbolism of the moment, the new president went straight from his inauguration to pay homage at the Panthéon to previous French socialist and resistance leaders. Equally symbolic of his humane intentions was his decision in September to abolish the detested, if little-used, death penalty. Yet what did his victory mean for France? The Socialist Party had promised a "break with the international capitalist order,"[13] although Mitterrand had based his campaign on his own "110 propositions for France" which avoided such sweeping language and itemized specific reforms. In victory he identified his top priorities simply as unemployment, growth, and social justice. It soon became evident that he would use the office of president as a powerful tool for the advancement of socialism, without accepting any dictation from the Socialist Party. Moreover, for all of his criticism of the Fifth Republic, he soon concluded that its institutions suited him "extremely well."[14] Indeed, a reduction in the presidential term to five years, proposed by Mitterrand during the campaign,[15] was only implemented by his Gaullist successor in 2002. However, Mitterrand did go some way to decentralize power, establishing regional authorities and, under the "Auroux law," formal workplace consultation.

For all his inherent pragmatism, during his first year in office Mitterrand gave free rein to his party's radical instincts. In essence, he sought to reflate the economy through a colossal injection of demand. There were substantial increases in pensions, family allowances, and the minimum wage, while the working week was cut from 40 to 39 hours (with an extra week's paid holiday per year). Reform was to be paid for by a wealth tax and by a state-managed dash for economic growth. The private banks and numerous leading firms were nationalized, increasing the public sector from 10 percent to 20 percent of the workforce. It was soon clear, however, that the reforms were not having the desired effect as, far from creating the expected 400,000–500,000 jobs, unemployment had soared to 2 million by October 1981. The injection of demand into an uncompetitive economy sucked in imports, resulting in higher inflation and three devaluations of the franc between 1981 and 1983. The dire economic figures and a series of sectoral protests by farmers and professional groups strengthened the advocates of austerity within the government, such as Jacques Delors, during 1982. The socialist experiment was formally abandoned in March 1983, when heavy defeats in local elections precipitated a governmental crisis and the adoption of strict deflationary policies. The first phase of Mitterrand's presidency had ended in historic failure, not only for French socialism, but also for the European left. Never again would a government claim an electoral mandate for such fundamental change: the defeat of the Mitterrand experiment pointed the way to accommodation with the market (firmly within the context of European integration) across western Europe.

Despite Mitterrand's "U-turn," the government was by no means left rudderless. Rising ministers such as Delors, Laurent Fabius, and Michel Rocard now redefined the government's mission as one of economic modernization and embarked on a shake-out of inefficient industries (aided by the fact that many were now under state control). However, the government faced mounting political pressure due to an ill-timed attempt to bring private (mainly Catholic) schools under state control. In June 1984 more than a million protested against the reforms in Paris, forcing Mitterrand to abandon the proposals and precipitating the resignation of Prime Minister Mauroy. Mitterrand's decision to replace him with the technocratic 37-year-old Fabius was the signal for the departure of the communists (under increasing political pressure due to the austerity measures) from the government. Fabius represented a retreat from traditional French *dirigisme*, commenting in July 1984 that "the state has met its limits and should not exceed them."[16] He presided over a limited economic recovery, but unemployment remained stubbornly high (reaching 2.6 million by 1986), and it was not enough to save the Socialist Party from defeat by the resurgent center-right in the March 1986 parliamentary elections.

In the international sphere, during this first phase of his presidency, Mitterrand offered a blend of traditional Gaullism and a new Atlanticism. As an instinctive anti-communist, Mitterrand brought France closer to the heart of NATO and (after initial criticism of Reagan's policy in Central America) was supportive of the US presence in Europe. He was also far more sympathetic towards Israel than many on the French left, although France continued to arm the Arab states. His Gaullism, meanwhile, was evident in his maintenance of the French nuclear deterrent, the military intervention in Chad (1983), and in the shameful decision to sink the Greenpeace vessel *Rainbow Warrior*, which was monitoring French nuclear tests in the South Pacific. Like de Gaulle, Mitterrand also forged close relations with West Germany, especially with the conservative Helmut Kohl. In September 1984 he invited Kohl (who had not been invited to attend the D-Day anniversary in June) to take part in commemorations of the battle of Verdun. Unlike de Gaulle, however, Mitterrand saw his relationship with Kohl as the basis for a surge towards European integration rather than as an endorsement of French leadership.

The supreme test of Mitterrand's political skills came when the Socialist Party lost control of parliament in March 1986. Many had predicted that the new conservative majority would seek to force him from office. Instead, he held his nerve, appointed the victorious Jacques Chirac as prime minister, and embarked on the Fifth Republic's first *cohabitation* (power-sharing) between political opposites. Chirac, over-anxious to impress ahead of the impending presidential elections, embarked on a frenetic program of privatization and educational reforms, backed up by tough law-and-order measures designed to appeal to supporters of the far-right National Front. The result was a series of politically damaging strikes and violent demonstrations which Mitterrand quietly exploited to deflate Chirac, who came to be seen as divisive and unmeasured. In 1988 Mitterrand, driving home the message with his slogan "La France Unie" ("France United") and pitching for votes in the political center, easily secured a second presidential term. The Socialist Party also regained control of parliament, although short of an absolute majority, and Mitterrand appointed the popular Rocard (his long-standing rival) as prime minister.

Mitterrand's second term was, at least on the domestic front, anti-climactic. The theme of an opening to the center (half of the ministers were nonsocialists) cast Rocard's government in a pragmatic, managerial mold, even though he genuinely sought to tackle the problems of urban deprivation. When Rocard resigned in 1991 France was again heading into recession, and his successor, Edith Cresson, proved a poor choice. Mitterrand was now far more absorbed in the development of European integration (see Chapter 9), the unforeseen shock of German reunification, and France's reluctant involvement in the Gulf War of 1991. In many respects the signing of the Maastricht Treaty (1991) marked the triumphant culmination of Mitterrand's presidency. His final years, smothered in a more emollient phase of *cohabitation* following the socialists' heavy defeat in the 1993 parliamentary elections, were dogged by ill health, corruption allegations, and renewed speculation about his past and private life.

Mitterrand was a deeply cultured statesman whose legacy went far beyond his beloved modernist *grands projets* (such as the Defense Arch) that transformed the Paris skyline. However, many of his achievements require heavy qualification. First, he had proved that the Fifth Republic was adaptable (which many had doubted), and had turned the socialists into a party of government. Yet his political tactics were often manipulative and cynical. For instance, his decision to introduce proportional representation for parliamentary elections in 1985 was primarily designed to promote the far-right National Front and thereby reduce the expected majority of the mainstream conservatives. Secondly, he had presided over the modernization of the French economy, which was by the 1990s more efficient, robust, and open to international competition. Yet evidence of greater social justice was hard to find: unemployment remained high, and there were severe problems of poverty and alienation amongst the urban poor, especially those of North African origin. Thirdly, he had been a great champion of European integration (and of reconciliation with Germany) but he had failed to persuade the French people of its benefits. The Maastricht Treaty passed by only the slenderest of margins in the referendum of September 1992.

Helmut Kohl and West Germany

Helmut Kohl, the third of the troika of dominant European leaders of the 1980s, in many respects had greatness thrust upon him by the sudden opportunity for German reunification in 1989–90. Until 1989 he had been widely viewed as an insecure, gaffe-prone Chancellor, and the idea that he might, in any sense, claim the mantle of Bismarck would have been regarded as ludicrous. Even so, it should be noted that, while he lacked the statesmanlike qualities of Schmidt and Brandt, Kohl was a gifted Rhineland politician with an intuitive understanding of the aspirations of middle-class Germans. He had done much to revive the CDU in the 1970s, and in 1976 had come close to leading it to victory over the SPD.

Kohl's prospects improved when the Christian Democrats, offering Franz Josef Strauss as candidate for Chancellor, were defeated in 1980. The election was dominated by personalities and in particular by the comparison between the bullish, reactionary Bavarian and the pragmatic, unflappable Helmut Schmidt. It was now clear that Strauss's strategy of building a majority to the right of the "social-liberal" coalition had failed, and that the CDU/CSU must move towards the center. At the same time, Strauss's defeat made it easier for the FDP (which was swinging towards neo-liberalism) to contemplate changing its coalition partner. Schmidt's own position, moreover, weakened rapidly after 1980. The German economy went into recession after the oil shock of 1979, and unemployment had risen to 2.2 million by the end of 1982. Schmidt's support for austerity placed him at odds with the SPD's trade union wing, while his advocacy of nuclear power and the NATO missile deployment lost him the support of younger party members, many of whom gravitated towards the Green Party. In September 1982 the FDP Economics Minister Count Otto von Lambsdorff brought the disagreements to a head by presenting a paper on economic policy to Schmidt. Lambsdorff's proposals, which called for sweeping cuts in expenditure on welfare in order to finance cuts in income tax and tax concessions for industry, were clearly unacceptable to the SPD. Soon afterwards the FDP ministers resigned and, under a constructive vote of no confidence, formed a new governing coalition with Helmut Kohl at its head.

While the FDP had not behaved unconstitutionally, there was initially much sympathy for Schmidt's allegation that his former allies were guilty of "treason" and had betrayed their 1980 mandate. Such sentiments undoubtedly added to the pressure on Kohl to seek a mandate of his own by forcing a new election (with somewhat dubious legality). In March 1983 he led the coalition to a landslide victory, although the FDP was punished by the electorate and lost a third of their previous vote. The CDU/CSU won 48.8 percent compared with a mere 38.2 percent for the SPD. The greatest shock, however, was the success of the Green Party (see below) which won 2.2 million votes and entered the Bundestag for the first time with 27 seats. Once it had become apparent that the Greens were not an ephemeral phenomenon, one of the main questions in German politics would be whether – or how – the SPD could forge a viable "Red–Green" coalition.

Kohl had won the election by repudiating Schmidt's poor economic record under the slogan "Now vote for an upturn!" In the process the CDU/CSU had taken some 2 million former SPD voters, many of them nonunionized workers alarmed at the rise in unemployment.[17] However, while there was much talk in Christian Democrat circles of a *Wende* (or change of direction), Kohl had no intention of initiating the radical economic policies advocated by Lambsdorff. Kohl undoubtedly wished to swing the pendulum back towards the social market, but he was aware that divisive supply-side economics were just as unpalatable to the CDU/CSU as they were to social democrats. As he would put it in 1987, the CDU had a "clear Christian democratic profile and it must remain attractive for people from all classes."[18] Likewise, in foreign policy, while Kohl took a more Atlanticist and pro-integrationist stance than Schmidt, there was no question of abandoning *Ostpolitik*. The ultimate guarantor of *Ostpolitik* was the FDP leader Hans-Dietrich Genscher, who continued in office as Foreign Minister. Evidently, one of Kohl's main challenges was how to balance out the different components of the coalition, especially given the policy differences and long history of animosity between the CSU and the FDP and the capacity of Strauss (who did not join the government) to cause trouble. Kohl's relentless pursuit of compromise and consensus was easily mistaken for indecisive leadership.

Kohl's government made a determined attempt to bring the economy under control. The CDU Finance Minister Gerhard Stoltenburg succeeded in trimming the budget deficit with a package of cuts (including unemployment benefit) and other measures (such as forcing students to repay grants once they had obtained jobs). However, tax cuts were slow to materialize. In fact, the recession had bottomed out in late 1982, and the Western world as a whole was benefiting from a dramatic decline in oil prices by the mid-1980s. On the back of an export boom (helped by the strength of the dollar) the West German economy went from negative growth (−1 percent) in 1982 to a healthier +2.5 percent in 1986. However, unemployment was lodged at over 2 million, and, while assuaged by generous benefits and retraining schemes, was actually higher than it had been under Schmidt. Even so, the underlying strength of the economy, allied to the political constraints, made Thatcher-style radical reform seem irrelevant in the later 1980s.

Kohl's successful economic stewardship should have guaranteed his reelection in January 1987, and it is a sign of the continuing doubts as to his leadership that the campaign was no walkover. The allegations of corrupt party funding by the Flick company, which had forced Lambsdorff to resign in 1984, had lapped at Kohl's own door. (Grave further allegations of corruption were made after his fall from power in 1998.) Kohl had also shown poor judgment, and managed to offend or embarrass both superpower leaders. His critical comments about Gorbachev were deeply resented, while his decision to take President Reagan to visit a military cemetery at Bitburg where, it transpired, SS soldiers were buried, caused a brief international furore in 1985. The SPD, meanwhile, had chosen a popular if dull candidate, Johannes Rau, who had recently enlarged his majority as premier of North Rhine Westphalia (the most populous of the *Länder*). Rau now claimed, somewhat implausibly, that the SPD could seek outright victory, without any alliance with the Greens. In the event, although Kohl's coalition eventually won a substantial victory, both the main parties lost votes to the FDP and Greens. The defeat meant the end of the long final phase of Willy Brandt's career as SPD National Secretary. Although revered by many in the party, he had proved an awkward figure for the SPD establishment during the 1980s as an advocate of greater openness towards the Greens.

Bitburg was symptomatic of Kohl's somewhat naive attitude to Germany's Nazi past. Kohl, who claimed to represent a generation too young to have any moral responsibility for Nazism, believed that West Germany needed to establish a new basis for national pride and patriotism. He did not seem to understand quite how sensitive this issue still was: witness his 1985 decision to address a congress of Germans expelled from Silesia at the end of the war. In the course of his speech banners were unfurled proclaiming "Silesia stays German."[19] Concerns about the interpretation of Nazism crystallized in the so-called *Historikerstreit* ("historians' quarrel") within the German academic profession. In 1986 the historian Ernst Nolte published an article in which he sought to relativize the Holocaust and even to argue that the Nazi racial murder of the Jews was a response to the Bolsheviks' liquidation of the Russian bourgeoisie. Nolte's views were extreme and easily rebutted, but a number of conservative historians broadened the debate. One consequence of the controversy, however, was that when Germany was unexpectedly reunified in 1990, a great deal of the ideological passion concerning modern German identity had already been spent.

The ferocity of these debates demonstrated that it was still far too early to close the book on the Third Reich, or to regard West Germany as simply a "normal" west European country. Indeed, in November 1988 the CDU president of the Bundestag was forced to resign when, in a speech to mark the 50th anniversary of the "Crystal Night" pogrom, he attempted to explain the attitudes of ordinary Germans of the time without sufficiently distancing himself from their views. At the same time (1987–8) the Austrian president, Kurt Waldheim, was mired in

Figure 8.1   Erich Honecker and Chancellor Helmut Kohl listen to national anthems in Bonn, September 1987. Photo © akg-images.

controversy following revelations concerning his wartime service with the German armies in the Balkans. However, there was no question that Kohl led a country that was democratic, prosperous, and not only closely integrated into NATO and the EEC but also tolerant and constructive in its relations with the East. In September 1987 the East German leader Erich Honecker visited the FRG (see Figure 8.1). He came as the leader of a foreign state, but at the same time this was a homecoming for a miner's son born in the Saarland in 1912. During the visit Kohl reminded him that the "awareness of the unity of the nation is as alive as ever,"[20] but there was little indication of how suddenly it would be manifested.

Breaking the Mold? New Political Movements

In 1981 the Social Democratic Party aimed to "break the mold" of British politics by offering an alternative to the ideological gridlock of the two-party system. The SDP had a serious political agenda (it was pro-European and hostile to trade union power) but also represented a cry of middle-class exasperation with the extremism of Mrs. Thatcher and her Labour opponents. Despite initial successes, however, by 1988 the SDP had fused with the Liberal Party to create an enhanced political center, and much of the early radicalism was forgotten. Arguably, the SDP's political thinking was ahead of its time, and its greatest influence would be on Tony Blair's "New Labour" in the mid-1990s. It was one of a number of new political movements in Europe during the 1980s which, with varying degrees of success, sought to transform national politics by articulating new issues and by mobilizing new constituencies.

Perhaps the most remarkable new force was the West German Greens, which in 1983 became the first new party to gain representation in the Bundestag for 30 years. The Green Party was only established on a national basis in January 1980, claiming in its Constitution to be "the alternative to the traditional parties."[21] It had coalesced out of the anti-nuclear protest movement and, more specifically, from a number of local "Lists" that had competed in *Länder* elections in the late 1970s. The Greens appealed primarily to the young, educated middle class who were susceptible to "post-material"[22] issues such as nuclear power. This was above all the generation that had come of age during the late 1960s and espoused grassroots, feminist, direct democracy and which, accordingly, found itself at odds with Schmidt's SPD. In March 1983, when the Green Party took 5.6 percent of the vote, the Greens won the support of 23 percent of first-time voters and 60 percent of their voters were under the age of 35, but very few were from the working class.[23] On taking their seats the new Green deputies immediately challenged the stuffy etiquette and hierarchy of German politics: pullovers took the place of dark suits and there were three annually elected spokespeople rather than a formal party leader. The deputies gave away most of their parliamentary salaries (living only on a skilled worker's wages) and were rotated every two years to forestall the growth of a leadership cadre.

Over the next four years the Greens consolidated their position in the *Länder* (a Red–Green coalition was formed in Hesse in 1985), and confirmed their national presence with 8.3 percent in the 1987 Bundestag elections. Yet their very success emphasized the inherent contradiction between the party's radical intentions and its widening political options. During the mid-1980s a bitter debate raged between the "realists" (who wanted to exploit the party's breakthrough by forming a coalition with the SPD and adopting a more conventional political style) and the "fundamentalists" (who wanted the Greens to remain a protest movement outside the political mainstream). Good media performers such as Petra Kelly and Joschka Fischer chafed at the restrictions placed on their ability to put the Green case. The balance steadily shifted in the realists' favor, and by the early 1990s the rotation of deputies had been abolished and the role of the leaders had been strengthened. The evolution into a more conventional party was hastened by the Greens' stunning reverse in the 1990 election, when they paid the price for their hostility to German reunification and fell short of the 5 percent hurdle for representation in the Bundestag. Ironically, for the next four years a Green voice was provided by their sister party (Bundnis '90) which had won 6.1 percent in the former East Germany. This was a temporary setback, however, and the Greens had clearly established themselves as a significant (if more conventional than originally anticipated) factor in German politics. Most tellingly, they had retained the support of their core voters despite the adoption of environmentalist policies by the other parties.

While the Greens articulated environmental concerns, a number of new political parties of the far right gave vent to racist views (often in the context of fears regarding immigration and asylum-seekers). Some were a flash in the pan, such as the Republikaner Party in West Germany, which was established in 1983 by two former CSU deputies unhappy with Strauss's newfound friendship with East Germany. The Republikaner, which fell under the control of former SS soldier Franz Schönhuber, won 7.1 percent in the European elections of 1989, but never recovered momentum after German reunification. More significant was the rise of the Austrian Freedom Party (FPO) under the leadership of Jörg Haider. The FPO was a long-standing party of the right which had edged towards political respectability and even, between 1983 and 1986, served in coalition government with the socialists. In 1986, however, Haider seized control and turned the FPO into the main opponent of Austria's suffocating political consensus, particularly on issues such as immigration and law and order. He also abandoned the far right's traditional pan-Germanism for Austrian nationalism, and provoked uncomfortable discussion of Austria's Nazi past (for instance, by referring to the SS as "men of character"). Haider's real success lay in the next decade, but already by 1989 the FPO had scored 29 percent in his political base of Carinthia and 16.6 percent in the national elections of 1990. His combination of charisma, populism, and Austrian nationalism proved extremely difficult for the establishment parties to combat.

Jean-Marie Le Pen's Front National (FN) achieved even greater success, quarrying a similar vein of fear and resentment. Le Pen, a former Poujadist deputy who had served with the paratroopers in Algeria in the 1950s, had created the FN in 1972. Although he failed to secure sufficient support even to stand for president in 1981, the FN burst onto the political scene with 11.2 percent in the elections for the European Parliament of 1984, and won 35 seats in the 1986 parliamentary elections. Le Pen's appeal bore many similarities to Haider's, not least in his rejection of the political establishment and a certain ambiguity towards the Nazi past (he infamously commented that the Holocaust was a mere "question of detail" of the war).[24] However, Le Pen was able to draw with less inhibition than Haider on the national traditions and symbolism of the far right. The FN built up a substantial membership in an arc that ran from southern France (especially amongst former *pieds noirs*) to Alsace and the industrial suburbs of Paris. Many of Le Pen's supporters were workers, including some former communists. Although Le Pen took 14.6 percent in the 1988 presidential elections, his main political impact was on the center-right parties, notably Chirac's RPR. They had to decide whether to adopt some of the FN's policies (witness the tougher, racially insensitive policing under Chirac's 1986–8 government) or, alternatively, to form coalitions with it (especially at the regional and local level). On the left, Le Pen helped to galvanize a popular anti-racism movement ("SOS-Racisme") which was quietly backed by Mitterrand.

The Northern League in Italy had many features in common with the parties of the far right, although it defies easy ideological categorization. It was created in December 1989, under the leadership of Umberto Bossi, out of a number of smaller regional organizations such as the Liga Veneta (established in 1980) and Bossi's own Lombard League. It was at the same time a regional and an anti-system party, reliant on grassroots activism. Resentment was directed against Rome (which was seen to be squandering the wealth of the north) and against the "lazy" southern Italian migrants who were now such an important element in northern life. Racist assumptions clearly underlay the League's appeal, although Bossi was adamant that he was an anti-fascist and refused to identify the League with the political right. The League achieved its political breakthrough in the 1990 local elections, when it won 18.9 percent in Lombardy, and in 1990 Bossi orchestrated a special assembly at which a "Republic of the North" was declared. However, the League's secessionist ambitions were placed in abeyance when it joined Silvio Berlusconi's first coalition government in 1994.

Southern Europe

Throughout southern Europe, the electoral success of socialist parties in the 1980s seemed to posit an alternative to the conservative hegemony in the north, although closer examination often revealed a yawning gap between leftist rhetoric and reality. Nowhere was this illusion more evident than in Italy where the socialist leader Bettino Craxi headed center-left coalitions between 1983 and 1987. This was not the first time that the Christian Democrats had ceded the premiership to a coalition partner, as the Republican Spadolini had held office between 1981 and 1982, but it reflected the very severe decline in their vote in the 1983 election (from 38.3 percent to 32.9 percent). Craxi was a domineering, ebullient politician whose party, perhaps more than any other in Europe, captured the upwardly mobile, "yuppy" zeitgeist of the 1980s. The socialists became the natural home for the enterprising, image-conscious middle class of the northern cities, above all Milan. In reality, however, the socialists still only commanded some 11 percent of the vote, and the DC were quick to regain control over the government when their vote partially recovered in 1987.

Craxi was unencumbered by traditional socialist concerns, and in 1984 pushed through a reduction of wage indexation in the face of union opposition. His business-friendly policies often shaded into impropriety: he was a close ally of the Milanese media entrepreneur Silvio Berlusconi and in 1984 came to his rescue when the courts sought to restrict his burgeoning television empire. However, Craxi's premiership undoubtedly restored a sense of stability and resolve after the crises of the 1970s. He became the longest-serving postwar prime minister (until Berlusconi), and embodied a new sense of national pride and self-esteem. In January 1987 he gloried in the claim that the Italian economy had "overtaken" that of Britain, while he also demonstrated a willingness to stand up to the USA. In 1985, for instance, he refused to hand over the Palestinian hijacker Abu Abbas, accused of murdering an American citizen, whose plane had been forced to land in Italy by US aircraft. Yet, ultimately, Craxi's political ambition was to ruin him and the Socialist Party, as he relentlessly milked the corrupt opportunities provided by Italy's new "economic miracle." The party-funding scandal that devastated Italian politics in the early 1990s (see Chapter 11) can hardly be blamed on the socialists alone, but the dark heart of *tangentopoli* lay in the greed of Craxi and his colleagues. It was fitting that the man who briefly dominated Italy should die (in 2000) in exiled disgrace in Tunisia.

In the Iberian peninsula the two dominant issues during the decade were the completion of the transition to democracy and integration with western Europe (both Spain and Portugal joined the EEC/EU in January 1986). The former issue was particularly significant in Portugal, where the revolution had been institutionalized under the terms of the 1976 Constitution. The presence of General Eanes as president was a constant reminder of the military's continuing role in politics, while the constitutional provisions for a large public sector inhibited economic restructuring. Well into the 1980s, therefore, Portuguese politicians were preoccupied with the need to revise the Constitution. Eanes was persuaded to relinquish his position as Chief of Staff and dissolve the Council of the Revolution, and the 1982 Law on National Defense established civilian control over the military. However, the formation of the pro-Eanes Democratic Renewal Party (which won

18 percent in the 1985 parliamentary elections) showed that the spirit of the 1974 revolution was not yet dead. Accordingly, the 1986 presidential elections (narrowly won by the socialist Mário Soares) were invested with extra significance, marking the final consolidation of civilian rule. Only now could the conservative government of Anibal Cavaco Silva begin in earnest to address Portugal's severe economic problems, which had left it trailing behind the rest of southern Europe.

The Spanish Socialist Party (PSOE), which swept to power with 47 percent of the vote in October 1982, was related in name only to the hard-bitten band of exiles that had kept the party alive during the dictatorship. During the 1970s a younger generation of Spanish-based leaders, notably the Andalusians Felipe González and Alfonso Guerra, had won control and begun to transform the PSOE into a modern reformist party. In 1979 González defeated the left and discarded Marxism from the PSOE's program. However, this was hardly a party devoid of ambition, as one of the socialists' campaign pledges in 1982 was to create 800,000 new jobs. Once in office González soon concluded that what was required was the painful restructuring of the Spanish economy, especially of the public sector, which had become bloated and corrupt under Franco, if Spain was to derive any benefit from its entry to the EC. Inflation was cut back and the Spanish economy grew at a rate well above the EC average in the boom of the later 1980s. But far from jobs being created, unemployment rose from 16.8 percent of the population in 1982 to peak at 21.7 percent in 1985. It had only fallen marginally when recession struck again in the early 1990s. Not surprisingly, the socialist government soon found itself at odds with the trade unions over its economic policy and, after a one-day general strike in December 1988, the PSOE was separated from its historic partner the UGT (General Workers' Union). In many respects, therefore, González was pursuing policies in line with neo-liberalism, such as a freer labor market and extensive privatization. However, it should be noted that he was responding to the statist inheritance of the Franco era (largely ignored by the previous Suárez government), and that Spanish structural reform relied far more heavily on the use of the state than neo-liberal orthodoxy allowed.[25]

The threat of military intervention was greatly reduced in Spain after the failed coup of February 1981. Even so, the desire to modernize, professionalize, and distract the army was an important element in the socialist government's controversial decision to campaign for Spain to remain in NATO (in apparent contravention of an election promise). Although the government was victorious in the March 1986 referendum on this issue, the campaign was colored by allegations of state manipulation of the media, and gave an opportunity for the Communist Party to revive as a focus for the Spanish left. In general, however, González was largely untroubled by opposition during the 1980s, and the PSOE easily won reelection, with absolute majorities, in 1986 and 1989. The UCD had collapsed by 1982, and the Partido Popular (the main conservative party) was far too tainted with Francoism to be electable. One consequence was a certain arrogance of power that began to affect González, whose attendance at the Cortes markedly declined in the later 1980s. Indeed, the principal blot on the record of the PSOE government was the "dirty war" conducted against ETA in the mid-1980s by a murder gang known as the GAL (Anti-Terrorist Liberation Groups) which was clearly sponsored from within the Spanish state. The GAL's activities inside France forced the French government to clamp down on ETA and extradite its militants, but they outraged Basque opinion and helped to perpetuate the conflict. Complex judicial investigations ensued and, while González escaped censure, his former Interior Minister was eventually jailed in 1998.[26] The socialists were also involved in a number of party-funding scandals which, like the GAL controversy, became susceptible to detailed investigation only when the PSOE lost its parliamentary majority in 1993. González's reputation, and that of his government, was severely damaged by these revelations of corruption and the abuse of power. However, it is important to acknowledge the government's role in modernizing the economy, promoting the decentralization of power to the regions, and helping the armed forces to come to terms with democracy. It was a sign of Spain's new maturity that the judiciary and press held González to account so effectively in the twilight of his administration.

Such maturity was difficult to detect in Greece, where the 1980s were dominated by the heady, infuriating populism of Andreas Papandreou (son of the prime minister overthrown in 1965). Papandreou returned from exile in the USA to establish the Pan-Hellenic Socialist Movement (PASOK) in 1974. His landslide victory in October 1981 with 48 percent of the vote was a remarkable achievement, even though his way had been smoothed by the elevation of Karamanlis (the hero of the transition) to the presidency in 1980. Papandreou successfully traded on a Greek sense of betrayal by the West (and above all the USA) over the junta and the invasion of Cyprus, promising voters nonalignment and a vague "third road to socialism." His rhetoric, which pitted the unprivileged majority against the privileged few, translated in office into a massive boost in public expenditure (which rose by 40 percent between 1982 and 1988) and job creation for the benefit of his supporters. There were undoubted gains – above all improvements in welfare and the establishment of a national health service – but the public sector was hopelessly inefficient, while private industry and agriculture responded poorly to the challenge of EC membership. Greece failed to attract significant US investment during the 1980s, whereas it rose by 90 percent in Spain and Portugal once they had joined the EC. By the mid-1980s Papandreou was forced to impose austerity measures, but the purse strings were loosened again in time for the 1989 elections. Internationally, meanwhile, for all his rhetoric Papandreou was remarkably pragmatic. The presence of US bases was successfully renegotiated in 1983, and Greece remained within NATO and the EC. Papandreou's popularity remained high, even when his health failed and he became vulnerable to allegations of corruption. In 1989–90 PASOK's vote held steady at some 40 percent in three bitterly contested elections, and Papandreou even survived an unholy alliance of the conservative New Democracy and the communists that was directed against him.

Conclusion

Despite the ideological differences that separated the three dominant leaders of western Europe in the 1980s, there was a very significant degree of convergence in economic policy during the decade following the failure of the French socialist experiment of 1981–3. No other European governments could match the anti-union, privatizing zeal of Margaret Thatcher, but by the late 1980s there was broad agreement on the need for sound finance, deregulation, and industrial restructuring. However, Thatcher's hostility to European integration prevented her from offering real leadership within the EC. She was also unusual in the closeness of her relationship with the United States: most west European governments were fearful of Ronald Reagan and the "New Cold War" and preferred détente. Meanwhile, there was rapid economic and political convergence amongst the new democracies of southern Europe, even though socialist governments were generally in power. Some theorists hailed the advent of a "postmodern" era in the 1980s, reflecting developments such as the long-term decline in traditional heavy industry, changing gender relations, and the new importance of leisure and the media.

9
European Integration
From Rome to Maastricht, 1957–1992

Perspectives on Integration

The process of integration has been the most significant European achievement of the postwar era. Ever-increasing numbers of states, far beyond the original Six, voluntarily yielded aspects of their sovereignty in return for economic and political benefits (see Map 9.1). The results in both areas were striking. The volume of intra-European trade massively increased, and a free market in goods, services, and capital was created. Integration also promoted the stabilization of western Europe (most notably through Franco-German reconciliation), while the desire for membership of the European Community drove liberal reforms in both southern and eastern Europe. However, significant questions need to be posed about why this particular path – apparently so much at odds with the nationalist traditions of the previous hundred years – was pursued. Could not, for instance, similar results have been achieved through the creation of a free trade area, or even by conventional bilateral arrangements?

Serious, systematic thought about the concept of European integration can be dated to the inter-war years, although there was little direct link between the federalist ideas of the 1920s, or even of the immediate post-1945 period, and the institutions that developed from the 1950s. The closest point of similarity between, say, the Pan-European Union of the 1920s and more recent integrationist thinking was that both were informed by the need for an end to Franco-German enmity, and both were essentially elitist constructions. World War II did much to promote the idea of a federal Europe – notably in resistance circles – as an alternative to the destructive nationalism of the 1930s. After the war such thinking also appealed to many conservatives, the most poignant example being Winston Churchill's call in September 1946 for "a kind of United States of Europe."[1] However, this overtly

Europe's Troubled Peace: 1945 to the Present, Second Edition. Tom Buchanan.
© 2012 John Wiley & Sons, Ltd. Published 2012 by John Wiley & Sons, Ltd.

political approach proved largely ineffectual given the lack of any strong support for it at the governmental level. The greatest early success for advocates of political union was the creation of the Council of Europe in 1949, which made a significant contribution to the development of norms of democracy and human rights,[2] but was not allowed to develop any supranational powers. Ever since the traumatic failure of the European Defence Community (EDC) in 1954, European political cooperation had consistently played a secondary role to economic integration. Jean Monnet himself commented, with reference to the EDC's proposed constitution, that it was wrong to think that European unity "would *begin* with the establishment of a federal political system."[3] Indeed, where integration was successful it started not with blueprints for federal institutions, but rather with specific projects that addressed individual states' economic and security needs: hence the attractiveness of the Schuman Plan for a Coal and Steel Community in 1950 (see Chapter 3).

European integration, as it evolved in the 1950s, was less concerned with visionary goals than with developing a process and a viable method of working. That process was enshrined in the preamble to the EEC Treaty of 1957, which aspired to an "ever closer union among the peoples of Europe."[4] This is broadly descriptive of the course of events since 1957, although there were periods (notably in the 1970s) when the process appeared frozen. There was also a tendency, as the Community enlarged and became more disparate, for some countries to opt out of aspects of integration and to wish to progress at different speeds. The method of integration was pioneered, in its purest form, by Jean Monnet in the ECSC (European Coal and Steel Community). Here, a supranational technocratic executive (the High Authority) operated with its own source of funding within a framework of legal, parliamentary, and ministerial supervision. Monnet and early theorists (notably Ernst B. Haas) believed that the integration of one sector would inevitably create "spillover" into other areas, generating the momentum that would ineluctably drive the whole process forwards. However, this "functionalist" approach did not initially appear to be borne out by events. The ECSC did not serve as a model for future developments, as the EEC was, quite deliberately, set up on an institutional basis that was substantially less supranational than that of its predecessor. Moreover, under the impact of de Gaulle, the EEC was – until the mid-1980s – driven primarily by intergovernmental cooperation. There was little sign of remorseless pressure for extending integration when for many years the only common EEC policy had been in agriculture. However, Monnet's belief in "spillover" was to some extent vindicated by the quiet growth in the importance of institutions such as the EEC's Court of Justice. For instance, the court's 1979 ruling on the import of French *cassis de Dijon* to West Germany established the principle of the "mutual recognition" of standards between member states which pointed the way to the single-market legislation of the mid-1980s.

It was initially something of a strength, and latterly a weakness, that European integration was very much an elite process. Its basis lay in traditional diplomatic

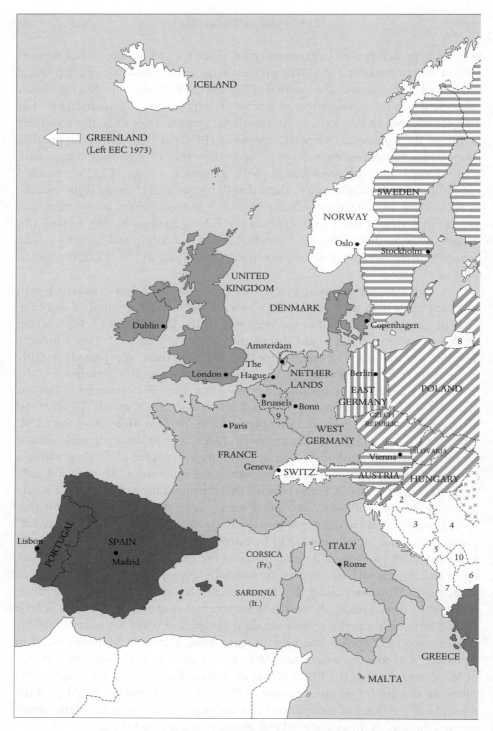

Map 9.1 From the EEC to the EU: the growth of European integration, 1957–2004. Members of the Eurozone in 2011: Ireland, Portugal, Spain, France, Malta, Cyprus, Greece, Italy, Belgium, Netherlands, Luxembourg, Germany, Austria, Slovenia, Slovakia, Estonia, Finland. Candidate countries 2011: Turkey, Iceland, Croatia, former Yugoslav Republic of Macedonia, Montenegro.

Date of entry into EEC

- 1957 (founding member)
- 1973
- 1981
- 1986
- 1990 (as a result of German unification, 3 October 1990)
- 1994
- 2004
- 2007

1 Slovenia
2 Croatia
3 Bosnia & Hercegovina
4 Serbia
5 Montenegro
6 Macedonia
7 Albania
8 Kaliningrad (Russian Federation)
9 Luxembourg
10 Kosovo

Potential candidate countries 2011: Albania, Bosnia and Herzgovina, Serbia, Kosovo (under UNSCR Resolution 1244) (Source: European Commission website, accessed 12/4/2011)
Source: Based on Derek Urwin, *The Community of Europe* (Longman, London, 1995), pp. 284–5. Reprinted with permission of Pearson Education

and interest group bargaining, and a belief that it was better to entrust crucial decisions to impartial experts than to national politicians. Moreover, little attempt was made to galvanize public support or even understanding. In Britain, for instance, the Community was generally – and somewhat misleadingly – referred to as the "Common Market" during the 1970s. By the early 1990s there was widespread concern at the EC's alleged "democratic deficit," given its lack of transparency and the relative weakness of its parliament. Indeed, a number of national referenda over the Maastricht Treaty in 1992 indicated a growing popular disenchantment with – and even fear of – integration. Meanwhile, the political basis of European integration had shifted considerably since the 1950s. Initially the EEC was closely associated with Christian Democracy and with business and farming interests. Liberals such as Ludwig Erhard tended to be more skeptical, favoring a free-trade area, while socialists realized that the Treaty of Rome had little to say about social policy. However, by the 1980s this had changed: indeed, the revival of European integration owed much to a socialist president of the Commission, Jacques Delors, working closely with the socialist French president François Mitterrand. In the late 1980s Delors persuaded trade unionists that the single market had to have a social dimension and encouraged them to work within the Community's structures. Between the 1970s and the 1990s, the British Conservative and Labour parties almost completely exchanged their positions for and against European integration (although in reality both parties remained deeply divided on the issue).

Reference to Delors raises the currently unfashionable question of the role of individuals in driving integration forwards. Clearly, no individual politician or servant of the Community – just as no individual country – has been able to advance the process single-handed. For instance, Jean Monnet's role as the "founding father" of European integration (see Figure 9.1) is now understood far more in rhetorical than practical terms.[5] Monnet had little direct input after resigning as president of the ECSC High Authority in 1955, and backed the wrong horse (Euratom) prior to the treaties of Rome. Yet his contribution to the vision of an integrated Europe was unparalleled, as was his ability to inspire a generation of collaborators with belief in the transformative power of institutions. His close connection with American policy-formers (having served French interests in Washington during the war, latterly as director of the French Supply Mission) was also extremely valuable. Delors, who served two and a half terms at the Commission (1984–95), demonstrated the impact that an activist president could make. However, it must be noted that his presidency coincided with the unique opportunity for progress offered by the Kohl–Mitterrand axis and German reunification. Conversely, the activism of the first president of the Commission, Walter Hallstein, foundered on the animosity of de Gaulle. Amongst politicians the most obvious influence has been wielded not only by those who wanted to advance integration, but also by those who, like de Gaulle, were inherently suspicious of it. In the 1980s Margaret Thatcher – while often an isolated figure – influenced the Community's evolution in a free market direction.

Figure 9.1 From left to right: Jean Monnet, Robert Schuman, Konrad Adenauer, and Walter Hallstein meeting to sign a draft treaty of the Schuman Plan, March 1951.
Photo © akg-images/Erich Lessing.

European integration has remained an uneasy balance between idealism and hard-headed national interest. Moreover, as the idealism of the 1950s waned, based as it was on the desire to avoid any further war in Europe, few in the 1990s were willing to articulate openly an alternative, federal European ideal. A draft reference to the EU's "federal vocation" was hastily withdrawn prior to the Maastricht Treaty negotiations in 1991. The historical record has, therefore, tended to vindicate those who have argued that, far from dissolving the nation-state, European integration provided a powerful new forum within which its interests could be articulated and defended.[6] Economic considerations took precedence, while governments consistently dragged their feet in areas where they did not wish to see integration, such as defense and social policy. No states were forced to join the Community, nor – until the extension of qualified majority voting (QMV) in the 1980s – could they be compelled to act contrary to their wishes. However, integration was above all about negotiation and compromise for mutual self-interest, and governments could make "package" deals that they later came to regret. A good example is that of Mrs. Thatcher, who was persuaded to allow institutional reform in return for sweeping economic deregulation in 1986.

The Foundation of the EEC

The failure of the EDC in 1954, overly ambitious and unnecessary as it proved, was taken to be a serious blow to European integration. However, a welter of more viable proposals soon emerged, resulting in what became known as the *relance* ("relaunching") of the European project. With hindsight, the most significant of these was the proposal by the Dutch Foreign Minister Jan Willem Beyen for a customs union, which had originally been intended to form part of the EDC, although Monnet's idea for the integration of the nascent European atomic industry was the more eye-catching. Monnet's proposal built on the ECSC "sectoral" approach and had the great advantage of appealing both to the USA and to the French (who were apprehensive about the liberalization of trade through a customs union). At the Messina conference of the ECSC foreign ministers in June 1955 a committee was established under the Belgian Paul-Henri Spaak to examine both proposals, thereby keeping the French on board, and eventually to devise concrete plans for their implementation. Spaak's report was approved in May 1956 and laid the basis for the twin Euratom and EEC treaties signed in Rome on March 25, 1957.

This successful outcome was by no means a foregone conclusion. At the heart of the difficult negotiation over the EEC Treaty lay the very different – if in some respects complementary – interests of France and West Germany. France, still mired in the Algerian conflict and traditionally protectionist, feared the potentially devastating impact of German competition on its industries. It also wanted to protect the interests of its colonies, and did not wish to suffer comparative disadvantage as a result of its more generous welfare provision. At the same time, however, it was desperate to gain access to the German market for its efficient and rapidly expanding agriculture. Meanwhile, within the West German government there was a division between Finance Minister Erhard, who disliked the common external tariff and wanted Britain to participate in the project, and Adenauer, who judged the EEC as being in Germany's long-term political and economic interests. The Chancellor was eager to find new export markets within Europe for Germany's booming manufacturing industries, but was also alive to the interests of German farmers who possessed an influential voice within the CDU. Establishing a workable balance between French and German interests was clearly crucial to the treaty, but other national considerations also had to be taken into account.

For instance, Italy – poorest of the Six – gave priority to labor mobility within the Community as a way of easing its unemployment. The Benelux countries, meanwhile, which had already established a limited customs union in 1948, wanted to maximize their voice within the EEC's institutions.

The eventual settlement met most of the French concerns: indeed, this was essential if the treaty were to be ratified given the weakness of French governments in the latter stages of the Fourth Republic. Above all, it was agreed that there would be a Common Agricultural Policy (CAP), although the exact details were yet to be worked out. The CAP was dedicated to ensuring a "fair standard of living for the agricultural community" and reasonable prices for consumers (Article 39), although the former concern was set to predominate. In addition, the interests of the French colonies were protected, and they were the main beneficiaries of a European Overseas Development Fund. At its core the treaty established a 12-year timetable for the progressive reduction of internal tariffs and the creation of a common market between the Six, sheltered by a common external tariff. It also established an institutional basis for the EEC which, on paper at least, resembled the ECSC. In fact, however, the ECSC had been widely seen as too independent and *dirigiste*, and the institutional balance within the EEC was designed to act as a check on supranationalism. For instance, the nine-strong Commission (which was charged with defending the EEC's interests) did not possess its own funding and its members were appointed by governments. The Commission was intended to initiate policy proposals, the fate of which was decided by a Council of Ministers (although this distinction between executive and decision-making roles subsequently became blurred with the rise of intergovernmentalism in the 1970s). Within the Council of Ministers voting was weighted according to size, but the treaty made provision for the eventual introduction of qualified majority voting in specific circumstances to prevent the biggest three states from simply imposing their will on the others. The Community's other two institutions were an Assembly (at this stage simply nominated from members of national parliaments) and a Court of Justice charged with ensuring the lawful interpretation and application of the treaty. Other aspects of the treaty, such as the harmonization of social policy, were far more nebulous, although a European Social Fund and a European Investment Bank were set up to ease the implementation of the common market (principally to help the poor south of Italy).

The most notable absentees were the British, who had been represented at Messina and on the Spaak Committee but had decided not to join the EEC. This was partly due to Britain's inherent dislike of integration, as well as a rather patronizing sense that – after the failure of the EDC – there was little prospect of success. Yet the British abstention also conformed to geopolitical and commercial realities at the time. In 1958 only some 30 percent of British trade was with western Europe, compared with 21 percent with the former Dominions and 25.6 percent with the Third World.[7] Britain also had a minuscule farming population by EEC standards (5 percent of the population, compared with 25 percent in France and 15 percent in Germany).[8] Moreover, British governments still prioritized the relationship with the USA (and to a lesser extent the Commonwealth) over Europe. However, it should be noted that the Eisenhower administration strongly supported the EEC, despite its potential disadvantages for US trade, and would have liked Britain to participate. The British response to the EEC was to float the idea of a European free trade area, within which the Six would form a united core, on the wider basis of the OEEC. This proposal had its supporters, such as Erhard, but was rejected by de Gaulle in November 1958. As a consequence, in November 1959 Britain joined with Portugal, Switzerland, Denmark, Norway, Austria, and Sweden in forming the European Free Trade Area. EFTA represented an alternative model of economic cooperation. Hence, there would be a progressive elimination of internal tariffs for manufactured goods, but no common external tariff, and the *modus operandi* would be strictly intergovernmental. EFTA's institutional base was very limited: its headquarters in Geneva employed a mere 80 staff compared with the 3,000 already employed by the EEC. While in many respects a success, EFTA – which mainly represented small economies around the periphery of western Europe – could never hope to compete with the EEC's much larger market. In any case, as early as July 1961 its largest member, Britain, applied for membership of the EEC.

The British application represented both recognition of how swiftly Britain's trade patterns were shifting towards Europe in the early 1960s, and also that the EEC was actually working to promote growth. Indeed, it soon became apparent that the EEC was a highly successful initiative, and that it – rather than Euratom – would henceforward be the driving force behind European integration. By April 1965 it had merged with the ECSC and Euratom to form the European Communities (EC). The EEC had succeeded because it offered something to all of the member states, while also promoting a general increase in trade from which all benefited. It had also been boosted by the very timely Rueff–Pinay economic reforms in France (1958–9), which allowed a liberalized French economy to play its full part. By 1961 trade within the Community was expanding at twice the rate of that with non-EEC countries. Although Monnet's role had been marginal, the EEC's progress vindicated his pragmatic strategy of advancing towards integration along the lines of common agreement. As he later wrote: "It was necessary to pull on the thread which would untangle some knots and, step by step, the rest would fall into place."[9]

De Gaulle and the EEC, 1958–1969

In many respects the EEC continued to flourish during the 1960s, and the core objectives of the Treaty of Rome were fulfilled. Internal tariffs were eliminated well ahead of schedule in July 1968, the same year that the free movement of labor was achieved. The Common Agricultural Policy became operational, after prolonged wrangling over its funding, in July 1967. The economy grew at some 7 percent per year across the EEC during this period, and even the Italian economy responded strongly to the vast new market. The economic attraction of the Community was such that enlargement almost immediately became an issue. Britain and a number of other EFTA members opened negotiations during the 1960s, while associate status was granted to Greece (1961) and Turkey (1963). In institutional terms, probably the most significant development was the growing assertiveness of the Court of Justice. Landmark rulings established that the EEC Treaty had created a new international legal order that impinged both on states and on their nationals (1963), and that EEC law took precedence over national law (1964). This sense of the Community as an international actor in its own right was encouraged by the Commission's first president, Walter Hallstein, a senior German civil servant who had previously served as Adenauer's State Secretary. Hallstein, an integrationist in the Monnet mold, believed that the Commission's task was to drive the process forward by opening up areas that had been only hazily sketched out under the Treaty of Rome. He enjoyed some success – for instance, the EEC was allowed to speak collectively for the Six in economic fora such as the General Agreement on Tariffs and Trade (GATT). However, his choice of language – he referred to himself as a kind of European prime minister and claimed that national sovereignty was a doctrine of "yesteryear"[10] – was ill advised and deeply provocative to de Gaulle.

De Gaulle's attitude to the EEC had initially proved surprisingly positive, given his outright opposition to the EDC. On returning to office he recognized the value of the EEC to the strengthening of the French economy, and above all wished to complete the introduction of the CAP. Moreover, de Gaulle saw the EEC as a potential vehicle for his ambitions for France, whereby a west European bloc – under French domination – would be free of both US and Soviet influence. As Harold Macmillan put it: "He talks of Europe, and means France."[11] De Gaulle was therefore supportive of the EEC, but only on his own terms. He detested supranationalism, and famously offered in its place the vision of a "Europe des patries." He opposed any extension of the Commission's powers, and was deeply suspicious of enlargement (which might dilute French influence). Accordingly, the de Gaulle era was marked by a series of crises which temporarily halted any further progress on either the widening or the deepening of the Community.

The tone was set for future relations by the controversy over de Gaulle's May 1960 proposal for European political cooperation (as formulated by the French diplomat Christian Fouchet and subsequently modified by de Gaulle in 1962). The final version of the "Fouchet Plan" was unacceptable to EEC Atlanticists such as Spaak and the Dutch Foreign Minister Joseph Luns. In particular, they objected to the absence of any reference to NATO in the document, as well as to the suggestion that the proposed (Paris-based) "Union of States" would have some economic functions. They saw this as an attempt by de Gaulle to encroach on the territory of

NATO and the Commission which would perpetuate the exclusion of Britain, and the proposal was abandoned in April 1962. This episode undoubtedly soured de Gaulle's relations with the EEC, and contributed to his remarkable decision to "veto" the British application to join the EEC at a press conference on January 14, 1963. De Gaulle's objection was twofold: first, he saw Britain as inherently incompatible with the Europe of the Six, "in the way it lives, in the way it produces, in the way it trades," and saw British membership as an obstacle to agreement on the CAP.[12] Secondly, he perceived Britain as a channel for US influence and a threat to French domination in Europe. In this case, the final straw had been Macmillan's meeting with Kennedy in December 1962 to negotiate British access to US nuclear weapons. The unilateralism of de Gaulle's "veto" (for which there was no legal provision) was particularly offensive to the other EEC members, who desired British membership precisely as a counterweight to this kind of behavior. As Luns commented, this was a "black day for Europe."[13] A second British application was also ruled out by de Gaulle in November 1967.

Meanwhile, Hallstein's activism placed him on a collision course with de Gaulle. In March 1965 the Commission advanced proposals which tied access to its own funding (from the import levy) to the financing of the CAP and the extension of the powers of the Assembly. At the same time, as agreed in the Treaty of Rome, the Council was intended to move towards majority voting in a number of areas by January 1966. De Gaulle deemed these measures an unacceptable dose of supra-nationalism, and railed against "the embryonic technocracy, for the most part foreign"[14] of the Commission. From July 1965 French officials refused to play a part in EEC decision-making, initiating the so-called "empty chair" crisis. Although too much was at stake to endanger the EEC itself, the crisis was undoubtedly a serious one, and it was resolved broadly on de Gaulle's terms under the "Luxembourg compromise" of January 1966. The Council noted the French position that unanimity was required on any issue affecting important national interests, although it was not made clear what would happen if a unanimous decision could not be reached. In effect, de Gaulle had achieved a "veto" for member states on matters of vital national interest, although it was ill defined and its effectiveness depended on the political context. For instance, in May 1982 Britain's attempt to veto a majority decision on agricultural price levels was ruled out on the grounds that this was not a vital British interest. More generally, de Gaulle had put a halt to further supranationalism and asserted governmental control over the process of European integration, at the expense of the Commission. Hallstein stood down in 1967, after France had ruled out a further term, and the next activist president of the Commission would be Roy Jenkins a decade later (1977–81). However, after the failure of the Fouchet Plan, de Gaulle had no new vision for the EEC and did not wish to turn the clock back, least of all on the CAP. The result was to consolidate the status quo.

De Gaulle's resignation in 1969 opened a window for further progress that was soon closed by the onset of recession and stagflation. Pompidou shared de Gaulle's suspicion of the Commission, but accepted that the greater economic and diplomatic strength of West Germany (expressed in *Ostpolitik*) now made Britain a potential counterweight within the Community. At the same time, however, he felt that integration should be deepened prior to enlargement, while agreement was urgently needed on the financing of the CAP and the EEC's self-funding. Accordingly, the Hague summit of December 1969 – itself an innovation – signaled an important change of direction. It gave the green light to talks on enlargement, but also set in train separate investigations into political unification and economic and monetary union, both of which reported in 1970. The Davignon report on political unification initiated a modest step towards intergovernmental cooperation, starting with regular meetings of member states' foreign ministers to discuss foreign policy issues. The more significant document of the two was the Werner report, which set out a staged process for achieving economic and monetary union (EMU) within the decade. The timetable was over-ambitious, but it was clear that – with governments now in the saddle – the logic of "ever closer union" was again in play. More prosaically, agreement was also reached in 1970 for the provision of the Community's own resources from a combination of levies on imported food, receipts from the external tariff, and up to 1 percent of the new Value Added Tax (VAT), imposed across the EEC.

Stagnation, 1970–1984

The economic crisis of the mid-1970s (see Chapter 7) compelled governments to prioritize their own national interests and prevented any significant progress towards the goals of monetary and political union established at the Hague. Indeed, let alone achieving EMU by 1980, many currencies struggled to survive within far more modest schemes for exchange rate stability. Even the enlargement of the Community, the greatest success of this period, brought its own new problems. For much of this period the EC, as it was now collectively known, seemed to have precious little to offer. The CAP, which remained the only substantial common policy, had grown to dominate the Community: it tied up 72 percent of its budget and 60 percent of its staff between 1968 and 1974.[15] It had also become a by-word for inefficiency and greed as EC taxpayers and consumers were, in effect, subsidizing the immense surpluses (the "lakes" and "mountains") generated by a highly productive industry. Meanwhile, the common market was still far from completion – notably in fiscal, monetary, and social policy – and nontariff barriers proliferated. The EC also found itself managing the decline of historic, but no longer internationally competitive, industries such as steel and textiles.

Even though this was the EC's most difficult decade, some progress was made. Most importantly, intergovernmentalism took an institutional form in the "European Council" (not to be confused with the Council of Ministers). From

1974 onwards it was agreed that there should be summits three times a year and a presidency which would revolve every six months amongst the member states. Although not formally part of the EC's structure, the Council was evidence of the closer interest that governments were now taking in the Community, and inevitably diminished the role of the Commission. The Council also offered a vehicle for the emerging Franco-German axis (based on the excellent relations between Giscard and Schmidt) and resulted in a number of significant initiatives – notably the European Monetary System (EMS). A second significant step was the development of the European Parliament, which had long seemed somewhat cosmetic. In 1979 the first direct elections were held across the EC, boosting the parliament's legitimacy. However, the five-yearly elections continued to reflect national political agendas, and direct election failed to stimulate the creation of "European" political parties or manifestos.

With the collapse of the Bretton Woods agreement and the suspension of dollar convertibility, exchange rate stability became a matter of pressing concern to EC governments, not least to ensure the smooth functioning of the CAP. Accordingly, in March 1972 the "snake" was set up to establish a 2.25 percent margin of variability between member currencies in relation to the dollar. However, the pressures were such that the pound sterling and the Irish punt (which had not yet formally joined the EC) had been forced to leave by July 1972. The franc was also forced out in January 1974, returning briefly in 1975–6. In effect, therefore, the "snake" became little more than a Deutschmark zone within which a number of non-EC countries (such as Austria, Norway and Sweden) could also be found. In the late 1970s the EMS, an altogether more sustained and elaborate project, was launched as a Franco-German initiative. Again, the objective was to control exchange rate volatility by imposing fixed bands (which central banks were compelled to uphold), although there was an additional objective of exporting West German anti-inflationary rigor. Moreover, the EMS was now backed up by official reserves and, for the first time, a common currency unit (the ecu) for internal accounting. Despite its success during the 1980s, however, the EMS (which operated through the Exchange Rate Mechanism) underlined the lack of unity within the Community. Britain remained outside the ERM until 1990, while those who joined it were divided into the stronger economies (which could fluctuate by 2.25 percent) and Italy and Ireland (which were allowed a 6 percent band). Monetary union still seemed a very distant possibility.

In January 1973 Britain, Denmark, and Ireland became the first countries to accede to the EC, to be joined in January 1981 by Greece. (In September 1972 Norway voted by 53.5 percent against taking up membership, mainly due to the concerns of its farmers and fishermen.) However, Euroskepticism remained strong in Britain and Denmark, which had been compelled by its strong commercial links to follow the UK's lead. In 1974 Harold Wilson's new Labour government immediately renegotiated Britain's terms of entry, sufficient to allow him to win a referendum by 2:1 on British membership in June 1975. However, the question of

Britain's excessive budgetary contributions resurfaced under Mrs. Thatcher, who shook the male camaraderie of the European Council with her determination to claim her "own money back" in November 1979.[16] Thatcher eventually succeeded in reaching a settlement at the Fontainebleau summit of June 1984, after a lingering and acrimonious dispute that had seriously distracted from the work of the Community. In Greece, too, Papandreou's new socialist government succeeded in winning greater regional aid in 1983. Indeed, with Spain and Portugal set to join the EC in January 1986, the question of national disparities of wealth was set to loom far larger than before in intra-Community bargaining.

By the early 1980s the EC seemed to have reached a low ebb. Summits were bogged down in seemingly endless squabbles over the budget and the CAP, governments were often sharply divided on ideological lines, and all economies were suffering in the new recession. There was even concern that the EC might fragment, and prior to the Fontainebleau settlement Mitterrand had spoken favorably of a "Europe of different speeds or variable geometry."[17] Attempts to enhance the powers of the parliament or the Commission, such as the 1984 Draft Treaty on European Union by the veteran federalist member of the European Parliament Altiero Spinelli, were easily ignored by governments. European political cooperation remained limited to an attempt to formulate common positions on foreign policy. There was much talk of "Euro-sclerosis": in other words, the institutions of the EC were hindering rather than promoting trade and enterprise. Suddenly, however, in the mid-1980s a new surge towards integration became possible, powered by a peculiar and unstable combination of Mitterrand's "discovery" of Europe, Thatcher's free market zeal, and the renewal of Commission activism under Jacques Delors.

The Single European Act and "1992"

The Single European Act (SEA), signed in February 1986 and implemented in July 1987, was the most important advance in European integration since the Treaty of Rome, which it amended. It set out to complete the internal market (allowing free movement of goods, people, services, and capital) by December 31, 1992. In the process, 300 nontariff barriers, ranging from technical regulations to customs formalities, which had been identified by the British Commissioner Lord Cockfield, would be eliminated. The beauty of the SEA was that it responded to the sense of failure and drift attached to the Community during the first half of the 1980s by advancing – as Monnet had predicted – on the one line on which all member states could agree. However, while the commitment to a free market brought Mrs. Thatcher on board and enthused business, the SEA also contained within it the germ of further developments – less welcome to the British government – such as regional and environmental policy, political union and, above all, the single currency.

   This strategic vision owed much to the new president of the Commission Jacques Delors, a French Catholic socialist who had previously worked for the progressive Christian CFTC trade union. Delors was a long-standing supporter of European integration who had briefly been a member of the European Parliament prior to serving – as a pillar of orthodoxy – as Mitterrand's Finance Minister. He believed strongly in what he referred to as the "European model of society," by which he meant capitalism tempered by the welfare state, workers' rights, and partnership between employers and employees. While he recognized that this model must adapt to respond to the challenge of global economic competition, he was adamant that "most people want to retain its spirit and its political foundations."[18] Delors also perceived an enhanced role for the Commission in organizing the European economy – especially in research and development – to enable it to compete with the USA and the Far East. He had come to the conclusion by October 1983 that "our only choice is between a united Europe and decline."[19] Such thinking was of course anathema to Mrs. Thatcher, who became Delors' principal adversary. However, it was pitched to appeal to both social democrats and Christian democrats across the EC, as well as to trade unionists. Delors was therefore the first president who could not only articulate a vision of the EC's future but also – at least temporarily – build a wide-ranging coalition of interests in support of it.

   Delors' ideas accorded closely with those of Mitterrand who, after the "U-turn" of 1983 (see Chapter 8), now saw the deepening of European integration as the salvation not only of his presidency but also of French socialism. Even so, the latest "relaunch" of the EC proved remarkably difficult as, while it was widely agreed that reform was necessary there was no consensus as to the direction that it should take. Most of the proposals of the mid-1980s (such as the Dooge Committee report presented in March 1985) concerned institutional reform and were unacceptable to Britain and a number of smaller states. However, at the Milan summit in June 1985 it was agreed – despite objections from Britain, Denmark, and Ireland – that an intergovernmental conference (IGC) should be convened to discuss reform. The IGC mechanism was an important innovation that proved crucial to reaching agreement and was repeatedly invoked during the 1990s. Like all stages in the development of European integration, the SEA represented a bargain between members' interests. Britain pushed strongly for the completion of the internal market, but was forced to concede the unwelcome extension of QMV to cover most aspects of its implementation (tax harmonization was specifically excluded). In effect, therefore, the SEA marked the end of the "Luxembourg compromise" veto and a very significant diminution of national sovereignty: a concession that Thatcher later regretted. As she wrote in her memoirs, "the trouble [with the SEA] was ... that the new powers the Commission received only seemed to whet its appetite."[20] The SEA also provided for a limited advance in political cooperation, including the establishment of a secretariat, although the role of the parliament was again largely neglected.

The simplicity of the SEA was beguiling, especially when rendered as a slogan: "1992." However, it remained open to a range of interpretations. For the Thatcherites, the SEA marked a shift towards a looser Europe that would favor business and enterprise. This was in line with contemporary developments such as the Commission's greater assertiveness on competition policy and the deregulation of capital markets. Conversely, Delors and most European leaders saw the logic of the "1992" program as requiring action to address other forms of market irregularity such as regional inequalities. By this reading the ultimate logic of the SEA was that a single market required a single currency, although this was hardly undisputed. In any case, the organization of the market would require more, not less, centralization. In July 1988 Delors told the European Parliament that the internal market could not be achieved unless "we see the beginnings of European government, in one form or another," and noted that within a decade 80 percent of all economic legislation would originate in the EC.[21] Delors, therefore, skillfully used the SEA in the late 1980s to promote his institutional agenda. First, the "Delors package" of February 1988 combined reform of the EC budget (favoring the Commission) with the enhancement of regional funding to help the new south European members (Spain and Portugal). The package was funded primarily by Germany, and marked the emergence of the EC as a vehicle for the redistribution of wealth at a national and regional level. Secondly, in May 1989 the Commission produced a "Social Charter." This contained nothing inherently new, but it encapsulated Delors' belief that the single market must be matched by a commitment to employees' rights. Finally, and most significantly, in June 1988 Delors was invited to produce, within a year, a report on EMU. The SEA had therefore not only kick-started European integration, but had also brought the lost ambitions of the 1970s back into play. Twin IGCs were commissioned to examine monetary and political union in the course of 1991.

Margaret Thatcher led a stubborn resistance to Delors. In her Bruges speech of September 20, 1988, she broke all protocol by stating explicitly what she feared: that ever greater centralization would result in a "European super-state exercising a new dominance from Brussels" and introducing "corporatism at the European level."[22] Beneath the hyperbole was a restatement of traditional British positions, from the quasi-Gaullism of a Europe of sovereign states to the overriding importance of NATO. By this stage, however, the tenor of her views, as well as her outright rejection of the single currency, had rendered her isolated and vulnerable. She even fell out with Lord Cockfield, an apostle of the free market who had come to believe that VAT should be harmonized and who, for his pains, was denied a second term as Commissioner. At the Rome summit in October 1990 Britain was outvoted by 11 to 1 on a proposed timetable for EMU, and this defeat triggered the moves within her own party that led to her overthrow in November. Although "Euroskepticism" was by no means dead, and indeed would resurface powerfully at the popular level in response to the Maastricht Treaty, its most vocal advocate had been silenced.

Maastricht and After

The twin IGCs resulted in the Treaty on European Union, concluded at Maastricht in December 1991 but only ratified a year and a half later. The entire process took place in the context of profound changes in the international environment, notably the ending of the Cold War and German reunification (see Chapter 10), which helped agreement but hindered implementation. German reunification undoubtedly hardened the resolve of Kohl and Mitterrand to deepen European integration as a means of locking Germany into western Europe and curbing its potential power. Kohl was willing to give up the Deutschmark, the sheet anchor of postwar German stability, in exchange for a single currency so long as some progress could also be made towards political union. Indeed, the problems that came in the wake of the Cold War, notably the EC's role in the reconstruction of eastern Europe and its weak response to the collapse of Yugoslavia, all emphasized the urgent need for the Community to act with greater unity and resolve in foreign policy. At the same time, however, the massive costs of reunification were not only reducing Germany's ability to finance European integration, but also were creating economic and financial turbulence that threatened the creation of the single currency. The United States, meanwhile, supported further integration but warned against any attempt to establish a European defense separate from NATO, such as the French proposal to make a revived western European Union (WEU) into the defensive arm of the EC.

By the time of the Maastricht negotiations, the key elements of the treaty – at least with respect to EMU – were well known, most of the groundwork having been done by Delors. At its core stood a three-stage timetable for the creation of a single currency, and the establishment of economic criteria for judging which countries would be allowed to participate. It was agreed that Britain could opt out of the final stage, but this concession was not made generally available. Aside from the British position, however, EMU was seen as relatively unproblematic at Maastricht. The French, in particular, had come to see monetary union as an opportunity to exert more influence over monetary and economic policy than was possible within the EMS, while the Netherlands and Belgium had long been accustomed to maintaining a stable rate against the Deutschmark. The countries of southern Europe, meanwhile, were more apprehensive about the potential costs, but could not afford to remain out of the EMU. It was not foreseen that Denmark, which would have had no problem in meeting convergence terms, would eventually vote against the treaty, partly due to fears that monetary union would undermine its welfare state. The negotiations concerning political union were, by comparison, less well formulated and more controversial. It was eventually agreed that the new European Union (EU) should stand on three separate "pillars," composed of, first, the economic community and single currency; secondly, a Common Foreign and Security Policy (CFSP) and, thirdly, joint judicial and home affairs (especially with regard to immigration, asylum policy and visas). The latter two "pillars" would be on an intergovernmental basis, and the details would not be finalized until a later stage. Significantly, although specific reference was made to the role of the WEU as an integral part of the new union, the treaty assuaged American fears by making clear that the CFSP would not conflict with the paramount role of NATO in the defense of Europe. Following British objections, social policy was treated as a separate protocol – the "social chapter" – which Britain did not sign. Maastricht also allowed a limited advance in the powers of the European Parliament, defining areas in which it would enjoy the right of "co-decision," and gave a range of new competencies to the Commission.

The treaty was, again, open to a range of interpretations. British Prime Minister John Major took comfort from Britain's opt-out on EMU and on the "social chapter" (although the latter was subsequently adopted by Tony Blair's government in 1997). From this perspective the treaty could be seen as a defense of national interests against federalism. Indeed, the treaty for the first time enshrined the concept of "subsidiarity" (Article 3b), whereby decisions would be taken at the lowest appropriate level, and would only be taken at the supranational level when they could not be taken nationally. However, this could be taken as a charter for promoting regional interests just as much as national ones. Meanwhile, the other member states had achieved the right to progress towards European integration – notably EMU – unencumbered by British objections. Germany had had its way on the independence of the proposed new European Central Bank and on the strict convergence criteria. However, the Germans – and the MEPs – had the most right to feel aggrieved as the immediate political attributes of the new union were relatively weak and primarily represented lines for future development. The treaty represented something of a setback for Delors, who had hoped that Maastricht would mark a point of no return for European integration. In fact, the "pillar" concept was a victory for intergovernmentalism, and marginalized the Commission. Even on EMU, which had been Delors' prime objective, the Commission would lose power to the new European Central Bank. As one of his staff put it, "We've lost the game on economic policy."[23] Maastricht, therefore, represented a series of compromises. It was a defeat for the outright federalists, but it opened the possibility of the eventual deepening of European integration in a wide range of areas.

Ratification proved an unexpectedly tortuous process. One of the first signs of trouble for the treaty was opinion-poll evidence that Germans were extremely unhappy at the thought of giving up their own currency, although they were denied the chance to express this in a referendum. Across Europe, meanwhile, broad coalitions united right and left in defense of national interests against a European integration that was seen as elitist and untransparent. In June 1992 the Danish voted against the treaty by the narrowest of margins (50.7 percent). This vote was eventually reversed in May 1993, but only after the Danes had been given their own "opt-outs." More damagingly, Mitterrand decided to call a French referendum for September 1992. He initially hoped that this would divide his conservative opponents and strengthen his own hand in the run-up to parliamentary elections in 1993 but, in fact, the treaty only scraped through with 51 percent. In Britain, despite Major's apparent success at Maastricht, Euroskeptics in parliament saw the chance to smash the treaty altogether, especially as Major had been left with only a small majority in the British elections of April 1992. Britain became the final country to ratify the treaty in July 1993, after a lengthy parliamentary process that drained Major's authority. By then the uncertainty over the fate of Maastricht, combined with the mounting cost of German reunification, had sparked a wave of currency speculation and forced a number of countries out of the ERM (see Chapter 11). For those who were left in, the margins of fluctuation were eventually slackened to 15 percent. Although the proponents of European integration held their nerve, the events of 1991–3 had been a salutary reminder that public support could not be taken for granted, especially on such far-reaching questions as monetary union. The political and financial crises also undermined Delors' presidency that had once been set to complete an ambitious third term. Given Germany's straitened circumstances, there were simply not the resources to fund another substantial expansion of the EC budget, and in February 1992 Delors had to accept a second budgetary "package" far more modest than he had originally wished. Moreover, his vision of a Commission-led response to Europe's recession, such as his June 1993 White Paper that envisaged the creation of 15 million jobs by 2000, was out of tune with the views of governments after Maastricht. He stood down as president of the Commission halfway through his final term in 1995.

Conclusion

European integration has, since the 1950s, become an ever more significant factor in the life of western Europe, and the benefits have been substantial. Integration has increased trade, enhanced Europe's security and given it greater collective weight in international relations. Meanwhile, membership steadily expanded from the "Six" of 1957 to the "Twelve" of 1992. However, this has not been a story of continuous, unchallenged success. De Gaulle had a separate vision of European integration in the 1960s, as did Thatcher in the 1980s, while between 1970 and 1984 there was concern that the whole project had stagnated. Ultimately, integration has succeeded where it has been in the perceived (economic) interests of the member states, and its history has been one of progress via elaborate "package" deals. Governments have been far more wary of political integration, and until the 1992 Maastricht Treaty this aspect was largely neglected. Even so, the main achievement at Maastricht was to set a timetable for monetary union. European integration has always been an elite project, and the problems faced by a number of governments in obtaining ratification for the treaty demonstrated a mounting public concern at the lack of transparency and democratic accountability.

10
The Fall of the Communist Regimes
The Soviet Union and Eastern Europe, 1980–1991

"All that is solid melts into air"[1]

The creation of the Solidarity trade union in Poland (August 1980) opened an 11-year crisis in "actually existing socialism" that ended with the collapse of the people's republics of eastern Europe in 1989 and the dissolution of the Soviet Union itself on December 31, 1991. Ever since, historians and political scientists have struggled to explain and categorize this stunning reverse. The processes of change at work were perhaps too diverse to be easily described as a "revolution," even though they did result in the most profound transformation not only of the political order but also of social and economic relations. No single factor is sufficient to explain the fall of the communist regimes, as each country offered a unique blend of pressures from below, pressures from without, and attempts to reform the system from above. The pressure that came from falling comprehensively and visibly behind the West was undoubtedly one of these external factors, but Western politicians were too quick to claim that their military build-up in the early 1980s had forced reform on the Soviet Union. Indeed, had a more traditional leader than Mikhail Gorbachev come to power in March 1985, it is quite plausible that the communist parties could have been entrenched in power for a further generation.[2] The examination of individual cases below will, therefore, emphasize the interplay of these different factors, while this introduction examines the generic economic and ideological failings of the communist regimes.

Europe's Troubled Peace: 1945 to the Present, Second Edition. Tom Buchanan.
© 2012 John Wiley & Sons, Ltd. Published 2012 by John Wiley & Sons, Ltd.

Throughout the communist world there was a mounting economic crisis during the 1980s. Although the severity and timing of the crisis varied by country, there were a number of common features. In particular, the east European states had become heavily indebted to the Western banks during the 1970s, but had generally spent money on propping up living standards rather than investing in a more productive economy. As a consequence, by the 1980s debt servicing consumed a very large proportion of national income (apart from in Romania, where Ceauşescu showed a suicidal zeal for repaying the debt) and growth stagnated. Governments were forced into rigorous austerity measures, but they lacked the political support to push through the painful restructuring seen in parts of western Europe. Moreover, with the fall in oil prices the willingness (and increasingly the ability) of the USSR to subsidize its satellites declined. Across the region, communism became associated with a failure to deliver basic standards of living, let alone an abundance of consumer goods. Shortages, even of food, had become routine and the black market essential. This failure of economic stewardship was exacerbated by a new awareness of the communist regimes' assault on the environment, from the open-cast lignite mines of East Germany to the once fertile Trakia Plain of Bulgaria, now poisoned by heavy metals. However, it should be noted that the fall of communism was not simply determined by economic failure, as the Communist Party also lost political authority in Hungary, which had been one of the more prosperous and market-oriented Comecon countries.

The economic failure of communism was inevitably accompanied by a sense of ideological bankruptcy. Indeed, the most devastating slogan of the East German demonstrators in the autumn of 1989, aimed at those claiming to act in their name, was "We are the people." By the 1980s Marxism-Leninism had become the mumbo-jumbo of the governing elite; it was mouthed and manipulated, but no longer believed in. Increasingly, the party apparatchiks had lost their ideological moorings and many came to admire any leaders, from Thatcher to Pinochet, who had forced through economic change without losing political control. What they found particularly disturbing about Mikhail Gorbachev was that he still truly believed in the transformative power of politics, if not in orthodox communism. But such idealism was rare by the late 1980s, when many had come to reject politics altogether. In 1988 a high-ranking Soviet economist shocked an audience of Western socialists when, asked to relate Gorbachev's policy of *perestroika* to social democracy and Leninism, he replied that: "We're sick and tired of all these isms! The main thing is that there should be sausage."[3]

Those members of the elite who rejected communism often – but by no means always – veered towards a rather brutal economic liberalism. The most notable exception was in Serbia, where extreme nationalism captured an important section of the intelligentsia. Here, a sense that Yugoslavia had worked to the disadvantage of the Serbs was amplified by claims that Serbs were being driven from Kosovo (a region with immense cultural and historical significance for them) by the Albanian majority. In January 1986 some 200 Belgrade intellectuals signed a petition claiming that "a rigged political trial of the Serb nation and its history has been going on for decades," and alleging "genocide" by the Albanians in Kosovo.[4] Such sentiments facilitated the rise to power of Slobodan Milošević and his policies of ethnic violence after 1987. Elsewhere, notably in the Soviet republics, many communist elites espoused nationalism as a new source of ideological legitimacy, often outmaneuvering more long-standing and genuine – but less politically astute – nationalists.

The suppression of Solidarity in December 1981 was a reminder that the Soviet Union was still not willing to concede any form of political opposition, let alone pluralism. Even so, apart from in an extreme police state such as Romania or Albania, forms of autonomous organization burgeoned during the 1980s. In the case of the Soviet Union, of course, this was connected to the attempt by Gorbachev to invigorate society in support of his reforms. By late 1987 there were some 30,000 "informal organizations" in the USSR, ranging from sports clubs and professional associations to Pamyat (an anti-Semitic Russian nationalist movement). In eastern Europe likewise there was a proliferation of organizations and campaigns that gave vent to the concerns of ordinary citizens. In Hungary, for instance, the two most emotive issues of the mid-1980s were the persecution of ethnic Hungarians in neighboring Romania and the proposed Nagymaros hydro-electric dam on the river Danube. In East Germany the churches played a very important role in nurturing small but vocal groups campaigning on issues such as the environment, peace, women's rights, and conscientious objection to military service.

Underlying these developments was a change in the strategy of opposition, away from heroic confrontation with the state and towards the creation of "civil society," where possible exploiting and subverting the rhetoric of the communist regimes. The Catholicism of Solidarity and the high-minded tone of Charter 77 gave way to a new, lighter mood amongst some young people. There was a recognition that, if anything, communism found gentle, surreal mockery, such as that practiced by the "Orange Alternative" satirists in Wrocław, even harder to deal with.[5] In the small Yugoslav republic of Slovenia, meanwhile, an altogether darker cultural movement led by the punk rock band Laibach (the German name for the Slovene capital) flourished in the 1980s. Taking advantage of Slovenia's relative freedom – even within the Yugoslav federation – Laibach (and their allied artist collective Irwin) set out to show that "every art is subjected to political manipulation except that which speaks the language of this very manipulation."[6] The "totalitarian," militaristic style of their performances and artwork conflated Nazi and communist imagery, while they also made provocative use of patriotic symbols. In 1987 a group of these Slovene artists scandalized Belgrade when it transpired that their winning poster design for a "Day of Youth" in Tito's honor had, in fact, been based on a Nazi image.

The advent of Gorbachev encouraged a new honesty and inquisitiveness about the recent past. There had already been glimmerings of this during the short-lived Solidarity "spring" in Poland,[7] but under Gorbachev there was a new willingness to confront the so-called "blank spots" of recent history, such as the 1939 Nazi–Soviet Pact. However, Soviet responsibility for the 1940 Katyn massacre was only fully admitted after the collapse of the USSR. Soviet censorship was relaxed, the works of authors such as Pasternak and Orwell finally became available, and a new investigative journalism flourished. By 1988 Stalin's most senior victims, such as Zinoviev, Kamenev, and Bukharin (but not yet Trotsky), had been posthumously rehabilitated, and in the final years of the USSR even the final taboo – criticism of Lenin – was broken. Meanwhile, an independent organization, Memorial, was set up to record and commemorate those who had perished in Stalin's Terror. In Hungary the Communist Party sought absolution for the events of 1956, recognizing that this was essential if it was to survive a transition to multi-party politics. However, this revival of memory was not always constructive or well-meaning. In Yugoslavia the wartime Croat ethnic violence was deliberately invoked by Serbia as part of a strategy of undermining Croatia's bid for independence, while the Soviet Union recalled the anti-Semitic violence of 1941 in Lithuania and Latvia as a riposte to the secessionist ambitions of the Baltic republics.

It was fitting that the past should loom so large in the late 1980s as the dramatic events of 1989–91 gave strangely little indication as to the future. Communism was overthrown by a short-lived but genuine coalition for change that united workers, intellectuals, and students with members of the churches and ethnic minorities. Through the ballot box when they had the chance, on the streets when they did not, the people of eastern Europe and the Soviet Union rejected a system that had failed them in favor of one which they believed would work in their interests. Amidst the joy of 1989 there was little appreciation that, as in any "revolution," there would be winners and losers, and that the latter category would disproportionately include women and the old. It was far from clear, for instance, that the main political beneficiary of the Czech "velvet revolution" would be the Thatcherite banker Václav Klaus, nor that those who voted for Solidarity candidates in June 1989 or for Boris Yeltsin in June 1991 would be voting for economic "shock therapy." The Cassandra voices of those who warned against the human costs of German unification were worth listening to: during 1990–1 industrial production fell by two-thirds and 1.8 million jobs were shed in the former East Germany.[8] In Bulgaria and Romania there was considerable apprehension about the depredations of raw capitalism, and the most successful politicians were those who promised a long-drawn-out process of transition. If the exhilaration of the struggle to topple the communist regimes had transcended conventional politics, the 1990s would see a return to grubby realities and hard choices.

Poland and Solidarity, 1980–1981

In 1980–1 the Polish Communist Party (and the Soviet Union) faced an unprecedented challenge from a movement that could truly claim to speak in the name of the Polish workers. The crisis had its origins in the policies pursued by the former Communist Party leader Edward Gierek in response to the working-class unrest of 1970 (see Chapter 6). The genial Gierek attempted to raise living standards by borrowing heavily from the West, but the loans were largely squandered, and the Polish economy became ever more heavily indebted. In June 1976 the government was forced to impose another swingeing price rise which again sparked violent resistance. Although the government backed down, the subsequent repression galvanized the formation of the Committee for the Defense of Workers' Rights (KOR) led by Jacek Kuroń, a former communist who had served two prison sentences for his criticism of the regime in the 1960s. This precursor to Solidarity began to break down the divisions between intellectuals, workers and Catholics that had previously hamstrung the Polish opposition. The regime's problems deepened when Karol Wojtyla, the Archbishop of Krakow and a staunch anti-communist, was elected Pope John Paul II in October 1978. Gierek had hoped that the Pope's historic visit to Poland in June 1979 would legitimate his regime, but in fact it did much to protect and promote Catholic lay activism.

In July 1980 Gierek introduced new pricing measures which stimulated a wave of strikes and, on August 14, the occupation of the Gdansk Lenin shipyard. Lech Wałesa, an electrician who had participated in the events of 1970 and been sacked in 1976, was hoisted back into the yard by the strikers and immediately emerged as their leader. Wałesa was a devout Catholic and Polish nationalist, but above all a pragmatist who represented the independent working-class spirit of the Baltic ports. A simple set of demands was formulated on August 16, at the center of which was free trade unionism, an end to censorship and greater religious freedom. It was soon clear that Solidarity was not only a trade union but also an embryonic national opposition movement. The key political input came from the leaders of KOR, Kuroń, and Adam Michnik (a former student radical jailed in 1968). Both hoped for fundamental political change, but appreciated that the overthrow of communism in Poland was impossible so long as the Cold War division of Europe lasted. Michnik's solution was his theory of the "self-limiting revolution," whereby Solidarity would steadily expand its role while giving no excuse for its suppression. The question that was not confronted, however, and which was to prove fatal to the movement's survival, was what would happen when the mere existence of Solidarity so weakened the communist regime that it faced collapse in any case?

The Gdansk strike, which soon spread to the neighboring port of Stettin, divided the authorities between the hardliners (who demanded a military clampdown) and moderates (who believed that a compromise could be reached). After unprecedented negotiations, the strike leaders reached an agreement with the government on August 31 under which Solidarity was recognized as the first independent trade union in a communist state, but on the condition that it recognized the "leading role" of the Communist Party. Wałesa signed the agreement, symbolically, with an outsize pen, a souvenir from the previous year's papal visit. Almost immediately a formal headquarters was established in Gdansk followed, on 17 September, by a national coordinating committee. Warsaw, and especially the Ursus tractor plant, soon emerged as a second center of militancy under Zbigniew Bujak. Solidarity's membership now rapidly expanded, and on October 3 it flexed its muscles with a one-hour national strike over pay involving an estimated 3 million workers. In addition, Rural Solidarity was legally recognized after a bitter struggle in May 1981, adding peasant farmers to a movement which by the autumn was some 9 million strong.

With the creation of Solidarity, Poland embarked on a bizarre and unique 16-month experiment in pluralism *within* a one-party state. Inevitably, there were many points of tension with the Communist Party, now led by Stanisław Kania. First, many members of the communist bureaucracy, as well as those in the government and secret police, found it impossible to reconcile themselves to the existence of Solidarity. There was a series of provocations in which the militants on both sides sought to force a crisis, and moderate leaders like Wałesa were engaged in ceaseless attempts to restrain their more hotheaded followers. On March 19, 1981, for instance, Rural Solidarity demonstrators occupying the prefecture at Bydgoszcz were severely beaten by the police. Secondly, Solidarity had dealt a heavy blow to the credibility of the Communist Party. Indeed, many of its members (some 750,000 of whom had also joined Solidarity) were themselves clamoring for political reform within the party. Delegates for the July 1981 party congress were freely elected for the first time, and the new and inexperienced delegates were, in turn, allowed a free vote on the leadership. In the ensuing massacre seven out of every eight Central Committee members, seven out of the 11 members of the Politburo and 40 out of 49 District Secretaries were voted out of office,[9] although Kania survived as First Secretary. Yet the party emerged from the congress more riven than ever, while Solidarity – at its own congress in the autumn – raised the political stakes by calling for free national elections. Thirdly, and most pressing for ordinary Poles, the rise of Solidarity had merely exacerbated an already critical economic situation, which by 1981 was turning into the possibility of famine.

The communist hardliners were strengthened by the knowledge that the USSR perceived Solidarity as a cover for "counter-revolutionary" forces that had to be defeated. However, the Soviet leadership was constrained by the political paralysis that overtook it in the last years of Brezhnev's life and also by awareness of the high price that would be paid for any overt Soviet intervention. Although invasion plans were drawn up, the Soviets dared not implement them for fear of destroying what was left of détente and seriously damaging economic links with western Europe. As the Soviet ideology chief Mikhail Suslov told a session of the Politburo on December 10, 1981 (immediately prior to the coup): "If troops are introduced that will mean a catastrophe. I think we have reached a unanimous view here on this matter, and there can be no consideration at all of introducing troops."[10] The crisis would, therefore, have to be resolved from within. During 1981 the Defense Minister, General Jaruzelski, quietly gathered the reins of power into his hands, acquiring in addition the posts of prime minister (in February) and First Secretary of the Communist Party (in October). His rise caused few qualms, as his image was that of a patriotic moderate who had avoided violence in the summer of 1980. However, on December 13, 1981 he declared martial law, banned Solidarity, and established the "Military Council of National Salvation." The official rationale was that military intervention by the Polish army was the only alternative to a Soviet invasion. Moreover, the reimposition of law and order was presented as the only alternative to complete social collapse in the face of economic crisis and unofficial strikes. Yet the second argument was more compelling than the first: the Soviet leaders not only knew that they could not intervene but were also urging Jaruzelski to take action.[11]

Solidarity was caught by surprise, wrongly believing that the army sympathized with it. The worst violence occurred near Katowice, where seven miners who had occupied their pit were killed. Wałesa and many of the Solidarity leaders were arrested, but so – in a display of even-handedness – were Gierek and the "corrupt" old guard of the Communist Party. However, the international response to martial law was muted. The US ran a special television program ("Let Poland Be Poland") and imposed sanctions, but Helmut Schmidt was afraid that any outright condemnation might derail *Ostpolitik*, while the socialist French Foreign Minister caused outrage when he described martial law as an "internal matter."[12] Jaruzelski had hoped to build a new consensus with the Catholic Church and moderate opposition leaders such as Wałesa, but neither was willing to collaborate. Solidarity, which was formally banned in 1982, maintained an effective underground existence, and the church's alienation from the new regime was confirmed when members of the secret police murdered the outspoken pro-Solidarity priest Father Popiełuszco in October 1984. Accordingly, although martial law was ended in July 1983, Jaruzelski was never able to legitimize his regime either through political reform or renewed prosperity. The point was graphically demonstrated in November 1987 when, confronted with accelerating economic decline, Jaruzelski called and lost a referendum[13] on his proposals for reform. Economic surgery would have to await a post-communist government.

Gorbachev and Soviet Reform, 1985–1990

The Polish crisis not only exposed the immobility of the Soviet Union in the late Brezhnev era but also raised fears that a similar pattern of events might be repeated in the USSR. Although the Soviet economy was not yet collapsing in the early 1980s, economic growth had fallen sharply over the previous decade, labor discipline had grown lax, and corruption and cynicism flourished. Yuri Andropov, who briefly governed after the death of Brezhnev in November 1982, sought to purge the Soviet system and promoted a group of younger, reform-minded leaders (notably Mikhail Gorbachev). However, he was incapacitated by ill health long before his death in February 1984, and he was succeeded by the equally frail Konstantin Chernenko, one of Brezhnev's cronies. Chernenko's rule proved a mere parenthesis during which Gorbachev consolidated his position, forged an important alliance with Yegor Ligachev (a puritanical opponent of corruption), and gained international exposure. On March 10, 1985, on the death of Chernenko, he was swiftly and unanimously voted into office by the Politburo. Despite the apprehension of many in the old guard, there was now a recognition that the economic and foreign policy challenges confronting the USSR demanded drastic measures.

Mikhail Gorbachev represented a new kind of Soviet leader, and not only because he became General Secretary of the CPSU as a vigorous 54-year-old. Admittedly, his rise through the party's hierarchy, first in his native Stavropol and then (from 1978) as a member of the Central Committee in Moscow, was hardly atypical. Gorbachev was adept at playing the game of Soviet politics and acquired influential patrons – above all, Andropov. However, he also displayed an unusual intellectual curiosity and openness to new ideas. His friendship while a student at Moscow State University with Zdeněk Mlynář, later a leader of the "Prague Spring," developed into a remarkable lifelong political dialogue. Gorbachev had also been deeply influenced by Khrushchev's 1956 "secret speech" and, despite the orthodoxy of his public views, felt private disappointment at the denial of reform in the late 1960s. By the mid-1980s he felt the need for change very keenly, confiding to his wife Raisa that "We can't go on living in this way."[14] It was less clear, however, exactly how he proposed to reverse the decline of the USSR. Gorbachev's stormy six-year leadership encompassed a personal political odyssey, whereby he slowly renounced communism for social democracy, as well as bringing about the historic democratization (and eventual collapse) of the Soviet Union. Yet his original intention had been to revitalize the Communist Party and reform the economy as a means to sustain the USSR. Whatever his true beliefs, the Gorbachev of 1985–8 was still very much a product of the Soviet system, able to couch reformist ideas in the language of Lenin. Ultimately this tension between radicalism and caution, allied at times to poor judgment, ensured that Gorbachev's reforms would end, if not in failure, at least not in the success that he had originally intended.

Initially Gorbachev had to tread cautiously, promoting like-minded allies and defining his new policies. Two key concepts emerged: *perestroika* ("restructuring") and *glasnost* ("openness"). Although neither was new to Soviet discourse, Gorbachev progressively redefined and radicalized their meaning. *Glasnost*, for instance, initially implied a more transparent government (reinforced by Gorbachev's shock at the secrecy concerning the Chernobyl disaster in April 1986) but evolved into unprecedented public debate and cultural freedom. Likewise *perestroika*, at first little more than the latest top-down attempt to reform the socialist economy, developed into an attempt to transform the socio-political order. Meanwhile, Gorbachev – who lacked his own network of clients – had to place sympathizers in the party bureaucracy and government. Crucial appointments, both radicals, were Eduard Shevardnadze, the Georgian party boss and anti-corruption campaigner who replaced the long-serving Foreign Minister Gromyko, and Alexander Yakovlev, who was rapidly promoted within the Central Committee and given responsibility for ideology. However, Gorbachev also had to work with those, such as Ligachev and Nikolai Ryzhkov, who wished to reverse decline but did not share his own reformist inclinations. Ligachev emerged as the main opponent of rapid reform until Gorbachev felt strong enough to demote him in the autumn of 1988. Moreover, some radicals could prove to be more of a hindrance than a help. The populist Moscow party boss Boris Yeltsin, appointed by Gorbachev, became too outspoken and was sacked in November 1987 (only to reappear as an extremely dangerous rival).

Gorbachev's initial concern was the economy, but this was precisely the area which was most resistant to change. He encountered powerful vested interests that were determined to block reform, as well as tremendous cultural inertia. A number of laws were passed between 1985 and 1988 to promote small businesses and the decentralization of state enterprises, but the overall impact was to under-mine the command economy without forcing a clean break to a new market-based system. In an economy in which the legal and institutional infrastructure for private enterprise barely existed, it was extremely difficult to tempt Soviet citizens out of the lethargy and relative comfort (sustained by the black market) to which they had become accustomed under Brezhnev. An excellent example of the failure of Gorbachev's moralistic and paternalistic attitude to reform was the anti-alcohol campaign of 1985–8. While carried out for the best intentions (alcoholism was a major health problem and harmful to the economy) the results of the clampdown were the rise of lethal illicit stills and a serious depletion of tax revenue. In these circumstances, economic reform was largely neglected until the discussion of the far more radical "500 days program" in 1990.

In 1987 Gorbachev, who now understood the capacity of the *nomenklatura* to block reform, turned his attention to the political system. His approach to political reform was essentially instrumental, as he was primarily concerned to undermine conservative forces by mobilizing public support for change. In many respects, Gorbachev was repeating the mistakes of the Czech reformers in 1968, as he had little understanding of the democratic forces that he was unleashing and no real mechanisms for controlling them. (This time, however, there was a joke that the hardline Czechs would have to send their tanks to Moscow to prevent reform![15]) In June 1988, at a historic CPSU party conference, it was agreed that there should be a new directly elected Congress of People's Deputies, with two-thirds of the deputies from territorial constituencies and one-third from public organizations, including 100 seats reserved for the Communist Party (the Congress would then indirectly elect the Supreme Soviet). The elections, held in March 1989 on an 89.9 percent turnout, aroused tremendous public interest and marked the advent of a new democratic politics. At the same time, however, democratization also contributed to the waning of Gorbachev's power. In his new role as Chairman of the Supreme Soviet (and from March 1990 Executive President) he was now publicly exposed to criticism from both radicals and conservatives. His stature was diminished and, further battered by the bewildering changes in eastern Europe, he seemed to have lost control of events.

The other unforeseen consequence of Gorbachev's democratic reform was the upsurge of regional and ethnic tensions triggered by the decline of central Soviet authority. Long-dormant questions such as the ownership of the enclave of Nagorno-Karabakh (disputed between the Soviet republics of Armenia and Azerbaijan) gave rise to serious inter-ethnic violence, while the Crimean Tartars, who had been dispossessed by Stalin, began to return to their homeland. Nationalist sentiments were often stoked by regional communist elites (indigenized under Brezhnev) as a means of ensuring their own political survival. Although Gorbachev was desperate to avoid violence, the intervention of Soviet troops to break up a nationalist demonstration in the Georgian capital of Tbilisi left 19 dead in April 1989. In January 1990 troops entered the Azeri capital of Baku following anti-Armenian rioting. The most serious challenge was the rise of powerful nationalist movements in the Baltic republics, calling for peaceful secession from the Soviet Union. In all three republics nationalist sentiment was fed by a deep sense of injustice at the Nazi–Soviet Pact of August 1939, the basis for their annexation by the USSR, which could now be publicly discussed. On the pact's 50th anniversary, August 23, 1989, 2 million Balts formed a human chain that stretched for 370 miles from Vilnius to Tallinn. Moreover, in two of the republics there was a genuine alarm and urgency at the rise of the Russian immigrant minorities, few of whom took the trouble to learn the local language. In Estonia the native proportion of the population had fallen from 74.6 percent in 1959 to around 61 percent in 1989, while in Latvia it had sunk from 62 percent to a mere 52 percent.[16] In all three republics pro-independence People's Fronts were the clear winners in the March 1989 elections.

Gorbachev appreciated that any domestic reform must be accompanied by a new look at foreign policy, as ending the Cold War and transferring resources from the military budget was essential for economic progress. As we have seen, after initial Western skepticism, a breakthrough was made in 1987 on nuclear arms reductions, and at the UN in December 1988 Gorbachev announced a unilateral cut in conventional Soviet forces. By now he was determined to woo the leaders and populations of western Europe, and his vision of a "common European home" served both to highlight common interests and to marginalize the position of the United States. Beyond Europe, Gorbachev was determined that the Soviet presence in Afghanistan, which he described in 1986 as a "bleeding wound," had to be ended. The final Soviet troops pulled out on February 15, 1989, after some 14,500 servicemen had perished in the conflict, although the pro-Soviet Najibullah government lasted until after the fall of the USSR (April 1992). Soviet support for a number of other regimes in the developing world, such as Cuba, was also greatly reduced. Gorbachev's willingness to turn his back on imperialist Soviet foreign policy delighted the West. However, old hands such as Gromyko were appalled that the new Soviet leadership seemed unable to "comprehend how to use force and pressure for defending their state interests."[17]

Nowhere was the new Soviet policy greeted with greater trepidation – or more warmly – than in eastern Europe. Gorbachev saw little of strategic, economic, or political value in the Soviet "empire" in eastern Europe, and hoped that it could be gradually reformed by like-minded leaders such as Jaruzelski and Kádár. However, he was loyal to the concept of Soviet "noninterference" in the internal affairs of the satellite states and appears to have done little to force the pace of change.[18] Meanwhile, the terms of the Soviet relationship with eastern Europe were definitively changed. In June 1988 the Brezhnev doctrine was renounced, and in October the Central Committee department that oversaw relations with the socialist states was abolished. On October 25, 1989 the Soviet spokesman Gennady Gerasimov famously joked that the Brezhnev doctrine had given way to the "Sinatra doctrine": each state must find its own way towards socialism. The rulers of eastern Europe could now no longer count on the Red Army – or even Soviet political influence – to keep them in power. Even so, the collapse of east European communism was – like the collapse of the USSR itself – still largely the unanticipated consequence of the radical changes that Gorbachev had set in train.

1989: The Fall of Communism in Eastern Europe

The processes by which the communist regimes of eastern Europe collapsed varied greatly from country to country, reflecting their divergent national experiences. In some cases (such as Hungary and Bulgaria) change was managed by the communists with a degree of success, while in others (such as East Germany and Czechoslovakia) they failed to adapt and suffered a catastrophic loss of political control. These latter cases seemed to bear out Gorbachev's warning to the East German Politburo on October 7, 1989: "If we fall behind, life will punish us immediately."[19] However, while the processes of change differed, there were also significant interconnections. For instance, the Hungarian decision to open its western borders precipitated the East German crisis by encouraging holidaymakers to flee to the West, while the breaching of the Berlin Wall inspired the demonstrators in Czechoslovakia and, to a lesser extent, Romania. And in every case the mesmerizing, liberating presence of Gorbachev in the Kremlin could not be ignored.

In Poland, Jaruzelski's failure to secure political legitimacy or support for economic reform meant that the government could do little more than keep the lid on protest. When price increases in 1988 were met with new strikes, it was clearly time for negotiation. In January 1989 Wałesa led Solidarity – against the wishes of many radicals – into "round table" negotiations with the government and the Catholic Church. Under the agreement of April 5, 1989 Solidarity was re-legalized, and semi-free elections were scheduled for June (with free competition for the whole of the Senate and 33 percent of the parliamentary seats). The communists still hoped to co-opt the opposition and retain political control, but any prospect of success was shattered when Solidarity won all but one of the contested seats in the first round on June 4. Even more damagingly, only a handful of communists won sufficient votes to be elected to the seats reserved for them, and many voters merely crossed out their names. The communists still controlled parliament after the second round, but had clearly been rejected by the Polish people. Although Solidarity did not relish taking responsibility for government (and being saddled with painful economic decisions) the political vacuum left it no real choice. On August 24 Tadeusz Mazowiecki, Wałesa's close adviser and a prominent lay Catholic, became the first noncommunist prime minister of a Warsaw Pact country. Soviet interests were guaranteed by the election of Jaruzelski as president in July, by the new government's pledge to remain in the Warsaw Pact, and by the presence of four communist ministers (controlling the defense and interior portfolios). Ironically, Poland's gradual and cautious transition, informed by two centuries of Russian and Soviet domination, was soon overtaken by the more dramatic pace of change elsewhere in eastern Europe. Free presidential elections were not held until late in 1990 (when Wałesa was elected), and unrestricted parliamentary elections were delayed until October 1991. However, the new government moved swiftly to implement drastic economic reform with finance minister Balcerowicz's so-called "shock therapy" of January 1, 1990 which, at a stroke, removed the remaining price subsidies.

A different kind of gradualism was evident in Hungary, where the political reform and economic liberalization which had started in the 1960s reached its natural terminus in the late 1980s. By the mid-1980s, although the opposition was still weak, there was mounting public discontent not only over the declining standard of living but also over less material issues such as the degradation of the environment. In May 1988 Janos Kádár, in power since 1956, was replaced by a younger generation of leaders who were willing to embrace more rapid change, notably Karoly Grósz and the liberal-minded Imre Pozsgay. Significant reforms of banking, taxation and rights for foreign investors were introduced between 1987 and 1989, while Pozsgay encouraged the formation of the opposition Hungarian Democratic Forum (MDF) in September 1987. Pozsgay realized that the Communist Party would only have a future if it could make its peace with the past, and he acquired an influential position as chairman of a committee investigating Hungary's recent history. In late January 1989 he stunned hardliners by announcing that the events of 1956 had been a "popular uprising" rather than a counter-revolution. At a stroke the whole Kádár era was discredited, and on June 16, 1989 Imre Nagy, the somewhat hapless hero of 1956, was officially reburied. At the ceremony, the young opposition firebrand Viktor Orban called openly for the withdrawal of Soviet troops from Hungary. In the autumn the opposition, which now also included the Alliance of Free Democrats (AFD) and the student-based

Alliance of Young Democrats (FIDESZ), negotiated the terms of a transition to multi-party democracy. The AFD succeeded, by means of a referendum, in blocking a proposal for a directly elected presidency which was thought to favor Pozsgay. The free parliamentary elections of March 1990 resulted in the defeat of the communists (who had been relaunched in October as the Hungarian Socialist Party) and the formation of a coalition government of opposition parties led by Josef Antall's MDF.

In Bulgaria, as in Hungary, the Communist Party sought to manage the transition to multi-party democracy, and succeeded in scapegoating their long-serving leader Todor Zhivkov (who was sentenced for corruption in 1992). Zhivkov was a pragmatist who had even attempted to go along with *perestroika*. However, he contributed to his own downfall by pursuing a policy of forced assimilation for Bulgaria's 1 million Turks from 1984 onwards. Turkish demonstrations in May 1989 were violently suppressed and resulted in a mass exodus to Turkey, crippling the harvest and annoying the USSR (which was seeking to improve relations with Ankara). These events galvanized Bulgaria's small opposition into holding a series of very public demonstrations coinciding with a meeting of the CSCE in Sofia between October 16 and November 3. On November 10, 1989 Zhivkov was overthrown by his Foreign Minister Petr Mladenov, who seems to have secured Moscow's backing and sought with some success to restore the Communist Party's authority. The fall of Zhivkov encouraged the opposition to press for more rapid change, with mass protests outside parliament, and by the spring of 1990 the communists (renamed as the Bulgarian Socialist Party) were ready to concede elections. The BSP held on to power with 47 percent of the vote in June 1990. However, Mladenov was soon afterwards forced to resign as president when evidence surfaced that he had threatened the use of tanks against the demonstrators in December 1989.

East Germany (see below), Czechoslovakia, and Romania were widely thought to be immune to the dramatic developments elsewhere in the region, and therefore change, when it came, took a far more overtly revolutionary turn. By 1989 Czechoslovakia had one of the most repressive and stagnant regimes in the communist bloc, and the replacement of Husák by Miloš Jakeš as party leader in December 1987 signaled no real change in direction. However, in November 1989 the regime was rapidly undermined by demonstrations, initially involving students and young people, inspired by the fall of the Berlin Wall. On November 17 a demonstration was violently attacked by the police and there were incendiary rumors – later proved false – that a protestor had been killed. As the protests intensified, leadership was provided by Václav Havel and fellow dissidents, who formed Civic Forum on November 19 (a Slovak equivalent called People against Violence was also established). Crucially, the workers also joined the opposition, mounting a brief general strike on November 27. Reeling under these blows, and with no recourse now to the Red Army for support, the communist regime swiftly collapsed. A new government was created from the ranks of the opposition and, with spectacular symbolism, Dubček was made Speaker of Parliament. Havel, who had shown great political determination throughout the crisis, was appointed president on December 30 following Husák's resignation.

Romania witnessed the only violent revolution of 1989. Although rich in minerals, it had suffered almost complete economic collapse in the 1980s as the dictatorship of Nicolae Ceauşescu diverted the nation's resources into repaying the foreign debt. There were extensive power cuts, even during the harshest winter, and food was scarce in the shops. Ceauşescu, who became eastern Europe's last Stalinist ruler, lurched into megalomania: a cult of personality was built around him and his close family, and his ambitious policies sought to remake Romanian society. The Hungarian minority in Transylvania were persecuted and thousands fled to Hungary; the basis of peasant life was destroyed through the process of village "systematization"; and much of the historic center of Bucharest was bulldozed to allow for grandiose new projects. Although there had been violent localized protests against the regime in 1977 and 1987, strict control was maintained through the Securitate secret police. However, on December 16–17, 1989 attempts to remove the Hungarian Protestant pastor László Tőkes from the Transylvanian city of Timisoara provoked an uprising which rapidly spread to the capital. On December 21 the dictator realized the dramatic change in the public mood when he was heckled at a rally, and fled when the army joined the protestors on the following day. The Ceauşescus were apprehended and executed on December 25. In Bucharest, meanwhile, four days of bitter fighting between the army and remnants of the Securitate left as many as 600 dead, and power was claimed by a number of former communists styling themselves the National Salvation Front. Their leader, Ion Iliescu, became acting president on December 27, but he and his prime minister, Petre Roman, took charge of much of the former communist apparatus. Although Iliescu won a convincing victory in presidential elections in May 1990, his methods (which included mobilizing coal miners to beat up his opponents and fomenting ethnic unrest in Transylvania) seemed to owe much to the old regime.

This readiness to stoke ethnic tensions was nowhere more destructive than in Yugoslavia, where the decline of "Yugoslav" idealism following the death of Tito and the growing desire for democracy coincided with a rebirth of violent national-ism. Yugoslavia's federal economy had largely broken down by the late 1980s, with inflation reaching 300 percent in 1989, as economic power devolved to the republics. Democratic politics were particularly advanced in the northern republics (Slovenia and Croatia), where secession and a reorientation towards western Europe seemed an ever more tempting option. Free elections were held in both republics in April 1990, bringing to power nationalists committed to secession from Yugoslavia. This desire for independence had been reinforced by the rise of Slobodan Milošević in Serbia, who had seized control of the Communist Party in 1986–7 by appealing to Serbian nationalism. Milošević played on the resentment felt by many Serbs against the loss of control over Kosovo, and openly sided with the Serbian minority living in the province. In 1988–9 he successfully restored central Serbian control over Kosovo and Vojvodina, and in elections held in late 1990 won a large majority for his Serbian Socialist Party. Milošević was formally committed to maintaining the integrity of Yugoslavia, but in reality was looking to build a greater Serbia out of its ruins. As we will see (Chapter 11), this inevitably brought him into conflict with Croatia (home to a 600,000 Serb minority) and Bosnia-Herzegovina (which was divided three ways between Slavic Muslims, Serbs, and Croats).

German Reunification, 1989–1990

In East Germany the collapse of communism meant far more than a change of regime: it also signified the end of the state and, indeed, of the Cold War which had been the *sine qua non* of East Germany's existence. Ironically, however, the regime seemed outwardly secure and successful by the 1980s. East Germany was now a full member of the international community and, as the Communist party (the SED) looked forward to the 40th anniversary of the state's foundation in October 1989, reunification seemed more distant than ever. The regime was actively constructing a distinct East German nationhood with its own historical lineage, while the DDR was emerging as an athletics superpower (albeit one powered by pharmaceuticals). There was a very high level of political conformity measured in terms of membership of the SED and its satellite organizations: for instance, 5.5 million East Germans (or a third of the population) were members of the German–Soviet Friendship Association. Opposition groups were still small and heavily penetrated by the Stasi, which by 1989 had as many as 109,000 employees and a legion of informers. Dangerous dissidents such as the singer Wolf Biermann and the radical philosopher Rudolf Bahro were routinely expelled to the West. Official statistics masked the extent of the country's economic problems, and East Germans certainly experienced a higher standard of living than that found elsewhere in the socialist world.

The reality was very different, although it was not only Western analysts who were deceived as East Germany's communist leaders only woke up to the chronic economic problems in the late 1980s. As one leader commented apropos a seminar given by Economics Minister Günter Mittag in 1988, "Then it was crystal clear to us: the GDR was totally bankrupt and there was no way it could get out of the now fatal circle of indebtedness … new credits and the growing burden of interest payments."[20] When Gorbachev met the new East German leader Egon Krenz on November 1, 1989 he was "astonished" to be told that the DDR owed $26.5 billion to the West and that its budget deficit for 1989 was $12.1 billion: "he had not imagined the situation to be so precarious."[21] The economy had, in effect, been sustained by financial assistance from West Germany and its privileged access to EC markets. There were other more visible signs of decay. The environment was severely degraded, the housing stock was of very poor quality, and much of the industrial base was antiquated. Citizens might display public conformity, but the regime had long ceased its attempts to prevent them from watching West German television at home. Moreover, the opposition was becoming more assertive in the mid-1980s (inspired by Gorbachev's reforms) and diversifying into independent environmental and peace campaigning. One very significant factor was the agreement signed between the regime and the Protestant churches in March 1978. The agreement suited the institutional objectives of both parties, but it also allowed the churches to provide an increasingly significant shelter for dissenters. Ironically, by 1988 the government was becoming so concerned about the destabilizing effect of Gorbachev's reforms that it was forced to ban the Soviet journal *Sputnik*.

The East German crisis was, however, triggered by Hungary rather than the USSR. In May 1989 the Hungarian government took down its barbed wire fence on the Austrian border and thousands of East Germans flocked to Hungary during the summer, many taking refuge in the West German embassy. On September 11 the Hungarian government announced that it would allow free passage for the refugees. These events not only provided a means of escape for young, ambitious East Germans, but also emboldened dissidents, who began to mount regular demonstrations for reform, notably around the St. Nicholas church in Leipzig. Significantly, these early protestors made it clear that they had no intention of joining the exodus, but wanted to work for a better DDR. The regime suffered a further reverse when Gorbachev arrived for the 40th anniversary celebrations on 7 October, and made clear his support for political reform. Eleven days later the party leader Erich Honecker was overthrown in favor of Egon Krenz. There was, however, little evidence that Krenz could meet the ever-growing demand for reform, as he had recently congratulated the Chinese authorities on their suppression of the Tiananmen Square protests. No such solution was practicable in East Germany, however. The key moment had come on October 9, when the authorities mobilized to crush the Leipzig protests but backed down: a tribute to the moderation of elements of the leadership and the disciplined nonviolence of the demonstrators.

By November 4, 1989 at least 500,000 were demonstrating for reform in Berlin and the regime was losing cohesion. Meanwhile, by the end of October over 188,000 people had applied to leave East Germany. On November 9 the SED leadership agreed to make concessions on travel to the West, which were read out, prematurely, by Berlin party secretary Günter Schabowski at 7 p.m. The crucial passage stated that: "Applications for travel abroad by private individuals can now be made without the previously existing requirements. The travel authorizations will be issued within a short time." When asked when this would come into effect he replied: "immediately, without delay."[22] These few words delivered a death sentence to the Berlin Wall and, indeed, to East Germany. Huge, peaceful crowds began to flock to the crossing points where bemused border guards, lacking any briefing, eventually waved them through amidst mounting excitement and disbelief. The botched lifting of travel restrictions was an attempt to relieve popular pressure and allow the state to survive, but it merely decided its fate. With hindsight the events of the following year, culminating in Germany's formal reunification on October 3, 1990, appear as a lengthy coda to the delirium of that night, but this was hardly apparent at the time. Before reunification could become a reality three distinct debates had to be conducted: amongst East Germans, amongst West Germans, and between the Germans and the victorious wartime powers.

The fall of the Berlin Wall accelerated the political decay of the SED, which until November had been determined to hang on to power. Now not even a communist reformer such as Hans Modrow, who became prime minister, could contain the growing popular hostility to the party (fuelled by revelations of the good life lived by its leaders). At first it seemed that the initiative would be taken by the dissidents who had led the protests in the autumn, grouped in organizations such as New Forum. They had no desire for reunification, which suggested a colonization by the materialist West, but rather hoped to preserve the best of East Germany – above all its welfare provisions and social solidarity. One slogan humorously captured this fear of trading one kind of servitude for another: "After Honecker and Krenz, not Daimler Benz." By the spring of 1990, however, the putative material benefits of rapid unification were proving irresistible to the majority of the population. When free elections were held on March 18, 1990, the pro-unification parties won a stunning victory, notably the Christian Democrats, who had been strongly backed by Helmut Kohl. Kohl made six personal appearances during the campaign, and offered East Germans a vision of a "flourishing land,"[23] a claim which later returned to haunt him. All that was left for the new government of Lothar de Mazière, who formed a coalition with the defeated social democrats, was to negotiate the best possible terms for unification.

Within West Germany the fall of the Berlin Wall caused both delight and consternation. There was genuine concern that West Germany's democracy and prosperity, as well as its integration with the West, could be undermined by any hasty action which might provoke a revival of German nationalism. However, Kohl was quick to seize the moment. On November 28 he presented a ten-point plan for handling the crisis to the Bundestag, and affirmed that unification would come "if it is wanted by the German people." Although he conceded that German reunification could not be planned "with our appointment calendars" in hand, he had put it firmly back on the political agenda.[24] In doing so, Kohl was not only grasping a historic opportunity, endorsed by a surge in public support, but also responding to the danger that an imploding East Germany might cause even greater difficulties for the West. Even so, the SPD leader Oscar Lafontaine warned, with some justification, that the costs of reunification would be far greater than Kohl admitted to. The SPD also argued, unsuccessfully, that reunification should take place under Article 146 of the Basic Law, whereby the two governments would negotiate a new Constitution. In fact, reunification took place under the more direct Article 23, according to which the five East German *Länder* (abolished in 1952) would be reconstituted and apply to join West Germany. In effect, therefore, there would be a takeover of the East by the West.

The third stage of reunification required international agreement. Kohl benefited from the warm support of the Bush administration, but there was initial hostility from Mitterrand and Thatcher. Both feared the consequences of a revival of German power in Europe and a reorientation of Germany towards the East. Mitterrand, however, was willing to see the solution as lying in an acceleration of European integration, leaving Thatcher isolated. The Soviet Union remained the major obstacle to reunification, and Gorbachev's initial reaction to the fall of the Berlin Wall had been to warn Western leaders against any "emotional denials of the postwar realities, meaning the existence of two German states."[25] He was affronted by Kohl's "ten points," which he regarded as "an ultimatum" and an attempt to destabilize East Germany.[26] However, the USSR was now so absorbed in its internal political and economic problems that it was, in practice, willing to negotiate. Gorbachev came to accept the principle of unification, but initially hoped that a unified Germany would be neutral (as well as long postponed). On July 15, 1990, however, Kohl traveled to Moscow and achieved a breakthrough. The Soviet Union now accepted that a united Germany could remain in NATO, and proposed to withdraw its 380,000 troops from East Germany. In return, Kohl offered generous economic assistance, reduced West German troop levels, and conceded special transitional security arrangements for East Germany. The other outstanding issue was the status of the Polish border. Kohl had caused some alarm by dragging his feet on this issue, but was forced to confirm the existing borders as the price of unification in late June. (A formal border treaty was concluded with Poland in January 1991.) With these substantive issues settled the "Two Plus Four" talks (the two Germanies plus the Allied powers) resulted in a final agreement ending the four-power status of Berlin on September 12.

Even before resolution of the diplomatic issues, the formation of a currency union and the ending of passport controls between the two Germanies on July 1, 1990 had brought about effective unification. The terms were very generous given the worthlessness of the East German Mark: currency was exchanged at 1:1 for wages and savings under 4,000 Marks (although less was offered for debts and foreign accounts). The currency union brought a short-term consumer bonanza, but the extent of the economic problems that lay ahead could not be concealed. Already, a *Treuhandstadt* (trust) had been established to manage East German assets, and rapidly evolved into a vehicle for mass privatization. However, it soon became apparent that the East German economy was hardly the much-vaunted "planned miracle." Few factories were viable in a market economy, and there were acute problems of pollution and overmanning. Even so, the surge of living costs and unemployment during the latter part of 1990 could not impede the logic of unification. A unification treaty was signed on August 31 which made a few temporary concessions to East German practice (for instance, in relation to abortion rights). In December 1990 Kohl received his reward with victory in the first all-German elections since 1932. The SPD was punished for its critical stance on unification (although many of Lafontaine's gloomy predictions were coming true) and was particularly hard hit in the former East Germany, where it won only 23.6 percent of the vote.

The End of the Soviet Union, 1990–1991

By 1990 Gorbachev's reforms appeared to be failing on every front. The Soviet gross national product actually fell by 2 percent during 1990 as the command economy collapsed into hoarding and barter, but Gorbachev was unwilling to implement the radical Shatalin plan that promised to create a market economy within 500 days. Meanwhile, democratization had undermined the ability of the Communist Party to run the Soviet Union (the CPSU formally renounced its claim to a "leading role" in February 1990) but produced no new governing order at the federal level. Gorbachev's own authority was diminished by his association with the Communist Party, but he dared not relinquish his post as General Secretary for fear of the party falling into conservative hands. Moreover, as Soviet politics polarized between the advocates and opponents of radical change, his own centrist position became increasingly isolated. Finally, Gorbachev was now engaged in an unexpected struggle for the survival of the Soviet Union itself. In May 1990 Lithuania declared independence – which was met with sanctions from Moscow – while the other Baltic republics, along with Georgia and Armenia, waited on events. Most dangerous of all was the emergence of a new desire for Russian sovereignty. Russia was by far the largest of the republics, and was itself a federal entity containing a number of ethnic minorities. However, Russian identity had previously been subsumed within the Soviet Union and – since Stalin's time – had been largely coexistent with it. Until 1990, for instance, Russia did not possess its own Communist Party. This invisibility was now coming to an end, to the advantage of Gorbachev's most bitter rival. In May 1990 Boris Yeltsin was appointed president of the Russian federation and, in June 1991, won the first democratic elections for this office with 57.3 percent of the vote. Yeltsin was not only becoming a more popular politician but also, unlike Gorbachev, now possessed a democratic mandate.

In the winter of 1990/1, confronted with the failure of *perestroika* and the threat to the integrity of the USSR, Gorbachev temporarily swung towards the hardliners. He parted company with many of his reformist advisers, and their replacements often proved unreliable. (Shevardnadze resigned in December 1990, warning of the "onset of dictatorship"). The consequences were most evident in the Baltic states, where there were a number of attempts to crush the independence movements. In January 1991 pro-Soviet militias stormed the TV station in the Lithuanian capital of Vilnius, and a week later took control of the Interior Ministry building in Latvia. Fourteen unarmed protestors were killed in Vilnius and four in

Riga. However, although bloody provocations continued into the summer, it became clear that the hardliners lacked a strategy for sustaining the USSR by force, and their behavior merely stiffened the resolve of the radicals (some 500,000 demonstrated in support of Boris Yeltsin in March 1991).

By the spring, therefore, Gorbachev was willing to break with the conservatives and to negotiate with the emerging power brokers: the presidents of the republics. The context for the negotiations was a majority view that the Union should be maintained (a position supported by 76 percent of voters in a referendum held in March 1991).[27] The result was a draft treaty under which the Union (and Gorbachev's role as president) would survive but with greatly reduced central powers. The decision to sign the treaty on August 20, before which Gorbachev would go on holiday in the Crimea, presented its opponents (many of them trusted allies of the president) with a final opportunity to prevent what they saw as the dissolution of the USSR. The plot was well supported: the prime minister, the head of the KGB, and the Defense Minister were amongst its leaders, and it was tacitly backed by the Chairman of the Supreme Soviet. On August 18, a delegation visited Gorbachev and demanded that he authorize emergency powers. When he refused he was placed under house arrest and, on August 19, a "State Committee for the State of Emergency" seized power. However, the coup was poorly planned and soon unraveled when many military units refused to support it. Most damagingly, Yeltsin, in his finest hour, established the Russian "White House" (the parliament building of the Russian Federation) as a center of resistance and appealed to the army to oppose the coup.

The collapse of the hardliners after three days allowed a disorientated Gorbachev to return to Moscow, but it soon became evident that his authority had been fatally weakened. Power had effectively passed to Yeltsin, who immediately suspended the Communist Party and sequestered its property. A plot intended to save the Soviet Union had merely accelerated its demise, as the new treaty was now a dead letter and all of the republics eventually claimed independence (which was conceded to the Baltic states in September). An overwhelming vote in Ukraine for independence in December demonstrated that no new federation was now possible, even within the Slavic core of the USSR. The agreement by most of the republics to form a new Confederation of Independent States, with no centralized functions at all, made Gorbachev redundant, and he formally resigned as president on December 25, 1991, a week before the USSR itself passed into history.

Conclusion

The fall of the communist regimes was largely unforeseen, and stunning in the rapidity and the completeness of the collapse. The underlying conditions were provided by the long-term failure of the regimes to provide adequate standards of living for their citizens, especially compared to those in the West. However, it was the advent of Mikhail Gorbachev as the new Soviet leader in 1985 that made radical change possible. Ironically, Gorbachev had been determined to avert the collapse of the Soviet Union by "new thinking" in relation to every aspect of Soviet life. However, in order to defeat the opponents of change he set in train a process of democratization that ultimately proved fatal. Meanwhile, his international policy sought to end the Cold War as the basis for a new economic relationship with the West. Within eastern Europe the different regimes underwent very different processes of political collapse, ranging from the gradual to the rapid and violent. However, in every case the rulers were aware that they could no longer have recourse to the Red Army for salvation. The true victory rested with the bravery of those citizens who were willing to demonstrate on behalf of reform in the autumn of 1989: on many occasions, however, they did not reap the political benefits in the post-communist world.

11
Europe after the Cold War

Building Europe?

Within a few years of the fall of communism and German reunification, it became apparent that the most fearful scenarios would not become reality. A wounded, humiliated Russia had not become a dangerous new version of the Weimar Republic, and the unified Germany was no "Fourth Reich." If anything, by the end of the 1990s it was Germany's weakness that was causing concern, while Western governments were rather grateful for Vladimir Putin's neo-Soviet authoritarianism in Russia. For most of the countries of central Europe, if not for the Balkan states, this was a decade of steady transition towards economic and military integration with the West. For the countries of western Europe, with the prime exception of Italy, the events of 1989–91 had a surprisingly limited impact beyond the knock-on effects of higher German interest rates. There was little that was distinctively new in the 1990s, apart from a growing awareness of the vast economic potential of information technology. Instead, there was a continuation and generalization of the trends – such as market liberalization and intensified European integration – established in the previous decade. Western European governments were, in particular, preoccupied with fulfilling the provisions of the Maastricht Treaty for economic and political union.[1] As the Cold War had ended on the West's terms there seemed to be no reason for it to question its own political and economic values, which were now to be exported to the former Soviet bloc.

The most significant mark of stability was the survival – and indeed the advance – of NATO. This was by no means implicit in the events of 1989–91, as it was quite conceivable that the collapse of Soviet power might have caused western Europe and the USA to pull apart in the 1990s. Such a departure was unlikely at first, given the traditionalist foreign policy of George Bush, but far more so under the globally

Europe's Troubled Peace: 1945 to the Present, Second Edition. Tom Buchanan.
© 2012 John Wiley & Sons, Ltd. Published 2012 by John Wiley & Sons, Ltd.

minded Bill Clinton (1993–2001), who actively encouraged European governments to play a more active role in resolving local conflicts. Moreover, in the early 1990s there were a number of potential rivals to NATO's hegemony. François Mitterrand was keen to revive the west European Union (WEU) as the EC's security arm, following the adoption of a Common Foreign and Security Policy (CFSP) at Maastricht, while Russia would have preferred to see an enhanced role for the Conference on Security and Cooperation in Europe (CSCE).[2] In fact, there was very little "Transatlantic drift"[3] during the 1990s as the Europeans had little stomach for an independent foreign policy – especially if there was any fighting to be done. Instead, from the Gulf War of 1991 to Bosnia (1995) and Kosovo (1999), the United States reasserted its military leadership of the West. The claim of Jacques Poos that "the hour of Europe" had dawned, speaking for the EC presidency apropos the Yugoslav crisis, proved hollow. If anything, as Delors put it, Europe had behaved during that conflict like "an adolescent confronted by an adult crisis."[4] Meanwhile, the countries of the former Soviet bloc desired above all to join NATO. A first step (inevitably somewhat tentative for fear of antagonizing Russia) was taken with the 1994 "Partnerships for Peace," and Hungary, Poland, and the Czech Republic became full NATO members in March 1999. Therefore, despite the absence of any common enemy, the USA and NATO remained central to European security, while other agencies established complementary roles (such as that of the CSCE in conflict resolution).

The conflicts of the post–Cold War decade were profoundly different from those which military planners had long prepared for. Soviet nuclear and armored superiority had been conceded even before the collapse of the USSR: now the greatest nuclear threat was the decay – or even the sale into undesirable hands – of its stockpile. Conflicts of the 1990s were low-tech affairs, characterized by the brutal ethnic violence in the former Yugoslavia or around the margins of Russia (notably in the Caucasus). If western Europe were to mount an intervention – either in these areas or in the developing world – it would require the ability to deploy troops rapidly at a distance, suitably trained for complex humanitarian missions. This encouraged a fundamental reassessment of the role of the military in national life. Many countries, such as Spain and France, truncated their compulsory military service to create more professional armed forces, while in November 1989, with the end of the Cold War in sight, 35 percent of Swiss adults voted in favor of abolishing their army altogether. The 1994 decision by the German Constitutional Court to allow use of the Bundeswehr outside the NATO area (within the framework of the UN) was the subject of a great deal of introspection, which itself placed further political limits on the uses of German power. Only the two greatest ex-colonial powers had the capability to act independently outside Europe. Hence, Britain intervened in Sierra Leone to restore the elected government in 2000 while French troops were sent to Rwanda in 1994 following the outbreak of genocidal civil conflict. It was unclear to many observers, however, whether this was a genuine humanitarian mission or an attempt to save France's Hutu allies from defeat.[5]

A sense of external military threat gave way to new concerns about mass immigration. West European countries had emerged from the Cold War as a beacon for the new poor in eastern Europe and elsewhere, as well as for those fleeing ethnic persecution (such as Bosnian Muslims and Gypsies from the former Czechoslovakia). The desirability of western Europe was such that in 1991 Albanians crammed onto boats to seek refuge in Italy, while the bodies of North Africans who had died attempting the short but perilous crossing were regularly washed up on the shores of southern Spain. In fact, levels of migration (admittedly, notoriously difficult to calculate) remained relatively steady across the EC/EU in the 1990s, but rose significantly in Britain, Italy and above all Spain.[6] The problem facing politicians was how to balance Europe's professed liberal and humanitarian values, as well as the need to redress skills shortages and population decline in countries such as Germany and Italy, against the rise of a powerful and destabilizing xenophobia. In Austria and France, for instance, the 1990s saw growing support for anti-immigration parties, which avoided overt racism by cleverly playing on fears of crime and concepts of cultural difference. Even more striking was the rise of the iconoclastic Pim Forteyn, who punctured the image of Dutch liberalism by arguing that Muslims were incapable of assimilation. The strains were most evident in Germany, where Article 16 of the Basic Law provided a right to asylum, originally for the small numbers who might escape the Soviet bloc. The rapid rise in numbers of asylum-seekers in the early 1990s caused particular tensions in the former East Germany where there had been little experience of multiculturalism and a number of immigrant hostels were attacked. Eventually, in 1993 Helmut Kohl received cross-party support to amend the Constitution, greatly reducing the numbers who could legitimately claim asylum. The EU might not yet have become "Fortress Europe" for immigrants by the late 1990s, but the terms of political discussion had undoubtedly altered to the disadvantage of all but a small privileged elite of potential immigrants.

The pressure of immigration reinforced an emerging negative sense of "Europeanness" as something which was desired by others. More positively, developments such as the implementation of the Schengen agreement on cross-border travel without passports (1995) and the advent of the euro in 1999 meant access not only to high standards of living and welfare, but also to new opportunities for working on a trans-national basis. In practice, however, labor mobility was far lower than in the United States, and only 1.5 percent of EU citizens worked in another member state.[7] Despite the introduction of a greater degree of European symbolism, such as the EU passports, flag, and anthem, it was clear that any emergent "European" identity was complementary, and almost inevitably secondary, to more long-standing national and sub-national loyalties. A "Eurobarometer" poll in December 1993 showed that 45 percent of those questioned identified equally with their nation and with Europe, 40 percent identified only with their nation, and a mere handful identified with Europe first.[8] Meanwhile, levels of participation in European elections (which continued to be fought on largely national issues) fell during the 1990s. The EU might have some of the attributes of a state, but as yet had none of those of a nation.

With so much focus on the completion of monetary union (see below), other aspects of integration made slower progress after Maastricht. Delors's successors lacked his vision and drive, and also had to cope with the decline of the Franco-German axis and a weakening of the Commission itself. Indeed, the entire Commission of Jacques Santer was compelled to resign in 1999 due to financial mismanagement. Attempts were made to give substance to the CFSP at the Amsterdam intergovernmental conference in 1997, and some significant steps were taken in the late 1990s, such as the appointment of Javier Solana as the first "High Representative of the CFSP", and the decision to create a Rapid Deployment Force for peacemaking duties. However, Britain and France held on to their permanent seats on the UN Security Council (having agreed at Maastricht to represent EU interests), and any pretension of a common foreign policy was shredded in the run-up to the Iraq war of 2003. Yet for all of the survival of national interests and agendas, there was also a steady process of "Europeanization"[9] under way, both in terms of national governments' need to respond to the flow of EU initiatives and in terms of the framing of policy. Europe's influence could also be indirect. For instance, in 1997 the British government gave the Bank of England freedom to set interest rates even though it was not yet ready to join the single currency. Moreover, just as governments had learnt to work together to obtain their desired policy outcomes from Brussels, so, increasingly, had trans-national networks of, say, trade unionists and environmentalists.

The EU's most palpable success was achieved in terms of enlargement, although this posed fundamental questions as to the Union's cohesiveness. The only countries that could ignore the pull of European integration were those which were wealthy and secure enough to do so. Norway narrowly voted against EU membership for the second time in November 1994, while in December 1992 Switzerland voted against joining the looser association known as the European Economic Area. However, the former neutrals (Austria, Finland, and Sweden) joined the EU in 1994 and a tranche of eight former Soviet and eastern bloc states (plus Malta and Cyprus) followed in May 2004.[10] Even so, by the time that many east European countries came to qualify for EU membership its appeal was already beginning to wear thin, not least because the deal on offer was a poor one. The new members would not benefit from regional aid, CAP assistance or (at least initially) full labor mobility within the EU. Although they still voted for accession, this was largely on the grounds of security and a desire to "return to Europe" rather than any immediate material benefits. Increasingly politicians saw advantage in hostility to integration, such as the Polish nationalist Andrzej Lepper, who argued that Poland had exchanged domination by Moscow for domination by Brussels. Ironically, just as European integration reached its zenith in the late 1990s, there was mounting disenchantment at its historic core – France and Germany. For Germany, now facing its own economic worries, the days of subsidizing its European partners were gone, while France seemed increasingly uneasy in a Union that was ever wider, looser, less federal, and less "French."[10]

The continuing enlargement of the EU and NATO raised very acutely the question of how Europe is – and will be – defined. The end of the Cold War had suddenly made possible de Gaulle's Europe united "from the Atlantic to the Urals" as well as Gorbachev's "common European home." A decade of political and economic reform had considerably eroded the divisions between western and former communist Europe, even though differences of wealth and culture clearly survived, as demonstrated by the continuing divisions between former East and West Germans (the *Ossis* and *Wessis*). In many respects the concept of "Europe" had come to represent a bundle of economic, social, and political philosophies – broadly humanist and liberal – that had grown detached from any specific geographical or historical moorings. Yet how far, then, should Europe extend, and on what criteria? Expressions of unease at the emergence of Turkey as a serious candidate to become the EU's first Muslim member state seemed to reflect more than concern at its human rights record, vulnerable strategic location and economic backwardness. However, concerns that Turkish membership would dilute Europe's Christian culture did little justice to the extensive secularization of the later twentieth century, or the substantial Muslim populations that already lived in many EU states.

West European Politics

The main characteristic of west European politics in the 1990s was the decline of ideological difference and an increasing convergence on the center ground. This tendency was strongly reinforced both by the strict economic regime imposed by the EU in preparation for the single currency and by the historic defeat of socialism (in communist form) during the 1980s. For the left as a whole the 1990s were a period of adaptation in the face of the liberal triumphalism and "end of history"[11] theorizing that marked the end of the Cold War. The traditional levers of social democratic management were no longer available to governments as economies became increasingly globalized and integrated. Even the Swedish social democrats fell back on the market in the early 1990s and took Sweden into the EU. Where the left was most electorally successful, it was as a centrist force that could appeal to middle-class voters: hence the victories of Britain's "New Labour" and the German SPD's "New Middle" in 1997 and 1998. (Although in both cases this success was partly due to running against parties – and in the German case a Chancellor – that had long overstayed their welcome.) This did not mean, however, that the left had lost all claim to political distinctiveness: above all, it remained the champion of social justice. Despite its economic orthodoxy, Tony Blair's New Labour government introduced a minimum wage and greatly increased public spending on health and education. In France, the socialist administration of Lionel Jospin (1997–2002) combined tax-cutting and privatization with the truly radical introduction of a 35-hour week in France. Jospin's credo was "Yes to the market economy, but no to the market society."[12] In Greece the return of PASOK to power in 1993 brought a combination of liberal modernization, welfare and strident nationalism (in opposition to the international recognition of an independent republic of Macedonia following the break-up of Yugoslavia).

Conservative parties did not benefit as much as might have been expected from the end of the Cold War. Indeed, they too faced an existential crisis. The collapse of communism took away a major source of their political cohesion just as they had to confront divisive issues such as European integration and immigration. Conservatives found themselves under attack from more populist parties to their right, as well as – later in the decade – center-left parties which had stolen many of their policies. The Italian Christian Democrats fragmented during the early 1990s, requiring a thorough recasting of the center-right. In Britain the Conservative Party lost its way under Thatcher's successor, John Major. Despite his election victory in April 1992, the subsequent currency crisis and bitter party in-fighting over Europe doomed his government to a lingering death between 1992 and 1997. In Germany, the reunification "bonus" was a diminishing asset for the Christian Democrats and, indeed, their defeat in 1998 was partly due to a loss of support amongst former East Germans disillusioned with Chancellor Kohl's failure to deliver on the promises of 1990. Jacques Chirac won the French presidency in 1995 for the center-right, but, at least until the presidency of George W. Bush offered him a perfect foil, it was far from clear what his Gaullism stood for in an age of European integration. Following an ill-judged decision to call parliamentary elections he was forced to "cohabit" with a socialist government from 1997, although he achieved a political apotheosis in 2002 when he defeated Le Pen in the run-off for the presidential elections. On this occasion many left-wing French voters opted for a man that they regarded with distaste in order to defeat a man that they regarded as a fascist. The Spanish conservative People's Party, under the leadership of José Maria Aznar, wrested power from the socialists in 1996 by proving that it was no longer tainted with Francoism.

Meanwhile, the conventional spectrum of European politics visibly narrowed. Most Western communist parties either faced political oblivion or reinvented themselves on democratic socialist lines. In Italy, for instance, the old PCI was reborn in 1991 as the Party of the Democratic Left (PDS), affiliated to the Socialist International, although a die-hard minority fought on as Communist Refoundation. Such changes aside, the 1990s did not witness the emergence of new parties so much as the entry into government of many of the radical forces of the 1980s. The German Greens joined a coalition with the SPD in 1998, while the Italian neo-fascists (under the banner of the National Alliance (AN)) served along with the Northern League in Berlusconi's 1994 government. In Austria, the entry of Jörg Haider's Freedom Party into a coalition with the conservative ÖVP in 2000 briefly provoked EU sanctions. Elsewhere, anti-immigrant parties such as the Vlaams Blok in Flanders and the Danish People's Party remained in opposition but could rely on substantial electoral support.

The success of such parties was reinforced by the persistent revelations of corruption during the 1990s, both at the national and the EU levels. Party-funding scandals contributed to the overthrow of the entire Italian political system after 1992 (see below) but also damaged the fortunes of socialist governments in Spain and France, and retrospectively tarnished the career of Helmut Kohl. Overall, the saving grace for politicians was that political parties of both left and right were implicated, although this did nothing to reassure voters that politics was a noble calling. In Britain, meanwhile, allegations of "sleaze" did much to undermine the Conservatives in the mid-1990s, although in this case the issue often tended to be British prurience about sex – combined with the power of the tabloid press – rather than financial irregularity. Throughout Europe, corruption scandals reinforced fears of political apathy due to the declining turnout in elections, although many young people were still drawn to extra-parliamentary politics: witness the rise of the anti-globalization movement. Indeed, although the 1990s were largely a decade of political quiescence, protest still had its part to play. Tony Blair's otherwise secure government was stunned in the autumn of 2000 by actions in protest at high fuel taxes that briefly paralyzed the country. Silvio Berlusconi was forced to back down over pension reforms by union-led protests in 1994, while the controversial welfare reforms of the conservative French Prime Minister Alain Juppé were defeated by nationwide strikes during the winter of 1995 that evoked memories of 1968.

Another important feature of the 1990s was the rising power of regionalism. Existing federal arrangements were strengthened, while some nonfederal states experimented with devolution. This trend was encouraged by the EU's rhetoric of "subsidiarity" and a "Europe of the regions," as well as by the establishment of a Committee of the Regions under the Maastricht Treaty. Many regions began to establish cross-border alliances, such as the economically powerful "Four Motors of Europe" group that united Württemberg, Catalonia, Lombardy, and Rhône-Alpes. The German *Länder* won the right to represent Germany at the EU Council of Ministers in their main policy areas (notably education and culture). Spain continued to move in a federal direction and the Catalan Convergència i Unión Party not only dominated the regional *Generalitat* but also, for much of the decade, held the balance of power in the national parliament. In Britain varying degrees of devolution of power to Wales and Scotland were agreed by referenda in 1997, temporarily curbing any momentum towards full independence. Indeed, as regionalism waxed secessionism seemed to be in retreat. There was little support for Umberto Bossi (leader of the Northern League) when he declared independence for a north Italian state of "Padania" in September 1996, or for the supporters of an independent Venetia who carried out an armed "uprising" in May 1997. Similarly, the peace process established in Northern Ireland under the 1998 "Good

Friday" agreement recognized that Europe's most violent regional conflict was unlikely to be resolved by a transfer of sovereignty. Instead, the solution appeared to lie in the devolution of power combined with greater equality between the communities and the "decommissioning" of illegally held weapons. Unfortunately, even this limited progress could not be achieved in the Basque country, where the advent of Aznar's more centralizing government in Madrid revived ETA militancy.

Troubled Waters: Italy and Germany

The Italian crisis was essentially one of political authority, as there was considerable consensus over the need for economic rigor to ensure that Italy met the criteria for membership of the single currency. The context was the ending of the Cold War, which had guaranteed the power of the Christian Democrats and their allies, combined with the rise of a new activism (centered on young people and professionals) on behalf of a cleaner Italian public life. In the mid-1980s, for instance, the mayor of Palermo, Leoluca Orlando, had campaigned courageously against the power of the Mafia. The crisis opened with the April 1992 elections in which both the Christian Democrats and the PDS (the successor to the Communist Party) lost votes heavily compared to new parties such as the Northern League (which won 8.7 percent). In the aftermath of the election judicial investigations into "kickbacks" (*tangente*) in the socialist bastion of Milan accelerated and spread to other cities and political parties. The scandal eventually destroyed the Socialist Party and discredited the Christian Democrats, lapping around such pillars of the republic as former prime minister Giulio Andreotti. In effect the political parties (although the communists were only marginally affected) had fallen victim to a paradigm shift in Italian public life, whereby practices of party funding and clientelism which had been broadly tolerated for many years were now repudiated. There were three further shocks to the system. First, in May and July 1992 two judges who had been involved in prosecuting the Mafia were assassinated in Sicily, in a direct assault on the authority of the state. Secondly, during the currency crisis of September 1992 the lira was forced out of the ERM and subsequently devalued, casting fresh doubt on Italy's ability to join the euro. Thirdly, there was mounting pressure for political reform, to allow for more decisive leadership. Following a referendum on political reform in April 1993 it was eventually agreed that there should be a combination of a majoritarian system of election (for 75 percent of the seats in parliament) and proportional representation.

As the main political parties disintegrated, it remained unclear who would inherit the former Christian democratic constituency. The Northern League was, by definition, a regional force, while the neo-fascist AN drew most of its support from the south. This gap in conservative politics was filled by the remarkable rise of Forza Italia! ("Come on, Italy!") which was formed in November 1993 by

Silvio Berlusconi, the media tycoon and owner of AC Milan football club. Berlusconi's decision to enter politics was in part taken for reasons of self-preservation, as he feared being the subject of judicial investigation, but it was also a fascinating experiment in the power of modern media and celebrity (termed by some a "videocracy").[13] Although he was detested by many intellectuals as a purveyor of low-brow culture with authoritarian tendencies, Berlusconi's image as a self-made man was appealing to many ordinary Italians. The new party's politics were neo-liberal, even Thatcherite, and anti-communist, but also promised an end to the corruption investigations (which, according to Berlusconi, were politically motivated). Berlusconi swept to power in the elections of March 1994 at the head of a "Pole of Freedom" alliance with the Alleanza Nazionale and the Northern League. This fractious coalition government collapsed in December 1994. At last, after almost 50 years, it was the left's turn to govern. In April 1996 an "Olive Tree Alliance" of former communists and Christian Democrats won a slender election victory under the leadership of Romano Prodi. All of the government's efforts were soon bent towards Italy entering the euro in the first wave, despite the severe austerity measures that this required of a center-left government. Prodi's efforts were successful, and soon after Italy's entry into the new currency he departed to become the president of the European Commission. However, Berlusconi was far from finished and returned to power on a more lasting basis in May 2001.

Germany, by contrast, absorbed far more fundamental political and economic shocks than Italy with surprisingly little visible impact. Even though Helmut Kohl had grievously misjudged the costs of reunification, the existing political system survived the 1990s largely unchanged, and the discontent of the former East Germans was successfully contained. The central problem was that East German industry and labor were far less productive than had been estimated in 1990, while the proceeds of privatization were likewise less than expected. Prospective investors were deterred by the uncompetitiveness of East German factories and the high costs of cleaning up pollution and contamination. Moreover, the harmonization of wages (which had been insisted on by the West German trade unions) was a further blow to economic recovery given the relatively lax labor discipline of the old DDR. Accordingly, the West had to make large financial transfers to pay for job creation, infrastructural renewal and the crippling unemployment in the east (officially 15 percent by 1994, but probably closer to 25 percent).[14] Given that Kohl was prevented by election promises from raising taxes, the Bundesbank was forced to raise interest rates, which contributed to recession in western Europe. The main burden of reunification was, however, borne by the former East Germans, who faced unemployment, early retirement or, for the more fortunate, reskilling and a job in one of the few new factories. Discontent and disorientation were rife: one of the unemployed described their condition as that of "hard-working and honest people … cast aside like dirt from a dustpan."[15] However, East Germany had gone for good, and despite continuing support for the former communists, or even for the far right, such discontent had little political purchase on Germany as a whole.

Kohl's gamble on reunification had paid off, and a brief revival of the far-right Republican Party in 1991–2 was headed off by the revision of the right to asylum in 1993. Aided by the end of the recession, the Chancellor won a slender victory in the 1994 election, although the CDU/CSU vote dipped to 41.4 percent. Kohl's final term of office was dominated by European issues, above all economic and monetary union, which he saw as essential for anchoring a reunified Germany in an integrated Europe. However, his decision to stand again in 1998 was ill advised. Unemployment had continued to rise (to stand at 4.66 million in 1997) and there was apprehension at the impending loss of the Deutschmark. Moreover, the SPD had finally produced a viable candidate for Chancellor, the telegenic Gerhard Schroeder, whose centrist appeal was sufficiently vague to allow him to forge a Red–Green coalition without alarming voters. In September 1998 Kohl became, remarkably, the first German Chancellor to be defeated at the polls. However, Schroeder's first term was politically incoherent and inept, although serious corruption allegations against the CDU provided a timely distraction. Schroeder was irresolute on important but controversial measures such as the reform of citizenship laws and the running down of the nuclear power program. Part of this incoherence was resolved when the influential left-winger Oskar Lafontaine resigned as Economics Minister and SPD Chairman in March 1999, allowing Schroeder to pursue a more modernizing policy thereafter.

Western Europe: The Economy and EMU

Throughout the decade, economic policy-making was dominated by the deadline of January 1, 1999, the date set at Maastricht for the third and final stage of European monetary union. The transition to full implementation would be completed in 2001. Not only did the strict convergence criteria result in low growth and higher levels of unemployment across much of the EU, but it also remained far from clear which member states would ultimately be able – or willing – to join the new single currency at the first attempt. (In the event, Britain, Denmark and Sweden all exercised their "opt-out" and postponed any decision on membership). The establishment of the euro on time by 12 EU members was therefore a remark-able achievement, even if it required some finessing of the accounts to ensure membership in certain cases. For instance, French governments of right and left cut the deficit by raiding the pensions and profits of the French Telecom company, although an attempt by the German government to revalue the Bundesbank's gold reserve was successfully fought off in 1997.

The EMU project evolved considerably after Maastricht, and was the subject of much political debate. Broadly, Germany (which was, of course, crucial to the whole enterprise) had its way on the major unresolved issues such as the location of the new European Central Bank (in Frankfurt), its founding president (the Dutch banker Wim Duisenburg), and the name of the currency (the "euro" rather than the French-sounding "ecu"). Moreover a "Growth and Stability Pact" was concluded in 1997 in an attempt to ensure that states kept their deficits in check once they had joined the euro. However, although the convergence criteria were never formally relaxed, the purpose of EMU was somewhat redefined, especially with the return to power of the center-left in a number of major countries. At the Amsterdam IGC in 1997 it was agreed that EMU must also be concerned with growth and jobs, and an Employment Pact was concluded in 1999 to set appropriate targets. In reality, however, this was a long way from the "economic government" of Europe that the French in particular would have liked to see, and many economic issues continued to be dealt with at the national level. Meanwhile, in the late 1990s the EU calculated that some 15 percent of its population still lived at risk of poverty.

The establishment of the euro had looked a decidedly remote prospect in the autumn of 1992 when currency speculation, encouraged by the raising of German interest rates due to the costs of unification, sent the British pound and the Italian lira crashing out of the ERM and brought about the virtual collapse of the European Monetary System. The subsequent response of these two states was indicative of the very different national attitudes towards EMU. In fact, "Black Wednesday" was something of a blessing in disguise for the British economy, as the devaluation of the pound made British exports more competitive and laid the basis for a strong recovery in the mid-1990s when the economy grew by 3 percent per year. This very success, and the advantage enjoyed over the other EU members, in turn made it less likely that the new Labour government would take Britain into the euro after 1997. In Italy, conversely, membership of the euro became a point of national pride, especially when it became clear that there would be no common front in favor of relaxing the convergence criteria among fellow south European governments. After a brief wobble when Prime Minister Romano Prodi warned that Italy wanted to participate in EMU "alive, not dead,"[16] the center-left government buckled down, rejoined the ERM, and introduced a "euro tax" to cut Italy's budget deficit. Despite this imposition, by the late 1990s popular support for the new currency was higher in Italy than anywhere else in Europe.

One of the most striking features of the 1990s was the faltering of the German economy, with record levels of unemployment and an annual growth rate (1.5 percent) below the EU average. In the mid-1990s there was even a question as to whether Germany could meet the EMU criteria. By no means could all of the blame be attributed to the costs of unification or EMU, as Germany was also suffering from longer-term problems of uncompetitiveness related to labor market inflexibility, generous welfare provision, and an ageing population. German governments had been complacent about these issues for many years, and in the mid-1990s serious reform was hampered by the political weakness of the Kohl government in its latter stages. To his credit, Schroeder was able to pass a controversial reform of the tax system in July 2000, and was aware that more drastic and unpopular measures were required. For the first time since the 1950s, Germany had to acknowledge the superior performance of other economies, such as those of the Netherlands and even the United Kingdom. British success, built on deregulation, low labor costs and a large number of unskilled, part-time jobs in the service sector (now constituting a remarkable 80 percent of the labor force) seemed to offer little to Germany. The same could not be said of the Netherlands, however, where a rather "German" combination of economic rigor and negotiation between government and all partners in the economy (the so-called "Polder model") had resulted in the 1990s in a competitive, low-wage economy where the welfare budget had also been tamed.

The greatest economic benefits of EU membership were visible on the periphery. Greece's fortunes improved dramatically during the 1990s, when governments of both left and right learnt to turn Europe to their advantage, as a rigorous financial discipline as well as a source of infrastructure funding. For Finland, EU membership offered a new economic orientation for its increasingly competitive economy (notably the production of mobile phones) following the collapse of its trade with the Soviet Union in the 1980s. The most remarkable success was, however, in Ireland, where a combination of economic policies in the late 1980s, extensive EU subsidy, and a drive to encourage inward investment by leading high-tech companies brought high levels of growth. By 1997 foreign-owned firms represented 30 percent of the Irish economy and 40 percent of exports. One sure indicator of the new prosperity was that the long-term pattern of Irish emigration was reversed, and there was a steady increase in the population in the later 1990s. Economic change was accompanied by rapid social and cultural change, notably the decline in the social authority of the Catholic Church and the rise of an urban, professional middle class. Dublin, at the epicenter of the boom, took on all of the trappings of a modern European city.

Post-Communism: Eastern Europe and the Former USSR

There was no precedent for the remarkable transformation of the countries of eastern Europe in the 1990s, as the southern European countries emerging from dictatorship in the 1970s, which offered the closest parallels, had already possessed capitalist economies and a degree of integration with the West. In many respects the portents – both economic and political – had not been propitious in the early 1990s. The inherent uncompetitiveness of the east European economies, combined with the collapse of established trade patterns through Comecon, precipitated a sharp recession. In 1991 Hungary's GDP fell by 21.5 percent, Czechoslovakia's by 24.7 percent, and Poland's by 11.9 percent,[17] and levels of unemployment, poverty, and crime all rose steeply. Ethnic minorities became a target for resurgent nationalisms, while the growth of Western investment brought jobs but also sharpened resentment. Politically, the initial situation was often shambolic as the broad anti-communist alliances of 1989–90 fragmented into a myriad of small, squabbling political parties and interest groups. In Poland the resumption of normal politics soon reopened dormant divisions between liberal intellectuals and the Catholic Church, while the presence of Solidarity in government was not sufficient to assuage working class fears and grievances. The former communists returned to power by electoral means in Poland in 1993, and in Hungary and Bulgaria in 1994, as champions of a somewhat gentler route to capitalism. Throughout the region there were also many signs of disorientation and quite understandable naivety. For instance, "pyramid" savings frauds offering rapid returns as high as 800 percent proved extremely attractive to investors with no experience of capitalism. The collapse of the Albanian pyramid scheme in early 1997 provoked an armed uprising and the fall of Sali Berisha's government, while some 3 million Romanians lost money in the failure of the "Caritas" scheme in 1994.

In these circumstances, the achievements of many east European states were very striking. By the late 1990s their economies were recovering to 1989 levels and political stability was much more in evidence. As we have seen, between 1999 and 2004 the majority entered both NATO and the EU. With the obvious exception of the former Yugoslavia, violence and hyper-nationalism had largely been avoided; nor was there an excessive desire to dwell on – or seek vengeance for – the communist past. The so-called "Velvet Divorce" between Czechs and Slovaks (as of January 1, 1993) was achieved cleanly and without violence. Nowhere was this post-communist achievement greater than in the Baltic states which, many feared, had, faced cultural extinction under Stalinism.[18] Yet, following the national revival in the Gorbachev era, they became the only former Soviet republics to join the first wave of EU eastern enlargement even though, in 1990, they had lacked any independent institutions or even a currency.

These improved fortunes were due in part to the circumstances in which eastern Europe found itself in the early 1990s. In effect, there was no alternative to integration with the West on the West's terms, although individual governments might seek to control the pace of transition. Russia was neither willing nor capable of offering an alternative pole of economic attraction, and the implosion of Yugoslavia was a constant reminder of the dangers of militant nationalism and economic collapse. The lure of membership of Western institutions, as well as of IMF loans, guided all eastern European governments down a path of neo-liberal economic reform, but the EU and NATO also set standards for the development of democratic governance and minority rights. The impact was very evident in Slovakia, which spent much of the 1990s under the idiosyncratic, authoritarian rule of Vladimir Meciar, a former boxer who opposed liberal reform and discriminated against the substantial Hungarian minority. However, when he was voted out of office in September 1998 a broad coalition of his opponents seized the chance to consolidate democracy and catch the first wave of entry to the EU. Western pressures also encouraged the Baltic states to improve the terms of citizenship for their Russian minorities.

It would, however, be patronizing to suggest either that all of the West's prescriptions were helpful (some, indeed, were highly damaging) or that change in eastern Europe only came when imposed from without. The growing maturity of east European politics also came from within. For instance, it was notable that Lech Wałesa, the hero of Solidarity, proved a divisive and somewhat authoritarian president of Poland (1990–5) compared with his successor, the former communist Alexander Kwaśnieski. Indeed, in both Poland and Hungary the ex-communists – unlike their Bulgarian counterparts – were committed to integration with the West on their return to government. It was the government of former communists in Hungary that imposed swingeing welfare cuts in March 1995 in order to secure economic assistance from the West. The appeal of extreme nationalism was also successfully contained. In Hungary the conservative prime minister, Josef Antall, rid his MDF party of an anti-Semitic minority led by the playwright Istvan Csurka in June 1993.[19] In Romania, President Ion Iliescu forged and then broke an alliance with extreme nationalists between 1992 and 1996. On his return to the presidency in 2000 he posed as a defender of minority rights. In Lithuania Vytautas Landsbergis, the first independent president and the proponent of an intense, backward-looking Catholic nationalism, was defeated in 1992 by the pragmatic ex-communist Algirdas Brazauskas, who promised that he would not "get lost in those Moscow corridors."[20] The presence of so many former communists in government throughout the region demonstrated not only that the past was no hindrance to political success, but also that the anti-communist card was one played with some peril. The archives of the former regimes held such complex secrets that many innocent victims were liable to be caught up in any wholesale purge, which was only seriously attempted in the Czech Republic.

For all of these achievements, however, any assessment of post-communism in eastern Europe must also record the failures. Above all, while there may have been no alternative to economic transition, how appropriate was the West's unrelenting pressure for rapid free market reforms, especially given the West's reluctance to offer a new "Marshall Plan" for the region? A decade of change left immense inequalities of wealth between western and eastern Europe, between the countries of eastern Europe themselves, and between social groups within those countries. There were now unprecedented divisions between the new rich (many of them former communist bureaucrats and managers who benefited from privatization) and a large section of the population whose lives had been blighted by unemployment, reduced welfare services and decaying infrastructure. The turbulent 1990s favored – alongside the more nimble apparatchiks – the young (who could learn new skills and languages) over the old, the unskilled, and those (mainly women) with family commitments. The growth of massive open-air markets such as that at Gariūnai in Lithuania offered opportunities for entrepreneurs: so long as the young, mainly male, traders were willing to travel regularly to China to acquire merchandise.[21]

While women stood to benefit from the advance of democracy and greater opportunities for prosperity, the post-communist era in many respects brought a backlash against the limited female emancipation that had occurred under socialism. Ideologically, the revival of nationalism and Catholicism favored a return to very conservative views of women's role in society (put at its crudest: "less talk, more births!").[22] Many women were also eager to reclaim a more traditional femininity after the drabness of the communist era as well as the acute burdens that had been placed on them as both workers and home-makers. Pro-natalist attitudes, when combined with neo-liberal policies, resulted in the cutting of the state social provision (such as child-care for working mothers) that women had previously enjoyed, while under pressure from the Catholic Church abortion rights were greatly reduced in countries such as Poland and Hungary. At the same time many women were driven to work in the sex industry that was rife in post-communist eastern Europe, especially in areas close to the borders with the West. Women had also been well represented in the toothless parliaments of the communist era, if not at senior leadership levels, but post-communist politics was largely male-dominated and chauvinist. A rare exception was Hanna Suchocka's period in office as prime minister of Poland in 1992–3. In a number of countries, such as Lithuania and Russia, women felt compelled to found their own political parties.

The post-communist balance sheet was still more uneven in the case of Russia (although Russia's performance far outstripped that of the other slavic former Soviet republics, Belarus and Ukraine). After a decade of change 30 percent of Russia's population lived in poverty, and unemployment stood at some 12 percent (9 million). Those in work (especially those employed by the state) faced infrequent payment of wages and were often forced to take second jobs. Thirty-eight percent still lived in an impoverished countryside, barely touched since the Soviet era.[23] Seventy percent of Russians felt that they had "lost" during the 1990s, while only 6 percent felt that they had significantly gained.[24] Those who gained most were members of a small, hyper-rich, and increasingly internationalized elite who enjoyed immense material wealth as well as political and media power. Meanwhile, Russia enjoyed little of the clout of the former Soviet Union, and the dismal performance of its armed forces during the first Chechen war (1994–6) mocked any pretensions to Great Power status. Russia was further humiliated by the fact that some 25 million Russians were stranded by the break-up of the USSR in the "near abroad" (the former Soviet republics). Here, the tables had been turned and Russians were now treated as second-class citizens. Again, however, the worst-case scenarios were averted. For all of the social cost of transition there was little prospect of the Communist Party returning to power; nor was there any real taste for a strongman such as the former general, Alexander Lebed. And despite the success of the radical nationalist Vladimir Zhirinovksy in the November 1993 elections (when his party won almost 23 percent), Russia did not lurch into expansionism or an attempt to restore the USSR by force (even though opinion polls showed that most Russians regretted its demise).

For most of the decade it was unclear whether the president, Boris Yeltsin, was part of the problem or part of the solution. Though often ill, drunk, and irascible, he remained the "principal (if not the only) guarantor of democratic reform in the country."[25] His spectacular comeback in 1996 to win reelection in June/July, after his popularity had stood at a mere 8 percent in January, was testimony to this indispensability as well as to his ability to mobilize the "oligarchs" (the new wealthy elite) in his support. Yet Yeltsin epitomized the contradictions of Russian reform. His governing style was personalist and unpredictable, reliant on shifting cliques and regional barons rather than parliamentary majorities. He failed to build a powerful democratic reform party and eventually dispensed with his liberal supporters in favor of dull conservatives such as Victor Chernomyrdin (the head of the state gas production company, who was prime minister from 1993 to 1998). All too often Yeltsin, who once wrote that he could "only feel alive in a crisis,"[26] allowed a political triumph to be followed by a lengthy period of inertia. His use of military force to defeat his political rivals in the Russian parliament in October 1993 resolved an unhealthy stalemate but deeply shocked domestic and international opinion. Likewise, the decision to invade the rebel republic of Chechnya in December 1994 was a hideous mistake that revived Chechen separatism, dismayed Russian liberals, and caused untold civilian suffering.

The true extent of Yeltsin's commitment to reform – both political and economic – was questionable. He was determined to bury the Communist Party and the Soviet command economy, but he felt unable to dispense with the old Soviet bureaucracy. In 1993 he revised the Constitution to concentrate more power in the presidency, although while Yeltsin was president the potential for authoritarianism was offset by his willingness to make concessions to regional interests. In economic reform, the "shock therapy" of price liberalization in January 1992 (when shop prices immediately soared by 300 percent) followed by "voucher" privatization in 1992–3 was somewhat deceptive. The legal and financial framework for a market economy was not so easily created, and a great deal of subsidy remained in place, for instance of housing and energy. Moreover, a very substantial public sector remained intact (notably the oil and gas industry, which was the key to Russia's economic survival) and no attempt was made to privatize the land. In the mid-1990s Chernomyrdin ran up a huge budget deficit at a time of falling oil prices. The political cost was borne by his inexperienced successor, the 35-year-old Sergei Kirienko, when many Russians lost their savings during the catastrophic financial collapse of August 1998. The crash, which left a legacy of disenchantment with reform, was fatal to Yeltsin's presidency. Having eventually identified a successor in Vladimir Putin, who was appointed prime minister in August 1999, Yeltsin resigned on December 31, 1999. To his credit, he became not only the first modern Russian ruler to stand down voluntarily, but also the first to admit frankly that he had failed the Russian people.[27]

Putin represented a sharp contrast as, unlike Yeltsin, the young ex-KGB man was healthy, decisive, and purposeful. As prime minister he signaled his intentions by launching a second invasion of Chechnya in October 1999, which was successful enough to guarantee his victory in the presidential election of March 2000, if not to finish off Chechen guerrilla resistance. Putin's goal was to restore the authority of the Russian state both within its own borders and internationally. Powers conceded by Yeltsin to the regions were reclaimed, and an attack was launched on the "oligarchs": above all, on their control over the media. His blunt message to Russia's wealthy was that they could keep their ill-gotten gains, but only if they paid their taxes and stayed out of politics.[28] In many respects Putin represented the post-Soviet identity that many Russians felt most comfortable with: even the popular Soviet anthem was restored, with new lyrics. His masterful image, shored up by a tamed media, underpinned the creation of a twenty-first-century democratic authoritarianism, smiled on by Western governments, who saw Putin as a strong ally in unstable times.

The Balkan Wars

Between 1991 and 1999 a series of conflicts unfolded across the former Yugoslavia (see Maps 11.1 and 11.2). As we have seen, these conflicts were framed and inflamed by memory of the inter-ethnic violence of 1941–5, but they were driven forwards by the political ambitions of governing elites seeking to survive in a post-Yugoslav, post-communist environment. The most dangerous exponent of this new politics was undoubtedly the Serbian leader Slobodan Milošević, a master tactician but weak strategist, who had ridden the wave of Serb nationalism in the late 1980s. His goal, aside from retaining power, was to recreate Yugoslavia on the basis of Serbia, Montenegro, and the Serb-populated regions within Croatia and Bosnia. Accordingly, he was willing to allow the secession of Slovenia, the ethnically homogeneous northernmost republic, with only nominal resistance in June 1991. His rival and accomplice in the destruction of the old Yugoslavia was Croatia's nationalist president, Franjo Tudjman who, in addition to seeking Croat independence, also harbored ambitions to annex the Croat-populated south of Bosnia. In military terms, however, Milošević held the upper hand as he controlled the Yugoslav national army (JNA) and its arsenals, while Croatia still only possessed a lightly armed National Guard. This advantage was frozen in place by a blanket UN arms embargo in September 1991.

Warfare started in earnest when Croatia attempted to follow Slovenia into secession in June 1991. Rebel Serbs had already declared an independent republic in the Krajina area of Croatia (the region settled by Serbs when it had represented the military border between Christian and Ottoman Europe). They were now joined by JNA and Serb militia forces in seizing a swath of territory in Slavonia. The shattered ruins of Vukovar on the Danube fell to the Serbs after a three-month siege on November 19, whereupon many of its defenders were massacred. Further

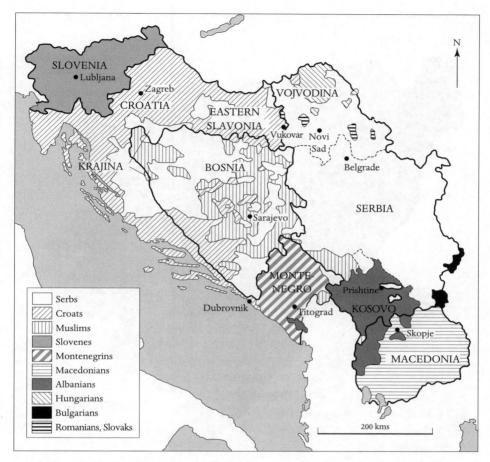

Map 11.1 National and ethnic distribution in Yugoslavia.

Source: Branka Magaš, *The destruction of Yugoslavia: Tracking the break-up, 1980–92* (Verso, London, 1993). Reprinted with permission.

pressure was placed on Croatia by a wantonly destructive JNA attack on the historic coastal city of Dubrovnik, to which the Serbs could lay no claim. The conflict caused mounting concern to the EC, which had initially hoped that it could help to broker a settlement. In practice, white-coated EC observers were powerless to prevent the violence on the ground. By December European attitudes, which initially had favored the preservation of the federation, began to change. Germany in particular, which had a substantial Croat population, was instrumental in forcing the EC to recognize the independence of Croatia and Slovenia (as well as other republics which wished to join them) in January 1992. Croats sang "Danke Deutschland" ("Thank you, Germany"): but a third of their territory remained under Serb control.

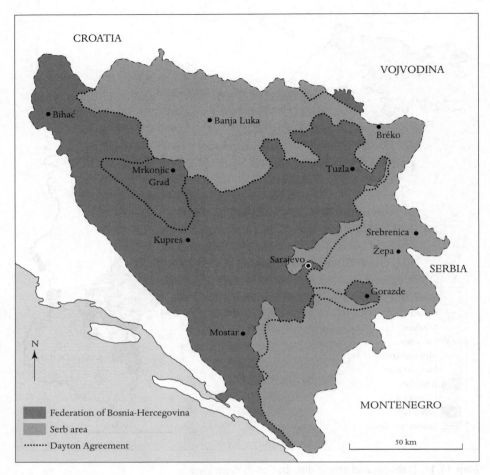

Map 11.2 The Dayton Peace Accord; shaded areas mark lands held in October 1995.
Source: James Gow, *Triumph of the lack of will: international diplomacy and the Yugoslav war*
(Hurst & Co., London, 1997).

The temporary cessation of the fighting in Croatia merely displaced the conflict
to neighboring Bosnia, which was divided three ways between Slavic Muslims
(44 percent), Serbs (33 percent), and Croats (18 percent). The government of the
Muslim Alija Izetbegović was now forced to make an unpalatable choice between
secession (with the prospect of civil war) and remaining within a Serbian-
dominated Yugoslavia. A referendum in February 1992, boycotted by the Serbs,
supported independence; however, this result was somewhat deceptive, as many
Croats who voted for Bosnian independence in fact wished for the union of
Croat-dominated areas of the south with Croatia. The EC recognition of Bosnia
on April 5 resulted immediately in a Serb revolt, again assisted by the JNA. This
represented the nadir of the EC's involvement in the conflict: it had recognized

a bitterly divided state that lacked the power to protect itself from aggression, while refusing to offer any means for its defense. The capital, Sarajevo, now came under siege from Serb artillery, while snipers terrorized the civilian population. Serbian militias stormed through the north and east of the country in a murderous orgy of "ethnic cleansing." Images of Muslim prisoners penned behind barbed wire, all too evocative of the Holocaust, horrified the West but failed to galvanize any change in policy. By the autumn most Muslims had fled these regions, apart from enclaves such as Goražde and Srebrenica, which were euphemistically entitled UN "safe areas" in 1993. Muslim fortunes worsened in mid-1993 when a Muslim–Croat conflict broke out for control of central Bosnia and Hercegovina, especially the city of Mostar. However, in March 1994 the US government brokered a new Muslim–Croat federation (while quietly encouraging the development of the Croatian national army).

After three years of desultory conflict, by 1995 the balance of power had begun to shift decisively against the Serbs for four main reasons. First, with the Serbian economy crippled by sanctions, Milošević was increasingly desperate to end the war on terms short of total victory – even if his Bosnian allies were not. Ironically, now Milošević seemed to be the West's partner in seeking a peace settlement. Secondly, the Muslims, having survived a genocidal assault, had emerged as determined and well-trained adversaries. Thirdly, the United States was increasingly intolerant of Serbian atrocities, and willing to contemplate military intervention. In July 1995, in the worst single massacre of the war (and, indeed, Europe's worst atrocity since 1945), some 8,000 Muslims, who were ostensibly under UN protection, were murdered when Serb forces overran Srebrenica. Finally, a rearmed Croatia was now in a position to reclaim its lost territory by force, which it did after a lightning campaign in August 1995. The Serbs' debacle in the Krajina area, accompanied by NATO bombing to lift the siege of Sarajevo, finally forced them to the negotiating table. Under the peace accord signed at Dayton, Ohio, in November 1995 Bosnia was to survive as a single state, but divided into separate Serbian and Muslim–Croat "entities" of almost equal size. A NATO-led "Implementation Force" (IFOR) was charged with overseeing a process of reconciliation and democratization, along with the pursuit of war criminals. However, it soon became apparent that the IFOR presence would be semi-permanent and that, for the foreseeable future, Bosnia would be little more than an international protectorate.

In 1999 the Balkan Wars came full circle to Kosovo, where Milošević's rise to power had started in 1987. Here, the Albanian majority (some 90 percent of the population) had long conducted a peaceful campaign for greater autonomy under the leadership of Ibrahim Rugova. Mounting frustration with Rugova's strategy, as well as the anarchy in neighboring Albania in 1997 which gave greater access to weapons, favored the guerrilla struggle of the Kosovo Liberation Army (KLA). Milošević was now the victim of his own earlier posturing as it was politically impossible for him to negotiate with the rebels. At the same time, military action against the KLA and their supporters merely convinced Western opinion that the horror of Bosnia was being repeated. The Rambouillet discussions of February 1999 came to nothing when Milošević refused to allow NATO troops access to Yugoslav territory. The West had now grown impatient with Milošević, and on March 24 NATO bombing commenced. The immediate consequence was, however, to produce an exodus of Albanians from Kosovo, mainly into Macedonia, encouraged to flee by Serbian threats and violence. The bombing was militarily ineffective within Kosovo itself, but the destruction of Serbia's infrastructure was more persuasive. Milošević eventually caved in after 78 days, abandoned even by his ally Russia, and Serbian forces withdrew from Kosovo as NATO-led KFOR peacekeeping troops arrived. Kosovo would remain part of Serbia, under the control of a UN mission, and its status would be reviewed after five years. Meanwhile, returning Albanians drove out many of the remaining Serbs.

Kosovo was not quite the end, as in 2001 members of the Albanian minority – assisted by former KLA fighters – rebelled in neighboring Macedonia. On this occasion, however, the international community swiftly sent in peacekeepers, while the Macedonian government made enough concessions on linguistic and educational issues to defuse the crisis. By this time Milošević had already gone, having called and lost direct elections for the Yugoslav presidency in September 2000. Despite attempts to steal the election, Milošević had clearly been defeated by his opponent Vojislav Koštunica and, following mass demonstrations reminiscent of 1989, he was forced from office on October 5. Soon afterwards he was extradited by the new government of Zoran Djindjic to face war crimes charges before the tribunal in the Hague. Even with his ignominious departure, however, Serbia remained far adrift from its neighbors – let alone from western Europe. Nationalism remained a potent force in this bruised, bankrupt society, in which crime and corruption had for too long been allowed to thrive. Djindjic, the leading exponent of pro-Western political and economic reform, fell victim to an assassin in March 2003.

Conclusion

The tragic violence that attended the break-up of Yugoslavia reflected poorly on both the governing elites of the Yugoslav republics and the international statesmen who allowed the crisis to run such a brutal course. Even so, the conflict was contained, and it proved unrepresentative of the pattern of change elsewhere in central and eastern Europe. The most remarkable aspect of the post-communist transition was that it was carried out, despite the heavy social cost, with very little recourse to violence. The seal was set on this success by the entry of many of these states into NATO and the EU. The situation was far less satisfactory in Russia, which hovered between the chaos of the Yeltsin era and Putin's Soviet revivalism.

Western Europe was relatively unaffected by these dramatic events, although the Italian political crisis was to a degree precipitated by the ending of the Cold War, and the German economy was hard hit by the cost of reunification. Throughout the decade most EU member states were transfixed by the looming prospect of monetary union, and the steps required to meet the convergence criteria. The politics of the 1990s were centrist and light on ideology: the quintessential figure was, perhaps, the charismatic tycoon Silvio Berlusconi, whose success rested on a personal union of wealth, football, and the media. The relaxed, even soporific 1990s ended for western Europe not with the fireworks at the coming of the new millennium, but with the "9/11" terrorist attacks in New York in 2001.

12
Europe in the New Millennium

Diversity and Union

On May 1, 2004, the European Union (EU) expanded to incorporate ten new member states, principally the new democracies of central and eastern Europe (including the former Soviet Baltic republics).[1] They were joined in 2007 by Romania and Bulgaria, while a number of other Balkan states waited for the chance to follow them. The EU now contained twenty-seven states, with a population of almost 500 million. By the end of the first decade of the twenty-first century, therefore, Europe was united as never before in peacetime, and the EU was now (apart from on its eastern borders) almost coterminous with continental Europe. Yet enlargement brought new challenges in its wake. When the German foreign minister Joschka Fischer spoke in 2000 of the "finality of European integration," he was referring not so much to the vision of an EU ultimately containing as many as thirty states, but rather the political integration (via a "European Federation") that would be needed to make such an enlarged entity work.[2] However, full political and economic union proved elusive, and the defeat of the proposed EU constitution in a number of national referenda in 2005 demonstrated that many Europeans did not share Fischer's vision of Europe's final destination. The compromise Lisbon Treaty of 2007 offered a less ambitious reform of EU governance arrangements, personified in the appointment of the low-profile Belgian politician Herman Van Rompuy as the first full-time President of the European Council. The EU appeared, therefore, to be treading water. It may, indeed, have reached its meridian in terms of both its institutional development and (apart from the absorption of the remaining Balkan states) future enlargement. As the drive towards "ever closer union" faltered, a snapshot of

Europe's Troubled Peace: 1945 to the Present, Second Edition. Tom Buchanan.
© 2012 John Wiley & Sons, Ltd. Published 2012 by John Wiley & Sons, Ltd.

Europe in the new millennium revealed a continent still characterized by considerable political, social, and economic diversity.

There was, of course, far more to "Europe" than the EU. According to one of the more generous definitions, the Council of Europe contained forty-seven member states, including Russia and other former Soviet republics stretching as far as Azerbaijan.[3] The single exception was Belarus, Europe's one surviving dictatorship, which was excluded due to flagrant human rights abuses. The Council's primary aim was to create a "common democratic and legal area throughout the whole of the continent," embodying the "fundamental values" of human rights, democracy, and the rule of law.[4] These values were deemed normative, and had been adopted as membership criteria by core institutions such as the EU and NATO. Indeed, one of the great triumphs of late-twentieth-century Europe had been the integration of so much of the former communist world into this realm of human rights, bringing to fruition a process started by the European Convention on Human Rights (1950) and the Helsinki Accords of 1975. However, just because values are deemed normative by elites does not guarantee their permanence. In early twenty-first-century Europe, there were many examples of a reduction in democratic accountability and increasing intolerance towards minorities. In January 2011, for instance, Viktor Orban's nationalist government in Hungary was accused of creating a "full-fledged illiberal democracy" following the introduction of a controversial media law – just as the country embarked on its six-month rotating presidency of the European Union.[5] Beyond the EU's borders, meanwhile, a new form of polity was emerging in Russia that combined democratic practices with authoritarian traditions.

Europe was still a continent divided by states, but in many cases the nature of the state was increasingly in question. In Italy, for instance, federalism was kept firmly on the political agenda by the Northern League, despite the rejection of sweeping federalist reforms by 61 percent to 39 percent in a referendum held in June 2006. The proposals were defeated not only – as one might expect – in the poorer south, but also in the major cities of the north. However, a creeping "fiscal federalism" (devolving taxation powers to town councils and regions) had made significant progress since 2008. The 150th anniversary of Italian unification in 2011 was greeted with cynicism and hostility from some northerners and minorities, and an effigy of Garibaldi (the hero of the *Risorgimento*) was burnt in the Veneto region. Belgium, an even older state which was divided between the more prosperous Flemish north and French-speaking Wallonia, became ever more dysfunctional. It survived a year of political deadlock after June 2010 with no official government, although with no obvious ill-effect. In Britain and Spain, two countries that had adopted devolution as a means to contain pressures for independence (in Scotland and Catalonia, respectively), outright secession began to appear more plausible. The Scottish Nationalists, who won an outright majority in the Scottish Parliament in May 2011, promised to hold a referendum on independence from the United Kingdom. Likewise, some 95 percent of Catalans voted in favor of independence (albeit on a turnout of only 30 percent) in locally organized "symbolic" referenda in December 2009. When the Constitutional Court in Madrid amended and rewrote key passages in the new Catalan autonomy statute, more than a million took to the streets in protest in June 2010 under the slogan "We are a nation: we decide." Eastern Europe had, of course, suffered greatly from secessionist tendencies during the 1990s, but one piece of business was still unresolved. In February 2008 Kosovo declared independence from Serbia, with the approval of most EU member states (although, pointedly, not that of Spain, which feared setting a precedent). The declaration was strongly contested by Russia, backed by many non-European states, and both the EU and the UN took no formal position. Meanwhile, despite the best efforts of the international community since the end of the Kosovo conflict in 1999,[6] it remained to be seen whether an economically viable new state (which still contained a significant and disenchanted Serb minority) could be created.

Large economic and social disparities also remained within Europe, not only between members and nonmembers of the EU, but also within the European Union itself. Economic activity within the EU was now predominantly concentrated in the service sector (73 percent) rather than manufacturing (25 percent). Agriculture made only a miniscule contribution to GDP, but still employed some 17 percent of the labor force in Poland, compared with a mere 2.4 percent in Germany and 1.6 percent in Britain. There was a sharp gradient of wealth (leaving aside Russia's abundance of natural resources) running from east to west within Europe. For instance, in terms of GDP per capita Ukraine ($3,483), which lay outside the EU, trailed far behind Romania ($8,156) in 2011, let alone Germany ($43,204), while the EU average was some $32,000. Luxembourg (the EU's wealthiest country per capita) had a Purchasing Power Standard six times higher than that of the poorest member state, Bulgaria. These differences could also be expressed in terms of life expectancy: in 2011 the average in Ukraine was 68.5 years (although far lower for men than women), in Romania almost 74, and in Germany 80.7: across the EU, the average was nearly 79.[7] There was also a gradient from south to north, albeit far less sharp. Membership of the EU had greatly increased the prosperity of countries such as Greece, Spain, and Portugal, but the economic crisis that started in 2008 began to reverse some of these gains. Striking disparities also existed *within* EU member states, above all Germany where, 20 years after unification, very real differences in wealth and living standards persisted. Per capita GDP was 30 percent lower in the former East Germany (excluding Berlin) than in the former West, and unemployment levels were almost twice as high. The population of the East shrank by 1.5 million during these two decades[8] as younger skilled workers headed west, in some cases leaving behind virtual ghost towns.

There were also sharp divisions between the experiences of women in western and post-communist Europe.[9] Across the EU the employment rate for women rose to 59 percent in 2008 (compared to 72.8 percent for men), although there were clear differences between Italy and Greece (both of which had a rate of under 50 percent) and Sweden, Denmark, and the Netherlands (all of which exceeded 70 percent). Women were far more likely to be engaged in part-time work than men (by 31.1 percent to 7.9 percent), and there was a persistent gender gap in pay of some 17.6 percent across the EU. In the west, women continued to extend their participation at the highest level in politics and the professions, but remained underrepresented in business. According to a law passed in Norway in 2006, all companies listed on the Oslo bourse were required to have at least 40 percent of women on their boards. However, the EU average was still a mere 11 percent, and only Finland and Sweden began to approach the Norwegian target. In Italy, meanwhile, the cause of female equality appeared to suffer a reverse under the governments of Silvio Berlusconi, whose TV channels had long flooded the screens with titillating sexuality. In February 2011 thousands of women protested against the tycoon's controversial private life (see below), as well as against the media "dictatorship" of looks and submissive female behavior in modern Italy.[10] In eastern Europe, women continued to be affected by the reaction to the state-decreed equality of the communist era. Cuts in childcare provision (such as workplace crèches) drastically reduced female participation in the work force, while in Poland the resurgent Catholic Church and its political allies succeeded in placing strict limits on abortion rights. Women in Hungary, Poland, and the Baltic states were the most highly educated in the EU (more than 65 percent had been educated to graduate level), but jobs commensurate to their skills were very difficult to find.

No social and political question was more highly charged than that of immigration. In 2008, 93.8 percent of the EU population was composed of "national" (or usually resident) citizens. There were, therefore, 30.8 million resident foreigners, two thirds of whom came from nonmember states. The vast majority of these foreigners lived in the EU's largest states, such as Germany (7.3 million, or 8.8 percent of the population), Spain (5.3 million, or 11.6 percent), and Britain (4 million, or 6.6 percent).[11] There had been successive waves of immigration into Europe since 1945, but these had impacted unequally, and different states had very different self-perceptions. Germany, for instance, had traditionally seen itself as a "no immigration" country (turning a blind eye to the fact that many *gastarbeiter* or guest workers, had settled there since the 1970s). This was only publicly reversed in August 2001 when Interior Minister Otto Schilly recognized the need for highly skilled immigrants.[12] After the Cold War the question of immigration was transformed by the rise in numbers of asylum-seekers, who were not only fleeing the collapse of Yugoslavia but also conflicts as far afield as Afghanistan, Somalia, and Iraq. Although the largest numbers settled in Germany (alongside a million "ethnic" Germans from Russia), the impact was felt most sharply in smaller states. In Denmark and Austria, in particular, the reception accorded to asylum-seekers soon cooled, and contributed to the rise of parties of the far right. A further wave of migration followed EU enlargement in 2004. As many as 1 million Poles went to work (and in some cases to settle) in Britain, while some 800,000 Romanians migrated to Spain. Large numbers of east European Roma (Gypsies) also moved west following enlargement, but the treatment that they received in Italy was no less hostile that that which they had left behind in Hungary, Slovakia, and elsewhere.[13] Immigration brought new skills, fashions, and tastes to cosmopolitan cities such as London, Paris, and Amsterdam. Yet it also tested the liberalism of many Europeans. A 2001 survey, for instance, showed that Dutch citizens generally saw the benefits of cultural diversity, but 35 percent felt that minorities should give up their own culture, and 75 percent believed that they should give up those aspects of their religion and culture that conflicted with Dutch law. The EU average on this latter point was 56 percent, but the figures for Denmark (85 percent) and Sweden (79 percent) were even more striking.[14]

Memory and the "European Identity"

In 2001 the German philosopher Jürgen Habermas commented that: "What forms the common core of a European identity is the character of the painful learning process it has gone through, as much as its results. It is the lasting memory of nationalist excess and moral abyss that lends to our present commitments the quality of a peculiar achievement."[15] The very idea of a common "European identity" is, of course, questionable given that Europe is still a conglomeration of national and sub-national communities, each with its own appreciation of the "learning process" that started with World War I. Even so, attempts to confront and commemorate the horrors of the twentieth century undoubtedly intensified after the end of the Cold War. For instance, a striking "Memorial to the Murdered Jews of Europe" was completed in 2005 in the heart of Berlin, only a short distance from the site of Hitler's bunker and the former ministries of the Third Reich. Unlike more traditional figurative representations of the Holocaust, Peter Eisenman's memorial was intended to create a sense of "uncanniness," as visitors were encouraged to wander through undulating rows of 2,711 tomb-like slabs covering almost five acres.[16] This vast and strategically located site could leave no visitor to Berlin in doubt about the dark past of Germany's resurgent capital (Figures 12.1 and 12.2).

Across western Europe few would question that Hitler's Reich – and more specifically the Holocaust – epitomized the "moral abyss" of the mid-twentieth century. In the former communist states, however, the situation was rather different. Countries which had been subject to decades of Soviet domination drew little distinction between the crimes of Nazi and communist "totalitarian" regimes, and increasingly urged western Europe to share their perspective. The "Prague Declaration" of June 3, 2008 branded such regimes as "the main disasters which blighted the twentieth century," and the call for August 23 (the anniversary of the Nazi–Soviet Pact) to become a day of remembrance for their victims was subsequently adopted by the European Parliament.[17] Despite the even-handedness of this approach, however, across east-central Europe the legacy of communist

Figure 12.1   Holocaust Memorial, Berlin. Photo © akg-images/Florian Profitlich.

Figure 12.2   Memorial to the forced laborers at Auschwitz concentration camp, Pere la Chaise cemetery, Paris. Photo: Tom Buchanan.

repression (which formed a core component of modern national identity in these countries) often tended to eclipse memory of the Holocaust. In the Baltic states, for instance, the memory of the Soviet repression of the 1940s was reinforced by the continuing perceived threat from modern Russia. In Latvia elderly Waffen SS volunteers and their supporters continued to march in Riga on March 16, in defiance of a dithering government, marking the date when they fought against the oncoming Red Army in 1944.

In post-communist Europe, the question was not only how to commemorate the communist past but also to decide how far that past should determine the present. For instance, the transition to democracy in east-central Europe had been accomplished with surprisingly little recrimination in the 1990s. However, in the new millennium politicians such as the Kaczyński twins in Poland or Viktor Orban in Hungary made anti-communism – and the removal of those tainted by their communist past – central to their political appeal. A sweeping extension of the law on "lustration" (political purification), which would have forced many thousands of Poles in the public eye to be subjected to a vetting procedure, was declared unconstitutional in May 2007. However, earlier in the year the newly appointed Archbishop of Warsaw was forced to resign over allegations that he had collaborated with the secret police. Similar allegations continued to be made against Lech Wałesa, the hero of the Solidarity movement, even though his name had been repeatedly cleared in the courts. Meanwhile, memorial museums, which have flourished in east-central Europe since 2000, often became the center of political controversy. For instance, the Budapest *Terrorháza* ("Terror House"), which was opened during Orban's first term in office in 2002 and received a million visitors in its first three years, was criticized for giving far more space to the communist than to the fascist "terror regimes," and for allocating only one room to the Holocaust.[18]

The past and present coincided most tragically over the memory of the 1940 Katyn massacres, when thousands of imprisoned Polish officers were murdered on Stalin's orders. Great steps had been taken since the collapse of the Soviet Union to establish the facts (concealed by decades of Soviet obfuscation) and to promote reconciliation between Poland and Russia. On April 7, 2010 Vladimir Putin and his Polish opposite number Donald Tusk took part in a first joint commemoration at the site, and the movie *Katyn* – a graphic account of the massacres by the director Andrzej Wajda, who had lost his own father there – was shown on Russian television. However, three days later a plane carrying Poland's President Lech Kaczyński crashed at Smolensk North airport *en route* to a further commemorative ceremony in the nearby Katyn forest. Alongside the president and his wife, almost ninety of Poland's military, administrative, and political elite also died in the crash. The scale of this new calamity was difficult for many Poles to accept, and spawned conspiracy theories which threatened once more to poison relations between the two countries.

Nowhere did the twentieth century's violent past return more forcefully – or unexpectedly – than in Spain. From 2000 onwards, groups of volunteers began to

Figure 12.3 The Valley of the Fallen, Spain. Photo © Jose Fuste Raga/Corbis.

carry out excavations at some of the unmarked mass graves of Franco's Republican victims (generally civilians, shot in cold blood in the early months of the Civil War). By the middle of 2008 more than 4,000 bodies had been exhumed from 171 sites, each case reviving traumatic memories in the small towns and villages of central Spain. This grassroots movement of activists and family members demonstrated the incompleteness of Spain's transition to democracy, and placed the unfinished business of the Civil War on the political agenda. In 2007 the new socialist government passed a landmark "Law on Historical Memory," which went some way to address these issues: most remaining physical traces of the dictatorship (such as statues of Franco) were to be removed, and local authorities were required to facilitate the efforts of bereaved family members to find the remains of their loved ones. However, there was to be no concerted effort by the state to complete the exhumations, or to bring any surviving perpetrators to justice. When Judge Baltasar Garzón, Spain's best-known advocate of human rights, attempted to open such an investigation in 2008, he was blocked by a higher court and suspended. Meanwhile, the future of the Valley of the Fallen – Franco's grotesque mausoleum, hewn from the solid rock north of Madrid by Republican prisoners of war, and still a site of Francoist homage – remained undecided (Figure 12.3). For many, therefore, the new law did not go far enough. But for others – despite explicit claims to the contrary – it represented an attempt to construct a "supposed 'collective memory'" of the Civil War that posthumously vindicated the defeated Republic.[19]

Garzón had made his name in seeking to bring General Augusto Pinochet to justice, and, indeed, the former Chilean dictator was detained for seventeen months in London (1998–2000) before being allowed to leave on grounds of ill health. The Pinochet case showed that Europe would no longer offer a safe haven for those accused of severe violations of human rights. This was confirmed by the record of the International Criminal Tribunal for the Former Yugoslavia, which was set up by the UN at The Hague in 1993, at the height of the conflict in Bosnia. Since then the tribunal has considered more than 160 cases – principally, though by no means exclusively, Serbs and Bosnian Serbs. The most high profile cases were those of the former Serbian leader Slobodan Milošević (who died while on trial in March 2006) and the Bosnian Serb leaders Radovan Karadžić and General Ratko Mladić (who was accused of responsibility for the Srebrenica massacre of 1995). The arrest of Mladić in Serbia in May 2011, which outraged a minority of ultra-nationalists, provided clear evidence of the Serbian government's determination to press for admission to the European Union and draw a line under the nationalist violence of the 1990s. The tribunal was cumbersome and time-consuming, but it successfully demonstrated that such violent acts could not be carried out with impunity on European soil.

The "War on Terror" and the Security of Europe

The readiness of the United States to act in a unilateral manner under the presidency of George W. Bush (2001–9) coldly disabused Europe of any fond assumptions about its relationship with the USA. There was tremendous sympathy in Europe for America's losses in the "9/11" attacks, as well as broad support for the overthrow of the Taliban regime in Afghanistan, which had sheltered the leaders of al-Qaeda. However, Bush's determination to invade Iraq in 2003 – to overthrow Saddam Hussein and remove his alleged "weapons of mass destruction" – was a different matter, and bitterly divided America's European allies. Tony Blair emerged as the principal European advocate for the invasion; with Jacques Chirac and Gerhard Schroeder its leading opponents. US Defense Secretary Donald Rumsfeld contrasted the obstructive "old Europe" (France and Germany) with the new, post-communist NATO member states which formed an important component of Bush's "coalition of the willing."[20] The crisis was symptomatic of the new tensions within the Atlantic alliance. The world's remaining superpower increasingly expected support – or at least acquiescence – from its long-standing European partners as it turned to meet perceived threats in the Middle East and Asia. However, for many Europeans it was impossible to turn a blind eye either to the illegality of the invasion – against which millions protested across Europe in March 2003 – or to the abuses of human rights apparently inherent in America's "Global War on Terror."

The damage caused by the Iraq crisis to transatlantic relations was severe, but should not be exaggerated.[21] For instance, Bush was quick to seek European support once a successful invasion had turned into a costly occupation and counter-insurgency operation. Conversely, many of Bush's strongest supporters in the "new" Europe felt disappointed that their support for the war did not receive the anticipated economic and diplomatic rewards. Changes of leadership on both sides of the Atlantic helped to smooth over the controversy. Both Angela Merkel and Nicolas Sarkozy were markedly more pro-American than their predecessors – indeed, Sarkozy went so far as to lead France back into the NATO joint command in 2009. Relations were greatly improved by the election of Barack Obama as Bush's successor in November 2008. Here was a president that Europeans felt far more comfortable with – intellectual, measured, inspirational, and multilateralist. In July 2008, while still on the campaign trail, he was greeted ecstatically by a crowd of some 200,000 in Berlin. "America," he told them, "has no better partner than Europe." However, Obama's principal task was to appeal to the recession-hit American public rather than to European audiences, and in the same speech he added that in the future both Europe and the United States would be "required to do more – not less."[22] Indeed, during his presidency there was a marked reluctance for an overstretched and economically weakened United States to pull Europe's irons out of the fire. During the NATO military intervention in Libya in the spring of 2011, for instance, the USA swiftly pulled back and left control of the operation to its European allies.

The emergence of al-Qaeda and its associated networks increased Europe's exposure to terrorist attack after a period in which such threats had appeared to be in decline. The Northern Ireland peace process had made remarkable progress since 1998, culminating in the "decommissioning" of the IRA's hidden arsenal. Indeed, by 2007 Sinn Fein's Martin McGuinness was Deputy First Minister in a devolved government. Although far less progress was made in the Basque country, the level of ETA violence also declined steeply after 2000. This greater sense of security was shaken by the Islamist terrorists who carried out the bombings of Madrid commuter trains on March 11, 2004 (which claimed 191 lives) and the four suicide bombers who killed fifty-two people in London in July 2005. The latter atrocities were all the more shocking in that the perpetrators were young Muslims born or raised in Britain. Across Europe, the specter of Islamist terrorism sharpened hostility towards Islam more generally, and played into the hands of the populist right (see below). Accusations of intolerance were leveled against both sides. Islam could be presented as the enemy of freedom of expression: hence the Iranian "fatwa" against the British writer Salman Rushdie in 1989, the brutal murder in 2004 of the Dutch filmmaker Theo van Gogh (who had made a film critical of the treatment of women in Islam), or the violent response in the Muslim world to the publication of caricatures of the prophet Mohammed in the Danish newspaper *Jyllands-Posten* (2005). Conversely, those in authority in Europe could also be seen as intolerant and anti-Muslim. For instance, France banned women from publicly wearing the Burqa (or veil) in April 2011, and

Switzerland prohibited any further building of minarets. This latter step had been approved by 57.5 percent of voters in a referendum called by the right-wing Swiss People's Party in November 2009. In 2010 a book by Thilo Sarrazin, a Social Democratic board member of the Bundesbank, attacking German multi-culturalism, proved a publishing sensation. In an interview he warned against Germany becoming a "mostly Muslim country" in which "the day is measured out by the muezzin's call to prayers."[23]

The controversy over the "War on Terror" coincided with – and failed to derail – attempts to give substance to the EU's Common Foreign and Security Policy (CFSP), which had been agreed as a sphere of intergovernmental action under the Maastricht treaty. The EU's humiliating failure to intervene effectively in the break-up of Yugoslavia had highlighted its weakness in this regard, and in December 1998 Blair and Chirac, in their "St Malo Declaration," argued that the EU needed a "capacity for autonomous action."[24] The result was the formulation of a European Security and Defence Policy (ESDP), as an element of the CFSP. The new policy was intended to complement rather than supplant the military security offered by NATO. However, it presented a broader definition of "security," and recognized the importance of peace-making and state-building within complex conflicts (however remote) that might affect the security of Europe. The new structures allowed the EU for the first time to mount military interventions beyond its borders, beginning with "Operation CONCORDIA" in Macedonia in March 2003. Subsequent EU missions (civilian and military) were sent as far afield as Bosnia, Gaza, and – most strikingly – the Democratic Republic of Congo (Figure 12.4). Under the Lisbon Treaty of 2007 the ESDP was renamed the "Common Security and Defence Policy" and placed under the control of a new High Representative for Foreign Affairs and Security Policy. This new post – which combined the former roles of the High Representative of the CFSP with that of the EU Commissioner for Foreign Affairs – was intended to address Henry Kissinger's famous question: "If I want to call Europe, who do I call?" However, the first incumbent (the British peer Baroness Ashton) struggled to create a new diplomatic infrastructure in the face of substantial institutional resistance, and did not immediately resolve that old conundrum.

The "War on Terror," and more specifically the invasion of Iraq, arguably distracted Europe from more significant long-term threats to its economic security (including food and energy supplies) and to the environment. Obama's successful visit to Europe in May 2011 suggested that the Bush years did, indeed, represent "just another major crisis" in a constantly changing transatlantic relationship.[25] However, European enthusiasm for the new president (symbolized in the rather premature award of the Nobel Peace Prize to Obama in 2009) ignored the fact that the Guantanamo Bay detention camp remained open and that Obama initially chose to intensify the US-led war in Afghanistan. Meanwhile, despite the EU's sporadic international interventions since 2003, its collective voice in foreign affairs

Figure 12.4   German troops in Kosovo, 1999. Photo © akg-images/ullstein bild.

remained far less than that of the sum of its principal states. Tellingly, the first great unforeseen crisis of the new decade, the "Arab spring" of 2011, found the European states as disunited as ever.

West European Politics

Across western Europe there was an intensification of the political trends established in the 1990s: an increasing ideological convergence between the main political parties, which jostled in the political center; the decline of the social democratic left; and the continuing rise of the "neo-nationalist" or "populist" right. The terms of political debate were set by a pressing awareness of the challenge that the "globalized" economy posed for western Europe's prosperous and secure population. China overtook Japan as the world's second largest economy in 2011 and the rapidly developing "BRIC" economies (Brazil, Russia, India, and China) beat on the door of the western-dominated G-8 (Russia joined in 1997). "Globalization" posed manifold challenges. Above all, how could European economies adapt to compete with the leaner emerging economic powers, whose high growth rates were fuelled by lower wage costs and younger populations? There were no easy answers. The population flows both into and within Europe offered a solution to the problem of an ageing population, but also generated fears amongst the most economically vulnerable elements in European society. Politicians (at least those with any prospect of office) had little choice other than proposing the short-term pain of "modernization" as the key to longer-term prosperity and security.

These challenges posed particularly acute problems for the parties of the center-left. They had lost much of their traditional working-class electorates during the industrial restructuring of the previous two decades, and indeed such constituencies were often now attracted to the populist right. At the same time conventional social democratic policies – namely, the management of national economies by the state – were of ever less relevance within the context of globalization and the single currency. Those who had looked to the EU in the Delors era as a new vehicle for correcting the social impact of the free market were largely disappointed by his less ambitious or more market-oriented successors. Indeed, one principal reason why the 2005 referendum on the EU Constitutional Treaty was lost in France and the Netherlands was that socialist voters refused to follow the advice of their party leaders.[26] In the new millennium, therefore, the center-left struggled to present a clear alternative to liberal political and economic orthodoxies.

In the late 1990s the center-left did appear to have successfully repositioned itself as a modern governing force in Britain and Germany. However, in both countries the pleasure of ending long years of conservative rule soon gave way to the complex realities of government. In Britain the Blair government's genuine achievements in promoting peace in Northern Ireland, devolving power to Scotland and Wales, and improving state provision in health and education was overshadowed by the controversy over Blair's support for the invasion of Iraq. Although some measures – such as the introduction of a minimum wage – appealed to the left, New Labour's political orientation was towards the center, with a greater emphasis on economic deregulation and labor market flexibility. New Labour courted the wealthy and left its old allies in the trade unions on the sidelines. Peter Mandelson, one of the architects of New Labour, told an audience of computer executives in California in 1998 that his party was "intensely relaxed about people becoming filthy rich."[27] When Blair was eventually forced to give way to his colleague and great rival Gordon Brown in June 2007, he left office as the most successful leader in his party's history. However, while New Labour had succeeded in modernizing the British state and liberalizing British society, social inequality was greater than ever.

In Germany, Gerhard Schroeder, after a lackluster first term, eventually committed the SDP–Green coalition to a radical reform of the welfare system in 2003. The so-called "Agenda 2010" program was a package of tax cuts and reductions in welfare entitlements which derived in part from a commission chaired by the Volkswagen executive Peter Hartz. Schroeder's bold initiative divided the Social Democrats and alienated the trade unions, but he was able to pass his proposals through the upper chamber in December 2003 following an agreement with the opposition Christian Democrats. Schroeder had got his way by appealing to widely shared concerns about the future of the German economy. Given high levels of unemployment and low rates of growth, many accepted that Germany faced a choice between drastic reform and decline. However, the political cost was heavy – Schroeder's bitterest opponents abandoned the SPD and formed a significant new political force with the former east German communists known as "the Left" ("*Die Linke*").[28] Schroeder's final gamble was to seek early elections in September 2005, which he duly lost. The result was a Grand Coalition under the Christian Democrat leader Angela Merkel, an arrangement that had been foreshadowed by the consensus over welfare reform. Merkel was Germany's first female Chancellor and a former citizen of East Germany, albeit one who had played no role in the dissident movements of the later 1980s. The SPD – further divided and weakened by its role in the coalition – went into opposition after defeat in the elections of 2009, when Merkel found a more natural coalition partner in the liberal FDP.

The position of the center-left in France and Italy was even more parlous. Lionel Jospin, the socialist prime minister, performed disastrously in the 2002 presidential elections, and was ejected from the race after the first round when he won fewer votes than veteran right-winger Jean Marie Le Pen. The party's candidate in 2007, Ségolène Royale, was an intriguing choice, but was decisively defeated by the burningly ambitious right-winger Nicolas Sarkozy. In Italy, progressive forces (ranging from former communists to some former Christian Democrats) rallied behind Romano Prodi on his return from Brussels, but his government of 2006–8 only offered a brief and ineffective respite from Silvio Berlusconi's domination of Italian politics. Prodi's government also initiated illiberal measures against Italy's Roma population (the so-called "nomad emergency") which were later pursued more systematically by Berlusconi on his return to power. As Berlusconi's problems mounted after 2008, a hapless center-left (now known as the Democratic Party) seemed incapable of benefiting from his discomfort. The only exception amongst the larger European countries was Spain, where José Luis Zapatero's Socialist PSOE unexpectedly regained power from the conservative People's Party in March 2004. The election was decided in the final days of the campaign by the government's mishandling of the terrorist bombings in Madrid. The new government represented a sharp break in Spain's international relations (Spanish troops were immediately withdrawn from Iraq), but also in gender relations. Zapatero's first cabinet contained a majority of women (nine out of seventeen), and the defining image was that of a pregnant Carme Chacon, the new defense minister, taking the salute from an army guard of honor (Figure 12.5). Zapatero led the Socialists to a second victory in 2008, but his government was soon overwhelmed by Spain's severe exposure to the global financial crisis.

In France, the baton of reform was enthusiastically picked up in 2007 by Sarkozy, who was determined to make the French economy more flexible and dynamic during his presidency. Where the flagship of the last Socialist

Figure 12.5   Spain's defense minister Carme Chacon reviews a guard of honor during a ceremony at the defense ministry in Madrid, April 14, 2008. Photo © Susana Vera/Reuters.

government had been the thirty-five hour week, his pledge was to "rehabilitate work, authority, morale and respect."[29] Sarkozy had come to prominence as Interior Minister in November 2005, when violent rioting by immigrant youths in the suburbs of Paris caused four deaths and considerable damage to property. Sarkozy's comment that the riots were the work of a *racaille* (meaning a "rabble," or "scum") was inflammatory.[30] Indeed, one reason for his victory in 2007 was precisely his ability to take votes from Le Pen's National Front. However, although a man of the right, his first cabinet drew on talent from across the political spectrum – notably Bernard Kouchner, a socialist and leading human rights campaigner, who was appointed as foreign minister. Sarkozy promoted his domestic reform agenda energetically and with some success, although the financial crisis of 2008 diminished the allure of the "Anglo-Saxon" economic model that he so admired. Despite strong opposition from the trade unions, Sarkozy pressed on with controversial pension reforms, and, unlike Alain Juppé in 1995, was not forced into a humiliating climb-down. Even so, many French people remained unconvinced by their divisive new president. His short temper as well as his unusually public private life – he was divorced from his second wife soon after the election and then courted and married the model-turned-singer Carla Bruni in the full glare of the paparazzi – struck many as distinctly unpresidential (Figure 12.6).

Silvio Berlusconi also claimed to offer reform from the center-right, although it often seemed that his entire project was motivated by little more than a desire for self-preservation (Figure 12.7). Berlusconi had been pursued by prosecuting

Figure 12.6 Nicolas Sarkozy and Carla Bruni, Egypt, 2007. Photo © Khaled Desouki /AFP/ Getty Images.

Figure 12.7 Vladimir Putin (right) and Silvio Berlusconi. Photo © akg-images/RIA Novosti.

magistrates throughout his career in business and politics, and he was no stranger to the courtroom. Accordingly, his principal goal was to rein in what he referred to as the "left-wing" judiciary. As an interim measure, his government passed a law of legal immunity for the holders of the highest offices of state in 2003. Berlusconi was also constrained by the fact that both between 2001 and 2006 and again after 2008, he was governing in alliance with Umberto Bossi's Northern League and Gianfranco Fini's National Alliance (which formally merged with Berlusconi's Forza Italia! in 2007). Each tugged the government in a particular direction. The Northern League favored federalism (to the disadvantage of the poorer South) and tough measures against immigrants and Roma, while the National Alliance promoted family values and the right to life. Berlusconi's problems deepened after 2008 when he was the subject of seemingly endless, lurid allegations about his private life. His wife, Veronica Lario, filed for divorce in 2009 as a result of his indiscretions, and it was claimed that erotic "bunga bunga" parties had taken place at the prime minister's country house. Even more damagingly, Berlusconi became associated with an under-age prostitute from Morocco (although he denied any sexual relations). His life finally appeared to have descended into a farcical "Burlesquoni" (as *The Economist* put it in 2003[31]). However, his powers of survival were formidable, and he even garnered some sympathy when he was bloodily assaulted in December 2009 with a model of Milan cathedral. Berlusconi clung to power despite a challenge from Fini (now the President of the Chamber of Deputies), in 2010, but the damage to Italy's international standing caused by his antics was incalculable.

The Politics of Intolerance

In the new millennium, the populist right seized the political initiative by offering simple – often crude – answers to the problems facing contemporary Europe. This did not mean that it was on the verge of seizing power. Le Pen's initial success in the 2002 presidential election shocked French opinion, but his rejection by 82.2 percent to 17.8 percent in the second round showed that demagogues of the far right were still a long way from taking power by electoral means. Jörg Haider's Austrian Freedom Party received 27 percent of the vote in 1999, but fragmented after entering a coalition government. Haider withdrew to govern his adopted province of Carinthia, where he died in a car crash in 2008. However, the Austrian elections of that year confirmed the enduring electoral appeal of the far right, especially amongst younger voters. In the Netherlands Pim Fortuyn, the gadfly of the Dutch establishment, won a large following in the months prior to his assassination in May 2002. In the subsequent general election his followers (many of them political novices) won twenty-six seats on a wave of sympathy and entered a coalition government. However, they soon faced political oblivion and the government only lasted eighty-seven days. Such parties were arguably far more effective in holding the balance of power and thereby setting the political agenda from outside of government. This policy was pursued successfully by the Danish People's Party after 2001 (resulting in a strict new immigration law in 2002 and subsequent moves to reimpose border controls) and by Geert Wilders' Dutch Freedom Party after 2010.

The phenomenon of the "populist" or "neo-nationalist" right defies easy categorization. While the well-established parties of Haider, Fini, and Le Pen clearly had their roots in the far right, others did not. The Danish People's Party, for instance, had split away in 1995 from the Progress Party, an anti-tax protest party founded in 1972 that had only latterly adopted an anti-immigrant platform. Both Fortyun and Wilders presented themselves as libertarians who denied any link to fascism or the far right. They claimed to oppose Islam precisely because of its intolerance with regard to issues such as gay and women's rights. In Finland the True Finns, who achieved an electoral breakthrough in June 2009, were the successors to the populist Finnish Rural Party, and saw themselves as standing on the center-left. In 1996 Massimo d'Alema, the leader of the post-communist Italian left, described the Northern League – with their working-class support – as a "left limb."[32] Many of these parties were staunch defenders of welfare entitlements (while not wanting to share them with immigrants) rather than neo-liberals.

Despite these differences, a number of common characteristics could be observed. First, these parties were all strongly critical of further immigration and believed that instead of fostering multiculturalism the state should force immigrants to integrate into their host society. This view of the essential incompatibility between "cultures" (as opposed to a language of racial difference) owed much to the French "nouvelle droite" intellectuals of the 1980s. Above all, these groups expressed visceral hostility to Islam and to Islamic immigrants. Wilders compared the Koran to Hitler's Mein Kampf, while in Italy members of the Northern League resisted the construction of a mosque by spreading pig excrement on the site in October 2000.[33] This targeting of Islam by the right was, of course, magnified by the impact of "9/11," which drove states to pursue more stringent security policies and generated negative stereotypes of Muslims in the media. Secondly, these parties thrived on opposition to elites, whether within individual countries or the EU. When Haider joked that "I'm the only liberal [provincial] prime minister in Austria,"[34] he meant that he delighted in shaking up Austria's stifling political consensus. Thirdly, they were careful to operate within the law and within democratic politics: they were not, therefore, "extremists" other than in their language. Their success lay in breaking liberal taboos and redrawing the boundaries of what was politically acceptable, in many cases articulating views that were held far more widely within their societies. Finally, they tended to appeal to a similar constituency: the younger, male, urban, and less well-educated section of the electorate. Indeed, in many cases, the populist right had won over the voters of the old left. In 2001, for instance, the Danish People's Party electorate contained a higher proportion of workers than that of the Social Democrats.[35]

The impact of these parties was perceptible even in countries where the far right had not achieved substantial or lasting electoral success. For instance, in October 2010 Angela Merkel stated that multiculturalism had "failed utterly" in Germany; likewise, a few months later David Cameron (the new British prime minister) declared that the doctrine of "state multiculturalism" had "encouraged different cultures to live separate lives," and thereby encouraged radical Islamist movements.[36] Their speeches were deemed controversial, but in countries such as Sweden, Austria, the Netherlands, and Denmark, multiculturalism had been superceded as much as a decade earlier by laws actively promoting integration. However, if immigrant communities felt a chill from such policies, the implications of this new intolerance also had profound implications for the future of the European Union. An unwillingness to share national resources with immigrant communities could easily turn into unwillingness for the wealthier states of northern Europe to come to the assistance of the embattled economies in the south. The True Finns, for instance, achieved their political breakthrough in European Parliament elections in 2009 with a platform that opposed just such support.

On Europe's Borders

Under the firm hand of Vladimir Putin, a viable and stable post-Soviet Russian state finally began to emerge after 2000. His rule was based on repudiating the troubled 1990s, when a weakened Russia was ill-served by a frequently drunk president, rampant cronyism, and feuding political parties. As late as 2007 Putin still lashed out at those who would restore the "oligarchic regime, based on corruption and lies."[37] In its place he offered a strong, centralized presidency alongside a weak parliament dominated by his "United Russia" party (which was periodically challenged by pseudo-parties created by the Kremlin). As one of Putin's supporters argued, this was no longer the "deformed democracy" of the 1990s, but a "sovereign democracy," which would uphold the authority of the state against those who sought to weaken it.[38] Putin finally succeeded in ending the brutal Chechen War, which had done so much to undermine Yeltsin's authority, and installed Ramzan Kadyrov, the son of a former Chechen warlord, as president. The defining moment for Putin's presidency, however, was the *Yukos* affair of 2003, when the regime jailed the politically ambitious oil magnate Mikhail Khodorkovsky. Opposition was further cowed by a number of mysterious murders, including that of the London-based dissident Alexander Litvinenko (who was poisoned with

polonium) and the courageous journalist Anna Politkovskaya. While there is
no suggestion that the crimes were commissioned by the government, these
and other deaths demonstrated just how dangerous investigating official corruption and the abuse of human rights had become. Putin's main political
problem was that his second four-year term was due to end in 2008. Instead of
rewriting the constitution to allow a third term, as many supporters urged, he
engineered the election of his protégé – the younger and rather more liberal
lawyer Dmitry Medvedev – as president. Putin was then immediately appointed
as Medvedev's prime minister, thereby maintaining both his grip on power and
Russia's reputation as a constitutional state. A subsequent extension of the
presidential term to six years opened the distinct possibility of a further Putin
presidency from 2012 to 2024.

Putin had inherited a state whose military and technological decline was
symbolized by the loss of the nuclear submarine *Kursk* in 2000. He set about
reasserting Russian power on the international stage, helped by the rising energy
prices which transformed the fortunes of the resource-rich economy. While talk
of a new "Cold War" was wide of the mark, this was an unapologetic Russia,
proudly different from the rest of Europe and feared by its neighbors. When
Estonian banks and government institutions were subjected to an unprecedented
month-long "cyber attack" in April–May 2007, following a chill in relations with
Moscow, the Estonian government was privately quick to blame the Russian
government.[39] Russia's revival had a profound effect on the borderlands between
Russia and the EU. The extension of NATO and EU membership to countries
such as Poland, Hungary, and the Baltic states began to appear like a timely
"escape" to Europe during a period of unparalleled Russian weakness rather than
a template for the transformation of the former Soviet Union. The so-called
"color revolutions" in Georgia ("Rose" in 2003) and Ukraine ("Orange" in 2004)
captured the West's admiration and cleared out some remnants of the post-Soviet
order, but did not bring the fundamental break with the past that many had
hoped for. The Ukrainian revolution soon foundered on political differences
between the victorious politicians, while in Georgia the telegenic Mikheil
Saakashvili (who took the presidency from Gorbachev's former foreign minister
Eduard Shevardnadze) proved dangerously inexperienced. In January 2006
Ukraine was briefly paralyzed when Russia cut off its gas supplies, and in 2010
Moscow's favored candidate Victor Yanukovych (the villain of the Orange
Revolution) won the presidency. Saakashvili's hopes of leading Georgia into
NATO and regaining control over the "lost" Georgian territories of Abkhazia and
South Ossetia were crushed by Russia during a brief war in August 2008. Russia's
subsequent decision to recognize the independence of both territories (accompa-
nied by what some saw as a *de facto* annexation) was a pointed rejoinder to the
decision by many European States to recognize the independence of Kosovo.
Russia had clearly restated its sphere of interest and ruled out any prospect of the
further eastward expansion of Western institutions.

Turkey, which was apparently placed on course towards full European Union membership at the Copenhagen summit in 1999, offered a different kind of challenge for the EU. The "Copenhagen process" was eagerly embraced by the conservative Muslim "Justice and Development" party (AKP) as a means of promoting economic modernization and democratization. It recognized that the attraction of "Europe" offered a strong counterbalance to the constitutional, but undemocratic, powers of the Turkish army and state bureaucracy. The AKP leader Recep Tayyip Erdogan became prime minister in 2003, won an election landslide in 2007 following a bitter power struggle with the generals, and a third term in 2011. The conflict between the secular, authoritarian, and nationalist elite, loyal to the vision of the state's founder Atatürk, and the advocates of a "Muslim democracy," was therefore framed by the criteria for EU membership. However, the prospect of Turkish membership galvanized strong resistance in countries such as France, Austria, and the Netherlands. In 2005, during the debate on the EU constitution, President Chirac promised that there would be a French referendum on Turkish membership. A poll of EU citizens taken at the time showed that 52 percent opposed the Turkish bid (rising to 70 percent and 74 percent in France and Germany) and only 35 percent supported it. The reasons for opposition ranged from the economic and geographic to concerns about "values" and security.[40] Many Europeans were simply not ready to allow a populous, poor Muslim country bordering one of the world's most unstable regions to join their "club." Turkey's poor human rights record – especially its treatment of the Kurdish minority – also proved a major obstacle. The charges brought against the leading novelist Orhan Pamuk in 2005 (for claiming that the Ottoman Empire had presided over the genocide of 1 million Armenians during World War I) emphasized the distance that still remained. As the prospect of full EU membership receded, Turkey began to redefine itself as a powerful player in the Middle East and Caucasus rather than an EU member state-in-waiting.

To the south, Europe had no land borders aside from the ancient Spanish enclaves of Ceuta and Melilla on the coast of Morocco. However, the Mediterranean Sea represented a highly porous frontier between Europe and North Africa, only 14 kilometers wide at its narrowest point, and thousands of economic migrants from sub-Saharan Africa risked their lives on the dangerous crossing to Andalusia, Malta, or the Italian island of Lampedusa. It was clearly in Europe's interests to foster better relations with the states of North Africa and the Levant, whether to seek to control immigration or to promote political stability in a volatile region. The first major initiative in this regard was the Euro-Mediterranean Partnership (or "Barcelona process") of 1995, which was replaced in 2008 by the Union for the Mediterranean (UFM). This brought together all of the EU member states with the existing regional participants and some new ones (such as Bosnia, Croatia, and Montenegro). The new Union – which was the brainchild of Nicolas Sarkozy, and was seen by Turkey as a sop for

EU membership – provided a strengthened institutional framework for intergovernmental relations. Critics observed that it represented a retreat from the ideals of the Barcelona Process, which had emphasized support for democratic institutions and the rule of law in the Arab world, and encompassed relations with nongovernmental bodies as well as with (often repressive) governments.[41] In any case, the unforeseen explosion of anger against long-standing, undemocratic regimes across the Arab world in 2011 shattered the assumptions behind the UFM, and triggered a new wave of immigration. The fact that Italy and France immediately responded by calling for the suspension of the Schengen agreement (which guaranteed free movement across most EU borders) showed how easily crisis in the Arab world could disturb Europe's equilibrium.

From Financial Crisis to European Crisis

In 2008 the world economy was shaken by a crisis in the financial sector which quickly came to threaten a global depression as devastating as that of the 1930s. Although this danger was averted by prompt concerted action, the impact of the crisis on Europe was still profound. It not only precipitated a sharp recession, but also posed the most severe challenge that the single currency – and indeed the entire project of European integration – had yet faced. The banking crisis had its origins in the "sub-prime" loans-selling scandal in the United States, which had left many banks saddled with bad debts and "toxic" assets. These problems were magnified by the culture of risk-taking associated with complex new financial products that had grown up in the boom years. The iconic moment of the crash in New York – the bankruptcy of Lehman Brothers – occurred on September 15, 2008. A number of British banks also faced collapse – and were saved only by state intervention – as did those in Iceland and Ireland. The British Prime Minister Gordon Brown, who had helped to galvanize the joint international response, blamed the banking crisis on "chronic recklessness powered by unchecked greed." However, he was later forced to concede that his own deregulatory policies had also played their part. He had not, he said, appreciated "how entangled things are,"[42] and these "entanglements" soon began to affect continental banks as well. European politicians may well have felt vindicated by the crisis in the free-wheeling "Anglo-Saxon" world – but they ignored it at their peril.

The crisis not only dislocated economic activity through a short-term shortage of credit, but also exposed the structural flaws within the single currency. The fundamental problem was that the "Eurozone" (which contained seventeen states, with seven more *en route* to membership) had bound together very different and unequal economies which were engaged in a protracted process of economic convergence. Accordingly, the Eurozone was far from being an "optimal currency area," such as the United States, within which the benefits of a single currency clearly outweighed the disadvantages. The US economy has both the flexibility and the central resources to absorb and adjust to shocks (for instance, by means of labor migration from depressed areas). By contrast, the European Union lacked most of the attributes of a federal state, and its budget was only a fraction of that enjoyed by the federal government in Washington. Moreover, economic decision-making was divided between the new European Central Bank (which was concerned with exchange and interest rates), multilateral decisions taken at an EU and Eurozone level, and actions by individual member states. Although the introduction of the new currency had gone surprisingly smoothly, one leading expert referred prophetically in 2008 to the "still untested risk of inadequate institutional capacity to manage cross-national and contagious banking and financial crises."[43] In addition, the "euro" had been a political just as much as an economic project, and many corners had been cut in order to bring it to fruition within the agreed timetable. Hence, statistical sleights of hand were needed to demonstrate that some of the weaker economies, such as Greece and Italy, met the convergence targets under the 1997 Stability and Growth Pact. Even Germany and France failed to meet their targets on the scale of their budget deficits, and the pact was rewritten to reflect this in 2005. This high level of politicization inevitably undermined the credibility of the single currency when the weaker economies encountered difficulties.

Monetary union had offered member governments a deal: in return for giving up control over their currency and interest rates, their economies would benefit from low levels of inflation, increased trade, and cheaper transaction costs. Whereas in the past states might have sought to gain an advantage through competitive devaluation (as, in 1992, when Britain and Italy left the ERM), members of the eurozone would now have to gain an advantage through improving their productivity and competitiveness. In fact, however, the low level of interest rates during the euro's first decade had a rather different effect. Many weaker states borrowed heavily, and in Ireland and Spain there were unsustainable property booms. Ireland epitomized the economic and political malaise at the heart of the crisis. The Irish economy had made remarkable progress since the mid-1990s (when it grew at a rate of 7 percent per annum), but faltered after 2001 when productivity and exports declined. However, this was concealed by the property bubble, fuelled by historically cheap mortgages and talked up by politicians. Bertie Ahern, prime minister from 1997 to 2008, famously stated in 2006 that the boom times were "getting even more boomier."[44] However, in September 2008 the Irish government was forced to guarantee all of the six major banks, thereby committing the taxpayer to huge, unquantified risk. By 2009–10, when Irish GDP fell by 13.5 percent, house prices were in free fall and unemployment was steeply rising. As the journalist Fintan O'Toole commented, the rise and fall of the former "Celtic Tiger" made "Icarus look boringly stable."[45]

Dire as the Irish situation was, the center of the storm was Greece, where the crisis provoked a more violent response. Greece should not, arguably, have joined the single currency at all, as its entry was based on massaged statistical data.

Figure 12.8   2010: Greece, strikes and protest. Photo © akg-images/John Hios.

Accordingly, Greece's entry has been described as "misjudged, even fraudulent."[46] In reality, Greece had never brought its deficit below the 3 percent of GDP entry target, and its borrowing had grown substantially once within the euro. Moreover, the Greek economy suffered from endemic problems such as a bloated state sector, deadlock over pension reform, and low rates of tax collection. In May 2010 the Greek Socialist government imposed an austerity package, provoking violent riots on the streets of Athens in which three people died (Figure 12.8). Greece was subsequently forced to seek a €110 billion financial assistance package from the European Union and the IMF, and slightly smaller packages were negotiated in the case of Ireland (November 2010) and Portugal (May 2011). In each case, the "bailout" was accompanied by further austerity measures, which threatened to prolong the recession for these countries as well as provoking further social and political unrest. A vicious cycle had been set in motion and within a year Greece was seeking further assistance. By the summer of 2011 Greece faced an unpalatable choice between defaulting on its debt and leaving the euro, or taking ever-harsher austerity measures that threatened its social and political stability. The previously unimaginable prospect of a Greek default began to be talked of as the "Lehman Brothers moment" for Europe. (To this point only Iceland, outside of the EU, had refused to reimburse foreign investors in its collapsed banks.)

The political damage caused by the crisis was palpable. Everywhere, incumbent governments were defeated at the polls. In Britain a budget-cutting coalition of Conservatives and Liberal Democrats was formed in May 2010. In Ireland the once-dominant Fianna Fail party saw its vote more than halved in February 2011, and it was thrust into a humiliating third place. Even in Germany, which had recovered strongly from recession as a result of prudent management of the manufacturing sector, Merkel's Christian Democrats suffered historic reverses at *Länder* level. In Spain the Socialist government not only lost regional elections in June 2011, but was also shaken by demonstrators who occupied some of Madrid's public squares for three weeks in protest at youth unemployment. However, while much anger was directed at the political class (as well as the bankers), the dominant political and economic response remained highly orthodox. The cost of the banks' ill-judged generosity and governments' miscalculations, it seemed, would be borne by workers and taxpayers.

The crisis raised many profound questions for the future of European integration. In particular, the extreme reluctance of Germany to fund the Greek bailout represented a dramatic shift from the 1980s and 1990s, when German payments had oiled the wheels of "ever closer union." In the past the German people might have responded to the call of historic responsibility: now many expressed resentment that hard-working north Europeans would have to rescue the soft-living south. In the words of an infamous headline in the tabloid *Bild*: "Sell your islands, you bankrupt Greeks! And sell the Acropolis too!" The lack of sympathy pointed to a deeper problem within the European Union. The visionary leadership of the Kohl/Mitterrand generation was now a thing of the past, and national interests were increasingly to the fore. All that the current generation of leaders could offer was crisis management: as one expert put it in 2008, "we must indefinitely get used to living uneasily with leaderlessness."[47] Kohl and Mitterrand had, of course, seen monetary union as the corollary of closer political union, yet this had been ruled out for the foreseeable future by the failure of the Constitutional Treaty in 2005. Now the single currency was also faltering. Which way would the European Union turn? The odds were stacked against a dramatic relaunch of the European project, such as Delors had achieved in the 1980s: yet muddling through might no longer be an option. Although European integration had faced many setbacks since the 1950s, for the first time there was the prospect of a genuine reversal, with the withdrawal of Greece (and possibly other weaker economies) from the euro and the consolidation of a smaller, "two-speed" European Union around the powerful German economy.

Conclusion

The opening decade of the twenty-first century represented a chastening experience for Europe. In almost every regard, the visions and strategies that Europe's statesmen and women had adopted since the Cold War had fallen short. The single currency had tripped at the first hurdle – its weaknesses laid bare by financial shocks that rippled across the Atlantic. The European Union's institutions were clearly still too weak to withstand the power and volatility of the globalized world economy. European integration was by no means dead, but this decade – with its joint political and economic failures – surely represented a decisive moment. The EU appeared as likely to survive as a confederation rather than as Fischer's "European Federation" – a future imagined by Margaret Thatcher rather than Jacques Delors. The arrival of parties of the neo-nationalist and populist right as a permanent feature in European parliaments, if not necessarily in governments, made such an outcome more likely. Europe's voice in the world had also declined. Cuts to military budgets and the widespread abolition of national service meant that Europe's capacity for foreign intervention independent of the United States was highly circumscribed. In June 2011 the retiring US Defense Secretary Robert Gates warned that there would be a "dwindling appetite and patience" in Congress for the USA to expend "increasingly precious funds" on defending nations that were unwilling to devote resources to their own defense. Future US leaders, he went on, for whom the Cold War had not been the formative experience, "may not consider the return on America's investment in NATO worth the cost."[48] Compared to China, with its surging economic growth and global ambition, Europe no longer seemed dynamic or forward-looking. A longer-term threat to Europe's interests lay in demographic trends. "Eurostat" projected that the overall population of the EU would remain fairly stable until 2060 (although countries such as Britain and France would experience dramatic growth). However, the relationship between those of working age and those over 65 would shrink from 4:1 in 2008 to 2:1 in 2060, at which point the proportion of those over 65 would have risen from 17 percent to 30 percent. Decades of improved health care and diet had given a predictive quality to Rumsfeld's comment about an "old" Europe, with profound implications for Europe's economic prospects.[49]

While the future looked cloudier and less optimistic than had been the case at the turn of the century, there was, of course, much that was still positive about Europe in the first decade of the new millennium. In July 2011 Polish Prime Minister Donald Tusk sought to dispel the gloom by pointing out that "The European Union is great. It is the best place on Earth to be born and to live your life." He ridiculed the idea that the EU impinged on national sovereignty when, under Soviet domination, "we saw a real restriction on our sovereignty."[50] The view may well have looked rosier from Warsaw: Poland was enjoying its longest period of freedom since the eighteenth century, and it had benefited more than most from membership of the EU. Even so, Tusk had a point. Above all, Europeans led lives that were secure from the threat of war. In contrast to the 1930s, there was no prospect of conflict between European states, and – the tragedy of Yugoslavia apart – Europe continued to enjoy an unprecedented era of peace within its borders. The architects of the Schuman Plan were proven correct in arguing that a process of European integration which reconciled the interests of France and Germany would ultimately render war in western Europe unthinkable. Meanwhile, Europe's economy continued to generate immense wealth – about a quarter of world GDP came from the EU. Countries such as Norway and Switzerland (small states which had decided against formal EU membership) enjoyed a standard of living almost without equal. Much of this wealth was redistributed either on social welfare, education, or indeed on foreign aid. More than a half of all of the money spent on developing countries worldwide came from the EU and its member states. Meanwhile, despite the rise of xenophobia, there had also been a striking liberalization of attitudes towards sexuality during this decade. Hence, same-sex marriages were legalized in the Netherlands (2001) and Spain (2005), and civil unions in, amongst others, Germany (2001) and Britain (2005). Most of the remaining 11 EU states (mostly in the east and south) were moving towards some form of legally recognized union. Illiberalism and liberalism therefore coincided within modern Europe to a confusing and remarkable degree. It all added to a sense that Europe stood at a watershed. One path might lead to a revival of national tensions and the unraveling of the project of European integration, or at least a peaceful decline into luxurious irrelevance. Another might be the revival and extension of the EU into – in the words of the President of the EU Commission in 2007 – the first "non-imperial empire,"[51] whereby member states worked closely together and set norms for other states within and beyond Europe's borders. Certainly both the scale of the challenge and the stakes were greater than at any point since the end of the Cold War.

Notes

Introduction: Europe's Troubles

1 For Mitterrand's speech, see A. G. Harryvan and J. van der Harst, *Documents on European union* (Macmillan, Basingstoke, 1997), pp. 294–300.

2 Philip Williamson, "'Safety first': Baldwin, the Conservative Party, and the 1929 General Election," *The Historical Journal*, 25, 2 (1982), p. 387.

3 Peter M. R. Stirk, *A history of European integration since 1914* (Pinter, London, 1996), pp. 35–6, citing the memorandum of French Prime Minister Aristide Briand, May 1930.

4 Michael Burleigh and Wolfgang Wipperman, *The racial state: Germany, 1933–1945* (Cambridge University Press, Cambridge, 1991).

5 Walter Benjamin, *Illuminations*, ed. Hannah Arendt (Pimlico, London, 1999 edn.), p. 234.

6 Dawn Ades (ed.), *Art and power: Europe under the dictators, 1930–1945* (Thames & Hudson/Hayward Gallery, London, 1995).

1 The War and its Legacy

1 Mark Harrison (ed.), *The economics of World War Two: Six Great Powers in international comparison* (Cambridge University Press, Cambridge, 1998), p. 22.

2 Werner Abelshauser, "Germany: Guns, butter and economic miracles," in Harrison, *Economics of World War Two*, p. 158.

3 Lucy S. Dawidowicz, *The war against the Jews, 1933–45* (Penguin, London, 1990 edn.), p. 143.

4 Hermann Goering's order to Heydrich of July 31, 1941: Jeremy Noakes and Geoffrey Pridham, *Nazism, 1919–1945*, vol. 3, *War and racial extermination: A documentary reader* (Exeter University Press, Exeter, 1988), p. 1104.

5 Ibid., p. 1131.

Europe's Troubled Peace: 1945 to the Present, Second Edition. Tom Buchanan.
© 2012 John Wiley & Sons, Ltd. Published 2012 by John Wiley & Sons, Ltd.

6 Ulrich Herbert, "Labour and extermination: economic interest and the primacy of Weltanschauung in National Socialism," *Past and Present*, 138 (February 1993), p. 172.

7 Robert Gildea, *Marianne in chains: In search of the German occupation, 1940–1945* (Macmillan, London, 2002), pp. 84–5.

8 See Robert O. Paxton, *Vichy France: Old guard and new order, 1940–1944* (Knopf, New York, 1972); for films, see p. 155 below.

9 Julian Jackson, *France: The dark years, 1940–1944* (Oxford University Press, Oxford, 2001), p. 565.

10 Dwight D. Eisenhower, *Crusade in Europe* (Heinemann, London, 1948), pp. 349–50; M. R. D. Foot, "The liberation of France and restoration of democratic government," in Gill Bennett (ed.), *The end of the war in Europe, 1945* (HMSO, London, 1996), p. 102.

11 Jan Gross, *Polish society under German occupation: The General Gouvernement, 1939–1944* (Princeton University Press, Princeton, 1979), p. 184.

12 A. Moravia, *Two Women* (1st pub. 1957; Penguin, Harmondsworth, 1961), p. 179.

13 Walter S. Dunn, *The Soviet economy and the Red Army, 1930–1945* (Praeger, Westport, Conn., 1995), pp. 83–6.

14 David Ellwood, *Rebuilding Europe: Western Europe, America and postwar reconstruction* (Longman, London, 1992), p. 33.

15 See Martin Conway, "The liberation of Belgium, 1944–1945," in Bennett (ed.), *The end of the war in Europe*.

16 Jonathan Steinberg, *Why Switzerland?* (Cambridge University Press, Cambridge, 1996 edn.), p. 66.

17 Exact figures are still contested: see Brian Girvin and Geoffrey Roberts (eds.), *Ireland and the Second World War: Politics, society and remembrance* (Four Courts Press, Dublin, 2000), pp. 86–7, 92–4.

18 For more detail, see Christian Leitz, *Nazi Germany and neutral Europe during the Second World War* (Manchester University Press, Manchester, 2000), *passim*.

19 Philippe Marguerat, "German gold – Allied gold, 1940–5," in George Kreis (ed.), *Switzerland and the Second World War* (Frank Cass, London, 2000), pp. 69–80.

20 Leitz, *Nazi Germany and neutral Europe*, p. 74; Girvin and Roberts (eds.), *Ireland and the Second World War*, p. 78.

21 Norman Davies, in Martin McCauley, *Communist power in Europe, 1944–1949* (Macmillan, London, 1979), p. 40.

22 John Barber and Mark Harrison, *The Soviet home front, 1941–1945* (Longman, Harlow, 1991), p. 41.

23 Ibid., p. 40.

24 Ibid., pp. 40–2; John Erickson, "Soviet war losses: calculations and controversies," in John Erickson and David Dilks (eds.), *Barbarossa: The Axis and the Allies* (Edinburgh University Press, Edinburgh, 1998), pp. 255–77.

25 J. Otto Pohl, *Ethnic cleansing in the USSR, 1937–1949* (Greenwood, Westport, Conn., 1999), pp. 79–86 and 93–107.

26 C. M. Kohan, *The history of the Second World War: Works and buildings* (HMSO, London, 1952), p. 225.

27 Mark Mazower, *Inside Hitler's Greece: The experience of occupation, 1941–44* (Yale University Press, New Haven, 1993), pp. 40–1.

28 Norman M. Naimark, *The Russians in Germany: A history of the Soviet zone of occupation, 1945–1949* (Harvard University Press, Cambridge, Mass., 1995), p. 41.

29 Lothar Kettenacker, *Germany since 1945* (Oxford University Press, Oxford, 1997), pp. 5–6.

30 For a thorough discussion in the light of new archival evidence, see Naimark, *The Russians in Germany*, ch. 2.

31 A. J. Nicholls, *Freedom with responsibility: The social market economy in Germany, 1918–1963* (Oxford University Press, Oxford, 1994), p. 125; Abelshauser, "Germany," p. 146.

32 Figures are mainly taken from Michael R. Marrus, *The unwanted: European refugees in the twentieth century* (Oxford University Press, New York, 1985), pp. 296–345.

33 Volker Berghahn, *Modern Germany* (Cambridge University Press, Cambridge, 2nd edn. 1988), p. 186.

34 Ibid., p. 215.

35 Jean-Pierre Rioux, *The Fourth Republic, 1944–58* (Cambridge University Press, Cambridge, 1987), pp. 32–4. For a detailed analysis, see Peter Novick, *The Resistance versus Vichy: The purge of collaborators in liberated France* (Chatto & Windus, London, 1968), pp. 184–8 and 208.

36 Jean Lacouture, *De Gaulle: The ruler, 1945–1970* (Harvill, London, 1993), p. 78.

37 Martin Conway, "Justice in postwar Belgium: Popular passions and political realities," in István Deák et al. (eds.), *The politics of retribution in Europe: World War II and its aftermath* (Princeton University Press, Princeton, 2000), p. 134.

38 John R. Lampe, *Yugoslavia as history: Twice there was a country* (Cambridge University Press, Cambridge, 2000 edn.), p. 227.

2 Europe between the Powers, 1945–1953

1 Cited in Jussi M. Hanhimaki and Odd Arne Westad (eds.), *The Cold War: A history in documents and eyewitness accounts* (Oxford University Press, Oxford, 2003), p. 78.

2 Between July and October 1946 a peace conference in Paris concluded treaties with Germany's allies Italy, Romania, Hungary, Bulgaria, and Finland, but did not address the future of Germany and Austria.

3 John Lewis Gaddis, *The long peace: Inquiries into the history of the Cold War* (Oxford University Press, New York, 1987), p. 30.

4 See the discussion in John Lewis Gaddis, *We now know: Rethinking Cold War history* (Oxford University Press, Oxford, 1997), ch. 4.

5 Joseph Stalin, *Speeches delivered by J. V. Stalin at meetings of voters of the Stalin electoral districts, Moscow* (Moscow, 1950), pp. 22–3.

6 *Foreign Affairs*, July 1947.

7 Gaddis, *The long peace*, p. 36.

8 Harry S. Truman, *Years of trial and hope, 1946–1953* (Hodder & Stoughton, Bungay, 1956), p. 111.

9 Alexander Werth, *France 1940–1955* (Robert Hale, London, 1957), p. 363.

10 Albert Resis (ed.), *Molotov remembers: Inside Kremlin politics* (Ivan R. Dee, Chicago, 1993), p. 59.

11 Henry Morgenthau Jr, *Germany is our problem* (Harper & Bros, New York, 1946), p. 48. See the frontispiece for a copy of the 1944 report.

12 For the text see Hanhimaki and Westad (eds.), *The Cold War*, pp. 82–6.

13 Alan Kramer, "British dismantling policies, 1945–8: A reassessment," in I. D. Turner (ed.), *Reconstruction in post-war Germany: British occupation policy and the Western zones, 1945–55* (Berg, Oxford, 1989), pp. 125–53.

14 Corey Ross, *The East German dictatorship* (Arnold, London, 2002), p. 84.

15 Byrnes' speech is available on the website of the US Diplomatic Mission to Germany, www.usembassy.de/usa/etexts.

16 Dominik Geppert, " 'Proclaim liberty throughout all the land': Berlin and the symbolism of the Cold War," in id. (ed.), *The postwar challenge: Cultural, social and political change in western Europe, 1945–58* (Oxford University Press, Oxford, 2003), p. 341.

17 Hanhimaki and Westad (eds.), *The Cold War*, p. 122.

18 Dean Acheson, *Present at the creation: My years in the State Department* (Hamish Hamilton, London, 1970), p. 231.

19 Michael J. Hogan, *The Marshall Plan: America, Britain and the reconstruction of western Europe, 1947–1952* (Cambridge University Press, Cambridge, 1987), p. 30.

20 Ellwood, *Rebuilding Europe*, p. 54.

21 Carlo Spagnolo, "Reinterpreting the Marshall Plan," in Geppert (ed.), *The Postwar challenge*, p. 280.

22 Hanhimaki and Westad (eds.), *The Cold War*, p. 52.

23 Hogan, *The Marshall Plan*, p. 415; Max-Stephan Schulze (ed.), *Western Europe, economic and social change since 1945* (Longman, London, 1999), p. 33.

24 Paul Hoffman, October 1950, cited in Hogan, *The Marshall Plan*, p. 349.

25 Werth, *France 1940–1955*, p. 414.

26 See in particular Alan S. Milward, *The reconstruction of western Europe, 1945–51* (Methuen, London, 1984).

27 Anthony Carew, *Labour under the Marshall Plan* (Manchester University Press, Manchester, 1987), p. 8.

28 The term was coined by Geir Lundestad in 1986. For a more recent formulation, see his *The United States and western Europe since 1945* (Oxford University Press, Oxford, 2003), ch. 2.

29 Maurice Crouzet, *The European renaissance since 1945* (Thames & Hudson, London, 1970), p. 141.

30 See Matthew Cullerne Bown, *Art under Stalin* (Phaidon, Oxford, 1991), pp. 207–9, 224.

31 David Caute, *The fellow travellers: A postscript to the Enlightenment* (Quartet, London, 1977), pp. 344–55.

32 Peter Coleman, *The liberal conspiracy: The Congress for Cultural Freedom and the struggle for the mind of postwar Europe* (Collier Macmillan, New York, 1989), pp. 49–50.

33 Orwell's lists are reproduced in Peter Davison (ed.), *The complete works of George Orwell*, vol. 20 (Secker & Warburg, London, 1998), pp. 240–59.

34 Rob Burns (ed.), *German cultural studies: An introduction* (Oxford University Press, Oxford, 1995), p. 223.

35 See Stephen E. Aschheim, "Comrade Klemperer: Communism, liberalism and Jewishness in the DDR. The later diaries, 1945–59," *Journal of Contemporary History*, 36, 2 (April 2001), p. 333, citing Klemperer's diary entry for February 10, 1952.

3 Restoration, Reconstruction, and Revolution: Europe 1945–1950

1 Lacouture, *De Gaulle*, p. 17.
2 See Ina Zweiniger-Bargielowska, *Austerity in Britain: Rationing, controls and consumption, 1939–1955* (Oxford University Press, Oxford, 2000).
3 Cited in Robert G. Moeller, *Protecting motherhood: Women and the family in the politics of postwar West Germany* (University of California Press, Berkeley, 1993), p. 13.
4 Eva Kolinsky, *Women in West Germany: Life, work and politics* (Berg, Oxford, 1989), p. 37.
5 See in particular William Hitchcock, *France restored: Cold War diplomacy and the quest for leadership in Europe, 1944–1954* (University of North Carolina Press, Chapel Hill, 1998); Richard Vinen, *Bourgeois politics in France, 1945–1951* (Cambridge University Press, Cambridge, 1995); and John W. Young, *France, the Cold War and the Western Alliance, 1944–49* (Leicester University Press, Leicester, 1990).
6 Rioux, *The Fourth Republic*, p. 106.
7 Schuman's statement is reproduced in Harryvan and van der Harst, *Documents on European union*, pp. 61–3.
8 Nicholls, *Freedom with responsibility*, p. 247.
9 Paul Ginsborg, *A history of contemporary Italy: Society and politics, 1943–1988* (Penguin, London, 1990), p. 117.
10 Wendy Carlin, "Economic reconstruction in western Germany, 1945–55," in Turner (ed.), *Reconstruction in post-war Germany*, citing *The Economist*, July 3, 1948, p. 56.
11 Knud J. V. Jespersen, *A history of Denmark* (Palgrave Macmillan, Basingstoke, 2004), p. 172.
12 Rolf Danielsen et al., *Norway: A history from the Vikings to our own times* (Scandinavian University Press, Oslo), p. 416.
13 Jean Grugel and Tim Rees, *Franco's Spain* (Arnold, London, 1997), pp. 109 and 110.
14 David H. Close, *The origins of the Greek Civil War* (Longman, London, 1995), p. 209.
15 Stalin, *Speeches* (February 9, 1946), p. 4.
16 Catherine Merridale, *Night of stone: Death and memory in Russia* (Granta, London, 2000), p. 311.
17 Y. Gorlizki and O. Khlevniuk, *Cold peace: Stalin and the Soviet ruling circle, 1945–1953* (Oxford University Press, Oxford, 2004), pp. 124–6.
18 Ibid., p. 75.
19 This comment was made to the Yugoslav Communist Milovan Djilas during his visit to Moscow in April 1945: see his *Conversations with Stalin* (Penguin, London, 1962), p. 90.
20 Karel Kaplan, *The short march: The communist takeover in Czechoslovakia, 1945–1948* (C. Hurst, London, 1987), p. 26. Stalin was referring specifically to the German and Hungarian minorities in Czechoslovakia although, in the event, the Hungarians successfully resisted forcible expulsion.
21 Milan Kundera, *The Joke* (1st pub. 1964; Penguin, London, 1984), p. 120.
22 Cited in Kaplan, *The short march*, p. 190.
23 See, for instance, Padraic Kenney, *Rebuilding Poland: workers and communists, 1945–1950* (Cornell University Press, Ithaca, NY, 1997); Melissa K. Bokovoy, *Peasants and communists: Politics and ideology in the Yugoslav countryside, 1941–1953* (University of Pittsburgh Press, Pittsburgh, Pa., 1998); Mark Pittaway, "The reproduction of hierarchy: Skill,

working-class culture and the state in early socialist Hungary," *Journal of Modern History*, 74, 4 (December 2002), 737–69.

24   Bennett Kovrig, *Communism in Hungary: From Kun to Kádár* (Hoover Institution Press, Stanford, 1979), p. 244.

25   Bruce McFarlane, *Yugoslavia: Politics, economics and society* (Pinter, London, 1988), p. 12.

26   *The Soviet–Yugoslav dispute* (Royal Institute of International Affairs, London, 1948), p. 68; Milovan Djilas, *Tito: The story from inside* (Weidenfeld & Nicolson, London, 1981), p. 31.

4   Consolidating Western Europe, 1950–1963

1   Alan Kramer, *The West German economy, 1945–1955* (Berg, Oxford, 1991), pp. 217–18.

2   Harold Macmillan, *Riding the storm, 1956–1959* (Macmillan, London, 1971), pp. 350–1.

3   Barbara Marshall, *Willy Brandt: A political biography* (Macmillan, Basingstoke, 1997), p. 48.

4   Patrick Major, *The death of the KPD: Communism and anti-communism in West Germany, 1945–1956* (Oxford University Press, Oxford, 1997), p. 266.

5   Cited in Richard Kuisel, *Seducing the French: The dilemma of Americanization* (University of California Press, Berkeley, 1993), p. 38.

6   See Tom Buchanan and Martin Conway (eds.), *Political Catholicism in Europe, 1918–1965* (Oxford University Press, Oxford, 1996); Ginsborg, *Contemporary Italy*, ch. 5.

7   Eric D. Weitz, "The ever-present other: Communism in the making of West Germany," in Hanna Schissler (ed.), *The miracle years: A cultural history of West Germany, 1949–1968* (Princeton University Press, Princeton, 2001), p. 227.

8   John Pollard, "Italy," in Buchanan and Conway (eds.), *Political Catholicism*, p. 89; Claire Duchen, *Women's rights and women's lives in France, 1944–68* (Routledge, London, 1994), pp. 53 and 60.

9   Elizabeth Ezra (ed.), *European cinema* (Oxford University Press, 2004), p. 121.

10   Ellwood, *Rebuilding Europe*, p. 217.

11   For a good overview, see N. F. R. Crafts, "The Great Boom, 1950–1973," in Schulze (ed.), *Western Europe*, pp. 42–62.

12   Michael Wildt, in Richard Bessel and Dirk Schumann (eds.), *Life after death: Approaches to a cultural and social history of Europe during the 1940s and 1950s* (Cambridge University Press, Cambridge, 2003), p. 222.

13   Mark Mazower, "The Cold War and the Appropriation of Memory: Greece after liberation," in Deák et al. (eds.), *The Politics of retribution*, p. 221.

14   Rioux, *The Fourth Republic*, p. 395.

15   David Forgacs and Robert Lumley (eds.), *Italian cultural studies: An introduction* (Oxford University Press, Oxford, 1996), p. 278.

16   Leif Lewin, *Ideology and strategy: A century of Swedish politics* (Cambridge University Press, Cambridge, 1988), p. 215.

17   Thomas W. Wolfe, *Soviet power and Europe, 1945–1970* (Johns Hopkins Press, Baltimore, 1970), p. 187.

18   Cited in Beatrice Heuser, *NATO, Britain, France and the FRG: Nuclear strategies and forces for Europe, 1949–2000* (Macmillan, Basingstoke, 1997), p. 17.

19   Cited in Andrew Moravscik, *The choice for Europe: Social purpose and state power from Messina to Maastricht* (UCL Press, London, 1998), p. 144. Moravscik argues against the view that Suez was vital in French acceptance of the EEC.

20   The term was first used by French demographer Alfred Sauvy in his article "Trois Mondes, une planète," *L'Observateur*, August 1952.

21   Christopher Hilton, *The Wall: The people's story* (Sutton, Stroud, 2001), p. 55.

22   For the text of Kennedy's speech see Hanhimaki and Westad (eds.), *The Cold War*, pp. 330–1.

23   This was the title of a book by Mark Abrams and Richard Rose (Penguin, London, 1960).

24   See Ronald Irving, *Adenauer* (Longman, London, 2002), ch. 5.

25   For a stimulating reappraisal of this subject, see Martin Conway, "Democracy in postwar western Europe: The triumph of a political model," *European History Quarterly*, 32, 1 (January 2002), 59–84.

26   Willy Brandt, *People and politics: The years 1960–1975* (Collins, London, 1978), p. 49.

27   Robert G. Moeller, "Remembering the war in a nation of victims: West German pasts in the 1950s," in Schissler (ed.), *The miracle years*, p. 96.

28   Percy Allum, *Politics and society in post-war Naples* (Cambridge University Press, Cambridge, 1973), p. 161.

29   Ginsborg, *Contemporary Italy*, pp. 258–65.

30   Cited in Antony Jay (ed.), *The Oxford dictionary of political quotations* (Oxford University Press, Oxford, 2004 edn.), p. 236.

31   See Matthew Connelly, *A diplomatic revolution: Algeria's fight for independence and the origins of the post-Cold War era* (Oxford University Press, Oxford, 2002).

32   Serge Berstein, *The Republic of de Gaulle, 1958–1969* (Cambridge University Press, Cambridge, 1993), p. 83.

33   Donald Sassoon, *One hundred years of socialism: The west European left in the twentieth century* (I. B. Tauris, London, 1996), ch. 10.

34   Alfred Grosser, *Germany in our time: A political history of the postwar years* (Penguin, London, 1974), pp. 234–5.

35   Tim Tilton, *The political theory of Swedish social democracy* (Oxford University Press, Oxford, 1990), p. 175.

5   Western Europe in the 1960s

1   Cited in Robert Lumley, *States of emergency: Cultures of revolt in Italy from 1968 to 1978* (Verso, London, 1990), p. 2.

2   Cited in Tariq Ali, *Street fighting years: An autobiography of the Sixties* (Collins, London, 1987), p. 170.

3   Cited in Arthur Marwick, *The Sixties: Cultural revolution in Britain, France, Italy and the United States, c.1958–1974* (Oxford University Press, Oxford, 1998), p. 306. Although rather compendious, Marwick's book is the best starting point for any study of the culture and politics of the 1960s.

4   Roel van Duyn, cited in David Winner, *Brilliant orange: The neurotic genius of Dutch football* (Bloomsbury, London, 2000), p. 15.

5   Franca Rame, cited in Lumley, *States of emergency*, p. 124.

6   Rudy B. Andeweg and Galen A. Irwin, *Governance and politics of the Netherlands* (Palgrave Macmillan, Basingstoke, 2002), p. 91.

7   Hans Daalder (ed.), *Party systems in Denmark, Austria, Switzerland, The Netherlands and Belgium* (Frances Pinter, London, 1987), p. 100.

8   Berstein, *The Republic of de Gaulle*, pp. 104–5.

9   Martin Clark, *Modern Italy, 1871–1982* (Longman, London, 1984), p. 349.

10   Marwick, *The Sixties*, pp. 361–2.

11   The term was coined by Alain Touraine.

12   J.-J. Servan-Schreiber, *The American challenge* (Atheneum, New York, 1968), p. 74.

13   Marwick, *The Sixties*, p. 285.

14   Gabriel and Daniel Cohn-Bendit, *Obsolete communism: The left-wing alternative* (Penguin, Harmondsworth, 1968), p. 41.

15   Burns (ed.), *German cultural studies*, p. 230; Kolinsky, *Women in West Germany*, p. 129.

16   Diarmaid Ferriter, *The transformation of Ireland, 1900–2000* (Profile, Bungay, Suffolk, 2004), p. 573.

17   Cited in Hera Cook, *The long sexual revolution: English women, sex, and contraception, 1800–1975* (Oxford University Press, Oxford, 2004), p. 271.

18   Marwick, *The Sixties*, p. 393.

19   Serge Berstein and Jean-Pierre Rioux, *The Pompidou years, 1969–1974* (Cambridge University Press, Cambridge, 2000), p. 164.

20   Kolinsky, *Women in West Germany*, p. 219.

21   Sassoon, *One hundred years of socialism* (citing Marguérite Duras, 1973), p. 435.

22   The Hallstein doctrine was a response to Yugoslavia's opening of diplomatic relations with East Germany in 1957; it was not applied to the USSR.

23   Marshall, *Willy Brandt*, p. 65.

24   Ben Pimlott, *Harold Wilson* (HarperCollins, London, 1992), p. 304.

25   Alexander Werth, *The de Gaulle revolution* (R. Hale, London, 1960), p. 110.

26   In 1964, Mitterrand published his *Le Coup d'état permanent*.

27   Berstein, *The Republic of de Gaulle*, p. 83.

28   Heuser, *NATO, Britain, France and the FRG*, pp. 108–9.

29   In a comment made to Khrushchev during his visit of March 1960 (see Lacouture, *De Gaulle*, p. 390).

30   Henri Weber, cited in Ronald Fraser et al., *1968: A student generation in revolt* (Chatto & Windus, London, 1988), p. 190.

31   Kristin Ross, *May '68 and its afterlives* (University of Chicago Press, Chicago, 2002), p. 59.

32   Lumley, *States of emergency*, p. 74.

33   Jürgen Habermas, *Toward a rational society: Student protest, science and politics* (Heinemann, London, 1971), p. 46.

34   Berstein and Rioux, *The Pompidou years*, p. 12.

35   Charles Posner (ed.), *Reflections on the revolution in France: 1968* (Penguin, Harmondsworth, 1970), p. 131.

36   Preston, *The triumph of democracy in Spain* (Methuen, London, 1986), p. 15.

37   John Springhall, *Decolonization since 1945: The collapse of European overseas empires* (Palgrave, Basingstoke, 2001), p. 179.

6 The Soviet Union and Eastern Europe, from 1953 to the 1970s

1 I am aware that the term "eastern Europe" has very pejorative connotations for those who, until the postwar era, had thought of themselves as "central" Europeans. I use it here to reflect the reality of Soviet domination and communist rule throughout the region between 1947 and 1989.

2 François Fejtő, *A history of the people's democracies: Eastern Europe since Stalin* (Penguin, Harmondsworth, 1974), p. 76.

3 Geoffrey Swain and Nigel Swain, *Eastern Europe since 1945* (Palgrave Macmillan, Basingstoke, 2003 edn.), p. 122.

4 Fejto, *The people's democracies*, pp. 425–6.

5 David Crowley, "Warsaw's shops: Stalinism and the Thaw," in Susan Reid and David Crowley (eds.), *Style and socialism: Modernity and material culture in post-war eastern Europe* (Berg, Oxford, 2000).

6 Mark Pittaway, *Eastern Europe, 1939–2000* (Arnold, London, 2004), p. 95.

7 Fejtő, *The people's democracies*, p. 396.

8 Zsuzsa Ferge (1988), cited in Barbara Einhorn, *Cinderella goes to market: Citizenship, gender and women's movements in east central Europe* (Verso, London, 1993), p. 63.

9 Ibid., p. 93.

10 Zdeněřk Mlynář, *Night frost in Prague: The end of humane socialism* (C. Hurst, London, 1980), pp. 10–11.

11 Fejtő, *The people's democracies*, p. 417, citing Nagy, *On communism: In defence of the New Course* (1957).

12 H. Gordon Skilling, *Czechoslovakia's interrupted revolution* (Princeton University Press, Princeton, 1976), p. 827.

13 Fejtő, *The people's democracies*, pp. 363–7.

14 Mary Fulbrook, *Anatomy of a dictatorship: Inside the GDR, 1949–1989* (Oxford University Press, Oxford, 1995), p. 48.

15 W. J. Tompson, *Khrushchev: A political life* (Macmillan, Basingstoke, 1995), p. 173.

16 Ibid., p. 259.

17 Nikita Khrushchev, *Khrushchev remembers: The glasnost tapes* (Little, Brown, Boston, 1990), p. 198.

18 Edwin Bacon and Mark Sandle (eds.), *Brezhnev reconsidered* (Palgrave Macmillan, Basingstoke, 2002), p. 176.

19 Tompson, *Khrushchev*, p. 275.

20 Gyorgy Litvan (ed.), *The Hungarian revolution of 1956: Reform, revolt and repression, 1953–1963* (Longman, London, 1996), p. 17.

21 Ibid., p. 49.

22 Kovrig, *Communism in Hungary*, p. 350. "Whereas the Rakosiites used to say that those who are not with us are against us; we say that those who are not against us are with us" (January 1962).

23 Henry Kissinger, *The White House years* (Weidenfeld & Nicolson, London, 1979), p. 1141.

24 John Keep, *Last of the empires: A history of the Soviet Union, 1945–1991* (Oxford University Press, Oxford, 1995), ch. 11.

25 Ibid., p. 206; Geoffrey Hosking, *A history of the Soviet Union* (1985; Fontana, London, 2nd edn. 1990), p. 377.

26 Mark Harrison, "Economic growth and slowdown," in Bacon and Sandle (eds.), *Brezhnev reconsidered*, pp. 38–67: 45.

27 Hosking, *History of the Soviet Union*, p. 382.

28 Keep, *Last of the empires*, p. 229.

29 Text in George Saunders (ed.), *Samizdat: Voices of the Soviet opposition* (Monad Press, New York, 1974), pp. 399–412.

30 John Gooding, "The roots of *perestroika*," in Bacon and Sandle (eds.), *Brezhnev reconsidered*, pp. 195–6.

31 Fejtő, *The people's democracies*, p. 306; Berghahn, *Modern Germany*, p. 307.

32 McFarlane, *Yugoslavia*, p. 72.

33 Dennison Rusinow, *The Yugoslav experiment, 1948–1974* (C. Hurst, London, 1977), p. 234.

34 Ibid., p. 299.

35 Alexander Dubček, *Hope dies last* (HarperCollins, London, 1993), pp. 128 and 165.

36 Skilling, *Czechoslovakia's interrupted revolution*, p. 217.

37 See Mark Kramer, "The Czechoslovak crisis," in Carol Fink et al. (eds.), *1968: The world transformed* (Cambridge University Press, Cambridge, 1998), p. 127.

38 Mlynářř, *Night frost in Prague*, p. 177.

39 Kundera, author's preface to *The Joke*, p. viii.

40 Paulina Bres, "The politics of private life in post-1968 Czechoslovakia," in David Crowley and Susan E. Reid (eds.), *Socialist spaces: Sites of everyday life in the eastern bloc* (Berg, Oxford, 2002).

41 Swain and Swain, *Eastern Europe*, p. 111 (Djilas was writing in November 1956).

42 Kramer, "The Czechoslovak crisis," p. 168.

43 Steven Lukes, introduction to John Keane, Václav Havel et al. (eds.), *The power of the powerless* (Hutchinson, London, 1985), pp. 14–15.

44 Fejtő, *The people's democracies*, p. 463.

7 Western Europe in the 1970s: Downturn and Détente

1 S. J. Ball, *The Cold War: An international history of 1947–1991* (Arnold, London, 1998), p. 178.

2 John Keane, *Václav Havel: A political tragedy in six acts* (Bloomsbury, London, 1999), p. 244.

3 J. R. Frears, *France in the Giscard presidency* (Allen & Unwin, London, 1981), p. 98.

4 Willy Brandt, *My life in politics* (Penguin, Harmondsworth, 1992 edn.), p. 200; Marshall, *Willy Brandt*, p. 72.

5 Timothy Garton Ash, *In Europe's name: Germany and the divided continent* (Jonathan Cape, London, 1993), p. 73.

6 Ibid., p. 289.

7 Lundestad, *The United States and western Europe*, p. 180.

8 Barry Eichengreen, "Economy," in Mary Fulbrook (ed.), *Europe since 1945* (Oxford University Press, Oxford, 2001), p. 126.

9 John Ramsden, *Winds of change: From Macmillan to Heath, 1957–1975* (Longman, London, 1996), pp. 349–50.

10   This was the SPD's slogan in the 1976 Bundestag election.

11   Susan Crosland, *Tony Crosland* (Cape, London, 1982), p. 295.

12   Wayne Northcutt, *Mitterrand: A political biography* (Holmes & Meier, New York, 1992), p. 281, citing Mitterrand in 1974.

13   Marshall, *Willy Brandt*, p. 66.

14   Vincent Wright (ed.), *Continuity and change in France* (Allen & Unwin, London, 1984), p. 25.

15   Although the Scots voted in favor of devolution by 33% to 31%, the required support of 40% of the population was not achieved.

16   David Hanley (ed.), *Christian Democracy in Europe: A comparative perspective* (Pinter, London, 1994), p. 105.

17   Stefan Aust, *The Baader–Meinhof group: The inside story of a phenomenon* (Bodley Head, London, 1987), p. 154.

18   Robert Meade, *Red Brigades: The story of Italian terrorism* (Macmillan, Basingstoke, 1990), p. 134.

19   Ibid., p. 235.

20   David Drake, *Intellectuals and politics in post-war France* (Palgrave, London, 2002), p. 161.

21   Jean-François Lyotard, "What is postmodernism?" in Charles Jencks (ed.), *The postmodern reader* (Academy, London, 1992), pp. 138 and 149.

22   Burns (ed.), *German cultural studies*, p. 314.

23   Samuel P. Huntington, *The Third Wave: Democratization in the late twentieth century* (University of Oklahoma Press, Norman and London, 1991).

24   See Helen Graham and Jo Labanyi (eds.), *Spanish cultural studies: An introduction* (Oxford University Press, Oxford, 1995), chapter 19, pp. 332–54.

25   Kenneth Maxwell, *The making of Portuguese democracy* (Cambridge University Press, Cambridge, 1995), p. 95.

8   Western Europe in the 1980s: The Era of Thatcher, Mitterrand, and Kohl

1   The term was coined by the American sociologist Daniel Bell in the late 1950s and developed in his book *The coming of post-industrial society: A venture in social forecasting* (Basic Books, New York, 1973). Bell's main concern was with the rise of a service economy and the growing importance of a class of professional and technical workers.

2   Maurice Kirby, "Industrial and Structural Change," in Schulze (ed.), *Western Europe*, pp. 81–104.

3   Kolinsky, *Women in West Germany*, pp. 152 and 155.

4   Burns (ed.), *German cultural studies*, p. 288.

5   Ibid., p. 262.

6   Jencks (ed.), *The postmodern reader*, p. 73.

7   Kuisel, *Seducing the French*, p. 228.

8   The term "new" (or "second") Cold War has become widely used, although in reality this was simply a new phase in the postwar ideological conflict. A recent scholar refers to these years as "Dark Times," which certainly captures the feel of the period. Wilfried Loth, *Overcoming the Cold War: A history of détente, 1950–1991* (Palgrave, Basingstoke, 1996), ch. 7.

9   Ramsden, *Winds of change*, p. 421.

10   Margaret Thatcher, *The path to power* (HarperCollins, London, 1995), p. 362.

11   See especially John Gillingham, *European integration, 1950–2003: Superstate or new market economy?* (Cambridge University Press, Cambridge, 2003), pp. 164–8.

12   Wright (ed.), *Continuity and change*, p. 43.

13   Northcutt, *Mitterrand*, p. 76.

14   Ibid., p. 13.

15   One of Mitterrand's "propositions" was for either a five-year presidential term or a seven-year term with no reelection.

16   Mairi Maclean, *The Mitterrand years: Legacy and evaluation* (Macmillan, Basingstoke, 1998), p. 33.

17   Karl H. Cerny, *Germany at the polls: The Bundestag elections of the 1980s* (Duke University Press, Durham, NC, 1990), pp. 79–82, 106.

18   Clay Clemens and William E. Paterson (eds.), *The Kohl chancellorship* (Frank Cass, London, 1998), p. 102.

19   Richard J. Evans, *In Hitler's shadow: West German historians and the attempt to escape from the Nazi past* (I. B. Tauris, London, 1989), p. 17.

20   A. J. Nicholls, *The Bonn Republic: West German democracy, 1945–1990* (Longman, London, 1997), p. 308.

21   Gene Frankland and Donald Schoonmaker, *Between protest and power: The Green Party in Germany* (Westview, Boulder, 1992), p. 179.

22   The term was coined by Ronald Inglehart: see his *The silent revolution: Changing values and political styles among Western publics* (Princeton University Press, Princeton, 1977).

23   Cerny, *Germany at the polls*, pp. 161–2.

24   Piero Ignazi, *Extreme right parties in western Europe* (Oxford University Press, Oxford, 2003), p. 98.

25   See Paul Heywood, *The government and politics of Spain* (Macmillan, Basingstoke, 1995), ch. 10.

26   For a detailed account, see Paddy Woodworth, *Dirty war, clean hands: ETA, the GAL and Spanish democracy* (Yale University Press, New Haven, 2001).

9 European Integration: From Rome to Maastricht, 1957–1992

1   David Cannadine (ed.), *The speeches of Winston Churchill* (Penguin, London, 1990), p. 311. It should be noted that Churchill envisaged a regional organization of Europe which Britain and its Commonwealth would remain outside.

2   The European Court of Human Rights was created in 1959.

3   Jean Monnet, *Memoirs* (Collins, London, 1978), p. 394.

4   Harryvan and van der Harst, *Documents on European union*, p. 104.

5   See, above all, Alan Milward, *The European rescue of the nation state* (1st pub. 1992; Routledge, London, 2nd edn. 2000), ch. 6; Gillingham, *European integration*.

6   Milward, *The European rescue*.

7   Sassoon, *One hundred years of socialism*, p. 235.

8   Moravcsik, *The choice for Europe*, p. 89.

9   Cited in George Ross, *Jacques Delors and European integration* (Polity, Cambridge, 1995), p. 1.

10 Cited in Derek Urwin, *The community of Europe: A history of European integration since 1945* (Longman, London, 2nd edn. 1995), p. 103.

11 Cited in Lacouture, *De Gaulle*, p. 345.

12 Harryvan and van der Harst, *Documents on European union*, p. 134.

13   Ibid., p. 141.

14   Miriam Camps, *European unification in the Sixties: From the veto to the crisis* (London, 1967), p. 81.

15   Gillingham, *European integration*, p. 127.

16   Stephen George, *An awkward partner: Britain in the European Community* (Oxford University Press, Oxford, 2nd edn. 1994), p. 149.

17   Stirk, *A history of European integration since 1914*, p. 207.

18   Daniel Wincott, "The idea of the European social model," in Kevin Featherstone and Claudio M. Radaelli (eds.), *The politics of Europeanization* (Oxford University Press, Oxford, 2003), p. 287.

19   Cited in Charles Grant, *Delors: Inside the house that Jacques built* (Nicholas Brealey, London, 1994), p. 55.

20   See Margaret Thatcher, *The Downing Street years* (HarperCollins, London, 1993), p. 556.

21   Harryvan and van der Harst, *Documents on European union*, p. 241.

22   Ibid., pp. 244–6.

23   Moravcsik, *Choice for Europe*, p. 445 (citing François Lamoureaux).

10   The Fall of the Communist Regimes: The Soviet Union and Eastern Europe, 1980–1991

1   Karl Marx and Friedrich Engels, *The Communist Manifesto*, in *Selected Works*, vol. 1 (Lawrence & Wishart, London, 1953), p. 36.

2   I find Archie Brown persuasive on this point; see *The Gorbachev factor* (Oxford University Press, Oxford, 1997), pp. 225–30.

3   Zdeněk Mlynář and Mikhail Gorbachev, *Conversations with Gorbachev* (Columbia University Press, New York, 2002), p. 81.

4   Reproduced in Branka Magaš, *The destruction of Yugoslavia: Tracking the break-up, 1980–92* (Verso, London, 1993), pp. 49–52.

5   This and other grassroots movements of the 1980s are described in Padraic Kenney, *A carnival of revolution: Central Europe 1989* (Princeton University Press, Princeton, 2002).

6   Aleš Erjavec, "New Slovenian art," in id. (ed.), *Postmodernism and the postsocialist condition: Politicized art under late socialism* (University of California Press, Berkeley, 2003), p. 145.

7   See, for instance, the book of interviews with Poland's former Stalinist rulers by Teresa Toranska, *Oni: Stalin's Polish puppets* (Collins/Harvill, London, 1987), or Andrzej Wajda's film *Man of Iron*, which closely records the Solidarity movement.

8   Konrad Jarausch, *The rush to German unity* (Oxford University Press, Oxford, 1994), p. 155.

9   Neal Ascherson, *The Polish August: The self-limiting revolution* (Allen Lane, London, 1981), p. 271.

10   See Mark Kramer, "Declassified Soviet documents on the Polish crisis," Cold War International History Project (CWIHP), virtual archive.

11   Witness Brezhnev's November 21, 1981 oral communication to Jaruzelski: "Doesn't this suggest to you that a failure to take harsh measures against the counterrevolution right away will cost you invaluable time?" (in Kramer, "Declassified Soviet documents").

12   Drake, *Intellectuals and politics*, p. 171.

13   Although 66% supported economic reform and 69% political reform, the turnout was such that Jaruzelski failed to achieve the required support of 51% of voters.

14   Brown, *The Gorbachev factor*, p. 81.

15   Cited in N. Hawkes (ed.) *Tearing down the curtain: The people's revolutions in eastern Europe* (Hodder & Stoughton, 1990), p. 102.

16   Anatol Lieven, *The Baltic revolution: Latvia, Lithuania, Estonia and the path to independence* (Yale University Press, New Haven, 1993), pp. 432–4.

17   Vladislav M. Zubok, "New evidence on the 'Soviet factor' in the peaceful revolutions of 1989," *CWIHP Bulletin*, 12–13 (2001), 6.

18   See Jacques Lévesque, *The enigma of 1989: The USSR and the liberation of eastern Europe* (University of California Press, Berkeley, 1997).

19   Jarausch, *The rush to German unity*, p. 53.

20   Fulbrook, *Anatomy of a dictatorship*, p. 38, citing comments by Manfred Uschner.

21   Hans-Hermann Hertle, "The fall of the Wall: The unintended self-dissolution of East Germany's ruling regime," *CWIHP Bulletin*, 12–13 (2001), p. 144.

22   See ibid., pp. 157–8, for a transcript of Schabowski's press conference.

23   Jarausch, *The rush to German unity*, p. 125.

24   Kohl's speech is reproduced in M. Donald Hancock and Helga A. Welsh, *German unification: Process and outcomes* (Westview, Boulder, 1994), pp. 329–37.

25   Gorbachev's message to Mitterrand, Thatcher, and Bush, November 10, 1989, printed in Hertle, "The fall of the Wall," p. 159.

26   As he told the German Foreign Minister Genscher on December 5: see Anatoly Chernyaev, *My six years with Gorbachev* (Pennsylvania State University Press, University Park, 2000), p. 237.

27   The referendum was not held in the more independence-minded republics: the three Baltic states, Armenia, Georgia, and Moldova.

11   Europe after the Cold War

1   The provisions of the Maastricht Treaty establishing the European Union formally came into force on November 1, 1993.

2   The CSCE was established as a result of the Helsinki process in 1975; from December 1994 it became the permanent OSCE (Organization for Security and Cooperation in Europe).

3   To quote Geir Lundestad's phrase in *The United States and western Europe*, ch. 10.

4   Poos, cited in Brendan Simms, *Unfinest hour: Britain and the destruction of Bosnia* (Penguin, London, 2002 edn.), p. 54; Delors cited in Ross, *Jacques Delors*, p. 169.

5   See Alan J. Kuperman, *The limits of humanitarian intervention: The genocide in Rwanda* (Brookings Institution, Washington, DC, 2001), pp. 44–51.

6   *Eurostat Yearbook 2004* (EU Publications Office, 2004), p. 52.

7   Loukas Tsoukalis, *What kind of Europe?* (Oxford University Press, Oxford, 2003), p. 118.

8   Paul Taylor, *The European Union in the 1990s* (Oxford University Press, Oxford, 1996), p. 163.

9   For a discussion of this relatively new concept, see the introduction to Featherstone and Radaelli (eds.), *The politics of Europeanization*.

10   In Germany, the proportion of those who deemed EU membership a "good thing" fell from 73% to 59% in 1990–2002, while in France it fell from 66% to 52% (Tsoukalis, *What kind of Europe?*, p. 39).

11   The term was coined by Francis Fukuyama in his article of the same name in *The National Interest* (Summer 1989).

12   David Howarth, "The French state in the euro-zone: 'Modernization' and legitimizing *dirigisme*," in Kenneth Dyson (ed.), *European states and the euro: Europeanization, variation and convergence* (Oxford University Press, Oxford, 2002), p. 170.

13   Paul Ginsborg, *Italy and its discontents, 1980–2001: Family, civil society, state, 1980–2001* (Penguin, London, 2001), p. 295.

14   Christopher Flockton, "The economy," in Klaus Larres (ed.), *Germany since unification: The development of the Berlin Republic* (Palgrave, Basingstoke, 2nd edn. 2001), pp. 67–9.

15   Eva Kolinsky, *Between hope and fear* (Keele University Press, Keele, 1995), pp. 79/80.

16   Dyson, *European states and the euro*, p. 223.

17   Pittaway, *Eastern Europe*, p. 218.

18   See for instance, Czesław Miłosz, *The captive mind* (1st pub. 1953; Penguin, London, 1985), pp. 229–31.

19   Csurka went on to found the small Hungarian Justice and Life Party, which just cleared the 5% electoral threshold in 1998.

20   Lieven, *The Baltic revolution*, p. 268.

21   Pernille Hohnen, *A market out of place? Remaking economic, social, and symbolic boundaries in post-communist Lithuania* (Oxford University Press, Oxford, 2003), p. 28.

22   The Croatian nationalist MP Vice Vukojevic, cited in Richard E. Matland and Kathleen A. Montgomery, *Women's access to political power in post-communist Europe* (Oxford University Press, Oxford, 2003), p. 285.

23   Figures taken from Robert Service, *Russia: Experiment with a people* (Macmillan, London, 2002), pp. 284 and 300–2.

24   Dale R. Herspring (ed.), *Putin's Russia: Past imperfect, future uncertain* (Rowman & Littlefield, Lanham, Mass., 2003), p. 32.

25   Lilia Shevtsova, *Yeltsin's Russia* (Carnegie Endowment, Washington, DC, 1999), p. 164, citing Lev Timofeyev.

26   Ibid., p. 271.

27   Service, *Russia*, pp. 339–40.

28   Cited in Herspring (ed.), *Putin's Russia*, p. 148.

12   Europe in the New Millennium

1   The ten were Poland, Hungary, the Czech Republic, Slovakia, Slovenia, Estonia, Latvia, Lithuania, Malta, and Cyprus.

2   See http://www.ena.lu/speech_joschka_fischer_ultimate_objective_european_integration_berlin_12_2000-2-17984

3   Other definitions were even more flexible: the Union of European Football Associations (UEFA) contained 53 members in 2011, including Kazakhstan, while 51 states have participated in the Eurovision Song Contest since its launch in 1956.

4   See the Council of Europe website, http://www.coe.int.

5   Istvan Deak, "Hungary: The threat," *New York Review of Books*, April 28, 2011.

6 Bryan Hopkinson, "The international administration of Kosovo," in Brad K. Blitz (ed.), *War and change in the Balkans* (Cambridge University Press, Cambridge, 2006), pp. 169–76.

7 The figures given in this paragraph are taken from *The World Factbook* (CIA) and the IMF's *World Economic Outlook Database, 2011*.

8 Catherine Stephan, "United Germany celebrates its 20th year," report issued by BNP Paribas, March 2011.

9 For a helpful statistical overview, which provides most of the basis for this paragraph, see the EU Commission's *Report on equality between women and men, 2010* (EU, 2009).

10 Paul Ginsborg has commented apropos Berlusconi's Mediaset channel that "rarely had the 'erotic gaze' been so crudely constructed"; see P. Ginsborg, *Silvio Berlusconi: Television, power and patrimony*, Verso, London, 2004, p. 43; the writer Lorella Zanardo referred to the "dictatorship" of media images of women in Italy (see http://uk.reuters.com/article/2011/02/14/uk-italy-berlusconi-women-idUK-TRE71C0R720110214).

11 See *Europe in Figures: Eurostat yearbook, 2010*, p. 192.

12 Andrew Geddes, *The Politics of Migration and Immigration in Europe* (SAGE, London, 2003), p. 89.

13 See the chapter by Nando Sigona, "'Gypsies out of Italy!' Social exclusion and racial discrimination of Roma and Sinti," in Andrea Mammone and Giuseppe A. Veltri (eds.), *Italy today: The sick man of Europe* (Routledge, London, 2010).

14 Geddes, *Politics of migration and immigration*, p. 113.

15 Justine Lacroix and Kalypso Nicolaides (eds.), *European Stories: Intellectual debates on Europe in national contexts* (Oxford University Press, Oxford, 2010), p. 87.

16 Paul Williams, *Memorial museums: The global rush to commemorate atrocities* (Berg, Oxford, 2007), p. 2.

17 The "Prague Declaration on European Conscience and Communism" was issued by a conference of politicians and intellectuals from east-central Europe (most notably Vaclav Havel): see http://www.praguedeclaration.org.

18 Williams, *Memorial museums*, p. 17 and pp. 116–17.

19 For a good overview, see Carlos Jerez-Farrán and Samuel Amago (eds.), *Unearthing Franco's legacy: Mass graves and the recovery of historical memory in Spain* (University of Notre Dame Press, Notre Dame, Indiana, 2010), esp. the chapter by Giles Tremlett, pp. 327–44.

20 "You're thinking of Europe as Germany and France. I don't. I think that's old Europe. If you look at the entire NATO Europe today, the centre of gravity is shifting to the east and there are a lot of new members" (Donald Rumsfeld, cited in *The Guardian*, January 24, 2003).

21 For a discussion, see Geir Lundestad (ed.), *Just another major crisis? The United States and Europe since 2000* (Oxford University Press, Oxford, 2008).

22 See http://www.nytimes.com/2008/07/24/us/politics/24text-obama.html.

23 *The Guardian*, September 2, 2010: Sarrazin's book was entitled *Germany abolishes itself*.

24 Frédéric Bozo, "The US changing role and Europe's Transatlantic dilemmas," in Lundestad, *Just another major crisis?*, p. 102.

25 Lundestad, *Just another major crisis?*

26 Matt Qvortrup, "The three referendums on the European Constitution Treaty in 2005," *The Political Quarterly*, 77, 1, January–March 2006, pp. 89–97.

27 Mandelson was keen to qualify this: "as long as they pay their taxes." See Peter Mandelson, *The third man: Life at the heart of New Labour* (HarperPress, London, 2010), p. 265.

28 Thomas Saalfeld, "Conflict and consensus in Germany's Bi-cameral system: A case study of the passage of the *Agenda 2010*," *Debatte: Journal of Contemporary Central and Eastern Europe*, 14, 3, December 2006, pp. 247–69.

29 Nick Hewlett, *The Sarkozy phenomenon* (Societas, 2011), p. 47.

30 Ibid, p. 45.

31 Ginsborg, *Berlusconi*, p. 2.

32 Mammone and Veltri, *Italy today*, p. 133.

33 Ibid, p. 140.

34 Ian Traynor's obituary of Haider in *The Guardian*, October 13, 2008.

35 Jens Rydgren, "Explaining the emergence of radical right-wing populist parties: The case of Denmark," *West European Politics*, 27, 3, 2004, pp. 474–502, esp. p. 490.

36 The Guardian, October 17, 2010; for Cameron's speech of February 5, 2011, see http://www.number10.gov.uk/news/pms-speech-at-munich-security-conference.

37 Quoted in Richard Sakwa, *The crisis of Russian democracy: The dual state, factionalism and the Medvedev succession* (Cambridge University Press, Cambridge, 2011), p. 236.

38 Ibid., p. 24.

39 See the diplomatic material published by "Wiki leaks": http://wikileaks.foreignpolicy.com/posts/2010/12/07/who_was_behind_the_estonia_cyber_attacks. The Russian government denied the claims. The crisis followed an Estonian decision to move a Soviet war memorial.

40 M. Hakan Yavuz, *Secularism and Muslim democracy in Turkey* (Cambridge University Press, Cambridge, 2009), p. 220.

41 See Oliver Schlumberger, "The ties that do not bind: The Union for the Mediterranean and the future of Euro–Arab relations," *Mediterranean Politics*, 2011, 16, 1, pp. 135–53.

42 Gordon Brown, *Beyond the crash: Overcoming the first crisis of globalisation* (Simon and Schuster, 2010), p. 95; BBC news website, April 11, 2011.

43 Kenneth Dyson, "The first decade," in Kenneth Dyson (ed.), *The euro at 10: Europeanization, power and convergence* (Oxford University Press, 2008), p. 3.

44 Fintan O'Toole, *Ship of fools: How stupidity and corruption sank the Celtic Tiger* (Faber and Faber, 2010), pp. 43 and 115.

45 O'Toole, *Ship of fools*, p. 9.

46 Kevin Featherstone, in Dyson, *The euro at 10*, p. 167.

47 Jack Hayward, "Introduction" to Jack Hayward (ed.), *Leaderless Europe* (Oxford University Press, Oxford, 2008), p. 9.

48 See http://blogs.wsj.com/washwire/2011/06/10/transcript-of-defense-secretary-gatess-speech-on-natos-future/.

49 *Europe in figures: Eurostat yearbook 2010*, pp. 161–2.

50 *The Guardian*, July 2, 2011. Tusk was speaking as Poland took over the presidency of the EU.

51 José Manuel Barroso, speaking at a press conference on July 10, 2007.

Guide to Further Reading

The literature on Europe since 1945 is large, if rather patchy in coverage. I have listed here the more general books, in English, that I found most helpful. I have indicated some more detailed references in the footnotes.

General

General Narratives

William I. Hitchcock, *The struggle for Europe: The turbulent history of a divided continent, 1945–2002* (Doubleday, New York, 2003).

Eric Hobsbawm, *Age of extremes: The short twentieth century, 1914–1991* (Penguin, London, 1994).

Harold James, *Europe reborn: A history 1914–2000* (Longman, Harlow, 2003).

Tony Judt, *Postwar: A History of Europe since 1945*, William Heinemann, London, 2005.

Mark Mazower, *Dark Continent: Europe's twentieth century* (Allen Lane, London, 1998).

Richard Vinen, *A history in fragments: Europe in the twentieth century* (Abacus, London, 2002).

J. Robert Wegs and Robert Ladrech, *Europe since 1945: A concise history* (Macmillan, Basingstoke, 1996).

Regions

David Arter, *Scandinavian politics today* (Manchester University Press, Manchester, 1999).

Tony Griffiths, *Scandinavia: A history from the Napoleonic era to the third millennium* (C. Hurst, London, 2nd edn. 2004).

Mark Pittaway, *Eastern Europe 1939–2000* (Arnold, London, 2004).

Joseph Rothschild, *Return to diversity: A political history of east central Europe since World War II* (Oxford University Press, New York, 1989).

Jacques Rupnik, *The other Europe* (Weidenfeld & Nicolson, London, 1988).

Geoffrey Swain and Nigel Swain, *Eastern Europe since 1945* (Palgrave Macmillan, Basingstoke, 2003 edn.).

Europe's Troubled Peace: 1945 to the Present, Second Edition. Tom Buchanan.
© 2012 John Wiley & Sons, Ltd. Published 2012 by John Wiley & Sons, Ltd.

Derek Urwin, *A political history of Western Europe since 1945* (Longman, London, 5th edn. 1997).

Thomas de Waal, *The Caucasus: An introduction* (Oxford University Press, Oxford, 2010).

National Histories

Dennis L. Bark and David R. Gress, *A history of West Germany*, 2 vols. (Blackwell, Oxford, 1989).

Peter Clarke, *Hope and glory: Britain 1900–1990* (Penguin, London, 1997).

David H. Close, *Greece since 1945: Politics, economy and society* (Longman, London, 2002).

Rolf Danielsen et al., *Norway: A history from the Vikings to our own times* (Scandinavian University Press, Oslo, 1995).

Diarmaid Ferriter, *The transformation of Ireland, 1900–2000* (Profile, Bungay, Suffolk, 2004).

Mary Fulbrook, *The divided nation: A history of Germany, 1918–1990* (Oxford University Press, Oxford, 1992).

Tom Gallagher, *Portugal: A twentieth century interpretation* (Manchester University Press, Manchester, 1983).

Robert Gildea, *France since 1945* (Oxford University Press, Oxford, 1996).

Paul Ginsborg, *A history of contemporary Italy: Society and politics, 1943–1988* (Penguin, London, 1990).

Jean Grugel and Tim Rees, *Franco's Spain* (Arnold, London, 1997).

Geoffrey Hosking, *A history of the Soviet Union* (1985; Fontana, London, 2nd edn. 1990).

Knud J. V. Jespersen, *A history of Denmark* (Palgrave Macmillan, Basingstoke, 2004).

John Keep, *Last of the empires: A history of the Soviet Union, 1945–1991* (Oxford University Press, Oxford, 1995).

Lothar Kettenacker, *Germany since 1945* (Oxford University Press, Oxford, 1997).

Patrick McCarthey (ed.), *Italy since 1945* (Oxford University Press, Oxford, 2000).

Kenneth O. Morgan, *The people's peace: British history 1945–1989* (Oxford University Press, Oxford, 3rd edn. 2001).

A. J. Nicholls, *The Bonn Republic: West German democracy, 1945–1990* (Longman, London, 1997).

Peter Pulzer, *German politics, 1945–1995* (Oxford University Press, Oxford, 1995).

Jonathan Steinberg, *Why Switzerland?* (Cambridge University Press, Cambridge, 1996 edn.).

Themes

Tom Buchanan and Martin Conway (eds.), *Political Catholicism in Europe, 1918–1965* (Oxford University Press, Oxford, 1996).

Geoff Eley, *Forging democracy: The history of the left in Europe, 1850–2000* (Oxford University Press, Oxford, 2002).

David Hanley (ed.), *Christian democracy in Europe: A comparative perspective* (Pinter, London, 1994).

Piero Ignazi, *Extreme right parties in Western Europe* (Oxford University Press, Oxford, 2003).

Brian Jenkins and Spyros A. Sofos (eds.), *Nation and identity in contemporary Europe* (Routledge, London, 1996).

Donald Sassoon, *One hundred years of socialism: The west European left in the twentieth century* (I. B. Tauris, London, 1996).

The Economy

Carlo M. Cipolla (ed.), *The Fontana economic history of Europe: The twentieth century*, parts 1 and 2 (Collins/Fontana, Glasgow, 1976).

M. M. Postan, *An economic history of western Europe, 1945–1964* (Methuen, London, 1967).

Max-Stephan Schulze (ed.), *Western Europe: Economic and social change since 1945* (Longman, London, 1999).

Frans J. L. Somers (ed.), *European economies: A comparative study* (Pitman, Bath, 1991).

Loukas Tsoukalis, *The new European economy: The politics and economics of integration* (Oxford University Press, Oxford, rev. edn. 1993).

Culture

Rob Burns (ed.), *German cultural studies: An introduction* (Oxford University Press, Oxford, 1995).

Maurice Crouzet, *The European renaissance since 1945* (Thames & Hudson, London, 1970).

Elizabeth Ezra, *European cinema* (Oxford University Press, Oxford, 2004).

Jill Forbes and Michael Kelly, *French cultural studies: An introduction* (Oxford University Press, Oxford, 1995).

David Forgacs and Robert Lumley (eds.), *Italian cultural studies: An introduction* (Oxford University Press, Oxford, 1996).

Helen Graham and Jo Labanyi (eds.), *Spanish cultural studies: An introduction* (Oxford University Press, Oxford, 1995).

Arthur Marwick, *The arts in the West since 1945* (Oxford University Press, Oxford, 2002).

World War II in Europe

John Barber and Mark Harrison, *The Soviet home front, 1941–1945* (Longman, Harlow, 1991).

Martin Conway and José Gotovitch (eds.), *Europe in exile: European exile communities in Britain, 1940–45* (Berghahn, Oxford, 2001).

István Deák et al. (eds.), *The politics of retribution in Europe: World War II and its aftermath* (Princeton University Press, Princeton, 2000).

Jan T. Gross, *Polish society under German occupation: The General Gouvernement, 1939–1944* (Princeton University Press, Princeton, 1979).

Mark Harrison (ed.), *The economics of World War Two: Six great powers in international comparison* (Cambridge University Press, Cambridge, 1998).

Julian Jackson, *France: The dark years, 1940–1944* (Oxford University Press, Oxford, 2001).

Roderick Kedward, *In search of the Maquis: Rural resistance in southern France, 1942–1944* (Oxford University Press, Oxford, 1993).

Martin Kitchen, *Nazi Germany at war* (Longman, London, 1995).

Vojtech Mastny, *The Czechs under Nazi rule: The failure of national resistance, 1939–1942* (Columbia University Press, New York, 1971).

Mark Mazower, *Inside Hitler's Greece: The experience of occupation, 1941–44* (Yale University Press, New Haven, 1993).

Richard Overy, *Russia's war* (Allen Lane, London, 1998).

R. A. C. Parker, *The Second World War: A short history* (Oxford University Press, Oxford, rev. edn. 1997).

Gerhard L. Weinberg, *A world at arms: A global history of World War II* (Cambridge University Press, Cambridge, 1994).

The Cold War in Europe

Anthony Carew, *Labour under the Marshall Plan* (Manchester University Press, Manchester, 1987).

David Caute, *The dancer defects: The struggle for cultural supremacy during the Cold War* (Oxford University Press, Oxford, 2003).

Peter Coleman, *The liberal conspiracy: The Congress for Cultural Freedom and the struggle for the mind of postwar Europe* (Collier Macmillan, New York, 1989).

Matthew Cullerne Bown, *Art under Stalin* (Phaidon, Oxford, 1991).

John Dunbabin, *The Cold War: The great powers and their allies, 1941–1947* (Longman, London, 1994).

John Lewis Gaddis, *The United States and the origins of the Cold War, 1941–1947* (Columbia University Press, New York, 1972).

John Lewis Gaddis, *The long peace: Inquiries into the history of the Cold War* (Oxford University Press, New York, 1987).

John Lewis Gaddis, *We now know: Rethinking Cold War history* (Oxford University Press, Oxford, 1997).

Francis H. Heller and John R. Gillingham (eds.), *NATO: The founding of the Atlantic Alliance and the integration of Europe* (Macmillan, Basingstoke, 1992).

Michael J. Hogan, *The Marshall Plan: America, Britain and the reconstruction of western Europe, 1947–1952* (Cambridge University Press, Cambridge, 1987).

David Holloway, *Stalin and the Bomb: The Soviet Union and atomic energy, 1939–1956* (Yale University Press, New Haven, 1994).

Wilfried Loth, *Overcoming the Cold War: A history of détente, 1950–1991* (Palgrave, Basingstoke, 2002).

Geir Lundestad, *America, Scandinavia and the Cold War, 1945–1949* (Columbia University Press, New York, 1980).

Geir Lundestad, *The United States and western Europe since 1945* (Oxford University Press, Oxford, 2003).

Vojtech Mastny, *Russia's road to the Cold War: Diplomacy, warfare and the politics of communism, 1941–1945* (Columbia University Press, New York, 1979).

Vojtech Mastny, *The Cold War and Soviet insecurity: The Stalin years* (Oxford University Press, Oxford, 1996).

Marc Trachtenberg, *A constructed peace: The making of the European settlement, 1945–1963* (Princeton University Press, Princeton, 1999).

Adam B. Ulam, *Dangerous relations: The Soviet Union in world politics, 1970–1982* (Oxford University Press, Oxford, 1983).

John W. Young and John Kent, *International relations since 1945: A global history* (Oxford University Press, Oxford, 2004).

Postwar Europe, 1945–1950

Richard Bessel and Dirk Schumann (eds.), *Life after death: Approaches to a cultural and social history of Europe during the 1940s and 1950s* (Cambridge University Press, Cambridge, 2003).

David H. Close, *The origins of the Greek civil war* (Longman, London, 1995).

John Coutouvidis and Jaime Reynolds, *Poland, 1939–1947* (Leicester University Press, Leicester, 1986).

Claire Duchen and Irene Bandhauer Schoffman (eds.), *When the war was over: Women, war and peace in Europe, 1940–1956* (Leicester University Press, Leicester, 2000).

David Ellwood, *Rebuilding Europe: Western Europe, America and postwar reconstruction* (Longman, London, 1992).

Dominik Geppert (ed.), *The postwar challenge: Cultural, social and political change in western Europe, 1945–58* (Oxford University Press, Oxford, 2003).

Yoram Gorlizki and Oleg Khlevniuk, *Cold peace: Stalin and the Soviet ruling circle, 1945–1953* (Oxford University Press, Oxford, 2004).

William I. Hitchcock, *France restored: Cold War diplomacy and the quest for leadership in Europe, 1944–1954* (University of North Carolina Press, Chapel Hill, 1998).

Karel Kaplan, *The short march: The Communist takeover in Czechoslovakia, 1945–1948* (C. Hurst, London, 1987).

Padraic Kenney, *Rebuilding Poland: Workers and Communists, 1945–1950* (Cornell University Press, Ithaca, 1997).

Alan Kramer, *The West German economy, 1945–1955* (Berg, Oxford, 1991).

Martin McCauley (ed.), *Communist power in Europe, 1944–1949* (Macmillan, London, 1977).

Alan Milward, *The reconstruction of western Europe, 1945–51* (Methuen, London, 1984).

Kenneth O. Morgan, *Labour in power, 1945–1951* (Oxford University Press, Oxford, 1984).

Martin R. Myant, *Socialism and democracy in Czechoslovakia, 1945–1948* (Cambridge University Press, Cambridge, 1981).

Norman M. Naimark, *The Russians in Germany: A history of the Soviet zone of occupation, 1945–1949* (Harvard University Press, Cambridge, Mass., 1995).

Paul Preston, *Franco: A biography* (HarperCollins, London, 1993).

Gareth Pritchard, *The making of the GDR, 1945–1953: From antifascism to Stalinism* (Manchester University Press, Manchester, 2000).

Jean-Pierre Rioux, *The Fourth Republic, 1944–1958* (Cambridge University Press, Cambridge, 1987).

I. D. Turner (ed.), *Reconstruction in post-war Germany: British occupation policy and the Western Zones, 1945–55* (Berg, Oxford, 1988).

Richard Vinen, *Bourgeois politics in France, 1945–1951* (Cambridge University Press, Cambridge, 1995).

S. J. Woolf (ed.), *The rebirth of Italy, 1943–50* (Longman, London, 1972).

Western Europe in the 1950s

Some books listed under "Postwar Europe, 1945–1950" also apply.

Matthew Connelly, *A diplomatic revolution: Algeria's fight for independence and the origins of the post-Cold War era* (Oxford University Press, Oxford, 2002).

Christopher Duggan and Christopher Wagstaff (eds.), *Italy in the Cold War: Politics, culture and society, 1948–1958* (Berg, Oxford, 1995).

Alistair Horne, *A savage war of peace: Algeria 1954–1962* (Macmillan, London, 1977).

Ronald Irving, *Adenauer* (Longman, London, 2002).

Patrick Major, *The Death of the KPD: Communism and anti-Communism in West Germany, 1945–1956* (Oxford University Press, Oxford, 1997).

Robert G. Moeller (ed.), *West Germany under construction: Politics, society and culture in the Adenauer era* (University of Michigan Press, Ann Arbor, 1997).

A. J. Nicholls, *Freedom with responsibility: The social market economy in Germany, 1918–1963* (Oxford University Press, Oxford, 1994).

John Ramsden, *The age of Churchill and Eden, 1940–1957* (Longman, London, 1995).

Hanna Schissler (ed.), *The miracle years: A cultural history of West Germany, 1949–1968* (Princeton University Press, Princeton, 2001).

Hans-Peter Schwarz, *Konrad Adenauer*, 2 vols. (Berghahn, Oxford, 1995).

Western Europe in the 1960s

Serge Berstein, *The Republic of de Gaulle, 1958–1969* (Cambridge University Press, Cambridge, 1993).

Carole Fink et al. (eds.), *1968: The world transformed* (Cambridge University Press, Cambridge, 1998).

Ronald Fraser et al., *1968: A student generation in revolt* (Chatto & Windus, London, 1988).

Jean Lacouture, *De Gaulle, the ruler, 1945–1970* (Harvill, London, 1993).

Robert Lumley, *States of emergency: Cultures of revolt in Italy from 1968 to 1978* (Verso, London, 1990).

Arthur Marwick, *The Sixties: Cultural revolution in Britain, France, Italy and the United States, c.1958–1974* (Oxford University Press, Oxford, 1998).

Kristin Ross, *May '68 and its afterlives* (University of Chicago Press, Chicago, 2002).

The Soviet Union and Eastern Europe, 1953–1970

Edwin Bacon and Mark Sandle (eds.), *Brezhnev reconsidered* (Palgrave Macmillan, Basingstoke, 2002).

David Crowley and Susan E. Reid (eds.), *Socialist spaces: Sites of everyday life in the Eastern Bloc* (Berg, Oxford, 2002).

François Fejtő, *A history of the People's Democracies: Eastern Europe since Stalin* (Penguin, Harmondsworth, 1974).

Charles Gati, *Hungary and the Soviet bloc* (Duke University Press, Durham, NC, 1986).

Bennett Kovrig, *Communism in Hungary: From Kun to Kádár* (Hoover Institution Press, Stanford, 1979).

Gyorgy Litvan (ed.), *The Hungarian revolution of 1956: Reform, revolt and repression, 1953–1963* (Longman, London, 1996).

Susan E. Reid and David Crowley (eds.), *Style and socialism: Modernity and material culture in post-war eastern Europe* (Berg, Oxford, 2000).

Dennison Rusinow, *The Yugoslav experiment, 1948–1974* (C. Hurst, London, 1977).

Timothy W. Ryback, *Rock around the Bloc: A history of rock music in eastern Europe and the Soviet Union* (Oxford University Press, New York, 1990).

H. Gordon Skilling, *Czechoslovakia's interrupted revolution* (Princeton University Press, Princeton, 1976).

William Taubman, *Khrushchev: The man and his era* (W. W. Norton, New York, 2003).

W. J. Tompson, *Khrushchev: A political life* (Macmillan, Basingstoke, 1995).

Kieran Williams, *The Prague Spring and its aftermath: Czechoslovak politics 1968–1970* (Cambridge University Press, Cambridge, 1997).

Europe in the 1970s

Serge Berstein and Jean-Pierre Rioux, *The Pompidou years, 1969–1974* (Cambridge University Press, Cambridge, 2000).
Claire Duchen, *Feminism in France: From May '68 to Mitterrand* (Routledge, London, 1986).
J. R. Frears, *France in the Giscard presidency* (George Allen & Unwin, London, 1981).
Timothy Garton Ash, *In Europe's name: Germany and the divided continent* (Jonathan Cape, London, 1993).
Barbara Marshall, *Willy Brandt: A political biography* (Macmillan, Basingstoke, 1997).
Kenneth Maxwell, *The making of Portuguese democracy* (Cambridge University Press, Cambridge, 1995).
Robert C. Meade, *Red Brigades: The story of Italian terrorism* (Macmillan, Basingstoke, 1990).
Víctor M. Pérez Díaz, *The return of civil society: The emergence of democratic Spain* (Harvard University Press, Cambridge, Mass., 1993).
Paul Preston, *The triumph of democracy in Spain* (Methuen, London, 1986).
John Ramsden, *The winds of change: Macmillan to Heath, 1957–1975* (Longman, London, 1995).
M. E. Sarotte, *Dealing with the devil: East Germany, détente and Ostpolitik, 1969–1973* (University of North Carolina Press, Chapel Hill, 2001).
Vincent Wright (ed.), *Continuity and change in France* (George Allen & Unwin, London, 1984).

Europe in the 1980s

Thomas C. Bruneau and Alex Macleod, *Politics in contemporary Portugal: Parties and the consolidation of democracy* (L. Reinner, Boulder, Colo., 1986).
John Campbell, *Margaret Thatcher*, 2 vols. (Jonathan Cape, London, 2000, 2003).
Karl H. Cerny (ed.), *Germany at the polls: The Bundestag elections of the 1980s* (Duke University Press, Durham, NC, 1990).
Clay Clemens and William E. Paterson (eds.), *The Kohl chancellorship* (Frank Cass, London, 1998).
Richard Clogg (ed.), *Greece 1981–1989: The populist decade* (Macmillan, Basingstoke, 1993).
Paul Heywood, *The government and politics of Spain* (Macmillan, London, 1995).
Mairi Maclean, *The Mitterrand years: Legacy and evaluation* (Macmillan, Basingstoke, 1998).
Wayne Northcutt, *Mitterrand: A political biography* (Holmes & Meier, New York, 1992).
John Vickers and Vincent Wright (eds.), *The politics of privatisation in western Europe* (Frank Cass, London, 1988).

European Integration

Stephen George, *An awkward partner: Britain in the European Community* (Oxford University Press, Oxford, 2nd edn. 1994).
John Gillingham, *European integration, 1950–2003: Superstate or new market economy?* (Cambridge University Press, Cambridge, 2003).

Charles Grant, *Delors: Inside the house that Jacques built* (Nicholas Brealey, London, 1994).

Alan S. Milward, *The European rescue of the nation state* (Routledge, London, 2nd edn. 2000).

Andrew Moravcsik, *The choice for Europe: Social purpose and state power from Messina to Maastricht* (UCL Press, London, 1998).

George Ross, *Jacques Delors and European integration* (Polity, Cambridge, 1995).

Larry Siedentop, *Democracy in Europe* (Allen Lane, London, 2001).

Peter M. R. Stirk, *A history of European integration since 1914* (Pinter, London, 1996).

Derek W. Urwin, *The community of Europe: A history of European integration since 1945* (Longman, London, 2nd edn. 1995).

The Fall of Communism

Neal Ascherson, *The Polish August: The self-limiting revolution* (Allen Lane, London, 1981).

Archie Brown, *The Gorbachev factor* (Oxford University Press, Oxford, 1997).

Lenard J. Cohen, *Broken bonds: The disintegration of Yugoslavia* (Westview, Boulder, Colo., 1993).

Aleš Erjavec (ed.), *Postmodernism and the postsocialist condition: Politicized art under late socialism* (University of California Press, Berkeley, 2003).

Mary Fulbrook, *Anatomy of a dictatorship: Inside the GDR, 1949–1989* (Oxford University Press, Oxford, 1995).

Mark Galeotti, *Gorbachev and his revolution* (Macmillan, Basingstoke, 1997).

Timothy Garton Ash, *The Polish revolution: Solidarity* (Granta, London, rev. edn. 1991).

Misha Glenny, *The rebirth of history: Eastern Europe in the age of democracy* (Penguin, Harmondsworth, 1990).

Konrad H. Jarausch, *The rush to German unity* (Oxford University Press, Oxford, 1994).

Padraic Kenney, *A carnival of revolution: Central Europe 1989* (Princeton University Press, Princeton, 2002).

David Lane, *Soviet society under perestroika* (Routledge, London, rev. edn. 1992).

Jacques Lévesque, *The enigma of 1989: The USSR and the liberation of eastern Europe* (University of California Press, Berkeley, 1997).

Anatol Lieven, *The Baltic revolution: Latvia, Lithuania, Estonia and the path to independence* (Yale University Press, New Haven, 1993).

Corey Ross, *The East German dictatorship: Problems and perspectives in the interpretation of the GDR* (Arnold, London, 2002).

M. E. Sarotte, *1989: The struggle to create post–Cold War Europe* (Princeton University Press, Princeton, 2009).

Vladimir Tismaneanu (ed.), *The revolutions of 1989* (London, Routledge, 1999).

Europe since the Cold War

Kenneth Dyson (ed.), *European states and the euro: Europeanization, variation and convergence* (Oxford University Press, Oxford, 2002).

Barbara Einhorn, *Cinderella goes to market: Citizenship, gender and women's movements in east central Europe* (Verso, London, 1993).

Paul Ginsborg, *Italy and its discontents: Family, civil society, state, 1980–2001* (Penguin, London, 2001).

Misha Glenny, *The fall of Yugoslavia: The Third Balkan War* (Penguin, London, 1992).

James Gow, *Triumph of the lack of will: International diplomacy and the Yugoslav war* (Hurst, London, 1997).

Dale R. Herspring (ed.), *Putin's Russia: Past imperfect, future uncertain* (Rowman & Littlefield, Lanham, Mass., 2003).

Klaus Larres (ed.), *Germany since unification: The development of the Berlin Republic* (Palgrave Macmillan, Basingstoke, 2nd edn. 2001).

Anatol Lieven, *Chechnya: Tombstone of Russian power* (Yale University Press, New Haven, 1998).

Donald Sassoon (ed.), *Looking left: European socialism after the Cold War* (I. B. Tauris, London, 1997).

Robert Service, *Russia: Experiment with a people* (Macmillan, London, 2002).

Lilia Shevtsova, *Yeltsin's Russia: Myths and reality* (Carnegie Endowment, Washington, DC, 1999).

Laura Silber and Allan Little, *The death of Yugoslavia* (Penguin, London, 1995).

Paul Taylor, *The European Union in the 1990s* (Oxford University Press, Oxford, 1996).

Loukas Tsoukalis, *What kind of Europe?* (Oxford University Press, Oxford, 2003).

Europe in the New Millennium

Brad K Blitz (ed.), *War and change in the Balkans* (Cambridge University Press, Cambridge, 2006).

Kenneth Dyson (ed.), *The Euro at 10: Europeanization, power and convergence,* (Oxford University Press, Oxford, 2008).

Andrew Geddes, *The Politics of Migration and Immigration in Europe* (SAGE, 2003).

Andre Gingrich and Marcus Banks (eds.), *Neo-nationalism in Europe and beyond: perspectives from social anthropology* (Berghahn, Oxford, 2006).

Paul Ginsborg, *Silvio Berlusconi: Television, power and patrimony* (Verso, London, 2004).

Jack Hayward (ed.), *Leaderless Europe* (Oxford University Press, Oxford, 2008).

Nick Hewlett, *The Sarkozy phenomenon* (Societas, 2011).

Justine Lacroix and Kalypso Nicolaides (eds.), *European Stories: Intellectual debates on Europe in national contexts* (Oxford University Press, Oxford, 2010).

Geir Lundestad (ed.), *Just another major crisis? The United States and Europe since 2000* (Oxford University Press, Oxford, 2008).

Andrea Mammone and Giuseppe A. Veltri, *Italy today: The sick man of Europe* (Routledge, London, 2010).

Richard Sakwa, *The crisis of Russian democracy: The dual state, factionalism and the Medvedev succession* (Cambridge University Press, Cambridge, 2011).

Paul Williams, *Memorial Museums: The global rush to commemorate atrocities* (Berg, Oxford, 2007).

Index

Page numbers in *italics* denote figures and "n" followed by page numbers denote Notes.

Abkhazia, 267
abortion, 103, 109, 124, 126, 149–50, 151, 240, 251
Abyssinia, 6, 11
Action Party (Italy), 59
Adenauer, Konrad, 26, 57, 58, 77, 78, 79, 83, 84, 87, 88–9, 91, 107, 108, 111, 145, 151, *191*, 192, 195
affluence, 75–6, 81, 82
Afghanistan, 142, 167, 214, 251, 256, 258
ageing, 236, 259–60, 273
Agrarian Party (Sweden), 95, 96
agriculture, 4, 20, 40, 43, 64, 65, 81, 104, 124, 128, 132–3, 163, 193, 197, 250
Ahern, Bertie, 270
AK. *see* Home Army
Akhmatova, Anna, 47
Albania, 16, 66, 135, 207, 238, 245
Albanians, ethnic group, 133, 206–7, 228
Algeria, 52, 80, 84, 91–4, 100, 110, 228
Algiers, Battle of, 1957, 92
Alliance of Free Democrats (AFD), 216
Alliance of Young Democrats (FIDESZ), 216
Alleanza Nazionale (AN) (Italy), 231, 233, 234, 264

Allied Control Commission (for Germany), 37, 39
Almodóvar, Pedro, 166
Al-Qaeda, 256, 257
Alsace-Lorraine, 10
Althusser, Louis, 100
American Federation of Labour/ Congress of Industrial Organisations (AFL/CIO), 43
anarchism, 2, 101, 102, 112, 115, 156
Andreotti, Giulio, 233
Angola, 117, 141, 160
Antonioni, Michelangelo, 101
Andropov, Yuri, 133, 211, 212
Antall, Josef, 217, 239
anti-Americanism, 76, 110, 112, 184
anti-communism, 54, 55, 66, 76, 87, 102, 129, 160, 168, 234, 239
anti-globalization, 280
anti-nuclear protest, 75, 102, 149, 179
anti-Semitism, 5, 12, 16, 26, 111, 131, 207, 208, 239. *see also* Holocaust
Anti-Terror Liberation Groups (GAL), 184
"Arab Spring", 2011, 259, 267
Aragon, Louis, 76
architecture, 165

Europe's Troubled Peace: 1945 to the Present, Second Edition. Tom Buchanan.
© 2012 John Wiley & Sons, Ltd. Published 2012 by John Wiley & Sons, Ltd.

Ardennes, offensive, 1944, 17
Argentina, 167, 169
Arias Navarro, Carlos, 157
Armed Forces Movement (MFA),
        (Portugal), 159
Armenia, 214, 223, 268, 288n
Aron, Raymond, 49, 106
Arrow Cross, 17
Ashton, Baroness, 258
asylum, 180, 228, 235, 251
Athens Polytechnic, 1973 massacre, 118
Atlantic Charter, 30, 32
Atlanticism, 76, 174, 176, 195
Attlee, Clement, 33
Auroux Law, 173
Auschwitz, 11, 23, 27, *253*
Austria, 54, 68, 73–4, 95, 147, 148, 151,
        178–9, 180, 194, 198, 220, 228, 229,
        231, 251, 264, 265, 266, 268
Austrian Freedom Party (FPO), 180,
        231, 264
Azerbaijan, 214, 249
Aznar, José Maria, 231, 283
Azores, 22, 65

Baader, Andreas, 99, 154
Baader-Meinhof gang. *see* Red Army
        Faction
Bad Godesberg, SPD congress, 1959, 94–5
Badoglio, Marshal Pietro, 58
Bahr, Egon, 143, 144
Bahro, Rudolf, 219
Balcerowicz, Leszek, 216
Barbie, Klaus, 27
Barcelona, 1951 strike, 79
Baku, 1990 violence in, 214
Baldwin, Stanley, 3
Balkan region, 17, 18, 32, 122, 178, 226,
        242–6, 248
Baltic States, 12, 23, 31, 52, 137, 208, 214,
        223–4, 238, 248, 251, 254, 267,
        288n. *see also* Estonia; Latvia;
        Lithuania
Bank Deutscher Länder, 58
Bank of England, 229
Barbarossa, Operation, 1941, 8, 10, 16
Barre, Raymond, 147, 150

Barroso, José Manuel, 274, 291n
Barthes, Roland, 100
Basque country (Spanish), 117, 153, 158,
        184, 233, 257
Baudrillard, Jean, 165
Bauhaus, 6
Beatles, 101
Beauvoir, Simone de, 77
Beckett, Samuel, 78
Belarus, 12, 240, 249
Belgium, 6, 10, 13, 14, 19, 20, 21, 28, 40, 53,
        54, 77, 80, 84, 102, 151, 202, 249
Bell, Daniel, 285n
Benelux, 44, 193. *see also* Belgium;
        Luxembourg; Netherlands
Beneš, Edvard, 20, 68, 71
Benjamin, Walter, 6
Benn, Tony, 169
Beria, Lavrenty, 68, 126
Berisha, Sali, 238
Berlin
    Battle of, 1945, 18, 53
    Berlin, East, 1989 protests in, 220–221
    Berlin Wall, 82, 85–6, *85–6*, 107, 125, 143,
        215, 217, 220–221
    Berlin, West, 43, 84, 86, 112, 143, 144
    blockade, 1948–9, 37
    crisis of 1958–61, 84–6, 96, 111, 140
    Berlin, Free University, 112
    status of, 144, 222
Berlinguer, Enrico, 150
Berlusconi, Silvio, 181, 182, 231, 232, 234,
        247, 251, 261, 262–3, *263*, 290n
Bertolucci, Bernado, 155
Bessarabia, 31
Best, George, 102
Bevan, Aneurin, 95
Beveridge, William, 48, 61
Bevin, Ernest, 33, 41, 47
Beyen, Jan Willem, 192
Bidault, Georges, 41
Bidonvilles, 104, 112
Biermann, Wolf, 219
birth control, 105–6, 124, 126, 240
Blair, Tony, 179, 203, 230, 232, 256,
        248, 260
Böll, Heinrich, 100, 153, 155

Bonn, 58
Bosnia-Hercegovina, 1, 23, 219, 227, 242,
    244, 244, 245, 246, 258, 268
Bosnian Muslims, 23, 133, 228, 244, 245
Bosnian Serbs, 244–5, 256
Bossi, Umberto, 181, 232, 264
Brandt, Willy, 86, 88, 102, 107, 108, 140,
    141, 142–5, 144, 149, 150, 151,
    175, 177
Brazauskas, Algirdas, 239
Brecht, Bertolt, 6, 49
Breton autonomy, 14
Bretton Woods, 1944 conference, 41,
    146, 198
Brezhnev Doctrine, 1968, 138, 215
Brezhnev, Leonid, 131–3, 138, 139, 141,
    210, 211, 212, 213, 214, 287n
"BRIC" (Brazil, Russia, India
    and China), 259
Brown, Gordon, 260, 269
Brundtland, Gro Harlan, 164
Bruni, Carla, 262, 263
Brussels Pact, 1948, 44, 83
Budapest, Battle of, 1944, 18
Bujak, Zbigniew, 210
Bulgaria, 11, 18, 32, 33, 66, 68, 69, 72, 123,
    125, 143, 206, 208, 215, 217, 239,
    248, 250
Bulgarian Socialist Party, 217, 238
Bundesbank, 58, 147, 234, 235, 258
Bundnis '90, 180
Bush, George Snr, 222, 226
Bush, George W, 231, 256, 257
Butler, RA, 79
Byrnes, James, 38, 69

Caetano, Marcello, 118, 159
Callaghan, James, 150
Cameron, David, 266
Canada, 111
Carinthia, 180, 264
Car ownership, 4, 81, 123, 132
Carrero Blanco, Luis, 152
Casablanca, 1943 conference, 30
Cassa per il Mezzogiorno, 89
Castle, Barbara, 109
Carter, Jimmy, 141, 142, 167

Catalonia, 117, 158, 232, 249–50
Catalan language, 158
Catholic Action, 54, 77
Catholic Church/Catholics, 5, 14, 54,
    64–5, 70, 76–7, 89, 102–3, 117,
    125–6, 151, 154, 207, 209, 237,
    238, 240, 251, 254
Catholic University, Milan, 114
Caucasus region, 13, 24, 227, 268
Cavaco Silva, Anibal, 183
Ceaușescu, Nicolae, 162, 163, 248, 263–4
Central America, 47, 167, 174
CCOO (Workers' Commissions), 47
Central Intelligence Agency (CIA), 15,
    48–9, 60, 100, 156
Centre Union (Greece), 118
Ceuta, 268
CFDT (France), 112
Chaban-Delmas, Jacques, 149
Chabrol, Claude, 78
Chacon, Carme, 261, 262
Chad, 1983 French intervention, 174
Challe, Maurice, 93
Charter 77, 141–2, 207
Chechens, 24
Chechen Wars (1994–6 and 1999-?), 240,
    241, 242, 266
Chernenko, Konstantin, 212
Chernobyl, nuclear accident, 1986, 165,
    166, 212
Chernomyrdin, Victor, 241
Chetniks, 15, 28, 72
China, 46, 99, 120, 128, 135, 140, 141, 154,
    220, 239, 259, 273
Chirac, Jacques, 149, 171, 172, 174, 181,
    231, 256, 258, 268
Christian democracy, 20, 35, 54–5, 75, 76,
    82, 87, 103, 151, 152, 171, 190, 200
Christian Democrat Union (CDU), 51, 57,
    58, 88, 89, 98, 107, 108, 144, 151,
    175–9, 192, 231, 235, 260, 272
Christian Democrat Union (in East
    Germany), 221
Christian Democrat Party (Netherlands),
    77, 103
Christian Social Union (CSU), 57, 58, 88, 89,
    94, 107, 144, 151, 175–9, 180, 235

Churchill, Winston, 15, 22, 31, 32, 33, 51,
    90, 186, 286n
Cinema, 6, 78, 81, 155, 254
Citrine, Walter, 54
Civic Forum, 217
Clay, Lucius, 35, 38, 40
Clayton, Will, 40
Clinton, Bill, 227
Club Med, 81
Cockfield, Lord, 199, 201
Co-determination (FRG), 57, 79, 149
"Cohabitation", in French government,
    174, 175, 231
Cohn-Bendit, Daniel, 112, 114
Coldiretti, 77
Cold War, 2, 27, 30–50 passim, 54, 59, 60,
    66, 76, 82–6, 140, 167–8, 185, 202,
    214–15, 219, 225, 226, 233, 267,
    273, 285n
Collaboration (World War Two), 12–14,
    19, 28, 62, 76
Comecon, 122, 124, 125, 206, 237
Cominform, 41, 71, 72
Commission. see EEC/EU Commission
Committee for the Defence of Workers'
    Rights (KOR), Poland, 209
Committee for the Liberation of Northern
    Italy, 16
Committee for the Liberation of the
    Peoples of Russia, 13
Committee of Public Safety (Algiers), 93
Common Agricultural Policy (CAP), 104,
    163, 187, 193, 195, 196, 197, 198,
    199, 229
Common Foreign and Security Policy
    (CFSP), 202–3, 229, 258
Common Security and Defense Policy
    (EU), 258
Common Market. see European Economic
    Community (EEC)
Commonwealth (British), 194
Communism, 16, 120–39, 150–151,
    205–25, 231
Communist (Third) International, 32
Communist Party
    Austria, 73
    Belgium, 53

Bulgaria, 217
Czechoslovakia, 71, 136, 137, 138,
    217–18
Finland, 73
France (PCF), 48, 49, 53, 55, 56, 76, 83,
    94, 150–151, 172–5
Germany (KPD), 38, 58, 76
Greece, 34, 66–7, 160, 184
Hungary, 69, 130, 208, 216–17
Italy (PCI), 20, 53, 58–9, 60, 87, 100, 139,
    148, 150, 231
Poland, 70, 129, 131, 208–11, 216
Portugal, 151, 159, 160
Romania, 135
Spain (PCE), 150, 151, 158, 183
Soviet Union (CPSU), 24, 126, 127, 128,
    131, 132, 211–15, 223–4
Yugoslavia, 16, 72
Communist Refoundation, 231
Confédération Générale du Travail
    (France), 43, 56, 112
Confederation of Independent States
    (CIS), 224
Confederazione Generale Italiana de
    Lavoro, 43, 163
Conference on European Economic
    Cooperation (CEEC), 41, 42
Conference on Security and Cooperation
    in Europe (CSCE), 141, 217,
    227, 288n
Congress for Cultural Freedom (CCF),
    49, 100
Congress of People's Deputies (USSR), 213
Conservative Party (UK), 51, 87, 90–91,
    109, 147, 151–2, 162, 168, 169, 190,
    231, 272
Constantine, King, 118
Constitutional Court (FRG), 58, 150, 227
Convergència i Unión, 232
corruption, 182, 184, 232, 233, 234
Coty, René, 93
Council of Europe, 52, 118, 187, 249
Council of the Revolution [Portugal], 159,
    160, 182
"Counterpart funds" (ERP), 42
Court of Justice. see EEC/EU Court of
    Justice

Craxi, Bettino, 150, 182
Cresson, Edith, 174
Crimean Tartars, 214
Croatia, 14, 134, 135, 218, 242–6, 268, 289n
Croats, 5, 72, 208
Crosland, Anthony, 95, 147
Cruise Missiles, 142, 168
Cruyff, Johan, 102
Csurka, Istvan, 239, 289n
Cuba, 99, 214
Cuban missile crisis, 1963, 82, 111, 128
Culture, 5–6, 47–59, 77–8, 98–103, 154–6,
        158, 165–7, 207
Cyprus, 160, 161, 184, 229
Czechoslovakia, 3, 20, 28–9, 41, 52, 54, 68,
        70, 71, 99, 108, 120, 123, 125, 131,
        135, 136–9, 141, 143, 208, 213, 215,
        217–18, 228, 237, 238. see also
        Prague Spring, 1968
Czech lands, Protectorate of 1939–45, 10,
        12, 13–14, 16–17, 18, 26
Czech Republic, 227, 238, 239

Daimler–Benz, 221
D'Alema, Massimo, 265
Darlan, François, 16
Davies, Joseph, 31
Davignon Report, 197
Dayton, 1995 peace accords, 244, 245
D-Day, June 1944, 16, 18, 23, 174
Déat, Marcel, 13
Debray, Régis, 99
Debré, Michel, 110
decolonization, 84, 96
De Gasperi, Alcide, 71, 108
de Gaulle, Charles, 13, 14, 15, 16, 17, 20,
        28, 52, 55, 60, 75, 83, 84, 88, 93, 94,
        98, 102, 103, 109–11, 112–14, 115,
        141, 149, 151, 187, 190, 194, 195–7,
        204, 230
Degrelle, Léon, 10
Delgado, Gen. Humberto, 117
Delors, Jacques, 164, 173, 190, 199, 200,
        201, 203, 204, 227, 229, 260, 272,
        273
"Delors Packages", 1988 and 1992,
        201, 204

De Man, Henri, 13
democracy, 2, 3, 53–4, 87–8, 149, 156–61,
        170, 186, 190, 238
Democratic Army of Greece (DSE), 66
Democratic Party (Italy), 261, 265
Democratic Renewal Party (Portugal),
        182–3
Democrazia Cristiana (Italian Christian
        Democrat Party), 45, 58–50, 77, 87,
        89–90, 107, 114, 148, 150, 151, 154,
        182, 231, 233
de-militarization, German, 37–8, 39
de-Nazification, 27–8, 35, 37
Denmark, 10, 17, 18, 21, 23, 40, 44, 62–4,
        80, 152, 194, 198, 200, 202, 203, 232,
        235, 251, 252, 257, 264, 266
Department of Economic Affairs (DEA,
        UK), 108–9
Derrida, Jacques, 100
Der Spiegel affair, 1962, 89
De Sica, Vittorio, 78
De-Stalinization, 126–31
Détente, 140–145, 161, 167, 168, 171,
        185, 210
Deutschmark, 163, 198, 202, 235
devolution, 149, 232, 233, 249, 257, 260,
        285n
Die Linke, 261
dissidence, 125–6, 131, 133, 139, 141–2,
        207, 217, 220
divorce, 103, 109, 151
Djilas, Milovan, 123, 138, 279n
Djindjic, Zoran, 246
Dönitz, Admiral Karl, 18
Dooge Committee, 200
Drabble, Margaret, 106
Draft Treaty of European Union, 199
Dubček, Alexander, 124, 134, 136–9, 217
Dubrovnik, 1991–2 siege, 243
Duisenberg, Wim, 236
Dulles, John Foster, 84
Dunkirk treaty, 1947, 44
Dutschke, Rudi, 99, 102, 113, 115

EAM (Greece), 52, 66
Eanes, Ramalho, 160, 182
Eastern Front (WW2), 8, 17, 18, 19, 22, 23

East Germany. *see* German Democratic Republic (DDR)

École Nationale d'Administration (ENA), 62

Eco, Umberto, 98, 166

economy (European), 4, 40–45, 53, 54, 62, 78–82, 103–6, 124–5, 145–8, 162–5, 235–7, 250, 262, 269–74

Eden, Anthony, 33, 90–91

EDES (Greece), 66

education, 104, 109, 122, 173

Ehrenberg, Ilya, 127

Eichmann, Adolf, 26, 27

Einsatzgruppen, 10, 23

Eire (Republic of Ireland), 198, 200, 237, 269, 270, 271, 272

Eisenhower, Dwight D, 16, 46, 83, 84, 85, 194

Eisenman, Peter, 252

Eisenstein, Sergei, 47

ELAS (Greece), 47

Elf-Aquitaine, 164

Elizabeth II, Queen, 81, 155

Empire, European, 6–7, 52, 91–4, 117, 159–60

encounter, 49, 100

ENI (Ente Nazionale Idrocarburi), 89

"Enosis", 160

Ensslin, Gudrun, 99

environmentalism, 116, 119, 179–80, 206, 229

Enzensberger, Hans Magnus, 100

EOKA, 160

Erdogan, Recep Tayyip, 268

Erhard, Ludwig, 39, 57, 58, 62, 79, 88, 89, 107, 108, 190, 192, 194

Erice, Victor, 158

Erlander, Tage, 96

Estonia, 214, 267

ETA, 117, 152, 153, 154, 158, 184, 233, 257

"ethnic cleansing", 1, 245

Euratom, 190, 194

"Eurocommunism", 11111139, 150

euro, 228, 235, 236, 269–72, 273. *see also* European Monetary Union (EMU)

Euro-Mediterranean Partnership, 1995, 268

European Central Bank, 203, 235, 270

European Coal and Steel Community (ECSC), 56, 83, 187, 190, 192, 193, 194

European Convention on Human Rights (1950), 249

European Cooperation Agency (ECA), 42–4

European Court of Human Rights, 286n

European Court of Justice, 187, 193, 195

European Defence Community (EDC), 83–4, 187, 192, 193, 195

European Disneyland, 166

European Economic Community (EEC), 79, 80, 81, 88, 91, 95, 103, 104, 105, 111, 117, 122, 148, 152, 156, 161, 163, 171, 179, 182, 184, 186–204 passim, *188–9*, 227, 228–9, 230, 231, 235–7, 238, 243, 244, 248–52, 256, 258, 260, 265, 266, 267, 268, 269–71 passim, 288n. *see also* EC and EU

EEC/EU Commission, 190, 193, 195, 196, 198, 199, 200, 201, 203, 204, 229, 234, 258

EEC/EU Council, 197, 198, 199, 248

EEC/EU Council of Ministers, 193, 196, 197, 232

EEC Treaty. *see* Treaty of Rome, 1957

European Economic Area, 229

European Free Trade Area (EFTA), 116, 194, 195

European identity, 228–9, 252–6

European integration, 42, 52, 84, 110, 148, 156, 171, 174, 186–204, 221, 248, 269, 272, 273, 274

European Investment Bank, 193

"Europeanization", 229

"European model of society", 200

European Monetary System (EMS), 198, 202, 236

European Monetary Union (EMU), 148, 197, 198, 201, 202, 203, 234, 235–7, 269–72

European Overseas Development Fund, 193

European Parliament, 1, 193, 198, 199, 200, 201, 203, 252, 266

European Payments Union (EPU), 51, 95

European Recovery Programme. *see* Marshall Plan/European Recovery Programme
European Security and Defense Policy, 258
European Social Fund, 193
"Euroscepticism", 198, 201, 204
Eurovision Song Contest, 289n
Evian, negotiations, 1962, 94
Exchange Rate Mechanism (ERM), 163, 198, 204, 233, 236, 270
Existentialism, 47
Extra-parliamentary Opposition (APO), 100, 107, 115

Fabius, Laurent, 173
Fagerholm, Karl-August, 74
Falange, 65, 117
Falklands Islands, 1982 conflict, 167, 169
Fanfani, Amintore, 89
Fanon, Frantz, 99, 107
Fassbinder, Rainer Werner, 155
Fejtő, François, 139
Fellini, Federico, 155
feminism, 106, 116, 119, 123–4, 149–50, 166
Festival of Britain, 1951, 61
Fianna Fail, 21, 272
Fiat, 79, 103, 104, 132, 1614
Fini, Gianfranco, 241, 265
Finland, 11, 18, 62, 63, 68, 70, 73–4, 229, 237, 251, 265
"Finlandization", 74
Fischer, Joschka, 180, 248, 273
Flemish nationalism, 14, 232, 249
Flick, 62, 177
Fo, Dario, 101
Fontainebleau, 1984 summit, 199
Force Ouvrière, 56
Fortuyn, Pim, 228, 264, 265
Forza Italia!, 234, 264
Foucault, Michel, 100
"Fouchet Plan", 1962, 195, 196
Fraga, Manuel, 117
Frahm, H. *see* Brandt, Willy
France
    culture, 141, 154, 155, 160, 257, 268
    economy, 4, 55, 56, 60, 62, 79–80, 103, 146, 173, 175, 194, 261–2

Empire (including Algeria), 6, 13, 24, 52, 56, 84, 91–4, 193
European integration (attitude towards), 84, 192, 193, 195–7, 198, 203–4, 229–30, 235, 260, 268, 270, 281n, 289n
Fifth Republic, 75, 93–4, 109–11, 115–16, 171–5
foreign policy, 35, 39, 46, 55–6, 83, 84, 90, 111, 142, 168, 174, 184, 202, 227, 229, 256, 258
Fourth Republic, 55–6, 75, 80, 91–3, 110, 111, 172
"May '68", 111–16, 118, 232
politics, 3, 4, 41, 53, 55, 77, 91–4, 109–11, 112–13, 115–16, 147, 148, 149, 150, 151, 171–5, 181, 228, 231, 261, 262, 268
society, 5, 53, 61, 62, 77, 81, 104, 105, 106, 149–50, 194, 227, 274
Third Republic, 4, 13
World War Two, 10, 12, 13, 14, 16, 23, 24, 28, 155
Franco, Francisco, 21–2, 33, 64–6, 76, 79, 80–81, 117, 152, 156, 157, 157, 158, 159, 166, 183, 231, 255
Frank, Hans, 10
Frank, Karl Hermann, 27
"Frankfurt school", 100
Free Democrat Party (FDP), 56–7, 58, 89, 107, 108, 148, 175, 176, 261
Freedom Party (Dutch), 265
Friedman, Milton, 147

Gagarin, Yuri, 127
Gaitskell, Hugh, 95
Galbraith, JK, 75
Garzón, Baltasar, 255–6
Gastarbeiter, 104, 116, 134, 251
Gates, Robert, 273
Gaullism, 55, 56, 83, 92, 155, 174, 201, 231
Gaza, 258
Gdansk, 209
General Agreement on Tariffs and Trade (GATT), 195
Geneva, 1954 accords, 91, 194
Genscher, Hans Dietrich, 108, 176, 288n

Georgia, 214, 223, 267, 288n
Gerasimov, Gennardy, 215
German Democratic Republic (DDR), 29,
        35–9, 49, 63, 77, 84–6, 108, 120, 123,
        124, 125, 137, 143, 144, 145, 153,
        179, 180, 206, 207, 208, 215, 219–23,
        228, 234, 250, 261, 283n
Germany (Federal Republic / FRG). *see also*
        DDR; Nazism
    Basic Law, 1949, 57–8, 77, 87, 221, 228
    Basic Treaty, 1972, 144–5
    culture, 78, 155, 177
    economy, 4, 61–2, 75, 76, 79, 80, 103,
        107, 108, 145, 146, 147, 176–7, 223,
        234, 236–7, 250
    European integration (attitude towards),
        192, 198, 201, 203, 229–30, 235, 270,
        272, 289n
    foreign policy, 45, 56, 57, 83, 107–8,
        142–5, 176, 243
    formation of, 35–9
    politics, 54, 56–8, 77, 87–8, 94–5, 107–8,
        112, 115, 149, 151, 175–80, 231,
        234–5, 260–261, 272
    reunification, 143, 175, 179, 180, 202,
        208, 219–23, 230, 234–5
    society, 53, 76, 77, 81, 104, 105, 106, 115,
        150, 151, 153, 154, 164, 166, 193,
        228, 250, 251, 266, 274
Gerő, Ernő, 129
Gheorgu-Dej, Gheorge, 135
Gierek, Edward, 131, 209, 211
Giraud, Henri, 16
Giscard d'Estaing, Valery, 110, 142, 149,
        150, 151, 172, 198
"Glasnost", 212
"Globalization", 259
Globke, Hans, 88
Goa, 84
Goebbels, Josef, 26, 168
Goering, Herman, 26
Gomulka, Wladyslaw, 71, 129, 131, 137
González, Felipe, 158, 159, 183–4
Gorbachev, Mikhail, 132, 133, 139, 167,
        168, 171, 177, 205, 206, 207, 211–15,
        219, 220, 221, 223–4, 225, 230, 238,
        267, 288n

Gorbachev, Raisa, 212
Gosizdat, 133
Gottwald, Klement, 69, 71
Gramsci, Antonio, 100
Grand Coalition, Germany 1966–69, 107–8,
        115
Grand Coalition, Germany, 2005–09, 261
Grass, Günter, 100, 155
Greater London Council (GLC), 170
Greece, 11, 16, 19–20, 25, 32, 34, 45, 52,
        66–7, 81, 116, 118, 160–161, 184,
        195, 198, 199, 231, 237, 250, 270,
        271, 272
Greek Civil War, 32, 66–7, 74, 118
Green Party (Germany), 149, 176, 177,
        179–80, 231, *235*
Greenpeace, 174
Grenada, 1983 invasion, 167
Grenelle negotiations, 1968, 113
Gromyko, Andre, 132, 140, 213, 215
Grosz, Karoly, 216
Guerra, Alfonso, 183
Guevara, Ernesto "Che", 99
Guillaume, Günter, 145
Guineau-Bissau, 117, 159
Gulag (USSR), 67, 126, 127, 141
Gulf war, 1991, 174, 227
Gypsies. *see* Roma

Haas, Ernst B, 187
Habermas, Jürgen, 115, 252
Hague summit, 1969, 197
Haider, Jörg, 180, 181, 231, 264, 265
Halliday, Johnny, 101
Hallstein, Walter, 190, *191*, 195, 196
"Hallstein doctrine", 107–8, 282n
Hammarskjold, Dag, 63
Harkis, 94
Harriman, Averill, 32, 42
Hartz, Peter, 260
Havel, Václav, 125, 142, 217–18, 290n
Heath, Edward, 109, 147, 151–2, 168, 170
Helsinki accords, 1975, 141, 142, 249, 288n
Herri Batasuna, 153
Herzog, Werner, 155
Heseltine, Michael, 171
Heydrich, Reinhard, 11, 12, 16

Himmler, Heinrich, 10, 26
Historikerstreit, 155, 177–8
Hitler, Adolf, 2, 3, 4, 10, 16, 11118, 19, 22, 24, 26, 65, 108, 143, 252, 265
Hoffman, Paul, 42, 44
Holocaust, 10–11, 19, 23, 155, 177, 181, 245, 252, 253, 254
Home Army, Poland (AK), 15, 16, 20, 70
Homosexuality, 109, 166, 170, 265, 274
Honecker, Erich, 125, 177, 178, 220, 221
Horthy, Miklós, 17, 23
Howe, Sir Geoffrey, 169, 171
Hoxha, Enver, 135
Human rights, 102, 117, 139, 141, 167, 172, 186, 249, 255, 256, 258, 262, 267, 268, 286n.
Hungary, 11, 17, 23, 68, 69, 120, 124, 125, 126, 128–31, 138, 143, 206, 207, 208, 215, 216–17, 220, 227, 237, 239, 249, 251, 252, 254, 267
Hungarian Democratic Forum (MDF), 216, 217, 239
Hungarian Justice Party, 289n
Hungarian Socialist Party, 217, 238
Hungarian uprising, 1956, 71, 76, 90, 128–31, 130, 133, 208, 216
Hungarians, 5, 135, 207, 217, 235, 279n
Husák, Gustav, 136, 138, 217, 218

Iceland, 45, 269, 272
IG Farben, 11, 62
Iliescu, Ion, 218, 239
Ioannidis, Dimitrios, 160
immigration, 80–81, 84, 158, 180, 181, 214, 227, 251–2, 259–60, 264–6, 269
India, 6, 52, 128, 259
Indochina, 52, 67, 84, 91, 92. see also Vietnam
Indonesia, 52
industrial unrest and strikes, 56, 79, 104, 109, 112–13, 114–15, 117, 123, 125, 131, 146, 152, 164, 170, 174, 209, 210, 232
Institute for Industrial Reconstruction (IR), 61, 164
Intermediate Nuclear Forces Treaty (INF), 1987, 168

International Criminal Tribunal for the Former Yugoslavia, 27, 246, 256
International Military Tribunal. see Nuremberg trials
International Monetary Fund (IMF), 41, 150, 238, 271
International Trade Organisation (ITO), 41
Ionesco, Eugène, 78
Iran, 34, 112, 257
Iraq war, 2003, 229, 256, 257, 258, 260, 261
Ireland, Republic of. see Eire
Irish Free State, 21–2
Irish Republican Army (IRA), 152–4, 257
Irwin (Slovenia), 207
Italy
    culture, 6, 78, 82
    economy, 59, 60, 80, 103, 115, 146, 163, 195, 233, 236
    Empire, 6
    European integration (attitude towards), 193, 198, 236, 270
    foreign policy, 45, 59, 182
    politics (post-1945), 41, 43, 52, 54, 58–60, 77, 87, 89–90, 107, 112, 114–15, 116, 148, 149, 181, 182, 231, 233–4, 249, 261, 263–4
    society, 5, 61, 77, 82, 104, 105, 106, 114, 146, 150, 151, 228, 249, 250, 251, 252
    World War Two, 11, 16, 17, 18, 20, 25, 28, 32, 58
Izetbegovic, Alija, 244

Jakeš, Miloš, 217
Japan, 6, 11, 19, 30, 33, 52, 146
Jaruzelski, Wojciech, 210–211, 215, 216, 288n
Jencks, Charles, 165, 167
Jenkins, Roy, 196
Jews, 5, 10, 12, 14, 116, 23, 25, 26, 54, 62, 88, 135, 141, 177, 252
John XXIII, Pope, 89, 102
John Paul II, 209
Joseph, Keith, 169
Jospin, Lionel, 231, 261
Juan de Bourbon, 65, 117

Juan Carlos, king of Spain, 65, 117, 156, 157, 157, 159
Juppé, Alain, 232, 262
Justice and Development Party (AKP), 268

Kaczyński, Lech, 254
Kádár, Janos, 71, 125, 130, 131, 215, 216, 283n
Kadyrov, Ramzan, 266
Kania, Stanisłaus, 219
Karadžić, Radovan, 256
Karamanlis, Constantine, 160, 161, 184
Katyn, massacres, 23, 32, 69, 207, 254
Kazakhstan, 24, 289n
KGB, 132, 224, 241
Keeler, Christine, 91
Kelly, Petra, 180
Kennan, George, 33
Kennedy, John F, 85, 86, 89, 196
Keynes, John Maynard, 4, 48
Keynesianism, 108, 146–7, 150, 169
Khodorkovsky, Mikhail, 266
Khrushchev, Nikolai, 82, 85, 120, 122, 126–31, 135, 139, 212, 282n
Kielce, pogrom, 26
Kiesinger, Kurt Georg, 107
Kirienko, Sergei, 241
Kirkpatrick, Ivone, 28
Kissinger, Henry, 131–2, 140, 159, 258
Klaus, Václav, 171, 208
Klemperer, Victor, 49
Koestler, Arthur, 71
Kohl, Helmut, 145, 151, 174, 175–9, 178, 190, 202, 221, 222, 228, 231, 234, 235, 236, 272
Korean War, 1950–53, 43, 46, 72, 79, 82, 126
Kosovo, 133, 206–7, 218–19, 227, 245–6, 250, 267
Kosovo Liberation Army (KLA), 245, 246
Koštunica, Vojislav, 246
Kosygin, Alexei, 125, 132
"Kosygin reforms", 125, 132
Kouchner, Bernard, 262
Krajina, 242, 245
Kravchenko, Victor, 48
Kreisky, Bruno, 148

Krenz, Egon, 219, 229, 221
Krupp, 62
Kundera, Milan, 69, 138
Kurds, 268
Kuroń, Jacek, 139, 209
Kursk, 1943 battle of, 17
KVP (Netherlands), 103
Kwaśnieski, Alexander, 239

Labour Party (Norway), 63
Labour Party (UK), 33, 35, 52, 53, 54, 60, 61, 90, 94, 95, 104, 108–9, 147, 148, 149, 150, 168, 169, 171, 179, 190, 198, 236, 260
Lacan, Jacques, 100
Lafontaine, Oskar, 221, 223, 235
Laibach (Slovenian rock group), 207
Lambsdorff, Otto von, 176
Lampedusa, 268
Landsbergis, Vytautas, 239
Lang, Jack, 166
Largac, environmental dispute, 148
Lario, Veronica, 264
Lasky, Melvin, 49
Latvia, 208, 214, 223, 254. see also Baltic states
Laval, Pierre, 13, 28
Law on Historical Memory (Spain), 255
Le Pen, Jean Marie, 181, 231, 261, 262, 264, 265
League of Communists (Yugoslavia), 72, 134
League of Nations, 3, 6
Lebed, Alexander, 240
Lefebvre, Archbishop Marcel, 103
Lego, 80
Lehman Brothers, 269, 272
Leipzig, 1989 protests, 220
Lend-Lease, 19, 33
Lenin, V.I., 32, 127, 133, 208, 212
Lenin Shipyard, Gdansk, 209
Leningrad, siege of, 1941–4, 24
Leopold III (Belgium), 20
Lepper, Andrzej, 229
Lévi-Strauss, Claude, 100
Levy, Bernard-Henri, 100
liberalism, 48, 61–2

Liberal Party (UK), 179, 272
Liberation Theology, 102
Libya, 33, 168, 257
Lidice, 1942 massacre, 17, 27
Lie, Trygve, 63
Liga Venetia, 181
Ligachev, Yigor, 212
Lip, factory occupation, 148
Lisbon Treaty, 2007, 248, 258
Lithuania, 68, 70, 208, 223, 224, 239. see also
        Baltic states
Litvinenko, Alexander, 266
Live Aid, 1985, 165
LO (Sweden), 95, 96
Loach, Ken, 101
Locarno, 1925 Treaty, 3
Lombard League, 181
Lombardy, 181, 232
Lublin, Polish government, 1944, 20, 32
Luns, Joseph, 195, 196
Luxembourg, 250
"Luxembourg Compromise", 1966,
        196, 200
Lyotard, Jean-François, 154, 165
Lysenko, Trofim Denisovich, 48

Maastricht, 1991 Treaty on European
        Union, 174, 175, 190, 191, 201,
        202–4, 226, 227, 229, 232, 235,
        258, 288n
Macedonia, Former Yugoslav Republic of,
        72, 231, 246, 258
Macmillan, Harold, 76, 83, 90, 91, 102,
        195, 196
Madagascar, 52
Madrid, March 2004 bombing, 257, 261
Mafia, 233
Major, John, 203, 204, 231
Makarios, Archbishop, 160
Malaysia, 52
Malenkov, Georgi, 126
Malle, Louis, 155
Malmédy, 1944 massacre, 23
Malta, 229, 268
Mandelson, Peter, 260, 291n
Mann, Thomas, 49
Mao/Maoism, 99, 100, 112, 135, 148

Maquis, 15
Marchais, George, 151
Marcuse, Herbert, 99
Marshall, Gen. George, 40, 41
Marshall Plan/European Recovery
        Programme, 39, 40–45, 50, 52, 54,
        60, 61, 64, 65, 74, 79, 239
Martens, Wilfred, 171
Marx, Karl, 171
Marxism, 100–101, 122, 134, 154, 183, 206
Masaryk, Jan, 71
Massu, Jacques, 92, 114
Matica Hrvatska, 134
Mattei, Enrico, 89
Mauroy, Pierre, 172, 173
Mazière, Lothar de, 221
Mazowiecki, Tadeusz, 216
Meciar, Vladimir, 238
Medvedev, Dmitry, 267
Medvedev, Roy, 96, 133
Meidener, Rudolf, 96
Melilla, 268
Memorial, 208
Mendès-France, Pierre, 34, 92, 93
Merkel, Angela, 257, 261, 266, 272
Merten, Max, 81
Messina, 1955 conference, 192, 193
Michnik, Adam, 209
Mihailović, Draža, 28
Mikołaijcyzk, Stanisław, 70
Milan, corruption in, 182, 233
Milan, AC. Football club, 234
Military Council of National Salvation,
        Poland, 1981, 211
Milošević, Slobodan, 207, 218, 242, 245,
        246, 256
Mindszenty, Archbishop, 70
Mitsotakis, Theodore, 171
Mittag, Günter, 219
Mitterrand, Francois, 1, 7, 12, 93, 106,
        110, 111, 114, 148, 151, 162, 163,
        164, 166, 168, 171–5, 181, 190, 199,
        200, 202, 203–4, 222, 227, 272,
        285n, 286n
Mladenov, Petr, 217
Mladić, Ratko, 256
Mlynář, Zdeněk, 124, 137, 139, 212

Moch, Jules, 56
Modernism, 165
Modrow, Hans, 221
Moldova, 288n
Mollet, Guy, 84, 92, 93
Molotov, Vyacheslav, 35, 41, 68
Monetarism, 147, 150, 169
Monnet, Jean, 187, 190, *191*, 192, 194, 199
Monnet Plan, 42, 60, 62, 74
Montenegro, 242, 268
Moravia, Alberto, 17
Morgenthau Plan, 37
Moro, Aldo, 90, 107, 152, 153, 154
Morocco, 6, 268
Moscow State University, 139, 212
Moscow Treaty, 1968, 138
Moscow treaty, 1970, 143
Mostar, 1994 conflict in, 245
Moulin, Jean, 16, 27
Mouvement Républicain Populaire (MRP),
       55, 56
Mozambique, 117, 141, 160
MSI (Italy), 51, 59, 89
multiculturalism, 165, 252, 258, 265, 266
Munich, 1938 agreement, 3, 20, 51, 68
Murdoch, Rupert, 164
Muslims, 228, 230, 257–8, 265, 268
Mussert, Anton, 10
Mussolini, 2, 3, 11, 17, 22, 28, 59, 60, 65, 87
Mutual Defence Assistance Programme, 43

Nagorno-Karabakh, 214
Nagy, Imre, 124, 128, 129, 130, 131, 216
Nanterre University, 112
Nasser, Gamal Abdel, 84, 90, 91
National Council of the Resistance (CNR),
       16, 55
National Democratic Party (NDP)
       (FRG), 107
National Economic Development Council
       (NEDC), 91
National Front (Czech), 51, 70, 137
National Front (France), 174, 175, 181, 262
National Health Service (UK), 61, 170
Nationalisation, 61, 66, 72–3, 74, 83, 114,
       115, 208
National Liberation Front (FLN), 91–4, 99

National Salvation Front (Romania), 218
Nazism, 4, 5, 6, 8–29 passim, 53, 88, 155,
       177, 178, 180, 181, 207, 252
Nazi-Soviet Pact, 1939, 3, 13, 16, 31, 207,
       214, 252
Negri, Antonio, 149
neo-liberalism, 162, 163, 164, 168, 183, 234,
       238, 265
neo-Realism, 47, 78
Netherlands, 6, 10, 13, 18, 20, 21, 23, 25, 52,
       54, 77, 80, 103, 105, 143, 168, 202,
       228, 237, 251, 252, 260, 264, 266,
       268, 274
"New Cold War", 167–8, 285n
New Democracy (Germany), 100, 184
New Economic Mechanism
       (Hungary), 125
New Forum (DDR), 221
New Labour (UK), 179, 230, 260. see also
       Labour Party
New Left, 102
"New Philosophers", 154
9/11, attacks in New York and
       Washington, 247, 256, 265
Nixon, Richard, 98, 140, 141, 146
Non-alignment, 73, 133
Nordic Council, 63, 74
"Normalisation" (Czechoslovakia), 138
Normandy, battle of, 1944, 18, 24
North Atlantic Treaty, 1949, 44–6, 111
North Atlantic Treaty Organisation
       (NATO), 44–7, 50, 60, 63, 65, 83,
       84, 87, 89, 94, 111, 142, 150, 161,
       168, 174, 176, 179, 183, 184, 196,
       201, 202, 222, 226, 227, 230, 238,
       245, 246, 249, 256–9, 267, 273
North Sea, oil and gas, 146
Northern Ireland, 102, 152, 153, 154, 232–
       3, 249, 264, 265
Northern League, 181, 231, 232, 233, 234,
       249, 264, 265
Norway, 10, 18, 20, 21, 44–5, 62–4, 142,
       164, 194, 198, 229, 251, 274
Nouvelle Droite, 265
Nouvelle Vague, 78
Novocherkassk, 1962 disturbances in, 122
Novotný, Antonín, 136

nuclear power, 146, 165, 176, 179, 192, 235
nuclear weapons, 33, 46, 67, 82, 83, 84, 95,
        111, 141, 142, 167, 168, 171, 174,
        176, 214, 227
Nuremberg Trials, 26–7, 62, 88

OAS (Secret Army Organisation), 93, 94, 114
Obama, Barack, 257, 258
Oberländer, Theodor, 88
Ohnesorg, Benno, 112
Olive Tree Alliance, 234
OPEC (Organisation of Oil Exporting
        Countries), 145, 147
Open University (UK), 109
Ophuls, Marcel, 155
Opus Dei, 81
Oradour, 1944 massacre, 23, 27
Orange Alternative (Wroclaw), 207
Organisation for Economic Efficiency and
        Cooperation (OEEC), 42, 61, 194
Orban, Viktor, 216, 249, 254
Orlando, Leoluca, 233
Orwell, George, 49, 208
Osborne, John, 77
Ostpolitik, 99, 108, 122, 142–5, 168, 176,
        177, 211
O'Toole, Fintan, 270

"Padania", 232
Palach, Jan, 138
Palme, Olof, 82, 96, 148
Pamuk, Orhan, 268
Pamyat, 207
Pan-European Union, 186
Papadopolous, 118, 160
Papandreou, Andreas, 161, 184, 199
Papandreou, George, 66, 118, 184
Papon, Maurice, 27
Paris
    1944 liberation, 14
    1968 "events", 98, 111, 112–13, 118
    1963 treaty of, 89
Parri, Ferruccio, 59
Partisans (Yugoslavia), 14, 15, 134
Partido Popular (Spain), 183, 231, 261
Partito Popolari (Italy), 59
Partnerships for Peace, 227

PASOK (Pan Hellenic Socialist Party), 161,
        184, 199, 231, 271
Pasolini, Pier Paolo, 114
Pasternak, Boris, 127, 208
Patocka, J, 142
PDS (Italy), 231, 233
Peasants Party (Poland), 70
People Against Violence (Slovakia), 217
People's Party (Austria), 73, 103, 151, 231
People's Party (Denmark), 232, 264, 265
Perestroika, 206, 212, 217, 223
Pershing missiles, 142, 168
Petain, Marshal, 10, 12, 13, 15, 28
Petkov, Nikola, 69
Petofi circle, 129
Pflimlin, Pierre, 93
Picasso, Pablo, 48
PIDE, 65
Piazza Fontana, Milan, 1969 bombing, 115
"pieds noirs", 84, 91, 93, 94, 181
Pierlot, Hubert, 19
Pilet-Golarz, Marcel, 21
Pineau, Christian, 43
Pirelli, 114
Pius XII, Pope, 77
Pléven, René, 83
"Pleven Plan", 83
Poland, 4, 10, 11, 12, 14, 16, 17, 18, 20, 23,
        25, 26, 31, 32, 33, 51, 68, 69–70, 108,
        120, 122, 123, 126, 128–9, 131, 127,
        143, 145, 168, 205, 207–8, 208–11,
        215–16, 222, 227, 229, 237, 238, 239,
        240, 250, 251, 254, 267, 274
Pole of Freedom (Italy), 234
Politkovskaya, Anna, 267
Pompidou, Georges, 110, 111, 112, 113,
        115, 116–17
Pontecorvo, Gillo, 92
Poos, Jacques, 227
Popiełuszco, Jerzy, 211
Portugal, 5, 6, 21–2, 45, 64–5, 84, 101, 116,
        117–18, 145, 159–60, 182–3, 194,
        199, 201, 250, 271
postmodernism, 155, 165–7, 185
post-structuralism, 100
Poszgay, Imre, 216
Potsdam, 1945 conference, 33, 37, 38

Poujade, Pierre, 92
Poujadism, 75, 92, 180
Poznan, 1956 revolt, 129
Prague coup, 1948, 54, 60, 71, 74
"Prague Spring", 1968, 71, 111, 120, 136–9,
    143, 150, 212
Praxis, 134
privatization, 170, 183, 222, 239, 241
Prodi, Romano, 164, 234, 236, 261
Profumo, John, 91
Progress Party (Denmark), 152, 265
Provos (Netherlands), 101
PSOE, 158, 159, 183–4, 255, 261, 272
PSU, 116
Punin, Nikolai, 48
Punk rock, 156, 207
Purges, post-World War Two, 28–9, 55, 59
Purges, post-communist, 239, 254
Purges, Stalinist, 79, 136, 137
Putin, Vladimir, 226, 241–2, 246, 254, *263*,
    266–7

Quadripartite Agreement (Berlin, 1971), 144
Qualified Majority Voting (EEC/EU), 191,
    193, 200
Quebec, 111
Quisling, Vidkun, 10, 14

racism, 180–181, 228
Radical Party (France), 56
Rajk, László, 71, 129
Rákosi, Mátyás, 128, 129, 130
Rallis, George, 20
Rambouillet, 1999 negotiations, 246
Rankovic, Alexander, 133, 134
rape, 25, 38
Rassemblement du Peuple Français
    (RPF), 55
Rassemblement pour la République (RPR),
    151, 181
Rau, Johannes, 177
Reagan, Ronald, 167, 174, 177, 185
Red Army, 24, 25, 30, *31*, 32, 38, 63, 67,
    68, 69, 72, 120, 128, 130, 137, 215,
    217, 254
Red Army Faction (West Germany), 152,
    153, 154

Red Brigades (Italy), 17, 152, 153, 154
Reform Communism, 124, 136, 138,
    139, 142
regionalism, 232, 249, 264
Rehn, Gosta, 96
"Rehn-Meidener Model", 96
Reitz, Edgar, 155
religion, 5, 54–5, 65, 70, 76–7, 102–3, 117,
    125–6, 151, 211, 237
Renault, 56, 62, 113
Renner, Karl, 73
Republican Party (Germany), 180, 235
Resistance, World War Two, 14–17, 29, 52,
    58, 62, 66, 155, 186
Rhineland, 30, 35, 175
Robbe-Grillet, Alain, 78
Rocard, Michel, 116, 173, 174
Rock music, 101, 131
Rokossowski, Konstantin, 128, 129
Roma ("gypsies"), 14, 23, 228, 251–2, 261
Roman, Petre, 218
Romania, 5, 11, 17–18, 32, 68, 69, 108, 113,
    120, 122, 123, 124, 125, 135, 206,
    207, 208, 215, 217, 238, 239, 248,
    250, 251
Roosevelt, Franklin Delano, 15, 31, 32,
    33, 40
Rosenberg, Alfred, 10
Royale, Ségolène, 261
Rueff, 103, 194
Rugova, Ibrahim, 245
Ruhr, industrial region, 18, 39, 61
Rumsfeld, Donald, 256, 274, 290n
Rural Solidarity (Poland), 210
Rushdie, Salman, 257
Russian Federation, 223, 226, 227, 238, 240,
    241, 246, 249, 250, 254, 259, 266–7
Russian Revolution, 1917, 5, 24, 31, 159
Russians, as a minority, 238, 240
Rwanda, French intervention in, 227
Ryzhkov, Nikolai, 213

Saakashvili, Mikheil, 267
Sa Carneiro, Francisco, 160
Saab, 64
Saarland, *35*, 179
Sagan, Françoise, 77

Sakharov, Andrei, 133
Salan, Raul, 93
Salazar, António de Oliveira, 21, 64–5, 116, 117, 118
Salò, Republic of, 17
SALT I, 141
SALT II, 141
Samizdat, 59, 133
Sampson, Nikos, 160
Sands, Bobby, 153
Santer, Jacques, 229
SAP (Sweden), 21, 63–4, 94, 95–6, 147, 148, 230
Saragat, Giuseppe, 59
Sarajevo, 1992–5 siege, 245
Sartre, Jean Paul, 47, 48, 49, 99, 154
Sarkozy, Nicolas, 257, 261, 262, 263, 268
Sarrazin, Thilo, 258, 290n
Saussure, Ferdinand de, 100
Schabowski, Günter, 220
Scheel, Walter, 108
Schengen Agreement, 228, 269
Schiller, Karl, 94, 108
Schilly, Otto, 251
Schleyer, Hanns Martin, 152
Schluter, Poul, 171
Schmidt, Helmut, 142, 145, 150, 175, 176, 179, 198, 211
Schönhuber, Franz, 180
Schroeder, Gerhard, 235, 236, 256, 260–261
Schumacher, Kurt, 56, 57, 88, 94
Schuman, Robert, 56, 191
Schuman Plan, 39, 56, 187, 191, 274
Sciascia, Leonardo, 153
Scotland, 149, 232, 249, 260, 285n
Second World War, 1, 3, 4, 8–29, 66, 143, 155, 177, 178, 186, 242, 252–4
Securitate, 218
SED (Socialist Unity Party, DDR), 38, 125, 219–23
Serbia, 72, 206, 208, 218–19, 242–6, 250
Serbian Socialist Party, 219
Serbs, 14, 23, 72, 134, 206, 218–19, 242–6, 250, 256
Servan-Schreiber, Jean Jacques, 99, 105
Sex Pistols, 156
sexuality, 106, 166, 251, 174, 290n

SHAPE (Supreme Headquarters Allied Personnel Europe), 46
Shevardnadze, Edward, 213, 223, 267
"Shock therapy", economic, 241
Sicily, 17, 19, 233
Sierra Leone, British intervention in, 2000, 227
Šik, Ota, 136, 138
Silesia, 177
"Sinatra Doctrine", 215
Singapore, surrender of, 1942, 11
Single European Act (SEA), 1986, 163, 171, 199–201
Sinn Fein, 153, 257
situationism, 101
Six Day war, 1967, 111, 131, 135
SKDL (Finland), 73, 74
Slánský, Rudolf, 136
Slavonia, 242
Slovakia, 14, 15, 28, 70, 136, 138, 238, 252
Slovenia, 10, 134, 156, 207, 218, 242, 243
Smallholders Party (Hungary), 69, 130
"Snake", (European currencies), 146, 198
Soares, Mário, 159, 160, 183
Social Chapter, 1991, 203
Social Charter, 1989, 204
social democracy, 2, 63–4, 82, 94–6, 97, 106–9, 146–7, 148, 164, 173, 200, 206, 212, 230, 259–61
Social Democrat Party (Italy), 59
Social Democrat Party (UK), 169, 179
Social Democratic Party (SPD), (Germany), 56, 58, 76, 88, 89, 94–5, 100, 106, 197–8, 115, 116, 144, 148, 149, 175–6, 177, 179, 180, 221, 223, 230, 231, 235, 286n
Socialist International, 156
Socialist Party,
  Austria, 54, 73, 95, 147, 148, 151, 180
  France
    SFIO, 35, 56, 94, 148
    PS, 116, 148, 151, 171–5, 231, 261
  Greece. see PASOK (Pan Hellenic Socialist Party)
  Italy, 59, 60, 99, 107, 150, 182, 233
  Portugal, 160
  Spain. see PSOE

Socialist Realism, 6, 47–8, 127
Solana, Javier, 228
solidarity, 125, 205, 207, 208–11, 215–16,
    238, 239, 254
Solzhenitsyn, Alexander, 127, 133, 141, 154
Sorbonne, 112
SOS-Racisme, 181
South Ossetia, 267
Spaak, Paul Henri, 42, 47, 192, 193, 195
Spadolini, 152
Spain, 3, 6, 21–2, 33, 45, 64–6, 79, 80–81,
    82, 101, 104, 111, 116–17, 156–9,
    166, 182, 183–4, 199, 201, 227, 228,
    231, 232, 249, 250, 251, 254–5, 261,
    268, 270, 272, 274
Spanish Civil War, 1936–9, 3, 5, 16, 21, 64,
    65, 254–5
Special Operations Executive (SOE), 15, 16
Speer, Albert, 19, 25, 26–7
Spinelli, Altiero, 199
Spinola, Antonio, 159
Springer, Axel, 115
Sputnik (satellite), 127
Sputnik (journal), 220
Srebrenica, "safe area" and 1995 massacre,
    245, 256
SS, 10, 13, 27, 177, 180, 252
SS-20, missiles, 142
Stalin, Joseph, 2, 20, 23, 24, 26, 31, 32, 33,
    35, 39, 40, 41, 46, 47, 50, 66, 67, 72,
    74, 83, 120, 122, 126, 127, 128, 133,
    135, 136, 208, 223, 254, 279n
Stalingrad, 1942/3 battle, 8, 17, 24
Stasi, 125, 143, 219
"State Committee for the State of
    Emergency", 224
Stepinac, Archbishop, 28
Stikker, Dirk, 42
Stirling, James, 165
Stoltenberg, Gerhard, 177
Strategic Defence Initiative (SDI/"Star
    Wars"), 167
Strauss, Franz Josef, 89, 108, 145, 151, 175,
    176, 180
structuralism, 100
Student protest, 102, 105, 111–16, 117, 131,
    134, 149

Suárez, Adolfo, 157–9, 183
"Subsidiarity", 203, 232
Suchocka, Hanna, 240
Suez Crisis, 1956, 84, 90–91, 130, 281n
Suslov, Mikhail, 210
Svoboda, President, 137, 138
Sweden, 21–2, 23, 61, 62–4, 94, 95–6, 142,
    147, 148, 164, 194, 198, 229, 235,
    251, 252, 266
Switzerland, 21–2, 80, 104, 194, 227, 229,
    258, 274
Szász, Béla, 129

Taliban, 256
Tbilisi, 1989 violence in, 214
Tehran, 1943 conference, 32
Tejero, Antonio, 159
television, 78, 81, 82, 91, 101–2, 104, 109,
    132, 149, 155, 158, 159, 166, 182,
    251, 254, 290n
Terror House (Budapest), 254
terrorism, 99, 101, 115, 117, 152–4, 182,
    184, 247, 256–9, 261
Thatcher, Margaret, 109, 152, 162, 163,
    166, 167, 168–71, 177, 179, 185, 190,
    192, 199, 200, 201, 204, 206, 222,
    231, 273
theatre, 77, 101
Third Force (France), 56
"Third World", 84, 99, 100, 119, 140, 141,
    154, 167, 193
Timisoara, 1989 uprising, 218
Tiso, Joseph, 14, 28
Tito, Josip Broz, 14, 28, 39, 66, 71, 72–3, 74,
    120, 129, 130, 133–5, 207, 218
    Togliatti, car plant, 132
Togliatti, Palmiro, 58–9, 60
Tőkes, László, 218
tourism and leisure, 4, 81–2, 101, 105, 116,
    117, 125, 137, 166
Touropa, 81
Touvier, Paul, 27
Trabant, 123
Trade Unions, 61, 63, 73, 77, 79, 95–6, 104,
    109, 112–13, 115, 117, 146, 147, 149,
    152, 163, 164, 170, 183, 200, 209,
    229, 232, 234, 260, 262

Transylvania, 5, 68, 135, 217
Treaty of Rome, 1957, 187, 190, 192–3,
    194, 195, 196, 199
Trent University, 112
Treuhandstadt, 222
Trieste, 59
"Tripartism", 56
Trotsky, Leon, 208
Trotskyism, 102
Trotte, Margarethe von, 155
True Finns, 261, 266
Truffaut, Francois, 78
Truman, Harry S, 33, 34, 35, 44, 66
Truman Doctrine, 34, 41, 66
Tudjman, Franjo, 134–5, 242
Tunisia, 182
Turkey, 21–2, 33, 34, 45, 104, 160, 161, 195,
    217, 230, 268
Turks, minority in Bulgaria, 217
Tusk, Donald, 254, 274

U Boat warfare (World War Two), 11, 24
UDBA (Yugoslav secret police), 133, 134
Ukraine, 12, 70, 137, 224, 240, 250, 267
Ulbricht, Walter, 25, 137
unemployment, 4, 145, 147, 162, 169, 172,
    173–4, 176, 177, 183, 234, 235, 236,
    240, 260, 272
Unión de Centro Democrático (UCD),
    158, 159, 183
Union de Défense des Commerçants et
    Artisans (UDCA), 92
Union de Démocratie Français (UDF), 151
Union for the Mediterranean, 2008, 268
Unión General de Trabajadores (UGT),
    164, 183
Union of European Football Associations
    (UEFA), 289n
Union pour la Nouvelle République
    (UNR), 110
Union of Soviet Socialist Republics (USSR)
    culture, 6, 47–8, 208, 213
    dissolution of, 205, 223–4
    Eastern Europe (domination over),
        2, 14, 20, 28, 32, 35, 47, 51, 54,
        67, 68–71, 73, 120–39, 205–25,
        252–3, 274

economy, 67, 125, 127, 128, 132, 143, 213
foreign policy, 3, 35, 46, 63, 82, 99, 111,
    126, 138–9, 140–142, 143, 168,
    214–15, 222
politics, 68, 126–8, 131–3, 168–71,
    211–15, 223–4
society, 67–8, 122, 124, 132–3
World War Two, 8, 19, 23
Unionists (Northern Ireland), 153
United Kingdom (UK)
    culture, 101, 155–6, 208
    economy, 4, 41, 60, 80, 91, 103, 108,
        145–6, 162–3, 169–70, 182, 193, 229,
        236, 250, 260, 269
    Empire, 6, 41, 52, 84, 109
    European integration (attitudes
        towards), 109, 152, 190, 193–4, 196,
        197, 1918, 199, 200, 201, 202, 203,
        204, 235, 236
    foreign policy, 33–4, 36–7, 66, 83, 90–91,
        109, 107–8, 171, 227, 229, 256, 258
    politics, 2, 87, 90–91, 95, 108–9, 151–2,
        179, 207, 208, 230–231, 232, 249,
        260, 272
    society, 104, 109, 146, 164, 169–71, 207,
        208, 228, 251, 260, 266, 274
United Nations (UN), 22, 32, 40, 46, 63,
    65, 73, 145, 227, 229, 242, 245, 246,
    250, 256
United Russia, 266
United States of America (USA), 4, 6, 11,
    19, 30–50 passim, 60, 61, 66, 78, 82,
    99, 104, 111, 118, 128, 140–142, 146,
    167–8, 174, 182, 184, 194, 196, 200,
    202, 211, 226, 227, 228, 256–8, 269,
    270, 273
Universities, 105, 109, 112–14, 122
Uomo Qualunque, 59
Urbanization, 81, 104, 132
Urban, Victor, 262
Ustasha, 14, 23, 28

Vaculík, Ludvík, 164
Valéra, Éamon de, 25
Value Added Tax (VAT), 237
Vatican II (Second Vatican Council,
    1962–5), 123–4

Verdun, battle of, 209
Vercors massif, 1944 battle, 17
Versailles, 1919 Treaty, 3, 4
Vichy, French regime, 11, 13, 15, 32, 66, 74
Victor Emmanuel, King of Italy, 21
Vietnam, 103, 119, 135, 143, 168, 175, 185
Vilnius, 82, 270
Vlaams Blok, 280
Vlasov, Andrei, 14
Vojvodina, 264
Volvo, 76
Vukovar, 1991 siege of, 293

Wajda, Andrzej, 254, 287n
Waldheim, Kurt, 178–9
Wales, 149, 232, 260
Wałesa, Lech, 209, 210, 211, 215, 216,
    239, 254
Wallonia, 249
"War on Terror", 256–8
Warsaw, 1944 uprising, 14, 25
Warsaw ghetto, 143
Warsaw Pact, 108, 122, 129, 130, 134, 135,
    136–7, 138, 216
Wehrmacht, 12–13, 18
Weimar Republic (1918–33), 2, 3, 6, 56, 57,
    58, 87, 115, 226
Welfare, 51, 54, 61–2, 63–4, 79, 146, 147,
    162, 165, 176, 200, 202, 221, 232,
    240, 260–261, 265
Wenders, Wim, 155
Werner Report, 1970, 197
West European Union (WEU), 83, 202,
    203, 227

Westwood, Vivienne, 156
Wilders, Geert, 265
Wilhelm Gustloff (sinking of, 1945), 25
Wilson, Harold, 61, 95, 102, 108, 109,
    150, 198
women, 3, 25, 53, 77, 95, 105–6, 123–4, 164,
    170, 208, 239, 240, 250–251, 261
World Federation of Trade Unions
    (WFTU), 43, 54
Wurmeling, Franz-Josef, 77
Wyszynski, Stefan, 70, 126

Yakovlev, Alexander, 213
Yalta, 1945 conference, 27, 32, 33, 35, 69
Yanukovych, Victor, 267
Yelstin, Boris, 208, 213, 223, 224, 241
Yom Kippur War, 1973, 141, 145
Yugoslavia, 1, 5, 15, 23, 27, 28, 43, 52, 59,
    66, 68, 72–3, 74, 104, 111, 120, 122,
    123, 125, 126, 130, 133–5, 139, 202,
    206–7, 208, 218–19, 227, 231, 238,
    242–6, 243, 256, 258, 274, 282n
Yugoslav National Army (JNA), 242, 243,
    244
"Yukos" affair, 266

"Zagreb Spring", 134–5
Zapatero, José Luis, 261
Zhadanov, Andrei, 41, 47, 68
Zhirinovsky, Vladimir, 240
Zhivkov, Ludmilla, 123
Zhivkov, Todor, 123, 125, 217
Zhukov, Marshal Georgi, 18, 68
Zweig, Arnold, 49